THE BOOK OF GREEK & ROMAN FOLKTALES, LEGENDS, & MYTHS

THE BOOK OF GREEK & ROMAN FOLKTALES, LEGENDS, & MYTHS

EDITED, TRANSLATED, AND INTRODUCED BY

William Hansen

WITH ILLUSTRATIONS BY

Glynnis Fawkes

PRINCETON UNIVERSITY PRESS
PRINCETON AND OXFORD

Published by Princeton University Press,
41 William Street, Princeton, New Jersey 08540
In the United Kingdom: Princeton University Press,
6 Oxford Street, Woodstock, Oxfordshire OX20 1TR
press.princeton.edu

Cover illustration by Glynnis Fawkes
Cover design by Amanda Weiss

First paperback edition, 2019
Paperback ISBN 9780691195926

The Library of Congress has cataloged the cloth edition as follows:

Names: Hansen, William F., 1941– editor, translator.
Title: The book of Greek and Roman folktales, legends, and myths / edited, translated, and introduced by William Hansen; with illustrations by Glynnis Fawkes.
Description: Princeton : Princeton University Press, 2017. | Includes bibliographical references and index.
Identifiers: LCCN 2016019001 | ISBN 9780691170152 (hardcover : alk. paper)
Subjects: LCSH: Mythology, Greek. | Mythology, Roman.
Classification: LCC BL312 .B66 2017 | DDC 398.20938—dc23
LC record available at https://lccn.loc.gov/2016019001

British Library Cataloging-in-Publication Data is available

This book has been composed in Garamond Premier Pro

Printed on acid-free paper. ∞

Printed in the United States of America

FOR JUDE, JULENE, AND JIM

CONTENTS

TRANSMIGRATION OF SOULS *135*

MAGICIANS AND WITCHES *138*

DIVINATION AND SEERS *145*

FATE *150*

JEWS, CHRISTIANS, AND PAGANS *156*

ANIMALS *186*

CHILDREN *194*

FRIENDS *198*

RULERS AND TYRANTS *202*

JUSTICE *205*

CHAPTER 4
TRICKSTERS AND LOVERS *216*

TRICKERY AND CLEVERNESS *216*

LOVERS AND SEDUCERS *228*

WEALTH VS. WISDOM *354*

THE CYNICS *355*

PHILOSOPHERS CRITICIZE ONE ANOTHER *360*

EDUCATION AND LEARNING *362*

DISCOVERIES AND INVENTIONS *364*

OTHER NUMSKULLS *402*

WITS *408*

MISCELLANEOUS *410*

ILLUSTRATIONS AND TABLES

ILLUSTRATIONS

TABLES

PREFACE

Since Greece and Rome were predominately oral societies, their narrative palette was richer than ours, both in the frequency with which they told stories and in the number and kinds of stories they told. Ancient literature teems with tales and with representations of persons telling and exchanging them. The Greeks and Romans had all the genres of oral narrative known to us, even ghost stories and urban legends, but they also told kinds of story that in most of the Western world no longer circulate orally, such as myths and fairytales, which for us have become book genres, stories that we now encounter in published compilations rather than as living narratives.

The great majority of these stories are set not in the distant mythological past, but in the historical period, the so-called human era, and their gaze is accordingly not upon the feats of gods and heroes but upon the doings of human beings of different sorts—rulers, merchants, sages, seers, priests, athletes, artists, statesmen, soldiers, farmers, thieves, and so on. Among them are famous and sometimes foundational figures of the Western world such as the lawgiver Solon, the fabulist Aesop, the mystic Pythagoras, the philosopher Plato, the dramatist Sophocles, the athlete Milo, the orator Cicero, the mathematician Archimedes, the conqueror Alexander the Great, the statesman Cato, the Egyptian queen Cleopatra, the Roman emperor Nero, and the Jewish prophet Jesus. These stories could well be labeled The Other Mythology. In the world of ancient narrative animals sometimes talk, Diogenes the Cynic and Alexander the Great converse, and deities intervene in human affairs if and when they wish. Although human beings are in the foreground, the world they move in includes gods and nature spirits (satyrs, centaurs, nymphs), shape-changers (lamias, werewolves), the quasi dead (ghosts, revenants), and other beings. These are the tales that Greeks and Romans recounted in their everyday lives, and they offer a unique window into the fantasies, anxieties, humor, passions, and values of ancient persons young and old, male and female, free and slave. They show us what made the ancients ponder or shudder or laugh.

The present volume offers a wide selection of traditional oral stories. It emphasizes informal narratives such as legends, novelle, anecdotes, jokes, fables, fairytales, and the like, many of which are not easily accessible even to classical scholars, and is the most extensive compilation of ancient popular tales ever made, exceeding in coverage the pioneering anthology of Greek tales published over a century ago by August Hausrath and August Marx, *Griechische Märchen, Fabeln, Schwänke, und Novellen aus dem klassischen Altertum* [*Greek Fairytales, Fables, Humorous Tales, and Novelle from Classical Antiquity*] (1913). I offer these tales for their crystallizations of ancient life and thought as well as for the pure enjoyment they afford as stories, as expressions of an old and exquisite art. In the introduction I provide an overview of the genres of ancient oral narrative, something attempted here for the first time. (Of course, readers who are impatient with talk *about* stories can proceed directly to the tales themselves.) All readers are invited to imagine themselves as guests of Helen, who, as Homer relates in the fourth book of his *Odyssey*, slips her wondrous drug nepenthe into the wine bowl, bids the chalices be filled, banishing grief and anger and all thought of miseries, and proposes that the company pass the time pleasantly in the telling of stories.

For help or inspiration along the way I thank Mario Andreassi, Robert Chavez, Lowell Edmunds, William Fortenbaugh, Ioannis Konstantakos, Moira Marsh, Richard P. Martin, Adrienne Mayor, Antonio Stramaglia, Cecil Wooten, and two scholars who departed life too early, Jack Winkler and Josep Miquel Sobrer. I owe debts of gratitude above all to my colleagues Gregory Schrempp and Henry Glassie and to my wife, Mary Beth Hannah-Hansen.

ABBREVIATIONS

ATU — Hans-Jörg Uther. *The Types of International Folktales: A Classification and Bibliography*. *FFC* 284–286. Helsinki: Academia Scientiarum Fennica, 2004.

CAG — *Commentaria in Aristotelem Graeca*. 23 vols. Berlin: G. Reimer, 1882–1909.

CIL — *Corpus Inscriptionum Latinarum*. Berlin-Brandenburgische Akademie der Wissenschaften. Berlin, 1867 ff.

CJ — *Classical Journal*

CQ — *Classical Quarterly*

CR — *Classical Review*

DK — Hermann Diels. *Die Fragmente der Vorsokratiker: Griechisch und Deutsch*. Edited by Walther Kranz. 6th ed. 3 vols. Berlin: Weidmann, 1951–1952.

EM — Kurt Ranke et al., eds. *Enzyklopädie des Märchens: Handwörterbuch zur historischen und vergleichenden Erzählforschung*. 15 vols. Berlin: Walter de Gruyter, 1977–2015.

FFC — *Folklore Fellows Communications*

FGH — Felix Jacoby, ed. *Die Fragmente der griechischen Historiker*. Berlin: Weidmann; Leiden: E. J. Brill, 1923–1958.

fr. — fragment

GRBS — *Greek, Roman, & Byzantine Studies*

HSCP — *Harvard Studies in Classical Philology*

Hsr — August Hausrath, ed. *Corpus Fabularum Aesopicarum*. 2nd ed. Edited by Herbert Hunger. Leipzig: B. G. Teubner, 1959–1970.

IG — *Inscriptiones Graecae*. Berlin-Brandenburgische Akademie der Wissenschaften. Berlin, 1873 ff.

JAF — *Journal of American Folklore*

JHS	*Journal of Hellenic Studies*
ML	Reidar Christiansen. *The Migratory Legends: A Proposed List of Types with a Systematic Catalogue of the Norwegian Variants. FFC* 175. Helsinki: Academia Scientiarum Fennica, 1958.
Motif	Stith Thompson. *A Motif-Index of Folk-Literature: A Classification of Narrative Elements in Folktales, Ballads, Myths, Fables, Mediaeval Romances, Exempla, Fabliaux, Jest-Books and Local Legends*. Rev. ed. 6 vols. Bloomington: Indiana University Press, 1955–1958.
MW	R. Merkelbach and M. L. West, eds. *Fragmenta Hesiodea*. Oxford: Clarendon Press, 1967.
Perry	Ben E. Perry. *Aesopica: A Series of Texts Relating to Aesop or Ascribed to Him or Closely Connected with the Literary Tradition That Bears His Name*. Urbana: University of Illinois Press, 1952.
PG	J.-P. Migne, ed., *Patrologia Graeca*. Paris, 1857–1858.
PL	J.-P. Migne, ed. *Patrologia Latina*. Paris, 1844–1845.
PMG	D. L. Page, ed. *Poetae Melici Graeci*. Oxford: Clarendon Press, 1962.
P. Oxy.	*The Oxyrhynchus Papyri*. Egypt Exploration Fund: Graeco-Roman Branch. London, 1898 ff.
RhM	*Rheinisches Museum für Philologie*
schol.	scholium, scholiast
SSR	Gabriele Giannantoni, ed. and comm. *Socratis et Socraticorum Reliquiae*. 4 vols. Naples: Bibliopolis, 1990.
TAPA	*Transactions of the American Philological Association*
Wehrli	Fritz Wehrli. *Die Schule des Aristoteles*. 2nd ed. 10 vols. Basel: B. Schwabe, 1967–1969.

THE BOOK OF GREEK & ROMAN FOLKTALES, LEGENDS, & MYTHS

INTRODUCTION

Give me a copper coin and you'll hear a golden tale!
—ROMAN STORYTELLER'S STREET CRY[1]

I begin with three instances of storytelling.

One hot day Socrates and a companion Phaidros sought relief from the sun by strolling alongside the cool stream of the Ilissos outside the walls of Athens. The place brought to Phaidros's mind an event from the distant past. "Tell me, Socrates," he said, "wasn't it from somewhere around here that Boreas is said to have carried off Oreithyia?" He was thinking of the myth according to which the Athenian king's daughter was playing on the banks of the stream when suddenly the god of the north wind snatched her up and carried her off to his cold kingdom. "Yes, that's what they say." "Was it from here, then?" "No," Socrates replied, "the spot is actually some distance downstream. There is an altar of Boreas there." Phaidros asked if Socrates believed the story was true. Socrates replied that although clever men might explain the story away, he did not care to waste time on such speculations and was content to accept the usual beliefs (Plato *Phaedrus* 229a–230b; cf. Finkelberg 2014).

On a different occasion, a group of persons was traveling and partying together aboard a ship. One of the men, Eumolpus, made a comment on the unfaithfulness of women, adding that he had in mind not women in the old tragedies and legends but a woman of their own day. When all ears turned to him, he told about a matron of Ephesos who was famous for her fidelity to her husband. When the man died, she kept company with his corpse in his tomb, fully intending to follow him in death. A soldier on guard duty nearby, noticing a light shining from the tomb, joined the widow in the underground chamber. Gradually the matron was won over by the comfort of the soldier's company, and in the end the two lay together in the tomb. As Eumolpus concluded his story, the sailors laughed, a woman blushed, and a man who had been cuckolded grumbled (Petronius *Satyrica* 109–113).

In an essay on the art of conversation Plutarch recommends that the questions posed by symposiasts should be simple and uncomplicated and the topics familiar, so as not to exclude the less intellectual guests. Persons who propose intricate subjects for discussion are no better fit for parties than are Aesop's fox and crane. A fox once entertained a crane at dinner, Plutarch explains, and served a broth, pouring it out upon a flat stone. The crane looked ridiculous as it tried to eat the broth with its bill. But it now invited the fox to dinner, serving the meal in a jar with a narrow neck. While the crane easily inserted its bill, the fox could not get its mouth inside. In the same way, Plutarch concludes, whenever philosophers plunge into subtle topics at a symposium, they are irksome to most of the guests, who cannot follow, and in consequence the other diners throw themselves into singing songs, telling silly stories, or talking business, with the result that the fellowship of the party is lost (Plutarch *Table-Talk* 1.5, *Moralia* 614d–615a).

The events recounted about the wind god and the princess, the widow and the soldier, and the fox and the crane are traditional stories (or, in the case of Boreas, an allusion to such a story), while the narratives themselves, the circumstances of their telling, and the intent of their narrators are quite different.

The myth of Boreas and Oreithyia was part of inherited Athenian tradition that was probably familiar to every resident of the city, so that Socrates and Phaidros could discuss it without actually having to narrate it. The event is set in the distant past, back when Athens was ruled by kings. It is precisely localized: the exact spot where the central action occurred—the abduction of a princess by the North Wind—was known and commemorated with an altar. The characters themselves are named, and they fit into known genealogies and sequences of events in Athenian prehistory. It is clear that, for all its improbability, the story was generally regarded as being true, although the question of its historicity was something one could discuss, as Phaidros and Socrates do as they walk along the Ilissos, much as today two Americans might explore a Civil War battlefield and talk about what is said to have happened here and there. It is significant that Socrates and Phaidros do not actually relate the story but merely discuss it, not only because both of them already know it but also because there is nothing to be accomplished by telling it. The story did not serve to make or clarify a point of some sort or to entertain or to console; that is, it had no immediate purpose or application. It came up as a matter of information because the two men happened to be strolling near the traditional location of the abduction.

The story of the widow and the soldier is much less anchored in history. Although the city of Ephesos is given as the site of the events, the characters themselves are nameless and the action is set at an unstated time in the vaguely recent past. The narrator declares that the events really happened, but his interest and that of his listeners are on the action and not on the question of its historicity. And the tone is different, for whereas the atmosphere of the myth is weighty and dignified, even solemn, with its important figures (a god, a princess) and dramatic event (abduction of a human by a supernatural being), the tone of the Ephesian tale is light and, for most of the listeners, humorous. It is essentially entertainment, a story told for its own sake.

The third narrative, the fox and the crane, is an entirely unrealistic tale. The characters are animals that behave like humans, they are generic (the fox is any fox, the crane is any crane), and the setting is as vague as can be (somewhere sometime in the past). There is no question of the narrator or his readers giving the tale a moment's consideration as being something that actually happened. Its tone is neither serious nor entirely humorous, but rather instructive in a light sort of way. Whereas the myth tells of an important event in early Athenian history and the Ephesian tale is a bawdy novella of sexual seduction set in the recent past and told to amuse, the fable is an extended metaphor that illustrates in a somewhat absurd fashion, via humanlike animals, how guests should not behave at a dinner gathering. The narrator's intent is to persuade.

Traditional narratives are not, then, a homogeneous kind of discourse with regard to their content, form, presumed historicity, and register. The Greeks and Romans, like other peoples, recognized that such stories are expressed in different genres, or conventionalized narrative forms (cf. Swales 1990; Bauman 1992:53), although they did not always give them distinct labels. The ancients possessed relatively specific terms for short narratives such as anecdotes, jokes, and fables, according these genres explicit recognition, but for most extended kinds of story they did not, referring to them simply by one or another general word for "story." The lack of a label did not necessarily mean the absence of a kind of story, only the absence of conscious and explicit cultural recognition of a kind of story. Thus, although urban legends are attested in classical antiquity, a term for them did not come into use until the twentieth century.

Broadly speaking, systems of oral-narrative classification are emic or etic. Emic genres are traditional categories of narrative discourse that members of a society themselves devise and employ in their daily lives. Etic genres are categories that analysts devise in order to classify and talk comparatively about the oral narratives of different cultural groups. Whereas native taxonomies arise piecemeal and serve mostly casual purposes, analytic categories tend to be more defined and systematic, since investigators create them for the purpose of scholarly study and communication.[2]

The genre categories that we English speakers ordinarily employ for ancient short narratives correspond approximately to the ancient emic categories: we distinguish anecdotes, jokes, and fables and employ specific terms for them, as the Greeks and Romans did. But for more extended forms of narrative the current practice does not match the ancient one. For example, scholars writing in English recognize certain kinds of realistic tales as "novelle" and generally lump together all stories of gods and heroes as "myths," whereas the Greeks and Romans had no emic terms for novelle or for mythological narratives, neither *mythos* nor anything else. So the emic system employed by the ancients and the etic system used today in Anglophone scholarship agree generally in their classification of simple narrative forms but disagree in their handling of complex narratives. Since neither the ancients nor the moderns make many discriminations among kinds of extended narrative, neither system is adequate for the scholarly study of ancient traditional narrative.

Our own use of the word "myth" to refer broadly to classical narratives of gods and heroes goes back only to the German philologist Christian Gottlob Heyne (1729–1812), who popularized the Greek word *mythos* and its forms as a replacement for the then more usual Latin term *fabula* and its forms. In the course of the nineteenth century the older term "fable" and the newer term "myth" competed for favor among English speakers, and "myth" eventually predominated.[3] It was a reflection of the times, then, that in 1855 when Thomas Bulfinch published his popular compendium of mythology, he called it *The Age of Fable; or, Stories of Gods and Heroes*, but that toward the end of the same century an editor renamed the book, giving it the title by which it is commonly known today, *Bulfinch's Mythology* (Hansen 2013:24–26). But the victory of the word "myth" in popular and scholarly usage did not mark an advance in analytic sophistication, since it amounted merely to the replacement of one more-or-less suitable term for fabulous stories for another such word.

The present-day understanding of ancient oral narratives is hindered by the fact that we have a wholly inadequate system of generic classification as well as an overall atomistic approach. By this I mean that mythologists study myths, fable scholars study fables, and others study the Greek novella, the Roman anecdote, and the like, but no investigators view the object of their study as being a part of a much larger whole, that of traditional narrative. Just as our understanding of classical art would be severely limited if it consisted only of studies of individual arts such as sculpture, architecture, painting, pottery, and jewelry, and possessed no notion of the ancient arts as an interrelated whole or an overall concept of classical art as such, so also our understanding of traditional narrative is constrained by our particularistic focus upon individual genres. For a clearer understanding of traditional narrative and its manifestations in antiquity we need a holistic vision of ancient story (Hansen 1983).

To distinguish the forms and variety of ancient popular narratives more clearly, I propose below a taxonomy of Greek and Roman oral-narrative genres. I begin with the emic categories that we find in use at different times among the ancients, and supplement them with etic categories that modern folk-narrative scholars find useful for cross-cultural study (e.g., Dégh 1972; Honko 1989). I distinguish genres mostly by internal criteria (i.e., form and content) because more is known about ancient texts themselves than about their contexts and the intentions of their narrators, who cannot now be interrogated, but sometimes I also give attention to the presumed communicative purposes of different genres (e.g., amusement, clarification, crystallization).

I use the term "credence narratives" for stories that ancient narrators shaped in such a way as to present, or imply, a claim to historicity. For example, in early Greek literature (epic poetry, lyric poetry, prose mythography) narrators handle narratives of prehistoric times respectfully as appropriate subjects for artistic treatment and retelling in dignified forms of literature. Although individual persons did not have to accept in full or even in part an implicit or explicit claim of veracity, hearers and narrators generally treated the issue of truth and historicity as something at least discussable by competent adults, as illustrated by the discussion of Socrates and Phaidros regarding the tradition of the North Wind's abduction of an Athenian princess. In short, credence narratives were subject to listeners' and readers' evaluation of their truth-value (cf. Nagy 1990:59–72). "We know how to speak many false things (*pseudea*) that seem genuine," declare the Muses to Hesiod, on whom they are about to confer poetic powers, "and we know how to utter true things (*alethea*) when we wish to" (Hesiod *Theogony* 27–28). Although the Muses constitute for human beings, and for bards in particular, the primary font of information concerning what happened in the remote past, they themselves announce to Hesiod that the information they choose to provide is not always reliable.

In the case of recent events, the sources are human beings alone, but human narrators are not necessarily trustworthy either. "Odysseus, as we look upon you, we don't regard you as one of those imposters and cheats whom the dark earth nourishes in abundance, persons who fashion falsehoods (*pseudea*) that no one can test," exclaims King Alkinoos, at whose court Odysseus has been recounting his extraordinary experiences (Homer *Odyssey* 11.363–366). While Odysseus was telling of his adventures, his listeners were silently judging the credibility of his report, for human narrators may introduce details of their own invention, as the poet Pindar (*Olympian* 1.28–29) observes when he declares that the narration of a "true story" (*ton alathe logon*) can become embellished with "elaborate lies" (*pseudesi poikilois*). Discriminating between truth and fiction was an integral part of listening to, or reading, a narrative, and it is doubtless a universal preoccupation of audiences.

Moreover, the system I set forth is tripartite in that it classifies individual oral narratives broadly as myths, legends, or folktales, a division that reflects the basic classification of traditional narratives that is found in many native systems of genre (Bascom 1965). The tripartite division of traditional narratives is usually traced back in European scholarly thought to the early nineteenth century, when the Brothers Grimm sorted German narratives into folktale (*Märchen*) and legend (*Sage*), and suggested that some of the fabulous tales of the present day were transformations of ancient myths.[4] These three categories are in common use by folk-narrative scholars, who analyze them into numerous subgenres (Bødker 1965), and the system is sometimes employed for ancient story.[5]

THE KINDS OF ANCIENT STORY

Traditional Credence Narratives

Myth

In the context of traditional Greek story, *myths* are traditional credence narratives whose principal characters are gods and other supernatural beings, whose events are set in the remote past during the formative era of the cosmos, and whose central topics, taken as a whole, are the origins of the physical world (cosmogony), of the gods (theogony), and of human beings (anthropogony), as well as the establishment of cosmic order.[6] Other notable topics of Greek myth are important events in the lives of the gods (birth, loves and conflicts, acquisition of prerogatives, founding of cult sites), the establishment of the conditions of human life such as the advent of toil and death, and cosmic catastrophes such as the Great Deluge. The lives of the gods are only partial biographies, for once divinities are born, they quickly mature and thereafter remain indefinitely at a particular developmental stage, usually mature adulthood (e.g., the elder Olympian deities) or youthful adulthood (the younger Olympians). Many mythic narratives are etiological in that they tell of how some familiar feature of the world came into being.

Toward the end of the mythic period, the physical cosmos possesses its present structure and nature in its essentials, the Olympian gods are in firm charge, the relationship of gods and humans has been defined, and the basic qualities of human existence have been determined. In short, the big matters have been taken care of.

The mythic era as described above is a feature of Greek more than of Roman tradition, at least initially, since Roman sources preserve little native tradition of myth. Such myths as the Romans once had either ceased to be told or were historicized by being converted into episodes of early Roman history. Subsequently the Romans reacquired myth by borrowing, primarily from the Greeks.

Although it is usual in anthropological and folkloristic scholarship to characterize myth as *sacred* narrative, this feature is not part of the present definition because sacredness does not make a good fit in the Greek and Roman case, and classicists rarely speak of myths and sacredness in the same breath. Myths do not appear to have been regarded as sacred stories in the classical lands, unless one means by "sacred" a narrative in which deities play a role, in which case the category of sacred story is too large to be of any practical use (Hansen 2002b:20–21). The Greeks did acknowledge a genre of traditional story to which they expressly attributed the quality of sacredness, namely, "sacred story" (*hieros logos*), to which I return later.

Heroic Legend

Heroic legends are traditional credence narratives set in the age of heroes, which in Greek tradition is the era that follows the mythic period and precedes our own era. In his Myth of the Ages the poet Hesiod tells of a species of person called heroes, or demigods, who lived upon the earth immediately before ordinary humans. These heroes fought in the great wars at Thebes and Troy. Some survived, some died there, and others were translated by Zeus to the Isles of the Blessed at the ends of the earth.[7] Heroes predominated on the earth for around nine generations (Cobet 2002:405–411).

In early Greek literature the term "hero" is approximately synonymous with "warrior." Although not all members of the heroic era were warriors, heroes characterize the age and give it its name (M. L. West 1978:190). They exceeded today's humans in mind and stature.[8] Hesiod can describe the heroes as a "divine species" (*theion genos*) and as "demigods" (*hemitheoi*) because many of them were literally the offspring of a deity and a human being. Perseus, for example, was the son of the god Zeus and the mortal woman Danae. It was presumably the divine component in persons of the heroic age that led them to achieve the extraordinary feats that made that age so splendid and memorable. The age of heroes came about as a result of the mating of deities and human beings, and it came to an end when this activity became less frequent.

Heroic legends, like myths, focus sometimes upon the doings of individual characters such as notable fighters (e.g., Achilleus, the foremost combatant at Troy), questers (Jason, who goes in search of the Golden Fleece), monster-slayers (Perseus, who slays the sea monster Ketos), tricksters (Odysseus, who devises the stratagem of the Trojan Horse), and seers (Melampous, who understands the speech of animals). Other heroic legends tell of group efforts such as the Argonauts' quest for the Golden Fleece, the hunting of the huge Calydonian boar, and engagement in two great wars, those at Thebes and at Troy, the Trojan War being the culminating endeavor of the age of heroes.

No sharp border separates the mythic and the heroic eras. Instead, there is a region of fuzzy overlap as the focus of narrative interest shifts from gods to demigods and other mortals, and similarly a murky period exists when early human communities are found and younger deities such as Apollon, Persephone, Hermes, and Dionysos, offspring of the elder Olympians, seek niches for themselves in the cosmos.

Taken together, these two genres of traditional story, myth and heroic legend, focusing respectively upon supernatural beings and heroic beings, the era of the gods and the era of the demigods, and providing between them a more-or-less continuous account of events from the beginning of the cosmos to the end of the heroic age, constitute what we have come to call Greek mythology, or, after its adoption and incorporation by the Romans, classical mythology. Although the Greeks themselves did not give this set of traditions the name "mythology" or any other special appellation (cf. Detienne 1986), they appear to have regarded these stories as belonging together and, as discussed below, as being in some ways distinct from stories set in later times. In a telling passage in which narratives of the distant past are distinguished from those of the recent past, the historian Herodotos (3.122) contrasts traditions about a figure of the heroic era, King Minos of Crete, with those about a ruler of more recent times, Polykrates of Samos, who lived in what Herodotos refers to as "the so-called human age."[9] For Herodotos, then, the present era is the age of humans, and it followed the age of heroes, just as, presumably, the age of heroes in its turn succeeded the age of gods.

As a historian of the Persian Wars, Herodotos is interested mostly in the events of the human, or historical, age, but there are other Greek authors who treat, in the form of prose compilations of Greek myths and heroic legends, the events that precede it. A work that survives mostly intact is Apollodoros's *Library*, a work of Hellenistic mythography that recounts events in the form of a continuous narrative from the mythic origins of the world to the aftermath of the Trojan War, the end of the heroic age. Greek prose mythography of this sort goes back to compilations of stories and genealogies made in the late sixth and early fifth centuries

BC by Hekataios, Akousilaos, Pherekydes, and others. The Greek epic poets and tragedians drew their plots almost exclusively from such myths and heroic legends. These practices constitute a tacit recognition that the mythological traditions of Greek prehistory constituted for the Greeks, and subsequently also for the Romans, a distinctive set of stories (Fowler 2000:xxvii–xxix).

The popular genres, as it will be convenient to call them, differ from the mythological genres in their characters, settings, and register. The focus of myths and heroic legends is upon the lives and deeds of divinities and heroes, while that of the other genres is upon the doings of human beings (or, in the case of fables, upon the activities of animals and plants and the like). Temporally, the events in mythological stories take place in the distant past, whereas popular stories are set in the historic era or in an indefinite past. With regard to register, the tone of the mythological narratives is one of weight and dignity. They are, as it were, high church, as shown by the fact that the composers of the loftiest and most dignified genres of ancient literature—epic and tragedy—drew almost exclusively upon them for their plots, as well as by the fact that mythological stories were frequently the subjects of parody, for nothing invites parody so much as high seriousness and dignity.[10] In contrast, the tone of the popular genres is less formal. They are, to continue the metaphor, low church, although not all to the same degree, ranging as they do in dignity from, say, historical legends at the heavier end to jokes and fables at the other.

Generically, popular stories can be sorted into two large groups: legends (or traditional credence narratives) and folktales (or traditional fictions). The opposition of legend and folktale is basic to folk-narrative scholarship, going back at least to the Brothers Grimm, who famously observe that "the folktale is more poetic, the legend more historic."[11] Their formulation is relative, since legends need not be devoid of aesthetic qualities nor folktales of historical elements (Röhrich 1991:12), but on balance the presence or absence of presumed historicity along with the corresponding implication for belief is the basic distinction by means of which ordinary traditional narratives are sorted into two great categories, legends and folktales, or traditional credence narratives and traditional fictions (Lüthi 1975).

Legends set in the historic period, as opposed to the heroic era, can be termed simply historic legends, but because of the large number and kinds of such legends it is useful to treat several kinds individually in accordance with their natures. Those distinguished here are historic legends as such, religious legends, belief legends, contemporary (or urban) legends, and anecdotes. In addition, it is convenient to include the quasi-legendary genre of the personal-experience narrative.

Historic Legend

Credence narratives set in the human age are *historic legends*. They include stories about important persons, places, and events—rulers, states and cities, settlement, wars and pestilences, and so on—as well as about notable persons of more modest station—philosophers, artists, athletes, thieves, and the like—and of small events of regional or local interest such as etiological traditions about the names of towns and the origins of natural features. In short, such legends focus upon supposedly real persons and events of the relatively recent past, that is, Herodotos's human era, as opposed to persons and events of the more distant heroic past. They range in magnitude from long saga-like narratives such as the traditional history of the Lydian Empire to short anecdote-like accounts such as that of the death of the poet Ibykos or how Ophiteia ("Snaketown") got its strange name.

An interesting example is the curious legendry, discussed by both Herodotos and Thucydides, that developed around the Athenian youths Harmodios and Aristogeiton.[12] In the late sixth century BC the city-state of Athens was ruled by tyrants, first Peisistratos and then his son Hippias. (The Greek term "tyrant" referred to a ruler who had taken control of a state by force; it did not necessarily imply that he ruled it oppressively.) In 514 BC, acting on a personal quarrel, the Athenian youths Harmodios and Aristogeiton assassinated the younger brother of the tyrant, Hipparchos, during a festival, and were themselves executed. The killing of Hipparchos did not put an end to the tyranny, which ended several years later, but after the expulsion of the tyrants political reforms taking place under the leadership of Kleisthenes led to the momentous creation of democracy in Athens. Despite the fact that Harmodios and Aristogeiton acted for personal reasons and despite the fact that they did not actually put an end to the tyranny, the two were transformed into culture heroes, celebrated in popular tradition as the liberators of Athens and the founders of the democracy. Statues of the so-called tyrannicides were erected in Athens, public sacrifices were made to them, drinking songs were composed in their honor, and civic privileges were granted to their descendants.

Religious Legend

Religious legends are credence narratives set in the historical period that recount the epiphany of a deity who performs a wonder of some kind or otherwise affects human affairs in a significant way.

This category usefully distinguishes narratives of divine epiphanies set in the human era from those set in the mythic or heroic eras. Compare, for example, two deluge stories, one a myth set in the remote past and the other a legend set in the recent past. According to Apollodoros (*Library* 1.7.2), Zeus decided to destroy the humans of the Bronze Age. The god Prometheus privately advised his mortal son Deukalion to build a chest, fill it with provisions, and embark on it with his wife Pyrrha. Presently Zeus brought about an immense flood that covered most of Greece and destroyed virtually all human life. Deukalion and Pyrrha floated in their chest for nine days and nights, landing finally on Mt. Parnassos. After the rains ceased, Deukalion disembarked and sacrificed to Zeus, who thereupon dispatched Hermes and allowed Deukalion to make a wish. He wished for people. The two survivors were instructed to throw stones over their heads, and those cast by Deukalion became men, while those thrown by Pyrrha became women. For this reason, having come from stones (*laas*), humans were called people (*laoi*): "people" from "pebbles," as it were.

In a different flood story Ovid (*Metamorphoses* 8.620–724) relates how the gods Jupiter and Mercury, in the guise of humans, came to a place in Phrygia where they sought shelter. A thousand homes rejected the travelers before finally an elderly couple, Philemon and Baucis, took them in and offered them the modest hospitality that their means afforded. Presently the two strangers revealed themselves to be gods and declared that the impious community would be punished. They instructed the couple to follow them on foot to the top of a nearby mountain. Philemon and Baucis did so, and when they turned around, they saw that every house in the region was covered by water, or rather every house except theirs, which had become a temple. Jupiter asked them what they might wish, and they answered that they wanted to serve as priests in the temple and, when their days reached their end, not to outlive each other. So the pious couple tended the temple until the time came for them to die, when they metamorphosed into two trees, which to this day the local peasants venerate with offerings.

These two narratives are constructed upon the same plot. (1) The principal god decides to destroy human beings, but (2) a pious couple is tipped off. When (3) the god causes a great flood, (4) the couple escapes by boat or on foot, and (5) comes safely to the top of a mountain. There (6) the gods offer the couple a boon of their choice, and (7) they state their wish, (8) which the gods fulfill. The stories conclude with a transformation and an etiology: stones metamorphose into people, or people metamorphose into trees.

What distinguishes the stories from each other is not their basic sequence of action, which is the same, but the scale and significance of the events. In the former story the world, or at least the world known to the narrator, is covered with water, and nearly all living creatures perish. The devastation is so complete that a new creation of human beings is called for. In contrast, the latter text describes a regional catastrophe. A Phrygian town is inundated; its houses disappear under water and its inhabitants perish. One story is a myth and the other a legend, not because of the plot but because of the implications of the events, which in one case are of cosmic significance and in the other have only regional implications (Hansen 2005:171–173).

Religious legends, set as they are in the human era, are narrated from the viewpoint of human beings, into whose world the divine makes a brief incursion. Several legends of this sort, for example, are found in the Lindian Chronicle, an inscription that was displayed in the sanctuary of Athena above the town of Lindos on the island of Rhodes (Higbie 2003). The text includes a description of an epiphany of Athena that took place around 490 BC when King Darius of Persia sent a naval expedition against the island. The Persians besieged the Rhodians at Lindos. A lack of water eventually wore down the inhabitants, who considered surrendering the city, but the goddess Athena appeared to a city official in a dream and urged him to take heart.[13] Presently a large cloud settled over the acropolis, and a great storm followed such that the besieged now had abundant water. According to the Lindian Chronicle the astonished Persian admiral sent offerings of his own to Athena, lifted the siege, and made a treaty of friendship with the people of Lindos.

ARETALOGY

The legend of Athena's epiphany at Lindos is an instance of what Greeks called an aretalogy (*aretalogia*), or narration of a miracle performed by a deity.[14] Correspondingly, an *aretalogos* was an expounder of such wonders, either a professional attached to a particular cult or an independent storyteller. It is perhaps unsurprising that such persons had a reputation for being garrulous and mendacious (Scobie 1979:240). The satirist Juvenal compares Odysseus's apologue to the Phaeacians in Homer's *Odyssey* (9–12), in which Odysseus regales his hosts with an account of his amazing adventures with the witch Circe, a Cyclops, the cannibalistic Laestrygonians, the ghosts of famous persons in the death realm, and so on, to that of a "lying aretalogist."[15] Many aretalogical texts have come down to us, such as the inscriptions displayed at the healing shrines of the Greek god Asklepios and of the Egyptian god Sarapis that told of miraculous cures effected by these deities.

SACRED STORY

Somewhat similar is what the Greeks called a sacred story (*hieros logos*). Although the term had multiple meanings, its central sense was probably that of an esoteric credence narrative associated with a sacred rite (Henrichs 2003). Knowledge of such a story was restricted largely to an inner circle. For example, Herodotos comments several times that the Pelasgians or the Egyptians tell a sacred story about a particular cultic practice, and each time he respectfully stops at that point, not revealing the content of the story.[16] Instances in which ancient writers actually reveal the plot of a sacred story are rare. In one of them, Lucian discusses the self-castration of priests belonging to the cult of the Syrian goddess, offers a possible etiology for the origin of the custom, and then mentions an alternative etiology: "Others recount a sacred story on this subject, saying that Hera, in her love for Kombabos, put the idea of castrating themselves into the minds of many men in order that Kombabos might not be alone in mourning his manhood. This custom, once adopted, has abided to our own day."[17] Lucian's sacred story clearly falls within the definition of, and can be classified as, a religious legend, and it seems likely that the sacred stories known to Herodotos are of the same sort. A sacred story, then, is like an aretalogy in being a form of religious legend, but the two are dissimilar in that an aretalogy is a virtual public advertisement that calls attention to the powers of a particular deity, whereas a sacred story is the arcane property of an in-group. Unfortunately, so secretive a category of story has limited usefulness for the present-day classification of ancient narrative.

Belief Legend

Like religious legends, *belief legends*, or legends reflecting a particular folk belief, concern human encounters with the supernatural.[18] Whereas religious legends may call forth pious feelings, belief legends, focusing as they do on controversial beliefs in ghosts, haunted localities, witches, werewolves (and in our day fairies, flying saucers, and extraterrestrials), tend rather to raise basic questions concerning the reality or nonreality of particular supernatural phenomena, and so of different listeners' stances toward them (Dégh 2001). An ancient example can be seen in Lucian's dialogue *The Lover of Lies*, in which the author portrays a group of men exchanging reports of the supernatural and disputing among themselves the credibility of each narrative.[19]

Belief legends range from well-constructed narratives to virtually formless statements with a bare claim to the label of story. These extremes can be illustrated in a single ancient document, the famous letter on ghosts written by the younger Pliny (7.27) to Licinius Sura. Pliny asks Sura whether he believes in ghosts or thinks they are merely creations of our own fears. He acknowledges that he himself is inclined to believe in their existence because of what he has heard about the experience of Curtius Rufus, who once encountered a female figure of superhuman size and beauty. She foretold Rufus's future, and events turned out just as she had said.[20]

Pliny goes on to relate two more stories of the supernatural. The first concerns a haunted house in Athens. In a large residence the clanking of iron was heard during the night. These sounds were followed by the specter of an old man with chains on his wrists and fetters on his legs. Because of the terror caused by the apparition the mansion stood empty. At this juncture the philosopher Athenodoros showed up in Athens and rented the haunted house. In the evening he positioned himself on a couch, and after a while the ghost approached. Entering the room, it beckoned Athenodoros to follow. The philosopher did so, and the ghost vanished suddenly at a certain place. Athenodoros marked the spot, and on the following day the magistrates dug in the ground, finding bones and chains and fetters. After the remains had been given proper burial, the spirit appeared no more. This first story, says Pliny, he recounts as it was told to him. By this statement Pliny says in effect that while he himself is a reliable narrator, he assumes no personal responsibility for so colorful a narrative.

But his second story, he declares, is one that he can vouch for himself. One of Pliny's freedmen was sleeping in bed with his younger brother, and dreamt that he saw someone sitting on the bed and cutting the hair on the top of his head with a pair of scissors. In the morning he found that the top of his head had been shorn and hair lay on the floor. A short time later a similar thing occurred to a slave boy who was sleeping in the slaves' quarters. Two men in white clothing entered through the window, cut his hair as he lay there in bed, and departed. When daylight came, the slave boy too discovered that his head had been shorn and his hair scattered about. Pliny speculates that these experiences were possibly a portent. In any case he concludes his letter with a request that Sura give his opinion on the question of ghosts so as to put an end to Pliny's doubts.[21]

Pliny's letter is belief legend in a nutshell. The story of the haunted house in Athens is an aesthetically well-structured, traditional narrative that begins with mystery and fear, introduces an intelligent protagonist, and concludes with a resolution of the problems of the house (haunting) and the ghost (improper interment). In contrast, the haircutting incidents are strange, rather formless events that are possibly connected with one another and possibly not, may involve supernatural agency and may not (ghost? practical joke? unreliable reporting?), and so remain unresolved and mysterious. In any case, the events challenged members of the household to take a position regarding the reality of ghosts and ghostlike beings.

Contemporary Legend

Contemporary legends, also known as *urban legends*, are short credence narratives that tell of an unusual event belonging to the very recent past. Unlike the typical historic legend, in which the events are usually set a generation or more in the past and often involve notable persons, the contemporary legend is set almost in the present day, often in the narrator's own community, and typically features ordinary people.[22] The narrator may support the credibility of the story by alleging that the events happened to a friend of a friend.[23] Although three degrees of separation is common in contemporary legends, it is not peculiar to them.

The contemporary legend frequently concludes with a surprise such as a reversal or irony that resembles the punch line of a joke. For example, in the modern legend known as the Solid Cement Cadillac a man driving a cement truck noticed a new convertible parked in his own driveway and his wife inside the house with a strange man. In jealous anger he filled the car with cement. Later he learned that the stranger was a car dealer who was delivering the convertible to the truck driver's house. His wife had ordered it as a birthday present for him.[24]

Although folk-narrative scholars initially supposed contemporary legends to be a new kind of legend, one expressive of a society that was no longer predominantly rural, scholars now perceive that stories of this sort have been in circulation for a long time. Indeed, there are ancient parallels to several contemporary legends that circulate in modern times, or at least to their principal motifs (Ellis 2001:46–57).[25] The existence of parallels between ancient and modern narratives is not in itself remarkable, but the urban-legend parallels seem more striking because such legends give the impression of being stories about current events and because, unlike many other traditional narratives, they are the sort of story that we ourselves hear, initially believe, and perhaps transmit. Because the legends are continually adapted to changing circumstances and are set in the very recent past, they have the feel of being new reports (Klintberg 1990).

Thus a Roman legend recounts how a craftsman created a glass bowl that was unbreakable. He secured an audience with the emperor, and when he was in the emperor's presence, he deliberately dropped the bowl onto the floor, picked it up, and repaired the dent with a hammer, expecting the emperor to be mightily impressed. The emperor asked him if anyone else knew of this technique for tempering glass, and the craftsman said no. Then the ruler had the man's head cut off, thinking that if the process should become general knowledge, gold would be worth no more than clay (Petronius *Satyrica* 51). In this story the ruler suppresses the secret of making unbreakable glass in order to protect the price of gold, just as in present-day rumors and stories a particular marvelous invention—an everlasting razorblade or lightbulb, an amazing additive for gasoline, and so on—has allegedly been suppressed, usually by a corporation that would suffer financially if the technology should become widely available.

Anecdote

Traditional *anecdotes* are credence narratives consisting of a brief incident that culminates in a memorable utterance or action by a named person, most often a humorous remark in direct speech.[26] They are told only of historical, not mythological, characters.[27] Ideally the story captures something deemed characteristic of the figure. Although the anecdote may seem to be a trivial form of expression, its importance is shown by the fact that it is the most abundantly represented genre of traditional story in Greek and Roman literature. Many hundreds of ancient anecdotes are known, far more than any other genre of traditional narrative.

Structurally, anecdotes are simple narratives. They typically consist of a single scene with two characters, the principal character and a lesser character whose narrative function is to provide the occasion for a comment or gesture made by the character of interest. For example, a Greek anecdote tells of an encounter between the philosopher Diogenes of Sinope and King Alexander of Macedon, known later as Alexander the Great. The philosopher was sunning himself in a grove as Alexander arrived in town. When Alexander stood over Diogenes and offered him anything he wanted, Diogenes merely asked him to move out of his light (Diogenes Laertios 6.38). The utterance fits the popular image of the Cynic philosopher, in particular his disdain for worldly possessions as well as his habit of frank speech (*parrhesia*).

As it happens, Diogenes was a magnet for anecdotes. Hundreds of stories circulated about him in antiquity, more than are told of any other ancient figure, and they continued to be recounted long after his death. As late as the second century of our era Dion Chrysostomos (*Oration* 72.11) remarks on the popularity of Diogenes stories. The philosopher was a local character who became an international figure.[28] And just as some persons such as Diogenes were the subject of many anecdotes, some anecdotes were attached to multiple persons.[29]

Although our word "anecdote" derives from Greek *anekdoton*, the Greek word did not bear its present meaning in the ancient language and was not an early term for the genre. Rather, the adjective *anekdoton* (etymologically, "not given out") signified something "unpublished" such as an unpublished text, or, by extension, something secret. In the sixth century the Byzantine author Prokopios employed the word in the plural as the title of a literary work, *Anekdota*, usually rendered *Secret History*, an intimate and scurrilous account of the regime of the emperor Justinian and the empress Theodora. Prokopios's *Anekdota* appeared in print in 1623, after which the word "anecdote" gradually acquired its modern sense in English and other languages.

The Greek narrative category that was closest to the present-day notion of anecdote was the *chreia*, which ancient rhetoricians defined as a concise reminiscence of an utterance or action attributed in a fitting way to a particular person.[30] Since the principal meaning of the noun *chreia* was "use, service," the ancients explained the term as being a reference to the usefulness of the genre. This perhaps unexpected idea is connected with the fact that in antiquity anecdotes were closely associated with the philosophic tradition. *Chreiai,* it was thought, crystallized and preserved teachings of the philosophers (Hock and O'Neil 1986:3–10). Thus the usefulness of a *chreia* was not so much that it allowed one to learn *about* an interesting character as to learn *from* such a character, and although many kinds of persons, from emperors to courtesans, star in anecdotal narratives, the ancient repertory of anecdotes teems disproportionately with philosophers.

APOTHEGM

A common subform of the anecdote is the *apothegm* (Greek *apophthegma*), a pointed utterance or retort.[31] Although apothegms can be transmitted as mere statements attributed to a particular person, more often they are given a setting, however minimal, and usually they have the form "A, when asked such and such by B, said C." For example, "Aesop, when asked by Kelaites what would produce the greatest disorder among humans, replied, 'If the dead should arise and demand their property back.'"[32]

Apothegms are also found contextualized and expressed in a more natural manner, as in Xenophon's account of the arrest and execution of the Athenian politician Theramenes. Upon being condemned to death, Theramenes was seized by an agent of the ruling oligarchy and dragged away through the agora. The victim cried out about the injustice he was suffering, prompting the goon to warn him to shut up or he would be sorry, to which Theramenes responded, "And if I do keep quiet, then I won't be sorry?" Later, when he was compelled to drink hemlock, he mockingly toasted the man who had condemned him to death. Xenophon comments that while such *apophthegmata* possibly do not merit recording, he himself admires Theramenes's self-possession and humor in the face of death (*Hellenika* 2.3.56).

Generically, the anecdote and the historical legend are close relatives, and many short belief narratives preserved in ancient literature in which authors tell about some remarkable person or event do not fit squarely into one category or the other. Depending upon the individual case, one might think of a particular narrative either as a short legend or as a diffuse anecdote, and for such stories the term "anecdotal legend" is perhaps descriptively apt.

CATCH TALE

Several comic anecdotes told in antiquity are cast in the form of a *catch tale*, a kind of narrative in which the speaker induces the listener to ask a particular question for which the speaker has a ready answer that makes the listener appear foolish.[33] Thus a story told of the orator Demades relates how he was once declaiming to the Athenians, who paid him little attention. So he asked if he might tell them an Aesopic tale. When they assented, he said that Demeter, a swallow, and an eel were traveling together. When they came to a river, the swallow took to the air and the eel went in the water. Then Demades fell silent. The listeners asked, "And Demeter, what did she do?" Demades responded, "She is angry with you for being content to listen to an Aesopic fable and neglect the affairs of the city!"[34] There was of course no tale for Demades to finish, for there was no such fable. The whole point was to embarrass the audience. In written texts, catch tales are necessarily represented as dialogues since they involve the spoken participation of both teller and listener.

Personal Narrative

The *personal-experience narrative*, or simply *personal narrative*, is a first-person narration based upon, or supposedly based upon, actual experiences that the narrator has had.[35] It is the sort of everyday, conversational story that we relate to friends and acquaintances when we tell of something that has happened to us. Personal narratives are sometimes called personal legends, but they are perhaps best regarded as a quasi-legendary form, since they are not traditional in the usual sense of the term. Special forms include the memorate and the personal fable, which I discuss below.

Homer relates how the royal couple Helen and Menelaos were relaxing in their palace with their young guests Telemachos and Peisistratos, when Helen slipped her grief-banishing drug into the wine and proposed that they pass the time telling stories: "Now sit in the hall and feast, and take pleasure in stories. I'll tell one myself that's apt" (*Odyssey* 4.238–239). She proceeded to tell of a personal experience (she described it as "apt" because it features Odysseus, whose son she is at that moment entertaining), after which her husband Menelaos recounted a personal experience of his own. Since the ancients had no special term for the genre of personal narrative, Helen speaks simply of exchanging "stories" (*mythoi*).

There is some generic sleight-of-hand here. Inasmuch as Helen and Menelaos are characters of the heroic age, stories that are personal-experience narratives for them may be heroic legends for us. Helen's story has to do with an occasion at Troy when Odysseus disguised himself and daringly made his way into the city, where Helen recognized him and secretly helped him. Menelaos's story describes the tense occasion when Menelaos, Odysseus, and other Greeks sat concealed within the Wooden Horse.

But there are many straightforward instances of the personal narrative in ancient literature. Lucian, for example, recounts experiences of his own in his essay *Alexander the False Prophet* (53–57).[36] The essay begins as a third-person account of the life and career of a religious charlatan, but toward the end the author himself enters the story, as Lucian charts Alexander's growing hostility toward him, which ends with an attempt on the author's life. Here, as in most personal narratives, the narrator's own experience takes center stage, but sometimes another person is the focus of narrative interest.[37]

MEMORATE

A subset of the personal-experience narrative is the *memorate*, or first-person account of a supernatural experience.[38] Whereas a belief legend is a third-person narrative of someone else's encounter with the supernatural, a memorate is a first-person account of one's own experience. An ancient example is the striking account that the poet Hesiod gives of his encounter with the Muses. Once, as Hesiod shepherded his sheep at the base of holy Mt. Helikon, the Muses appeared to him and addressed him, handed him a staff of laurel, "breathed into" him a divine voice with which to celebrate things future and things past, and told him to sing of the blessed gods (*Theogony* 22–34), whereupon he became a bard.[39]

While we possess Hesiod's own narration of his paranormal experience, for the memorate of Curtius Rufus, mentioned earlier, we are dependent upon retellings by Pliny and by Tacitus.[40] Is a retelling of Rufus's memorate still a memorate? It seems preferable to refer to a retelling of another person's story as a *vicarious* narration (Labov and Waletsky 1967:32, 34). Thus Rufus's first-person account of his encounter with a supernatural being is a memorate, whereas tellings by Pliny and Tacitus, at an unknown remove from Rufus's, are properly vicarious narratives, or vicarious memorates.

PERSONAL FABLE

The *personal-experience fable*, as we may call it, or simply *personal fable*, is a rare but interesting form that combines two narrative models, the personal narrative as a first-person account of the speaker's own experience and the fable as a simple metaphoric narrative possibly with an application to the immediate situation. Although the ancient instances of the personal fable are set in the heroic age, I locate it here among other personal narratives because the essential idea of the subgenre is not its content but its structure. It is at bottom a rhetorical device.[41] Thus Homer recounts how Odysseus came in the guise of an old beggar to the hut of the swineherd Eumaios. In the evening the weather turned rainy and windy, and Odysseus, hoping to induce his host to lend him a cloak, said he was going to express a wish in the form of a story (*epos*). He then told how, as a younger man at Troy, he and other soldiers had encamped for the night, and the weather turned bitterly cold. He had neglected to bring a cloak. He mentioned his plight to his commander, who cleverly devised a way for him to have the use of another man's cloak. When Odysseus finished his story, the swineherd commented, "That was a fine *ainos* you related, old fellow," and provided him with warm clothing for the night.[42]

The term that Eumaios uses for the beggar's story, *ainos*, signifies a narrative that has a hidden (i.e., metaphoric) meaning. Like the Aesopic fable, the personal fable is a traditional rhetorical device in which the speaker relates a brief story that is meant to be understood metaphorically and applied in some way to the present situation. The difference between the two lies in their content. The person who employs a personal fable draws upon a personal experience, or simply invents a realistic tale, as Odysseus does in the Homeric passage, and reports it as something he or she experienced. In contrast, the person who uses a fable of the Aesopic kind ordinarily draws upon a repertory of traditional fables and recounts an obviously fictitious tale featuring talking animals or the like. In the present scene the personal fable enables the guest to express a need without rudeness and presumption.

Traditional Fictions

Traditional fictions can be grouped together under the umbrella-term *folktale*, or simply *tale*. Since folktales are generally presented by narrators as fictional, they do not normally raise issues of historicity or belief. The

ANCIENT FOLK-NARRATIVE GENRES

Traditional Credence Narratives	*Traditional Fictions*
Myth	Wonder (or Fairy) Tale
Heroic Legend	Religious Tale
Historic Legend	Novella
Religious Legend	Milesian Tale
Aretalogy	Animal Tale
Sacred Story	Fable
Belief Legend	Short Fable
Contemporary (or Urban) Legend	Comic Tale
Anecdote	Joke
Apothegm	Tall Tale
Catch Tale	Chain Tale
Personal Narrative	
Memorate	
Personal Fable	

characters are usually nameless or bear generic folktale names, and the action is usually set in a generic location in the vague or timeless past. Narrators make little attempt to lend credibility to such narratives by claiming to have been present or by attributing their story to a reliable source, unless they do so in a playful spirit.

The principal genres discussed here are the wonder (or fairy) tale, the religious tale, and the novella, which are complex tales, and the animal tale, the fable, and the joke, which usually are simple tales. Frequently the tone is comic, especially in the shorter forms. Some of the genres may be regarded as nonbelief counterparts to particular credence genres, notably, the wonder tale to the heroic legend, the religious tale to the religious legend, and the tall tale to the personal narrative.

Wonder Tale

The stories known to English-speakers as *fairytales* are complex (that is, poly-episodic), artistically formed traditional tales of fantasy that mix the supernatural into the natural.[43] To folklorists they are *magic tales*

(*Zaubermärchen*) or *wonder tales* (*Wundermärchen*), since the element of magic along with an atmosphere of wonder are characteristic, whereas fairies rarely appear in them. I shall refer to them by the etic term "wonder tale" as well as by the familiar emic designation of "fairytale."

In many such tales a young hero or heroine goes out into the world, where at some point he or she encounters the supernatural, overcomes obstacles, and triumphs by means of kindness, perseverance, and/or luck, achieving wealth or elevated social status or both.[44] The wonder tale is the genre par excellence for happy endings in an atmosphere of the marvelous. Tales teem with such elements as enchanted spouses, supernatural adversaries (monsters, ogres, witches, etc.), mysterious helpers, talking animals, and magic objects, not to mention princes and princesses and kings and queens. Unlike characters of legend, who respond to supernatural phenomena as something extraordinary, characters in the wonder tale exhibit neither astonishment nor fear at giants, speaking animals, and other marvels, but treat them as perfectly ordinary.[45]

One such wonder tale has come down to us in classical literature, the enchanting story of Cupid and Psyche, which is recounted by the Roman novelist Lucius Apuleius in his *Metamorphoses*, also known as *The Golden Ass*. In this tale a beautiful princess, Psyche, was obliged to marry a mysterious supernatural being, who visited her nightly but forbade her ever to look upon him. When she was induced by her jealous sisters to break her husband's strange taboo, he departed, never to return. She regained him after a long and arduous quest, and they were happily reunited (4.28–6.24).

An abstract of the plot does not capture the tale's qualities of wonder, which are found mostly in the details. Thus Psyche, attired for her wedding, was led by her grieving parents to a cliff to be claimed by her mysterious husband-to-be, where the West Wind gently lifted the girl up and deposited her below in a flowery valley. From there she made her way through a woods to a palace of divine craftsmanship, full of treasure, and was welcomed by an invisible servant, who suggested that she rest, bathe, and proceed to the banquet table. And so on.

Although today wonder tales are generally treated as children's literature, historically they were a form of entertainment primarily for adults. Still, some traditional wonder tales are designed to appeal to children, and although none has survived entire from antiquity, we have tantalizing allusions to ancient children's tales and legends that attest to the existence of stories of this sort.

Religious Tale

Religious tales are traditional, noncredence narratives focusing upon some aspect of the relationship of humans and gods. An ancient Greek story, for example, relates how a man witnessed a ship sink with everyone onboard, whereupon he declared that the gods were unjust, since many innocent persons perished merely because, as he assumed, one impious man had been aboard. In the meantime some ants crawled upon him, and when one ant bit him, the man trampled on them. Thereupon the god Hermes appeared, saying, "So, then, won't you let the gods be your judges the way you are the judge of the ants?" (Babrios 117).

Religious tales are the folktale counterpart of religious legends. In religious tales, as in wonder tales, humans respond without awe to the appearance of the supernatural. So in the foregoing narrative the focus is upon what Hermes has to say, almost as though he were a human interlocutor, and not upon his sudden epiphany. In contrast, humans in belief legends and religious legends treat the supernatural as a startling intrusion into their world.

Novella

Like wonder tales, *novelistic tales*, or *novelle*, are complex narratives of traditional fiction, but they are realistic rather than fantastic.[46] The novella features domestic and urban themes such as love, seduction, cleverness, and thievery. Its heroes and heroines are ordinary people rather than royalty, the action takes place in realistic settings, and the protagonist faces social enemies rather than monstrous antagonists. When characters and places are named, they serve to create a realistic atmosphere rather than to lend serious credibility to the events.

An example of a novelistic tale of clever thievery is "The Treasury of Rhampsinitos." King Rhampsinitos of Egypt had a stone treasury constructed to house his valuables, but the man who built it secretly made one of the stones removable, and on his deathbed he revealed to his two sons this vulnerability of the king's treasury. The sons went to the building, removed the stone, and took away much of the king's money. The next time that the king visited his treasure-house, he was surprised to find that although the locks were intact, some valuables were missing. So he set a trap inside the treasury and when the two thieves struck again, one of them got caught. The ensnared thief instructed his brother to cut off his head in order to prevent his identification. The other brother did so, replaced the stone, and departed with his brother's head. Although the monarch tried again and again to catch the clever thief, the youth always outwitted him, until finally the king offered the thief a pardon and a reward. The youth presented himself to the king, who gave him his daughter in marriage (Herodotos 2.121).

MILESIAN TALE

A well-known ribald novella is exemplified by the tale "The Widow of Ephesos" mentioned earlier. A matron of Ephesos was famous for her fidelity, and when her husband died, she followed his corpse to his underground vault and remained there in constant mourning. Meanwhile, a soldier, seeing a light in the tomb, descended into the vault to investigate, and found the beautiful widow. He offered her food, which eventually she was persuaded to accept, and presently the two were passing their nights together in love. When the soldier discovered to his horror that one of the corpses he was supposed to be guarding had been stolen, the widow came to his rescue by replacing it with the dead body of her own late husband (Petronius *Satyrica* 110.6–113.9).

The bawdy novella of the widow is the sort of narrative that the Romans called a *Milesian tale*.[47] The appellation derives ultimately from a Greek literary work, *Milesiaka*, composed in the second century BC by a certain Aristeides, which seems to have been a compilation of amusing and licentious short stories in prose much like Boccaccio's *Decamerone*, possibly set in the city of Miletos. Its favorable reception is evidenced by the fact that it was translated into Latin, though very little survives of the original or the translation.[48]

Although Aristeides popularized the bawdy novella, the form predates him, for we find a ribald novella, lightly mythologized, centuries earlier in Homer's *Odyssey*. Ares and Aphrodite carried on an affair in her own home in the absence of her husband, the blacksmith Hephaistos. When the cuckold learned of the affair, he went to his smithy and forged fetters as fine as spiderwebs, which he draped around his bed. No sooner were the two lovers in bed together than they found themselves trapped in place and unable to move. Hephaistos summoned the other gods to view the discomfited pair (*Odyssey* 8.266–369). The mythic coloration here is superficial. The narrative is essentially a realistic tale of adultery and revenge set in the vague past in a nameless Greek village: a handsome soldier begins an affair with the beautiful wife of a lame blacksmith, but the cuckold has a trick of his own, trapping the lovers and displaying them publicly to their shame and for the amusement of others.

Animal Tale

The traditional *animal tale* is a short folktale featuring animals as characters, or animals and humans. A story told whimsically as an etiological tale about why dogs sniff one another relates how the dogs once sent ambassadors to Jupiter in order to complain of the poor treatment they received at the hands of humans, and to petition for a better lot in life. The ambassadors sniffed around for food on the way, took a long time to reach Jupiter's palace, and when they finally beheld the face of the mighty god, were so frightened that they shat all over the palace, whereupon they were driven away. The dogs then dispatched a second group of ambassadors, who took pains to guard against a similar mischance by stuffing their rear ends with perfume. But when they faced the father of the gods sitting on his throne and brandishing his thunderbolt, they promptly voided shit and perfume. The gods were indignant, and Jupiter decreed that dogs would evermore be tormented by hunger as well as experience bad treatment from humans. The dogs of today, who are still awaiting the return of their ambassadors, sniff the hind end of every new dog that shows up.[49]

Fable

Traditional *fables* are short tales that feature animals and, less often, humans, gods, plants, or the like as characters, and are meant to be understood both literally and metaphorically.[50] Like the anecdote (and, as we shall see, the joke), the fable is a simple form that typically consists of two characters and a single scene. Fables were not normally related as independent narratives having their own interest as stories, but rather played a subordinate role in several kinds of discursive context such as a conversation, speech, or essay. The fable's principal function was to convey the speaker's point metaphorically for the sake of emphasis or clarification, or to express a possibly unwelcome message by indirection.

An example of a fable in live social interaction is one employed by the philosopher Socrates in conversation with an acquaintance, Aristarchos.[51] After a dozen female relations had moved into Aristarchos's house, he provided them with wool so that they might engage in productive work. The work made them content, but now they chided him for being idle while they were working. Socrates said, "Why don't you tell them the tale (*logos*) of the dog? For they say that back when animals could talk a sheep said to her master, 'It's surprising that you give us sheep nothing beyond what we ourselves get from the land, though we supply you with wool and lambs and cheese, whereas you do share your own food with your dog, who supplies you with nothing of the sort.' Now the dog heard this and said, 'Yes by Zeus he does, because I keep you from being stolen by people or carried off by wolves. Without my protection you would not even be able to graze on your own for fear of being killed.' The sheep, they say, acknowledged that the dog should be honored above themselves. And so in your own case tell the women that you function as their watchdog and superintendent, and it is because of you that they live and work safely and happily."

This incident is characteristic of ancient fable-telling in a number of ways. First, ancient authors regularly represent fables as being communicated by an adult to other adults. Only recently in Western culture has the fable become a genre of story that is employed primarily for the edification and entertainment of children. Second, Socrates's fable is a simple tale consisting of one scene and two speaking parts (sheep, dog). The characters are animals that possess the faculty of human speech but otherwise preserve their animal relationships. The narrative offers enough of a story to be interesting, but just barely, so as not to distract from the point that its narrator wishes to make. Third, Socrates refers to his fable merely as "the tale of the dog," but he frames it with stereotypical expressions that were anciently associated with the fable. He begins with a common introductory formula ("back when animals could talk"), signaling that the narrative to come is a beast fable, and concludes with a coda or transitional formula ("And so in your own case . . ."), introducing the application of the fable to Aristarchos and his female relations.[52]

Most of the fables that have come down to us from antiquity have been preserved not in discursive contexts such as that of Aristarchos but in compilations. Inasmuch as fables in collections lack particular contexts, they can be equipped only with general, or ideal, applications. Accordingly, ancient literary fabulists frequently placed a generalized moral such as "This tale is suitable for an untruthful man" before (*promythion*) or after (*epimythion*) individual fables (Perry 1952:28). Over time *epimythia* predominated and developed into a regular feature of the literary fable, the familiar "morals" that conventionally follow fables in books.[53]

The Greeks and Romans referred to fables simply as "tales," as Socrates does above when he refers to his fable as the "tale of the dog." One could specify "fable" in particular by calling it an "Aesopic tale," since fables were closely associated with the figure of Aesop, an apparently historical person of the sixth century BC who in Greek tradition was a renowned teller of fables.

Animal fables, sometimes called beast fables, are not precisely identical with animal tales. Whereas the fable is told to instruct, the animal tale is told primarily to amuse.[54] Still, animal tales and animal fables do overlap in that both are simple narratives with sometimes stereotyped characters: clever fox, stupid wolf, and so on. And most of the animal tales that have come down to us from antiquity have been preserved in fable compilations, where fabulists convert them into fables or quasi fables by virtue of including them in a book of fables and sometimes equipping them with a moral. Although some fables and tales portray animals in a natural way, more often the animal characters speak and act to some extent like human beings, a phenomenon that has been termed "analogism."[55] Plants and nonliving things can also receive analogistic treatment.

SHORT FABLE

A minor subform of the fable is the *short fable*, or *fable-proverb*, a narrative only a sentence or so in length that may be regarded as a fable or a proverb or both.[56] This ambiguity is possible because some proverbs have the form of mininarratives, as in our "curiosity killed the cat."

An ancient example is "A mountain was in labor and gave birth to a mouse." The paroemiographer, or proverb scholar, Diogeneianos includes it in his compilation of proverbs, while the fabulist Phaedrus has it in his fable collection.[57]

Comic Tale

The traditional *comic tale* is a loose narrative category that includes humorous tales, both simple and complex (Oring 1992:81–93).

Humorous narratives, like anecdotes, sometimes cluster around a particular figure. An ancient instance is the cycle of tales about the simpleton Margites, who lacks an adult understanding of sexuality. An entire comic epic, now mostly lost, was composed about him.[58] Similarly, humorous cycles can develop around whole communities or regions or ethnic groups, a phenomenon found in many lands: the English tell of the silly people of Gotham, the Germans of the Schildbürger (inhabitants of the fictional town of Schilda), the Danes of the Molboer (inhabitants of Mols), the modern Greeks of the Chiotes (inhabitants of the island of Chios), the Italians of the inhabitants of Bergamo, and so on.[59] In antiquity proverbial Greek cities of fools included Abdera, on the north coast of the Aegean Sea, home of the dull-witted Abderites, and Kyme, on the east coast of the Aegean, home of the foolish Kymaians.[60] Differences between Abderite and Kymaian jokes are very minor, "Abderite" and "Kymaian" signifying little more than "numskull."[61]

A different sort of comic cycle features the delicate, luxury-loving Sybarites. A Greek city in southern Italy, Sybaris was renowned for its wealth and luxury (as our word "sybarite" continues to attest) until the city was destroyed in 510 BC. By the fifth century good-natured traditions about its self-indulgent inhabitants appeared (Herodotos 6.127), and in time a cycle of comic tales and jokes developed that treated Sybarite delicacy and extravagance with extreme exaggeration.[62] For example, Smindyrides the Sybarite went so far in delicacy that after sleeping on a bed of rose petals, he woke up complaining of blisters (Aelian *Historical Miscellany* 9.24). That so and so "went so far in delicacy" or "ran aground in delicacy" are conventional formulas that sometimes introduce Sybarite tales.[63]

Another kind of witticism about Sybarites consists not of tales but of descriptions of Sybarite culture in the spirit of caricature, such as that the Sybarites roofed over the roads that led to their country estates. This form of humor is called "caricaturism." A modern example is "He is so tall that he has to stand on a chair to brush his teeth" (Esar 1952:153–156).

JOKE

Traditional *jokes* are succinct, humorous tales featuring generic characters and consisting of a setup and a punch line.[64] Like anecdotes and fables, jokes are simple tales, consisting usually of two characters in a single scene. The narration provides a setting for a culminating utterance, which in ancient jokes is most often a foolish comment, just as in anecdotes it often is a clever put-down and in fables an epigrammatic statement that gives the point of the tale.

Many jokes turn upon what has been termed an "appropriate incongruity," which the listener must perceive in order to understand the joke and enjoy its humor.[65] For example, in an ancient Greek joke a numskull wanted to sleep but did not have a pillow, and so told his slave to place a clay jar under his head. When the slave pointed out that the jug was hard, the numskull told him to fill it with feathers (*Philogelos* 21). The listener must recognize that although stuffing a clay headrest with feathers is incongruous, there is a kind of appropriateness to it in that pillows are conventionally stuffed with feathers. If the numskull had told his slave to fill the jar with water, the incongruity would be arbitrary and there would be nothing humorous about the incident. So jokes, like fables, require a certain amount of decoding on the part of the listener for their point to be appreciated.[66]

After numskulls, the next most frequent kind of character in ancient jokes is a person of quick wit.[67] For example,

> When a talkative barber asked, "How shall I cut you?" a wit responded, "In silence."

This joke is structured as an apothegm, and indeed we find the same story told of a historical character and recounted as a comic apothegm:

> When a garrulous barber asked him [King Archelaos of Macedon], "How shall I cut you?" he responded, "In silence."

These texts illustrate how the same comic idea can be expressed through different genres.[68]

Obscene, or "dirty" (as we call them), jokes were recognized by the Greeks and Romans as a category of witticism, and several specimens survive.[69] Cicero, for example, declares that obscene humor is unworthy not only of public oratory but also of private parties (*On the Orator* 2.62.252).

TALL TALE

Tall tales, or *lying tales*, are traditional narratives of humorous and outrageous exaggeration.[70] Raconteurs tell of impossible or nearly impossible occurrences, frequently playing with the listener's credulity by dryly presenting the events as something that the speaker actually experienced. In such a case tall tales are jocular tales in the guise of personal narratives, or, more precisely, just as the personal narrative may be regarded as a first-person form of the historical legend, and the memorate as a first-person form of the belief legend, so the tall tale might be thought of as a first-person form of the comic folktale.

In his *True Stories* Lucian relates how he and his companions were sailing upon the sea when they encountered a fish that was over 150 miles in length. The monster came at them with its mouth open, and presently Lucian and his fellows were swallowed, ship and all. Inside the belly of the fish they saw wrecked ships, human bones, fish, and a large island. After cooking a meal they explored the island, whose perimeter was twenty-seven miles, and came upon a woods and a temple of Poseidon as well as a farmhouse. There they spoke with the farmer, who gave them an account of the different warring tribes that inhabited the great fish. After defeating them in battle, Lucian and his allies lived well for two years. Still, they wanted to escape their prison. Since they were unable to dig their way out, they finally started a forest fire, and after twelve days the creature was all but dead. They propped open its mouth and escaped with their ship into the open sea.[71]

Lucian's *True Stories*, a first-person account of the narrator's astonishing adventures, including a voyage to the moon, is a concatenation of traditional and original tall tales. Lucian himself asserts that the inventor of this sort of nonsense was Odysseus, for in his apologue to the Phaeacians, Odysseus tells of enslaved winds, one-eyed beings, cannibals, multiheaded creatures, and metamorphoses, and so is the prototype of the raconteur who tells lies to credulous listeners.[72]

Chain Tale

My taxonomy concludes with *chain tales,* which are cumulative narratives constructed upon a succession of linked items on a particular theme.[73]

In a traditional chain tale known in many countries the protagonist declares that a particular being (or thing) is the strongest thing in the world; however, there proves to be another thing that is stronger, and another that is yet stronger. The series of successively stronger items eventually concludes, sometimes with comic irony. An ancient example appears in a scene in a Greek comedy by Diphilos in which three girls are riddling. When someone asks what the strongest thing of all is, one girl answers, "Iron," since people use it to dig and cut everything. A second girl says that the blacksmith is stronger than iron, since he bends and softens it. But the third girl declares that the penis is the strongest of all, inasmuch as it pierces the blacksmith's rump (Athenaios 10.451b–c). Here the underlying chain is iron, blacksmith, penis.

In the foregoing taxonomy I offer an ordering and description of genres of traditional oral narrative found in the ancient Greek and Roman repertory. The taxonomy is mostly etic, and so is more extensive and systematic than the narrative categories of everyday Greek and Roman life. The native classification tells one that there is, for example, a narrative form known as *chreia*, but it does not tell one how this genre fits into the larger spectrum of ancient traditional story, whereas my descriptive taxonomy tells one that with regard to belief and setting the *chreia*, or anecdote, is one of several kinds of popular credence narrative set in the historical period, and that in its structural simplicity and pointedness it is closely allied to two fictitious genres: jokes and fables.

The purpose of this survey is to provide a clear and useful vocabulary and system of classification that more accurately reflect the realities of ancient narrative than the rough system that currently prevails among persons who work with ancient narrative. Still, one should keep in mind that the etic genres defined here are graded categories. While some texts are clear instances of a particular narrative genre, others escape neat classification. Like male/female, life/death, and other binary categories of our daily existence, analytic genre categories are useful even though they are challenged by fuzzy instances that do not make a clean fit.

THE PRESENT BOOK

The present work presents a generous selection of Greek and Roman traditional stories, illustrating genres and themes preserved in the rich literature that stretches from the earliest poets to the authors of late antiquity.

Three principles govern my choice of narratives from the ancient story-hoard, to borrow an image. First, I select those stories that, in the course of my reading classical literature over five or so decades, have persisted in my memory because of their artfulness or cleverness or bizarreness, or because they crystallize a feeling or attitude so well. They are stories that I hope you, my reader, will encounter as old friends or welcome discoveries. To this base of personal favorites I add tales whose popularity and widespread appeal is proven by the fact that they have remained generally familiar over many centuries. I mean such stories as the anecdote of the philosopher Diogenes walking the streets of Athens with a lantern in search of an "honest" man, the legend according to which the emperor Nero sang while Rome burnt, or the Aesopic fable of the tortoise that outraced a hare. I supplement these two groups of tales with narratives that further illustrate the generic range, typical content, and recurrent themes of Greek and Roman storytelling. I emphasize the popular genres because they existed in far greater numbers than the mythological genres and because they were the tales that the Greeks and Romans most frequently told. I treat the notion of "story" somewhat loosely, as a graded category, admitting some texts that could more accurately be described as "self-contained narrative units" than as stories.

I translate the stories directly from the ancient sources, letting the original authors speak for themselves, rather than synthesizing and paraphrasing. I do not modify the content other than to take the small liberties that translators allow themselves, such as to replace a personal pronoun with a proper name for the sake of clarity (thus, "Alexander" for "he"). To explain possibly obscure references I insert clarifying words in brackets here and there, or append a footnote.

One consequence of my presenting the original sources in translation is that the texts display their differences in tone, fullness, and purpose openly, since I do not coerce them into a uniform style and pace. Conscious artistry alternates with casual narration, a story told fully is neighbor to one related elliptically, verse mingles with prose, the restrained archaic style of a Hesiod stands next to the lively prose of a Lucian. The principal advantage is that I bring you, the reader, as close as possible to the ancient narratives, so that you experience something of their charm and their ordinariness, their familiarity and their otherness. In some instances I offer more than one version of a narrative, especially when a text offers interesting details that are not found in another.

My arrangement of the narratives reflects a mix of genre and theme, bringing out, I believe, interesting and occasionally surprising connections among the stories. A strictly generic ordering would be dull, it seems to me, in addition to the fact that not all narratives are easily classified by genre, which are only ideal categories. Although a strictly thematic arrangement might be interesting, it would also be somewhat arbitrary since almost any story displays more than one theme. So in the present work themes and genres weave in and out of one another. The selection begins with the famous fairytale of Cupid and Psyche and other fantasies of palaces and royal persons. It goes from there to stories of the supernatural and continues with a mix of legends on different themes, some bizarre and others familiar. Tales of tricksters and lovers are next, followed by stories of two kinds of public performer, artists and athletes. These stories lead into anecdotes and legends about other well-known persons, which are followed in turn by traditions about sages and philosophers and wisdom in general. The anthology concludes with jokes and other humorous tales.

A disadvantage of limiting myself to texts in translation is that I am obliged to exclude some stories that I would like to include, stories whose texts are too long for a book of this sort or that contain too much extraneous material or that are unsuitable in some other way. An example is an interesting portrait of the Athenian statesman Perikles and his young charge Alkibiades, not yet twenty years old. Alkibiades asked Perikles if the older man could explain to him what a law was. Certainly, replied the elder statesman, that wouldn't be difficult at all. As Perikles proceeded to instruct Alkibiades, the youth responded with one pesky question after another in the manner of a Socrates (of whom, of course, the young Alkibiades was an admirer). Perikles finally said, in effect, "You know,

Alkibiades, when I was your age, I too was very good at this, coming up with and trying out clever arguments." To which Alkibiades responded, in effect, "Ah, then, I wish I had known you back then when you were at your best" (Xenophon *Reminiscences* 1.2.40–46). I first encountered this story in Berkeley in the late 1960s in a course on Aristophanes's *Clouds* taught by the late K. J. Dover, who recounted it as evidence that adolescent rebelliousness against elders has a long history. Alkibiades was provoking Perikles, and Perikles recognized it because he had done the same when he was younger. Over the years the story stayed in my mind, and I was pleased to encounter it again when I read Xenophon's *Reminiscences*. Unhappily for my present purpose, Xenophon's narration is very long; he re-creates the entire dialogue. For Xenophon's ancient readers much of the interest of the narrative doubtless lay in the details of the give-and-take between the uppity youth and the prominent statesman, whereas for me it lies in the fact of the conflict of generations and in the portrayal of the particular personalities involved. The text has too much extraneous material for inclusion in the present compilation, and so it did not make the cut, although, as you see, I have managed to find a way to mention it anyway.

Some narratives that I would have liked to include have been omitted for reasons that have nothing to do with their textual qualities. Consider a striking story I remember, or think I remember, about the great church of Hagia Sophia in Constantinople. On the occasion of its dedication the guests entered the nave and presently fled in terror since the dome seemed to them to be floating in the air unsupported, somewhat as allegedly happened in 1895 during the first screening of Louis Lumière's film *The Arrival of the Train*, when the spectators are said to have run out of the Cinématographe Lumière in panic, thinking that the filmic locomotive was headed right for them.[74] Since I did not know offhand what the Byzantine sources for the Hagia Sophia story were, I pulled all the books on Hagia Sophia from the shelves of the Indiana University Art Library and went through them page by page, expecting soon to find many mentions of the story. To my bewilderment I encountered not a trace of it. I mentioned my quest to my friend and colleague Henry Glassie, who, as it happened, also recalled the story. He joined my search but likewise came up with nothing. I wrote to Byzantinists here and abroad, who suggested as a possible source this and that Byzantine work, each (for me) less familiar than the last. I am still looking.

At the back of the book I provide notes on the ancient sources of the translated texts, related texts of interest, and bibliographic references to the scholarly literature. These notes make no claim to be exhaustive. When a story is migratory, or widely distributed, and has been so classified in folkloristic indices, I include this information.

For many of the texts I append brief comments of a cultural or historical nature. I pay no attention, however, to the question of the extent to which individual stories have, or may have, a historical basis, a topic with which classical scholarship seems to me to be unduly obsessed; indeed, I myself assume that most traditional stories, regardless of genre, are historically untrue, if not entirely then for the most part. It is time to dispense with the oft-repeated article of faith that legends preserve a kernel of truth. Why should they? To take a familiar example from heroic legend: from ancient commentators to present-day scholars the Trojan Horse has often been rationalized as being a distorted memory of a siege engine. Speaking against this explanation is the fact that siege engines are not attested until centuries after the period in which the Trojan War is set. But even if that were not the case, nothing is gained by trying to explain the device away as distorted history, for what is striking and memorable about the stratagem of the horse is precisely its wonderful improbability, its boldly treating a fantastic idea with all the seriousness and weight of an actual event. The hollow horse may be bad history or not, but it is fine legendry.[75]

NOTES

1. Pliny the Younger *Letters* 2.20.1: *Assem para et accipe auream fabulam.*
2. Bascom 1965; Pike 1971; Ben-Amos 1976.

3. Graf 1993:9–13; Fulk 2002:226–228; Pàmias 2014:64–65.
4. In fact, the idea precedes the Grimms, though its widespread acceptance is probably owed to them (Hansen 2002a:25 n. 2).
5. For example, James George Frazer divides traditional ancient stories into myths, legends, and folktales ([1921] 1:xxvii–xxxii), and H. J. Rose sorts them into myths, sagas, and *Märchen* (1929:10–14).
6. On myth see, for example, Dundes 1984 and Schrempp and Hansen 2002. For a critique of sacredness as a criterion of mythic narrative see Hansen 2002b:20–21.
7. *Works and Days* 156–173; M. L. West 1978:190–196.
8. Aristotle *Politics* 7.13.3; cf. Hansen 1996:137–139.
9. *Histories* 3.122.2; Asheri et al. 2007:508. For Romans the historical era can be considered to begin with the foundation of Rome (Hawes 2014:166–167).
10. Accordingly, the plots of the comic poets are sometimes mythological parodies, sometimes adaptations of folktales, and sometimes inventions of the playwrights. See Hansen 1977.
11. The observation appears in the introduction to their collection of German legends; cf. Grimm (1981) 1:1.
12. See Herodotos 5.55–65, 6.123; Thucydides 1.20–21, 6.53–59.1; R. Thomas 1989:238–282; and M. W. Taylor 1991.
13. Athena's father, the sky god Zeus, is the deity in charge of weather.
14. Longo 1969; Scobie 1969:24–27, 1979:240–244.
15. Juvenal 15.13–16: *mendax aretalogus*.
16. Herodotos 2.51.4, 2.62.2, and 2.81.2.
17. Lucian *On the Syrian Goddess* 26. For the context see story 136 in this book, "The King's Trusted Friend."
18. On belief legends see, for example, Klintberg 1989; Dégh 1996; and Ellis 2001.
19. See Ebner et al. 2001 and Ogden 2007.
20. See further Felton 1999:29–34, 62.
21. See further Felton 1999:63–65.
22. For samplings see, for example, Brunvand 2001 and Bennett and Smith 2007. Brunvand 1993 (325–347) has produced a provisional type-index of contemporary legends recorded in the United States. For a bibliography of scholarship on the contemporary legend see Bennett and Smith 1993.
23. The "friend of a friend" connection has become so familiar that the International Society for Contemporary Legend Research (ISCLR) has whimsically adopted it as the name of their newsletter, *FOAFtale News*.
24. Brunvand 2001:400–401; Bennett and Smith 2007:93–94.

25. See Ellis 1983 (gang initiation), Mayor 1991 (a parent's request), Mayor 1992 (choking Doberman), Mayor 1995 (poisoned blankets), Lassen 1995 (improved product), Hansen 2002a:367 (cadaver arm), Bennett and Smith 2007:239–243 (the master craftsman and his apprentice), Ingemark 2008 (alligators in the sewer).
26. On anecdotes see, for example, A. Taylor 1970; *EM* 1:528–541; Bauman 1986:54–77; Hock and O'Neil 1986, 2002; Dillon 2004; Cashman 2008; and Goldhill 2009. I restrict the term "anecdote" to the sense described here. It does not advance the present purpose to employ it loosely, as some persons do, to refer to any short, humorous tale.
27. Dillon 2004:188 n. 14.
28. On anecdotes about the Cynics, especially Diogenes of Sinope, see, for example, Halliwell 2008:372–387. On local-character anecdotes see Stahl 1975; Mullen 1978:113–129; and Cashman 2008.
29. Some ancient anecdotes are told of as many as three or four different persons; cf. Hard 2012:217, nos. 350 and 353. On migratory anecdotes see Barrick 1976.
30. I synthesize the definitions of Theon, Quintilian, Hermogenes, Priscian, Aphthonios, and Nikolaos; see Hock and O'Neil 1986.
31. On apothegms see Gemoll 1924 and Russo 1997:57–64.
32. Perry 1952:249, no. 4; similarly, *Life of Aesop* 47.
33. On catch tales see Esar 1952:185–188; Hansen 2002a:75–79. The term derives from "catch" in the sense of "snare, trick." Ancient catch tales are recounted as anecdotes told of historical persons, for which reason I discuss them here, whereas in modern oral tradition they are normally playful fictions.
34. Perry 1952:63.
35. On personal-experience narratives see, for example, Labov and Waletsky 1967; Stahl 1989; Dégh 1995; and Georgakopoulou 1997.
36. Lucian's personal-experience narrative reads very much as though it were a response to the question that Labov and Waletsky (1967) asked their informants, which was, approximately: "Did you ever have an experience in which you felt your life was in danger?"
37. On other-oriented and self-oriented personal narratives see Stahl 1983.
38. On the memorate (rhymes with "thanks a lot") see, for example, Honko 1964; Jauhiainen 1998; and Dégh 2001:58–79. The Swedish folklorist Carl von Sydow (1948:73–74) proposed the term originally as a designation for first-person personal-experience narratives of any sort, distinguishing them as a genre from legends. Folk-narrative scholars have adopted the term (Anglicized also as "memorat") but in practice restrict it to personal narratives of supernatural experience.

39. Cf. M. L. West 1966:158–161. To West's list of parallels add that of *Life of Aesop* (Vita G) 4–8. Originally mute, Aesop encounters the goddess Isis and the Muses in the field where he is working. After he treats them kindly, they grant him speech and eloquence and inventiveness.
40. Pliny the Younger *Letters* 7.27; Tacitus *Annals* 11.21.
41. Other instances of the personal fable include Sophocles *Aias* 1140–1162 and, in the Old Testament, 1 Kings 20:38–43. See further Meuli 1954:73–77, 85–86; Perry 1959:23; and Verdenius 1962.
42. *Odyssey* 14.457–522. See further Minchin 2001:209–216.
43. On the wonder tale generally see, for example, Dégh 1969; Lüthi 1986; Holbek 1987; and Propp 2012:147–224. On correspondences between ancient traditional narratives and modern wonder tales see Siegmund 1984; Anderson 2000; and Hansen 2002a, 2008. Some authors reserve the term "fairytale" (a rendering of the French *conte de fées*) for literary tales composed in the manner of the oral wonder tale. On the literary fairytale see Zipes 2000.
44. Haney 1999:92: "The wondertale is basically an oral story about a young man's, or less often a girl's, initial venture into the frightening adult world." We know little about the ancient repertory of wonder tales, but the plots of several ancient hero legends (e.g., Perseus and Andromeda, Theseus and Ariadne, Jason and Medeia) agree essentially with those of particular modern wonder tales and seem to be adaptations of ancient wonder tales (Hansen 2002a:15–16 and passim).
45. See further Lüthi 1975.
46. On the traditional novella see, for example, Rohde 1914; Cataudella 1957; Trenkner 1958; and Propp 2012:225–274.
47. Greek *Milesiakos logos* (Lucian *Loves* 1), Latin *Milesia* (sc. *fabula*) (Apuleius *Metamorphoses* 4.32).
48. See further Harrison 1998; Schmeling 2011:358–359; and Bowie 2013.
49. Phaedrus 4.19 (Perry 1952:517). Phaedrus, however, does not venture to offer a moral for the tale. See ATU 200B *Why Dogs Sniff at One Another*.
50. On fables see, for example, Perry 1959; Karadagli 1981; Dijk 1997; and Holzberg 2002. For a bibliography of fable scholarship see Carnes 1985. On animal tales see Propp 2012:283–299.
51. Xenophon *Reminiscences* 2.7. For a survey of ancient fables recounted in situational contexts see Karadagli 1981:6–52.
52. The commonest introductory formulas for the Greek fable are "At the time when animals spoke the same language as humans" and "Now hear this tale." See Crusius 1879:134–135 and Karadagli 1981:99–100.

53. See further Perry 1940.
54. Perry 1959:21 n. 16.
55. Sydow 1948:134–135, 144.
56. "Fable-proverb" is Perry's term (1959).
57. Diogeneianos 8.75; Phaedrus 4.24. See further Otto 1890:234–235, no. 1173; and Perry 1965:xxviii–xxxiv.
58. On Margites see M. L. West 2003:224–253.
59. See, for example, Stapleton 1900 on Gothamites; Bausinger 1961 on the Schildbürger; Christensen 1939 on the Molboer; Orso 1979:81–84 on the Chiotes; and, in general, Clouston 1888.
60. Thierfelder 1968:16–17; Baldwin 1983:80–81. The ancient Greek jokebook, *Philogelos*, features a section devoted to Kymaian jokes (nos. 154–182) and another to Abderite jokes (110–127); it also includes some Sidonian jokes (128–139), although the Phoenician city of Sidon is not elsewhere treated as a city of stupid folk.
61. Beard (2014:192–193) perceives small differences among jokes told of the foolish inhabitants of Abdera, Kyme, and Sidon.
62. See Rohde 1914:587–589; Trenkner 1958:8, 175–176; Hansen 1997; Bowie 2013:252–255; and Gorman and Gorman 2014.
63. See further Gorman and Gorman 2014:212–238.
64. On jokes and comic tales see, for example, Freud 1960; Röhrich 1977; Baldwin 1992; Bremmer 1997; Graf 1997; and Andreassi 2004. The notion that punch-line jokes first emerged, or were recognized, only in the nineteenth century (Röhrich 1977:4, 8) cannot be maintained, since punch-line jokes are attested in antiquity.
65. Oring 1992:1–15 and 2003:1–12; however, see Schrempp 1995 on the presence of appropriate incongruities also in nonhumorous contexts.
66. Oring 1992:6 (jokes as puzzles with solutions); Perry 1959:23 (fables as metaphors), 35 (a fable has a *lysis*, or solution).
67. In his *Nicomachean Ethics* (4.8) Aristotle discusses the man of ready wit (*eutrapelos*) as a type, and contrasts related character types such as the buffoon and the boor.
68. The sources are, respectively, *Philogelos* 148 and Plutarch *Apothegms of Kings and Generals: Archelaos* 2 (*Moralia* 177a). See further Nicolson 1891; Andreassi 2004:75–76; and Beard 2014:213.
69. For example, *Philogelos* 45, 245, 251.
70. On the tall tale see, for example, Henningsen 1965; G. Thomas 1977; Mullen 1978:130–148; Bauman 1986:78–115; C. S. Brown 1987; and Rammel 1990.
71. *True Stories* 1.30–2.2. See further Hansen 2002a:261–264 and ATU 1889G *Man Swallowed by Fish*.

72. Lucian *True Stories* 1.3, with reference to Homer *Odyssey* 9–12.
73. On chain tales see Esar 1952:34–37, 49–52; and Propp 2012:275–282. Chain tales, like catch tales, are structurally defined forms. Folklorists classify them both as formula tales.
74. Loiperdinger 2004. He demonstrates, however, that there is no real evidence that the spectators reacted with panic to the fifty-second screening, and argues that the story is a cinematic legend.
75. See further Hansen 2002a:174–175.

CHAPTER 1

KINGS AND PRINCESSES

We begin with the famous tale of Cupid and Psyche, the earliest recorded fairytale in Western literature, and continue with two shorter stories set in the world of royalty and palaces.

I. CUPID AND PSYCHE

In a certain city there were a king and queen who had three beautiful daughters. Although the elder two were of pleasant enough appearance and it was thought that human praise could do them justice, the beauty of the youngest girl was so extraordinary and remarkable that human language was too poor to express or even adequately praise it. Indeed, many citizens and foreigners, brought together in eager crowds by word of so exceptional a sight and then stunned at her unequaled beauty, put their right thumb and fingertip upon their lips and offered the girl outright religious adoration as being the goddess Venus herself. Rumor had now spread through nearby cities and neighboring regions that the goddess to whom the deep blue sea had given birth and whom the foamy waves had brought forth was freely granting the grace of her godhead by mingling with mortals; or at least that, newly fertilized by drops from heaven, the earth rather than the sea had produced a second Venus in the flower of her maidenhood.*

This belief increased enormously day by day. As her fame spread, it reached the nearby islands, much of the mainland, and most of the provinces. Many persons, making long journeys and voyaging over the deep

*According to Greek myth the goddess Aphrodite (Roman Venus) emerged from the sea, which had been fertilized by Ouranos (Sky).

sea, flocked to observe this marvel of the age. No one sailed to Paphos or Knidos or even Kythera to view the goddess Venus herself any more. Her worship was forsaken, her temples disfigured, her couches threadbare, and her rites neglected. Her statues lacked garlands, her altars were bereft of offerings and shamefully cold. It was now the girl to whom people addressed their prayers, and it was in a human shape that the power of the great goddess was placated. At the maiden's morning appearance she was propitiated with sacrifices and banquets in the name of Venus, who in actuality was elsewhere. And as the girl strolled upon the streets, people crowded around and adored her with garlands and flowers.

This outrageous transference of divine veneration and honors to a mortal girl kindled anger in the real Venus, who, unable to contain her indignation, tossed her head and muttered loudly to herself, "Here I am, the ancient mother of nature, primordial origin of the elements, Venus the nurturer of the whole world! But I have to share my honor with a mortal girl, and my name, founded in heaven, is profaned with foul earth. It seems I myself must put up with shared adoration and vicarious worship, while a mortal girl walks around with my image. It was in vain, then, that that shepherd to whom great Jupiter gave his approval for fairness and impartiality preferred me for my unrivaled beauty to those other great goddesses!* But this girl, whoever she is, will feel no joy in usurping my honors. I'll see to it that she regrets this beauty of hers to which she has no right!"

Without delay Venus summoned that winged and reckless son of hers, who, armed with torch and arrows and wickedly scorning public morals, runs through the houses of others at night ruining everyone's marriages, behaving disgracefully with impunity, and never doing any good. Although he was already irresponsible by nature, she goaded him on even

---

*Venus alludes to the Judgment of Paris. The god Zeus (Jupiter) arranged for the shepherd Paris to judge a contest in beauty among the goddesses Hera (Juno), Athena (Minerva), and Aphrodite (Venus). He awarded the prize to Aphrodite.

more. Taking him to the city in question, she showed him Psyche—for this was the girl's name—in person and, fuming and muttering in indignation, laid before him the whole tale of her rival in beauty. "By the bonds of a mother's love," she said, "I implore you to avenge your mother fully by the sweet wounds of your arrows and the honeyed burns of your torch. Punish that insolent beauty without mercy, and do this one thing for me willingly in return for all else. Let the maiden be seized with a burning passion for the lowest sort of man, someone whose status, inheritance, and very self Fortune has cursed, a person so lowly that in the entire world he has no equal in wretchedness!"

So she spoke, and after pressing long, avid, and sensuous kisses upon her son, she made her way to the shore of the sea. She trod with her rosy feet upon the surface of the quavering waves and, lo, sat down upon the bright surface of the deep sea. As soon as she wished for it, as if she had issued orders in advance, her marine attendants promptly appeared. There came Nereids singing in chorus, shaggy Portunus with his sea-blue beard, Salacia with an armful of fish, and little Palaemon the dolphin rider. And on all sides troops of Tritons leapt about, one softly blowing his conch-shell trumpet, another blocking the heat of the hostile sun with a silken covering, and a third holding a mirror before his mistress's eyes, while still others, yoked in pairs, swam beneath her chariot. Such was the host that escorted Venus as she traveled to Ocean.

Meanwhile, for all her conspicuous beauty, Psyche reaped no enjoyment from her loveliness. She was gazed upon by everyone, she was praised by everyone, but no one, king or prince or even commoner, came as a suitor desiring her in marriage. To be sure, they marveled at her divine beauty, but only in the way that everyone marvels at a skillfully worked statue. Her two elder sisters, whose moderate good looks no one had much talked about, had long ago gotten engaged to royal suitors and were now happily wed, but Psyche remained at home as an unmarried maiden and wept at her solitary loneliness, suffering in body and hurt in mind, and hating that beauty of hers that so pleased the entire world.

The wretched father of the unfortunate girl suspected she was the object of heavenly hatred, and feeling anxious about divine anger, he consulted the ancient oracle of Apollon at Miletos. With prayers and sacrifices he asked the great deity for a marriage and husband for the slighted girl. Apollon, though he is Greek and Ionian, kindly gave his oracular response in Latin for this present author of a Milesian tale.*

> King, place the girl, dressed for a funereal wedding,
>   On the cliff of a lofty mountain.
> Expect not a son-in-law of mortal stock,
>   But a cruel, wild, and viperous calamity
> That flies in the air with wings and torments every creature,
>   Disabling them all with fire and iron,
> A being before whom Jove† himself trembles, the other gods are terrified,
>   And the dark waters of the Styx shudder.

After hearing the utterance of the sacred prophecy, the king who once was happy made his way home reluctantly and downcast, and explained the instructions of the inauspicious oracle to his wife. There followed several days of mourning, weeping, and wailing. But eventually the horrid fulfillment of the fearful oracle was at hand. Preparations were made for the poor girl's funeral-like wedding, the flame of the torch died down with ashes of black soot, the sound of the wedding pipes changed into the plaintive Lydian mode, the joyful wedding song ended in doleful wailing, and the bride wiped away her tears with her own bridal veil. The whole city joined in lamenting the sorrowful fate of the afflicted household, and

---

*The narrator declares playfully that the Greek god Apollon (Latin Apollo), whose oracles are uttered in Greek, gives the present oracle in Latin out of consideration for the narrator, who of course is a Roman writing in Latin. The narrator describes his work here and elsewhere (*Metamorphoses* 1.1) as "Milesian."

†Jove = Jupiter.

in sympathy with the general mourning a suspension of public business was forthwith decreed.

But the divine command had to be obeyed, and so poor Psyche proceeded to the punishment ordained for her. After the ceremony of the funereal wedding had been performed with great sorrow, and with the entire populace as escorts, Psyche was led forth, a living corpse, the tearful girl joining in the procession, not of her wedding, but of her funeral. When her parents, dejected by the calamity, were slow to execute the abominable deed, their own daughter urged them on, saying, "Why torture your unhappy old age by prolonging your weeping? Why exhaust your spirit—mine, really—with so much wailing? Why disfigure with useless tears your faces that I revere? Why harm my eyes by harming yours? Why pull out your gray hair? Why beat your chest, your holy breasts? This is your fine reward for my extraordinary beauty. Only now do you understand that you've been struck with a fatal blow of impious envy. When the nations and peoples were celebrating me with divine honors, when they united in calling me a new Venus, it was then you should have grieved and wept, then you should have mourned me as one already dead. Now I perceive and understand that I perish only from the name Venus. So lead me to the cliff to which fate has assigned me, and station me there. I hurry on to this happy marriage of mine, to see this noble husband of mine. Why should I put off meeting him who was born for the ruin of the whole world?"

Saying this, the maiden fell silent and with a vigorous step joined the procession of people escorting her. They went to the prescribed cliff of the lofty mountain, on the topmost summit of which they all placed the girl, and leaving behind the wedding torches by which they had lit their way and which were now extinguished by their tears, they returned home with bowed heads. Her wretched parents, worn out by the disaster, hid themselves in the darkness of their shuttered home, giving themselves over to unbroken night.

As Psyche stood terrified, trembling, and weeping on the summit of the cliff, she was slowly wafted up by the mild breeze of a gently blowing

Zephyr that made the edges of her clothing flutter here and there and caused its folds to billow, and was conveyed by its tranquil breath little by little down the slope of the high rock. Upon her descent she was gently laid down in the lap of blossoming sod in the valley below.

In this place of soft grass Psyche lay on a bed of dewy turf, her distressed mind calmed down, and fell sweetly asleep. Refreshed from her rest, she arose with her mind at ease. She saw a wood planted with immense trees and a glistening spring of glassy water, and in the middle of the wood beside the course of the spring there stood a palace built not by human hands but by divine art. As soon as you entered it, you would know you were gazing upon the splendid and delightful residence of some god. The paneled ceiling was fashioned from citrus wood and ivory, and columns of gold stood beneath it. The walls were all covered with silver reliefs of wild and tame animals that were on their way to meet the entrant at the door. It was a truly amazing man, or rather demigod or more likely god, who had worked all that silver with such art! The floor was divided up into different pictures in the form of mosaics made of precious stones. Twice blessed and more are those who tread on gems and jewels! The other parts of the house, precious beyond price and extending far and wide, and all the walls, which were solid blocks of gold, gleamed by their own luster so that the house created its own daylight whether the sun wished it or not. So shiny were the rooms, the portico, and the baths. The rest of the opulence answered in the same way to the magnificence of the house so that it seemed to be a heavenly palace built for great Jove to dwell among humans.

Enticed by the delights of the place, Psyche approached and, now a bit bolder, crossed the threshold. Soon her eagerness for the beautiful sight drew her on so that she examined everything in detail. On the other side of the palace she saw storehouses finished with sublime craftsmanship and filled with great treasures. There was nothing that was not there. Beyond even the marvel of such riches, what especially amazed her was that this treasure-house of the whole world was protected by no chains or locks or guards.

As she was looking at these things with the greatest pleasure, a disembodied voice manifested itself, saying, "Mistress, why are you amazed at this great wealth? It's all yours. So go to your bedroom, soothe your weariness in bed, and proceed to your bath when you wish. We whose voices you hear will diligently attend upon you as your maidservants, and a royal banquet will quickly appear for you after you have tended to your body." Psyche recognized that her felicity was owed to divine providence. In obedience to the instructions of the bodiless voice, she first dispelled her weariness with sleep and then a bath, whereupon instantly there appeared next to her a seat in the form of a half circle. From the dining utensils she understood that it was for her comfort, and gladly reclined. Abundant courses of nectar-like wine and different foods were placed before her, handled not by a servant but by a sort of breeze. She saw no one, only hearing words being uttered and so having only voices as servants. After the rich feast an invisible being entered and sang, while another played the lyre, which likewise was not visible. Then voices in concert reached her ears so that clearly a chorus was present, although no body appeared.

When these pleasures ended, Psyche went to her bedroom at the urging of the evening. Night was well along when there came a soft sound to her ears. Fearing for her virginity in so solitary a place, she trembled in terror, afraid of the unfamiliar more than of any particular danger. Then her unknown husband entered, joined Psyche in bed, made her his wife, and left quickly before sunrise. The voices attending her in the room took care of the new bride and her lost virginity. Things continued this way for a long time, and, as is natural, the strangeness of the situation turned into pleasure as Psyche became accustomed to it, and the sound of the unseen voices comforted her in her solitude.

Meanwhile, Psyche's parents were wasting away from tireless sorrow and grief, and, as news of the event spread, her older sisters learned everything, left their homes in sadness and mourning, and went eagerly to see and talk with their parents. That night Psyche's husband spoke to her as follows (for she had full contact with him in terms of touch and sound, but not sight), "Sweetest Psyche, my dear wife, cruel Fortune is threatening you with deadly danger, which I think you must pay attention to with special caution. Your sisters, upset and believing you are dead, are following in your steps and will soon reach the cliff. If you should hear their wailing, don't answer them or even look at them, for if you do, you will bring great grief on me and sheer ruin on yourself." Nodding her assent, she promised she would do as her husband wished. But after he and the night had both disappeared, the poor girl spent the whole day crying and beating her breast, saying again and again that she had now truly come to nothing, confined as she was in her opulent prison, deprived of human company, and unable to comfort her sisters in their grief or even to see them at all. After declining her bath and food and all other refreshment, and crying copiously, she fell asleep.

Presently, and sooner than usual, her husband came to bed, put his arms around his weeping wife, and remonstrated with her, asking, "Is this what you promised me, my Psyche? What am I, your husband, now to expect or hope from you? All day and all night long you keep tormenting yourself, even in your husband's embrace. Do then as you wish, and obey the ruinous urging of your heart. Only keep in mind my grave warning when you begin, too late, to be sorry." With prayers and threats of suicide, she forced her husband to accede to her wish, which was to see her sisters, soothe their grief, and speak with them. He yielded to the entreaties of his new bride and even permitted her to present them with gold or jewels, as she might wish. But he warned her repeatedly, sometimes frightening her, not to let herself be persuaded by the baleful advice of her sisters to seek to learn what her husband looked like and not to cast herself down from Fortune's heights because of impious curiosity, and so no longer partake of his embraces.

She thanked her husband and, her spirits now lifted, said, "I'd prefer to die a hundred times over than to lose my delightful marriage with you, for whoever you are, I love and adore you desperately, as I do my own soul. I wouldn't compare Cupid himself with you. But I beg you to grant me this wish as well. Order your good servant Zephyr to bring my sisters to me here just as he brought me." Planting persuasive kisses on him, plying him with soothing words, and entwining him with her arms, she added these words to her caresses: "My darling, my husband, sweet soul of your Psyche." Her husband unwillingly succumbed to the force and power of her amorous whisperings, and promised to do all she asked. Since daylight was approaching, he vanished from his wife's hands.

The sisters inquired about the location of the cliff where Psyche had been abandoned, quickly made their way there, and cried their eyes out and beat their breasts until the rocky cliffs re-echoed with sounds like their continuous wailing. Next they began calling their poor sister by name, until the penetrating sound of their howling went down the mountainside, and Psyche, out of her mind with alarm, ran out of her house and said, "Why are you tormenting yourselves for no reason with misery and lamentation? I, whom you're mourning, am here. Cease your sad cries and dry your cheeks that are drenched from your prolonged weeping, for you can now embrace the one you've been mourning." Then she summoned Zephyr, reminding him of her husband's order. Without delay he obeyed the command and straightway, with a very gentle breeze, carried them down safely.

Now they enjoyed embraces and eager kisses to the full, and tears that had been soothed welled up again, called forth by joy. "But cheer up and enter my hearth and home," said Psyche, "and restore your despondent spirits with your sister." Saying this, she showed their eyes the immense riches of her golden house, and their ears her staff of attendant voices. Afterward she restored their spirits sumptuously with an exquisite bath and a luxurious, supernatural feast, so that the sisters became sated with the abundance of celestial wealth and began to nurture envy deep within their hearts. And so one of the sisters kept inquiring with assiduous curiosity who the master of this celestial dwelling was, and who and what kind of person her husband was. Psyche did not treat her husband's instructions rashly or forget them in the depths of her heart, but on the spur of the moment fabricated a story that he was a handsome young man with a slight growth of beard on his cheeks who often spent his time hunting in the countryside and mountains. In order that no slip betray the admonition that she not reveal anything, she loaded them down with objects of gold and jewelry with gems, summoned Zephyr right away, and turned them over to him to be brought back up the cliff.

The conveyance took place right away, and the excellent sisters began their return home. Already burning with the bitterness of swelling envy, they now held forth noisily and at length in conversation with each other. "O blind, cruel, and unjust Fortune!" said one of them. "Have you decided that, though we are daughters of the same father, we are to put up with different lots in life? Must we, who in our case are older, be given as maids to foreign husbands and be banished from hearth and even country, living away from our parents like exiles, while our younger sister, who dropped out last in a wearying birth, gets great riches and a god for a husband—she who doesn't even know how to make use of so much wealth?

"You have seen, sister, how many pieces of jewelry are just lying about her house, the clothes that shine there, and the gems that glitter, not to mention how much gold one steps on all over the place. And if she has as handsome a husband as she claims she does, no woman in the entire world now lives a happier life. If their intimacy progresses and their affection becomes stronger, it may even be that her god of a husband will make her a goddess. By Hercules, that's how she was behaving and bearing herself. She kept looking up and giving off the air of a goddess—she who has voices for maidservants and even orders the winds around.

"But poor me, I've gotten as my lot a husband who, first of all, is older than our father and, second, is balder than a pumpkin as well as shorter than any boy you've seen, but keeps guard over the whole house with bars and chains."

"As for me," the other sister replied, "I put up with a husband who's so bent double from arthritis that he hardly ever cultivates my bed. I spend my time rubbing his twisted, stony fingers and burning these delicate hands of mine with stinking compresses, filthy rags, and disgusting poultices so that I play the toilsome role of a nurse more than the dutiful part of a wife.

"But, sister, you must see for yourself how patiently or, really, how slavishly—I'm speaking freely about how I feel—you can endure this. For me it's impossible any longer to put up with the fact that such blissful fortune has befallen so unworthy a person. Just recall how haughtily and arrogantly she behaved with us, and how with her excessive display of pomp she revealed just how puffed up with pride she is, and how out of her immense wealth she tossed us mere crumbs, and that unwillingly, and then, how when she tired of our company she speedily gave orders for us to be driven out, blown away, and hissed off. I'm not a woman and I'm not alive if I won't cast her down from her opulent heights. If you, too, were soured by the way she insulted us, as I imagine you were, then let's work together to come up with a solid plan. We'll not show the presents we received to our parents or to anyone else. Better yet, we'll not let on that we know anything at all about her well-being. It's enough that we've seen what we wish we hadn't, much less that we should spread her good news about. As they say, you aren't rich unless someone knows you are. She'll learn that we're her older sisters, not her maidservants.

"For the moment let's go back to our husbands and return to our poor but respectable homes. Armed for the long run with this clear plan, we'll come back in a stronger position to punish her pride."

The two evil women thought their evil plan was a good one, and after hiding away all their precious gifts, they pulled at their hair, scratched their faces (just as they deserved), and renewed their feigned wailing. Then straightway they went and plunged their parents back into grief, and quickly left them and, fuming with jealousy, made their way to their own homes, having contrived a wicked deceit, or murder really, against their innocent sister.

Meanwhile, Psyche's husband, whose identity remained unknown to her, once again gave her a warning during their nighttime talk. "Do you see how much danger you are in?" he asked. "Fortune is making attempts on you from a distance now, but unless you take very firm precautions, she'll soon approach you and engage in hand-to-hand combat. Those faithless little whores are working hard to prepare a heinous trap for you, the main idea of which is to persuade you to look upon my face. But as I told you before, if you do see it, you'll cease to see it. And so if those vile lamias should come again, armed with their criminal designs—and they will come, I know—then don't converse with them at all, or if you can't do that because of your natural lack of guile and tenderness of heart, then at least don't listen to anything they say, or answer anything about your husband. For we are about to increase our family. This young womb of yours is bearing for us a young one, who, if you preserve our secret in silence, will be divine, but if you profane it, mortal."

Psyche was exhilarated by the news, gloried in the solace of divine offspring, rejoiced in the thought of the pledged child, delighted at the dignity of the name of mother. She anxiously counted the days as they passed and the months as they ended, and at her first experience with an unknown burden, she marveled at how large her fertile womb had grown as the result of a mere puncture.

But now those plagues, those loathsome furies, were breathing forth their viperous poisons and sailing swiftly with ungodly haste. Then again Psyche's husband, during his brief stays, warned her, saying, "The last day, the final fall, the dangerous sex, and enemy blood have already taken up arms, struck camp, arranged their battle line, and sounded the signal for battle on the trumpet. Your treacherous sisters have drawn their swords and are going for your throat. Alas, with what great calamity we are beset, my sweet Psyche. Have compassion for yourself and me, and with scrupulous self-control free your house, your husband, yourself, and this little one of ours from the misfortune of the impending destruction. Don't look at or listen to those evil women—who ought not to be called sisters at all because of their murderous hatred of you and their trampling upon the bonds of blood—when they stand at the edge of the cliff and, like Sirens, make the rocks resound with their dangerous voices."

Sobbing, Psyche replied with barely audible speech, saying, "For a long time now, so far as I know, you have weighed the evidence of my trustworthiness and discretion. In the same way my resolve will also win your approval now. Order our Zephyr again to obey, and give me at least a look at my sisters in compensation for your sacred image, which you have denied me. By these cinnamon-fragrant tresses of yours that hang down on all sides, by your cheeks that are tender and smooth like mine, by your chest with its strange heat, as I hope to know your appearance in this little one at least, be persuaded by the pious prayers of your anxious suppliant and grant me the enjoyment of embracing my sisters, restoring with joy the spirit of Psyche, who is devoted and dedicated to you. I no longer seek to see your face, and the shadows of the night no longer obstruct my vision, for I hold you as my lamp." Enchanted by her soft words and embraces and wiping away her tears with his locks, her husband promised to do as she asked, and left immediately before the light of the dawning day.

The sisters, joined in their shared conspiracy, bypassed their parents and went in a headlong rush straight from their ships to the cliff, where without waiting for the appearance of a favorable wind they leapt forth with wonton rashness into the deep. Zephyr was not unmindful of the royal command, lifted them up in his breezy lap, however unwillingly, and returned them to the ground. Immediately and without delay the women penetrated the house in close order and embraced their prey, pretending in name to be sisters and covering with cheerful countenances their rich and deeply hidden deception. They flattered her, saying, "Psyche, you're not the little girl you used to be, but are already a mother! How much good you are carrying in that little pouch of yours, with how much joy you'll delight our whole household! How blessed are we, who will enjoy the nurturing of this golden infant! If he turns out to be as beautiful as his parents, as is bound to happen, he'll be born a veritable Cupid!" And so with feigned affection they invaded their sister's mind step by step.

Immediately Psyche offered them chairs to refresh them from the fatigue of traveling, had them tended splendidly with baths of steaming water, and delighted them in the dining room with rich and marvelous foods and savories. She ordered the lyre to play, and there was strumming; the flutes to perform, and they resounded; and the choir to sing, and there was song. Though no one was there, the music soothed the spirits of the listeners with the sweetest tunes. But not even the mellifluous charm of song could soften the evil women's wickedness, and, turning the conversation toward the deceitful snare they had in mind, they began to interrogate her deceitfully about what sort of husband she had, where he was born, and what his profession was. Owing to her excessive naïveté, Psyche forgot her earlier words and devised a new tale, saying that her husband was a wealthy merchant from the neighboring province, a middle-aged man with a scattering of white hair. She did not tarry in this discussion but again loaded her sisters with sumptuous gifts and returned them to their windy conveyance.

After they had been borne aloft by Zephyr's tranquil breath, they returned home, exchanging views with each other. "What are we to say, sister, about so monstrous a lie from the foolish girl? Previously her husband was a young man outfitted with a downy beard, and now he's a splendid middle-aged man with shiny white hair. Who is he anyway, whom a brief period of time has suddenly refashioned with old age?" "My sister, you will find no other explanation than that this wicked woman is making up lies or doesn't know what her husband looks like. Whichever is the case, we should drive her away from these riches of hers as soon as possible. If she is ignorant of her own husband's appearance, she has surely wed a god and with this pregnancy is bearing us a god. In any case, if Psyche is to be—god forbid!—the mother of a little divine child, I'll hang myself straightway with a knotted noose. In the meantime let's return to our parents' house and spin a colorful yarn about our plans."

Thus inflamed, they summoned their parents haughtily, disturbing them in the middle of the night. After suffering through a sleepless night themselves, they all but flew to the cliff in the early morning and from there hastened impetuously down with the usual assistance of the wind. Squeezing their eyelids to force out tears, they summoned the girl with cunning speech. "While you happily sit here doing nothing, blissful in your ignorance of great evil and unconcerned about the danger to you, we lie awake with ever-watchful concern for your situation, tortured miserably by the disaster that threatens you. For in fact we've learned and can't conceal from you, united as we are with you in your distress and fortunes, that an enormous snake creeping along with many coils, its neck bloody with venom and its gluttonous jaws agape, shares your bed with you nightly without your knowing it. Now recall to mind Apollon's oracle, which declared that you were destined to wed a savage beast. Many farmers, local hunters, and other persons dwelling in the neighborhood have seen it in the evening when it returns from feeding and swims in the shallows of the nearby stream. They all say it is fattening you up with pleasant offerings of nourishment, but not for long, for as soon as your pregnancy reaches maturity, it will devour you, endowed as you will then be with richer fruit. So, then, it's up to you to decide whether you agree with your sisters, who are concerned about your precious well-being, and so avoid death and live with us with no fear of danger, or are to be buried in the entrails of a gruesome beast. But if the desolation of this country-seat with its voices, its dangerous and disgusting copulation consisting of furtive lovemaking, and the embraces of a poisonous snake please you, then at any rate we will have done our duty as faithful sisters."

Poor Psyche, gullible and tenderhearted as she was, was carried away by the terror of these gloomy words. Driven out of her mind, she shed all memory of her husband's warnings and of her own promises, and threw herself headlong into an abyss of calamity. Trembling and pallid, she muttered and stammered with mouth half open, saying, "Dearest sisters, as is right, you remain true to your duty as sisters, and the neighbors who affirm these things to you are surely not making them up. I've never actually seen what my husband looks like and have no idea where he comes from. I merely listen to the words he speaks during the night, and cope with a husband whose nature is uncertain and who shuns light. You're right to call him some kind of beast. He always terrifies me with warnings not to try to look at him, and threatens me with great misery regarding any curiosity I may have about his face. If you can offer any help for your sister's welfare, support me now. Inaction would spoil the advantage of our foresight."

With Psyche's mind now defenseless, its gates standing open, the wicked women abandoned the concealment of their covered siege engine and occupied it, unsheathed their swords of guile, and invaded the gullible girl's fearful thoughts. One of the sisters replied, "Since the bond of family makes us mindful of any danger to your safety, we'll show you the only way that leads to safety, one that we have been thinking about for a long time. Take a really sharp knife, one that would cut the delicate palm of your hand at a touch, and secretly conceal it on the side of the bed where you are accustomed to sleep. Make ready a lamp, filled with oil and shining brightly, and cover it with a little pot. Keep all these preparations absolutely to yourself. After your husband has slithered his way there, climbed into his accustomed bed, stretched himself out, and begun to fall asleep and breathe deeply, then slip out of bed and, walking with bare feet and small steps like a tiny animal, uncover the lamp from the darkness of its guardhouse. Letting its light guide you to the right moment for your noble deed, raise your right hand and, holding that double-edged weapon, boldly and with all your might cut the joint between the neck and head of the deadly snake. We'll help, too, for as soon as you have secured your own safety by its death, we'll be waiting, full of concern for you. And when we've all carried off these riches, we'll arrange for you the marriage you really want—with another human being."

Psyche's heart, already burning, was inflamed by the fiery words of her sisters. They themselves, however, instantly left her, terrified of being in the vicinity of such a disaster. After they landed on the clifftop thanks to the usual boost from the winged breeze, they fled swiftly away, immediately boarded their ships, and departed. Psyche, left alone but not really alone, driven as she was by the fiendish Furies, tossed in her grief like the waves of the sea, and though she had made her decision and felt resolve, she still wavered when actually moving her hand to the deed, torn by the many emotions connected with the calamity. She hurried and delayed; she was bold and fearful; she despaired and raged. Worst of all, in one and the same body she hated the beast but loved the husband. Since, however, evening was now bringing on the night, she made her preparations in headlong haste. Night came, her husband came, and after a skirmish on the battlefield of Venus he fell into a deep sleep. Then the cruelty of Fortune lent strength to Psyche, who otherwise was weak in body and spirit, and taking out the lantern and laying hold of the knife, she acquired a man's daring.

But when the presence of light revealed the secret of her bed, she saw the gentlest and sweetest of beasts, Cupid himself, the beautiful god in beautiful sleep. At the sight of him the light of her lantern lit up in gladness, and her knife regretted its sacrilegious point. Terrified by so great a sight, Psyche lost control of herself. Trembling, pale, and feeling faint, she sank down. She tried to hide her weapon, to hide it in her own chest, and would certainly have done so if the weapon, out of the fear of so enormous a crime, had not fallen from her rash hand and flown away. Although she was exhausted and felt utterly lost, as she gazed again and again upon the beauty of his divine appearance, she began to regain her inner strength. She saw the rich hair, drunk with ambrosia, on his golden head, the nicely bound curls straying over his milky neck and rosy cheeks, some hanging down in front, others in back. They shone so brilliantly that the very light of her lantern flickered. On the shoulders of the winged god feathers glistened brightly with dew, and though his wings were at rest, the tender and delicate down feathers at the ends fluttered and frolicked restlessly. The rest of his body was smooth and shiny and such as Venus would not regret having given birth to. At the foot of the bed lay his bow, quiver, and arrows, the gracious weapons of the great god. With her insatiable spirit and innate curiosity, Psyche examined, picked up, and marveled at her husband's weapons. She drew forth an arrow from his quiver and tested its point by pricking her thumb, but since her hand was still trembling, she applied too much pressure and pierced herself too deeply, so that little drops of rosy blood trickled out onto the surface of her skin. So, without knowing it, of her own accord Psyche fell in love with Love. Then, burning more and more with desire for Desire,* she bent over him panting deeply and rashly smothered him with bold, openmouthed kisses, all the

*Love (*amor*) and Desire (*cupido*): the narrator plays of course on names of the god.

time fearing she might wake him up. While Psyche, aroused by so beautiful a sight and her mind wounded with love, thus wavered, that lamp, either from base treachery or from hurtful envy or because it too longed to touch and, as it were, kiss such a body, discharged a drop of burning oil from the tip of its spout onto the god's right shoulder. What! You rash and reckless lamp, worthless attendant in love, you burn the very master of all fire, when, as everyone knows, it was some lover who first invented you in order that he might enjoy his desires longer into the night!

Scorched, the god leapt up, and detecting the foul betrayal of his trust, he straightway flew away from the kisses and out of the embraces of his unfortunate wife without saying a word. As he arose, Psyche quickly took hold of the god's right leg with both of her hands. He soared aloft and passed through the regions of the clouds, while she hung on miserably like the tail end of an escort until at last, exhausted, she sank back down to the ground. Her divine lover did not abandon her as she lay there, but flew to a nearby cypress tree and from its high crest, and deeply disturbed, addressed her. "I too, my guileless Psyche, was unmindful of instructions, in my case those of my mother Venus, whose orders were that you should be overcome with desire for some worthless wretch of a man and then be condemned to a humiliating marriage. Instead, I myself rushed to you as your lover. But I did so frivolously, I see, since I, famous archer that I am, struck myself with my own arrow and made you my wife, with the result apparently that you thought me a monster and were going to cut off my head with your knife, this head whose eyes love you. I warned you over and over again to be on your guard and with kindly intent reminded you about this. Those excellent advisors of yours will be punished very soon for their ruinous counsel." When he finished speaking, he dashed up into the sky on his wings.

Psyche lay stretched out on the ground, watching her husband's flight as long as she could, and tormenting her soul with bitter lamentation. After his height and feathered flight had taken him utterly away from her, she flung herself headlong from the bank of a nearby stream. But the gentle river, honoring the god who, as we know, often makes even waters burn, and fearing for itself, immediately lifted her with a harmless surge and placed her on a bank with flowering plants.

At that moment Pan, god of the countryside, happened to be sitting by the edge of the stream, holding in his arms the mountain nymph Echo and teaching her to repeat sounds of all kinds in song. Young goats, grazing here and there upon the grass along the stream, were frolicking near the bank. The goatish god somehow was aware of what had happened to Psyche, who was wounded and exhausted. He called her over to him and soothed her with comforting words. "My pretty girl," he said, "I may be a rustic and a herdsman, but thanks to my extended old age, I've had a lot of experience. If I guess correctly—something that learned men call divination—from your unsteady gait, the extreme paleness of your body, your incessant sighs, and indeed by your mournful eyes, you are suffering from an overwhelming love. So listen to me. Don't leap to your death or put an end to yourself in some other way. Stop grieving and set aside your sorrow, and instead pay your respect to Cupid, greatest of the gods, by means of prayers and, since he's a wonton and voluptuous youth, win him over by flattering attention." So spoke the shepherd god. Psyche did not reply but only paid respectful homage to the kindly deity, and proceeded on her way.

After she had wandered wearily for a good distance and the day was waning, she reached by an unfamiliar track a city ruled by one of her sisters' husbands. Once she realized where she was, she announced her presence to her sister and soon was led in. When the two had embraced and greeted each other, her sister asked why she had come, and Psyche said, "Do you remember your advice to me, how you urged me to kill with a double-edged knife the beast that lay with me in the guise of a husband, before he could devour my poor self with his voracious jaws? As soon as I looked at his face by the light of my accomplice the lamp, as we had agreed, I saw an astonishing and indeed divine spectacle, the very son of the goddess Venus, I mean Cupid himself, peacefully and soundly asleep. While I was excited by so great a delight and overcome with a superabundance of pleasure and suffering and with my inability to enjoy it all, a terrible misfortune caused my lamp to spill burning oil onto his shoulder. Immediately startled from sleep, he saw me there armed with fire and sword, and said, 'For this terrible crime of yours, leave my bed this instant and take your belongings with you! As for me, I shall arrange a formal wedding with your sister'—and he named you—while straightway giving orders to Zephyr to waft me beyond the boundaries of his palace."

Psyche had not yet finished speaking when her sister, driven by mad passion and pernicious envy, devised a story on the spot to deceive her husband, to the effect that she had heard something about the death of her parents, immediately got onboard a ship, and proceeded straight to the usual cliff. Although a different wind was blowing, she stood with blind hope and gaping mouth, saying, "Receive me, Cupid, as a bride worthy of you, and you, Zephyr, catch up your mistress!" And with an immense leap she jumped down headlong. But she did not manage to reach the place, even in death, for her falling limbs were scattered upon the projecting rocks, so that, just as she deserved, she provided with her mangled flesh a meal for the birds and beasts.

Nor was the second act of revenge slow in coming, for in the course of her wandering Psyche came again to a city, in which, in the same way, her other sister lived. She too was fooled by Psyche's deceit, rushed to the cliff as a rival to the other sister's impious wedding, and fell to the same kind of death.

Meanwhile, as Psyche went around from people to people, intent on her search for Cupid, Cupid himself lay moaning in his mother's bedroom, suffering from the painful wound caused by the lamp. Then a tern, that white bird that swims with its wings above the waves of the sea, dove swiftly down to the deep bosom of Ocean and perched next to Venus, who was bathing and swimming, and disclosed to her that her son had been burnt and was lying in bed in serious condition and suffering from his painful injury. Moreover, the tern continued, Venus's family had gotten a bad name through the rumors and reproaches on everyone's lips to the effect that the family had withdrawn itself from the world, he by his whoring in the mountains and she by swimming in the sea, for which reason there was no longer any pleasure or grace or charm, but everyone was rude and boorish and coarse; furthermore, there were no more weddings, no friendships, no love for children, but only enormous squalor and disagreeable, sordid couplings. The talkative and meddlesome bird chatted these things into Venus's ear, doing harm to Cupid's good name. Quite furious, Venus instantly exclaimed, "So that fine son of mine has a mistress now? Out with her name, now! You're the only one who serves me affectionately. So who has seduced my tender young boy? Is she one of the band of nymphs or of the Hours or of the choir of Muses, or one of my own Graces?" The talkative bird did not hold back but said, "Mistress, I don't know. I believe the one he loves so desperately is a girl—she's called Psyche, if I remember correctly."

Then Venus shouted indignantly as loud as she could, "He actually loves Psyche, my rival in beauty and name? Apparently that little offspring of mine took me for a go-between to help him become intimate with the girl." As she shrieked, she swiftly emerged from the sea and made her way straight to her golden bedchamber, where, as she had heard, her ailing boy was to be found. Crying out as she entered, "What honorable behavior this is!" she said, "How fitting to our family origin and your fine morality that you tread upon your mother's, or really your sovereign's, orders! First, you don't torment my enemy with a base passion, and then, though a boy of your age, you even hold her in your own unbridled and immature embraces so that I have to put up with my own enemy as a daughter-in-law! You odious and good-for-nothing seducer, you doubtless suppose that you're the only one fit to breed and that I can't conceive anymore because of my age. Well, I'd like you to know that I'll produce a much better son than you, or better, to make you feel the reproach all the more, I'll adopt one of my young household slaves and give him these wings, torches, bow and arrows, all my gear, which I didn't give you to use the way you did. Certainly none of this outfit came from your father's estate.

"You've been brought up badly from your earliest days, battering your elders disrespectfully with your light-fingered hands I don't know how many times, abusing your mother—that is, me myself—daily by exposing me, and you often strike me, treating me like a widow. You're not afraid even of your stepfather, the strongest and greatest of warriors, and why should you be, since you have a regular habit of procuring girls for him, to torment me with his liaisons?* But now I'll see to it that you regret these games when I give this marriage of yours a sour and bitter taste.

"But now that I'm a laughingstock, what am I to do? Where am I to go? How am I to constrain this creature? Should I seek the help of my enemy, Sobriety, whom I've often offended through my son's riotous living? I shudder at the thought of dealing with so simple and unsophisticated a female. Still, the solace of revenge is not to be spurned, wherever it comes from. I've got to summon her and no one else to punish my good-for-nothing son as harshly as possible, emptying his quiver, blunting his arrows, unstringing his bow, extinguishing his torch, and subjecting his body to harsh remedies. I'll consider myself appeased of his insult to me only when she's cut off his hair, which I've often smoothed to a golden sheen with my own hands, and clipped the tips of his wings, which I have tinged with nectar from my own breast."

With these words she dashed outside, furious and angry as only Venus could be. There she encountered Ceres and Juno, who noticed her swollen face and asked her why she was letting a scowl spoil the sparkle of her eyes. "You've come at the right moment," Venus said, "no doubt to help me with the plan that my heart is burning to carry out. I beseech you to use all your might to find that elusive runaway, Psyche, for me. I'm sure that the infamous story of my household and the doings of my unspeakable son have not escaped you!"

Then the goddesses, who were aware of what had happened, tried to soothe Venus's raging anger. "Good lady," they said, "what wrong has your son done that brings you to attack his pleasures so obstinately and to destroy the woman he loves? Is it a crime for him to enjoy smiling at an agreeable girl? Don't you see he's a young man, or have you forgotten how old he is? Perhaps, since he carries his age so prettily, he always seems to

---

*Venus treats Mars as her husband and therefore as Cupid's stepfather.

you to be only a boy? But as a mother and also a sensible female—will you always be prying into your son's dalliances, finding fault with him for his excesses, suppressing his affairs, and criticizing your good-looking son for your own arts and pleasures? What god or human will tolerate your spreading passion among peoples everywhere if you repress love affairs in your own family and close down your workshop for female wantonness?" The goddesses, who themselves feared Cupid's arrows, spoke flatteringly and graciously in his defense, although he was not present. Indignant at the ridicule of her grievances, Venus cut them off and, proceeding hastily in a different direction, made her way to the sea.

Meanwhile Psyche went hither and thither, day and night, in her restless search for her husband, all the more desirous, however angry he might be, if not to soothe him with wifely caresses, then at least to win him over with slavish prayers. She spotted a temple on the top of a steep mountain. "Perhaps," she said, "my lord may live there?" She quickly made her way toward it. Though her pace was weak from her unbroken efforts, the hope that her wish might be fulfilled gave it strength. She diligently crossed the high ridges and approached the shrine. There she saw sheaves of wheat, some piled up and others plaited into garlands, and ears of barley. There were also sickles and other equipment that reapers use, though everything was lying around in casual disorder, as usual in the summer when workmen throw down their tools. Psyche carefully sorted them, separated them, and arranged them properly, thinking that she should not neglect the sanctuary or rites of any god but rather seek the kindly compassion of them all. Bountiful Ceres, coming upon Psyche as she was busily and diligently taking care of the equipment, immediately shouted to her from a distance. "Ah, is it you, poor Psyche? Venus in her rage is searching for you throughout the whole world, with the intent of punishing you severely. She demands revenge with all the resources of her divine power. And here you occupy yourself with taking care of my belongings and thinking of anything other than your own safety."

Then Psyche prostrated herself before her, moistening the goddess's feet with copious tears and sweeping the ground with her hair, and in an elaborate prayer implored her favor. "I beseech you by this fertile right hand of yours," she said, "by your joyous harvest rites, by the secret mysteries of your sacred baskets, the winged wagon of your servant dragons, the furrows of Sicilian soil, the abducting chariot and the tenacious earth, your daughter Proserpina's descent to a dark wedding and her ascent to a bright reunion, and by everything else that your sanctuary in Attica keeps hidden in silence for the people of Eleusis, come to the aid of the pitiful soul of your suppliant Psyche.* Let me hide myself away in that pile of sheaves for a few days, until the fierce anger of the mighty goddess softens with the passage of time, or at least until the fatigue from my constant toil is assuaged by a short period of rest."

"I'm moved by your tearful prayers and want to help you," Ceres replied, "but I can't incur the disfavor of my relative, with whom I maintain old ties of friendship and who is moreover a good woman. You must leave this sanctuary at once and consider yourself fortunate that I don't keep you here under guard."

Rebuffed contrary to her hopes and afflicted with a double grief, Psyche resumed her journey. In the faint light of a grove in a valley farther down she saw a shrine of skillful craftsmanship. Since she was unwilling to leave any means untried, however doubtful it might be, but wished to seek the favor of any god, she went to the sacred entrance. Affixed to the branches of the trees and to the doors she saw costly gifts and strips of cloth with golden letters that attested to the goddess to whom they had been dedicated, naming her and thanking her for her action. Psyche sank to her knees and embraced the warm altar with her arms, and wiping away her tears she prayed: "Sister and wife of great Jove, whether you're residing

---

*Psyche alludes to the myth according to which the lord of the dead abducted Ceres's daughter, Proserpina, in Sicily and brought her to his dark kingdom beneath the earth, where he wed her. Subsequently she spent, or spends, part of the year in the gloomy realm of the dead and part in the bright realm of the living. The story serves as the foundation myth of the famed Eleusinian Mysteries.

in your ancient sanctuary on Samos, the island that alone prides itself in being the place of your birth, your infant cries, and your early nurture, or whether you're visiting the blessed site of lofty Carthage, which reveres you as the maiden who descends from heaven on the back of a lion, or whether you are watching over the celebrated walls of Argos near the banks of the Inachos, who commemorates you as the Bride of the Thunderer* and the Queen of the Gods, you whom all the East venerates as Zygia, goddess of marriage, and all the West addresses as Lucina, goddess of childbirth, be Juno Sospita, Juno the Savior, for me in my extreme circumstances and free me, exhausted as I am from the toils I've endured, from the fear of the danger threatening me. You frequently come, even unasked, I think, to the aid of pregnant women at risk."

As she was praying, Juno appeared before her in the august dignity of her full divine power. "How much I should like," she said, "to give my assent to your prayers! But respect for my daughter-in-law Venus,† whom I've always loved like a daughter, doesn't permit me to show favor contrary to her will. Then too I'm prohibited by the laws that forbid harboring fugitive slaves against the wishes of their masters."

Psyche, frightened by yet another shipwreck of her fortunes and unable to find her winged husband, gave up all hope of salvation and took counsel with herself thus: "What kind of support can I try or bring to my troubles when even the favor of goddesses who are well-disposed hasn't done any good? Caught in such snares, where can I direct my steps or under what roof or in what dark place can I hide and not be seen by the inescapable eyes of mighty Venus? In the end I must take on a man's courage, renounce my faint gleam of hope, and surrender myself to my mistress voluntarily, softening her fury and vehemence by my submission, however late it comes. And for all I know, I may even find the one I've been searching for so long right there in his mother's house." So, prepared

---

*Thunderer = Jupiter.

†Venus is married to Juno's son, Vulcan.

for submission and its uncertain outcome, or rather for certain destruction, she thought about how to begin her supplication.

Venus, giving up her search of the earth, set her sights on heaven. She ordered to be readied the chariot that the goldsmith Vulcan had carefully adorned for her with delicate craftsmanship and presented to her as a wedding gift before their wedding night. It was conspicuous for what the craftsman's file had rubbed away, and precious for the very loss of gold itself. Of the many doves that nested around their mistress's bedchamber, four shiny ones came forward with lively steps as they turned their colorful necks, submitted to a jeweled yoke, and, once their mistress was aboard, flew happily upward. Sparrows followed the goddess's chariot, frolicking with noisy twittering, and other birds sang sweetly, pleasantly echoing them with honeyed tunes and announcing the approach of the goddess. The clouds parted, Heaven opened for his daughter,* highest Aether joyfully received her, and the mighty goddess's melodious escorts were met by no rapacious eagles or hawks.

She went right away to Jove's royal citadel and haughtily said she had need of the services of Mercury, god of the clear voice. Jove's dark brow nodded his assent. Exulting, Venus descended from the sky accompanied by Mercury, and earnestly spoke to him. "Arcadian brother,† as you know, your sister Venus hasn't ever accomplished anything without your help. In any case you're surely aware how long I've been searching in vain for my slave girl, who has been hiding from me. Nothing remains but for you to make a public proclamation of a reward for her discovery. See that you do my bidding with all haste and clearly describe the features by which she can be recognized, so that if anyone is charged with illegal concealment, he can't plead ignorance." As she said this, she handed him a placard bearing Psyche's name and other information and, as soon as that was done, withdrew into her house.

---

*Heaven, or Sky, is the father of Venus.

†According to a different genealogy, the father of Venus is Jove (Jupiter), in which case she and Mercury are siblings.

Mercury complied, traveling here and there on the lips of all peoples, carrying out his task of proclaiming: "If anyone can reveal the hiding place of the king's runaway daughter, the slave girl of Venus named Psyche, or can force her to return, he should meet the herald Mercury behind the turning posts of the Circus Maximus, where he'll receive by way of reward seven sweet kisses from Venus herself plus an additional, deeply honeyed kiss with her thrusting tongue."

Mercury made his proclamation, and the desire for so fine a reward aroused the competitive zeal of all mortal men, which completely did away with any hesitation on Psyche's part. She approached her mistress's door, and a member of Venus's household named Habit ran up to her and immediately started shouting at the top of her lungs, "You worthless servant girl, have you finally noticed that you have a mistress? Or, considering your usual impudence, are you pretending not to know how much effort we've expended in looking for you? It's a good thing you've fallen into my hands where you'll be as stuck as in Orcus's prison,* and you'll soon pay the penalty for your stubbornness." Thereupon she brazenly grabbed Psyche by the hair and began dragging her, though Psyche offered no resistance. As soon as she was brought inside and presented to Venus, the goddess gave a broad laugh such as people do when they are furious, tossing her head and scratching her right ear. "Have you finally deigned to call on your mother-in-law?" she asked. "Or have you rather come to look in on your husband, who's in critical condition thanks to the wound you gave him? Don't worry—I'll receive you as befits a good daughter-in-law. Where are my servants Care and Sorrow?" When they had been summoned, the goddess turned Psyche over to them to be tormented. Following their mistress's orders, they whipped poor Psyche and afflicted her with other torments, and then brought her back to face her mistress. Venus laughed again, saying, "Look how she's trying to arouse my pity with the allurement of her swollen belly, whose glorious issue is to make me a happy grandmother. I'm thrilled that in the very flower of my

*Orcus = Dis = ruler of the dead.

age I'll be called a grandmother and that the son of a vile slave girl will be called my grandson. I'd be a fool to call him a son, since the marriage isn't between equals and, what's more, took place in a country house without witnesses and without the father's consent, so that the marriage can't be regarded as legitimate and this offspring of yours won't be legitimate either, if I even allow you to carry your unborn child to term." Saying this she flew at Psyche, ripping her clothes to pieces, tearing her hair, shaking her head, and beating her violently.

Venus then made piles of wheat, barley, millet, poppy seeds, chickpeas, lentils, and beans, and combined them all into a single, mixed heap. "You're a hideous slave," she said to her, "who can win the favor of your lovers only by diligent drudgery. So I'm going to put your usefulness to the test. Sort this random heap of seeds, separating the different grains into individual stacks, and show them to me all put into order by this evening." After assigning her the task of the heap of seeds, Venus went off to a wedding dinner.

Psyche did not touch the confused mass, all but impossible to sort, but sat in silent stupefaction, overwhelmed by the enormity of the job. Then a little ant, that tiny country dweller, understanding the great difficulty of her task, pitying the great god's bed partner, and detesting the mother-in-law's cruelty, diligently scurried about and called together the entire body of ants in the neighborhood. "Have pity, all you energetic nurslings of Earth, mother of all! Have pity on the wife of Love, a pretty maiden in peril, and run quickly to her aid!" Wave upon wave of the six-legged creatures rushed forth. With the utmost zeal they took apart the entire heap grain by grain, and when they had distributed the grains into separate piles, they swiftly went away.

At nightfall Venus came back from her wedding banquet flushed with wine, fragrant with balsam, and wrapped in gleaming roses. When she saw the astonishing diligence with which the task had been performed, she said, "This isn't your doing, you worthless girl, nor that of your hands, but rather the work of the one you've allured, to your misfortune and his." With that, she tossed her a piece of coarse bread and retired to her bedroom.

Meanwhile, Cupid was being kept in strict solitary confinement in a single room in the inner part of the house, partly in order that he not aggravate his wound with his riotous living and partly in order that he not come together with his beloved. So the lovers, divided and separated under a single roof, endured a horrid night.

When Dawn appeared, riding on her horse, Venus summoned Psyche and said, "Do you see that grove stretching along the banks of the stream that washes the banks as it passes, and the low bushes there that stand above the nearby spring? Shiny sheep the color of gold wander around there and graze unguarded. I want you to obtain a flock of wool of that precious fleece, and bring it to me."

Psyche went on willingly, not indeed expecting to perform the task but to find respite from her miseries by leaping from a cliff into the river. But from the river below, a green reed, that nurse of delightful music,* divinely inspired by the gentle rustling of the sweet breeze, uttered a prophecy. "Psyche, oppressed by such great troubles, don't pollute my sacred waters with your miserable death. And this isn't the time to confront the terrible and savage sheep with their sharp horns and stony forehead, while they are absorbing heat from the blazing sun, which makes them wild with fierce rage so that often they vent their fury by killing humans with their toxic bites. But when midday has cooled the sun's warmth and the serenity of the river breeze has calmed the flock down, you'll be able to conceal

*Reeds can be called nurses of music because panpipes are made from them.

yourself beneath that towering plane tree over there, which along with me drinks from this stream. As soon as the sheep's fury has calmed down and their mood is relaxed, shake branches in the nearby woods and you'll find the golden wool stuck everywhere in the entwined branches." In this way the simple and kind reed instructed poor Psyche how to stay safe. She carefully acted upon its advice, doing all that she was told. With an easy theft she brought a lapful of soft, yellow gold back to Venus.

Even the danger of her second task did not earn a favorable judgment from her mistress, who, twisting her brows and smiling acidly, said, "It doesn't escape me that on this occasion, too, someone else has performed the task. Now I'm going to test carefully whether you're really endowed with a powerful mind and unparalleled intelligence.

"Do you see the top of the steep mountain that towers over that lofty cliff? The dark waters of a black spring flow down from it, and become enclosed in the basin of the nearby valley where they supply the marshes of Styx with water and feed the hoarse streams of Cocytus. You must draw some ice-cold water from the inmost bubbling top of the spring there and bring it to me in this little jar." As she spoke, she handed her a vessel of hollowed-out crystal along with more grave threats.

Psyche eagerly quickened her pace, making her way toward the highest peak of the mountain, sure to find there, if nothing else, an end to her miserable life. As soon as she drew near to the summit she perceived the deadly difficulty of her enormous enterprise. For a huge and lofty rock, too rugged and slippery to climb, spewed out a fearsome stream from the middle of its stony jaws. The stream emerged from a sloping cleft and then plunged deeply to hide itself in a narrow channel it had carved out, after which it fell inconspicuously into the nearby valley. On the left and the right ferocious serpents glided forth from the hollow rocks, their eyes unsleeping and watchful, their pupils on everlasting guard. Even the water tried to defend itself, shouting again and again, "Depart!" and "What are you doing? Look out!" and "What are you up to? Beware!" and "Flee from here!" and "You're going to die!" Psyche was petrified by the impossibility of her task. Although her body was present, her senses were not, and overwhelmed as she was by the weight of the inextricable danger, she lacked even the consolation of tears.

The troubles of an innocent soul did not, however, escape the notice of the august eyes of kindly Providence. For that regal bird of supreme Jove, the rapacious eagle, suddenly appeared, its wings spread out on each side. Remembering its compliance of old when, induced by Cupid, it carried up the Phrygian youth to be Jove's cupbearer,* it now came bringing welcome help. Honoring Cupid's divinity and his wife's distress, it left Jove's lofty pathways, flew down before the girl, and addressed her: "Do you, then, naïve as you are and without experience in such matters, hope to steal or even touch a single drop of that very holy and dangerous spring? You must have heard, if only by hearsay, that these Stygian waters are terrifying to the gods and even to Jove himself, and that just as you humans swear your oaths by the divinity of the gods, so the gods swear by the majesty of the Styx. But give me that little jar of yours."

Without waiting, the eagle snatched it away and hurried off to fill it. Spreading the mass of its swaying wings, it banked to the right and the left between the serpents' jaws with their ferocious teeth and flickering, tri-forked tongues. It collected some of the water, though the water was unwilling and threatened the eagle to depart while it still could. Instead, the eagle invented a falsehood, saying that it was seeking the water at the bidding of Venus and was acting as her servant, by which means it gained somewhat better access.

Psyche joyously took the full jar and brought it speedily back to Venus. Not even then could she appease the powerful, raging goddess. Threatening her with still greater and worse punishments, Venus said to her with a deadly smile, "I think you must be some kind of great and skillful witch, since you've obeyed these orders of mine so diligently. But you still have this to attend to, my little lass. Take this little box," she said, giving it to her, "and make your way directly to the land of the dead to the gloomy

*The allusion is to Ganymedes, a youth whom Jove's eagle once seized and carried up to Olympos to serve the god.

dwelling of Orcus himself. Bring the box to Proserpina, saying, 'Venus asks you to send her a little bit of your beauty, enough at least for one tiny day, since she has used up all that she herself had while tending her ill son.' And don't come back too late, since I have to put in an appearance at the assembly of the gods."

Then Psyche felt that her fortunes were coming to an end. The veil had been flung back, and she perceived plainly enough that she was being driven to her immediate destruction, for she was obliged to go on her own two feet to Tartarus and the spirits of the dead. Not putting it off, she made her way to a high tower in order to throw herself down from it. By doing so, she thought, she would make a proper descent to the realm of the dead below. But the tower suddenly broke into speech, saying, "Poor girl, why do you want to leap off and kill yourself? Why surrender yourself rashly to this latest danger and task? Once your spirit is separated from your body, you'll go directly to the depths of Tartarus, from which you'll never be able to return.

"Listen to me. Sparta, the renowned city in Achaea, is situated nearby. Go look for Taenarus, which lies on its border, hidden in a remote place. An opening of Dis is there, and through its gaping gates the forbidden road can be seen. Once you cross the threshold and commit yourself, proceed straight to the palace of Orcus. But you must not enter that dark region without provisions. You should carry in each hand a barley cake mixed with honey and wine, and you should bring two coins in your mouth. When you've gone a good part of the way on the infernal road, you'll come upon a lame donkey carrying wood, along with a lame driver who'll ask you to hand him some sticks that have fallen from his load, but you must say nothing and pass by in silence.

"Soon you'll come to the river of death, whose harbormaster is Charon. He'll demand his fare on the spot and only then convey passengers to the farther bank on his skiff made of skins. Greed thrives among the dead, and even the great god Charon, Dis's collector, doesn't do anything for free. A pauper who's dying had better get hold of his fare, for unless he has a copper coin ready at hand, no one will let him breathe his last. One of the two coins you're carrying you'll give to the filthy old man as your fare, but have him take it from your mouth with his own hand. Likewise, when you're crossing the sluggish stream, an old dead man floating upon its surface will lift his putrid hands and beg you to pull him into the boat, but you must ignore him, since no pity is allowed. After you've crossed the river and gone on a little way, some old women, weavers who are setting up their loom, will beg you to lend them a hand for a while. But you aren't permitted to touch it. All these and more are traps set by Venus to induce you to let go of one of your cakes. And don't think a mere barley cake would be a paltry loss, for if you lose either cake, you'll also lose the light of the sun. There's a huge dog, an enormous and frightening creature with three large heads, that barks with thunderous jaws at the dead, though it can't harm them any longer and terrifies them now in vain. It keeps perpetual guard at the threshold and dark hall of Proserpina and watches over the house of Dis with its shadowy inhabitants. Once you've tamed it with the reward of a cake, you'll easily pass by and come directly into the presence of Proserpina, who'll receive you courteously and kindly in order to persuade you to take a comfortable seat and dine sumptuously. But you must sit on the floor, ask for a piece of coarse bread, and eat only that.

"After you've explained why you've come and taken what she has handed you, start making your way back, bribe the fierce dog with the remaining cake, and after you've given the greedy boatman the coin you've kept and crossed his river, retrace your previous steps, and you'll return to this heavenly choir of stars. But of all the things you must heed, I regard this as the most important: don't open or look inside the box you're carrying, or peek stealthily at the treasure of divine beauty hidden in it." In this way the farsighted tower accomplished its prophetic task.

Without delay Psyche made her way to Taenarus. Having duly gotten coins and cakes she descended to the lower world, passed the crippled donkey driver in silence, gave the ferryman his river fee, ignored the wish of the floating corpse, rejected the crafty pleas of the weaver women, calmed the dog's terrifying rage with a piece of cake, and penetrated the house of Proserpina. Declining her hostess's offer of a soft chair and luxurious food, she sat on the floor at the goddess's feet, contented herself with a piece of coarse bread, and carried out Venus's mission. As soon as the box had been filled and closed up in private, she picked it up, silenced the barking dog with the ruse of the second cake, gave the remaining coin to the boatman, and came back from the realm of the dead far more lively than before.

Returning to the shiny light of day and giving it a greeting, she was in a hurry to conclude her task when her mind was rashly seized with curiosity. "Look at me," she said, "foolishly carrying divine beauty without drawing off a tiny bit for myself so as to please that handsome lover of mine." So saying, she opened the box. But there was nothing inside, not even beauty, only an infernal and truly Stygian sleep. As soon as she had lifted the lid, it invaded her, suffusing her limbs in the form of a dense cloud of slumber and taking possession of her as she collapsed in her tracks on the path. She remained there without moving, no more than a sleeping corpse.

Cupid, whose wound had now healed and whose strength had returned, was no longer able to endure his long absence from Psyche. He escaped through the high window of the bedroom in which he was being confined, his wings having gotten refreshed from his long rest, and flew out very fast. He rushed to his Psyche, carefully wiped off the sleep and put it back into its original place in the box, roused Psyche with a harmless prick from an arrow, and said, "Look, poor girl, you would have been ruined once again from curiosity, as before. But in the meantime you must quickly finish the mission my mother has assigned you, while I myself see to the rest."

Having said this, her lover entrusted himself to his nimble wings, and Psyche hastened to bring Proserpina's gift to Venus.

Meanwhile Cupid, consumed by his mighty love, looking unwell, and deeply fearing his mother's newfound strictness, returned to form and with swift wings penetrated the heights of heaven, where he supplicated great Jove and pled his case. Jupiter pinched Cupid's cheek and, putting his hand to his mouth, kissed it, saying, "Although you, powerful lad, have never respected the honor decreed me by the gods but with the repeated stings of your arrows have wounded this heart of mine, which ordains the laws of the elements and the movements of the stars, and have sullied it with many instances of earthly lust, and, moreover, although in defiance of the laws, the Lex Julia in particular, and public morality you've done injury to my esteem and reputation by the lowly transformations of my serene form into snakes, fire, wild animals, birds, and cattle, still, mindful of my moderation and the fact that I raised you with my own hand, I'll do all you ask—provided that you be on guard against your rivals, and provided also that if there's a girl of outstanding beauty on earth at the moment, you repay me with her in return for this present favor."

So saying, he ordered Mercury to call the gods together at once for an assembly and to announce that anyone absent from the divine gathering would be fined ten thousand sesterces. Because of this fear the heavenly auditorium was filled at once. Sitting on his exalted throne, lofty Jupiter spoke, "Gods inscribed in the roll of the Muses, of course you all know this youth whom I've raised with my own hands. In my judgment the hot impulses of his adolescence need to be bridled in some way. It's enough that he has been defamed in daily gossip on account of his sleeping around and other kinds of misbehavior. We've got to take away his opportunities for the sexual self-indulgence of boyhood by means of the bonds of marriage. He's chosen a girl and deflowered her. Let him have and hold Psyche, enjoying love from now on in her embrace."

Turning to Venus he said, "Don't feel gloomy, daughter, or have any fear for your great family or personal status as a result of a marriage with a mortal, for I'll now make this a marriage not of unequals but in accord with civil law." On the spot he instructed Mercury to take charge of Psyche and conduct her to heaven. Holding out a cup of ambrosia, he said, "Take this drink, Psyche, and be immortal. Cupid will never depart from your embrace, and your marriage will last forever."

Instantly there appeared a lavish wedding feast. The husband reclined on the top couch, embracing Psyche in his lap, and likewise Jupiter with Juno, and then all the other gods in order. Jove's cupbearer, that country

lad,[*] served him a goblet of nectar, the wine of the gods, and Bacchus served the others. Vulcan cooked the meal, the Hours adorned everything with roses and other flowers, the Graces scattered balsam, and the Muses made everything resound with song. Apollon sang to his lyre, Venus moved in time to the sweet music, dancing beautifully, after she had arranged the performance to suit herself so that the Muses sang as a chorus, a satyr played a flute, and a little Pan sang to the panpipes.

This was how Psyche duly passed into the hand of Cupid, and there was born to them in childbirth a daughter, whom we call Pleasure.

Apuleius

The tale of Cupid and Psyche is the first wonder tale, or fairytale, that we encounter in Western literature. As a traditional story it belongs genetically to a group of international tales with this basic plot: (a) a human female enters into a marriage or marriage-like relationship with a supernatural (or enchanted) being; (b) he treats her well but mysteriously forbids a particular action such as to look upon him; when (c) she breaks this taboo, (d) he abruptly departs; but (e) she seeks and finds him; and (f) they are reunited.

Our text of the tale appears in the ancient Roman novel Metamorphoses, *also known as* The Golden Ass, *written by Apuleius of Madauros. In the novel an old woman relates the tale to an adolescent girl in distress. The girl has been kidnapped on her wedding day by robbers, who take her to their hideout and place her in the charge of their housekeeper. In order to comfort and encourage the frightened girl,*

---

[*]Ganymedes.

the old crone tells her a wonder tale, one in which the heroine faces tremendous adversity but triumphs in the end.

The novelist does not recount the tale so straightforwardly as an oral narrator might have done; instead, he plays with the inherited oral story in a variety of ways. Notably, he assigns the central roles to Cupid and Psyche, or Love and Soul, who were traditional lovers in ancient art and also figured as themes in Platonic philosophy. Accordingly, the husband is not an enchanted mortal but a god, Cupid (a Roman rendering of Greek Eros), and Cupid's mother Venus inherits the role of the hostile, witchlike mother-in-law.

2. THE TREASURY OF RHAMPSINITOS

King Rhampsinitos possessed such a great wealth of silver that none of the kings who succeeded him could surpass it or even come close to equaling it. Wishing to store his treasure in safety he had a stone room constructed, one wall of which formed part of the outer wall of his palace. But the builder, scheming about the treasure, cleverly contrived to build the outer wall in such a way that one of the stones could easily be removed by two men or even by one. When the chamber was completed, the king deposited his treasure in it.

In the course of time the builder, nearing the end of his life, called his sons to him—he had two sons—and related to them that he had used some cunning in building the king's treasury, since he wanted to provide them with a life of plenty. He revealed to them everything about removing the stone, gave them its measurements, and said that if they observed these matters carefully they would become the keepers of the king's valuables. He died, and his sons did not remain inactive for long. They went to the palace at night, found the stone in the building, handled it easily, and carried away for themselves many of the king's valuables.

When the king opened the chamber, he was surprised to see that some of his valuables were missing from the chests, but he did not know whom to accuse since the seals were intact and the room was locked. After opening it on a second and again on a third occasion and seeing that his property was continually diminishing (for the thieves did not cease from their plundering), he ordered traps to be made and had them placed around the chests in which his valuables lay.

The thieves came just as they had done before, but when one of them entered and went to the chest he was immediately caught by the trap. Realizing the sort of difficulty he was in, he called immediately to his brother, explaining the situation to him and bidding him enter as quickly as possible and cut off his head in order that it not be seen and, once it was known who he was, cause the downfall of the other brother also. The suggestion seemed prudent, and the other brother was persuaded to carry it out. He fit the stone back in place and went home carrying his brother's head. The next morning the king went to his chamber and was shocked to see that the thief's body, but not his head, was in the trap while the chamber was undamaged and showed no sign of entry or exit.

Very puzzled the king decided to have the corpse of the thief hung from the wall and to station guards there with orders to arrest and bring to him anyone they saw weeping or showing signs of sorrow. The thief's mother was very upset at the hanging up of the corpse. Speaking to her remaining son, she enjoined him to contrive some way of taking down his brother's body and bringing it home; if he neglected to do so, she threatened to go to the king and reveal that her son had the valuables. Since the mother handled her surviving son roughly and could not be persuaded otherwise in spite of his pleas, he devised a plan for the purpose.

Readying some donkeys, he loaded them with wine skins filled with wine and drove them to the place where the men were guarding his brother's hanging corpse. When he was near, he pulled on two or three of the wine skins, untying the mouths that had been bound up. As the wine began to flow he struck his head and loudly yelled out as though he did not know which donkey to deal with first. The guards, when they saw that wine was flowing freely, quickly gathered in the road with their jugs and began to collect the wine as it ran out, considering it their gain. With feigned anger he cursed at them each in turn. The guards tried to pacify him and after a while he pretended to be appeased and give up his anger. Finally he drove his donkeys out of the road and began to repack them. Conversation arose, and when or another of the guards poked fun at him and managed to make him laugh, he presented them with one of the wine skins. With little delay they lay down intending to drink and invited him to stay and join them. He was persuaded, of course, and stayed. In the course of the drinking they became more and more friendly, and he presented them with another wine skin. Drinking to excess, the guards became very drunk and were overcome by sleep there where they were drinking. Since it was quite dark by that time, he took down the body of his brother, and he also shaved the right cheek of each of the guards in order to disgrace them. Then he placed the corpse on his donkey and drove it home, having accomplished what his mother had charged him to do.

When it was reported to the king that the corpse of the thief had been stolen away, he was furious. But he really wanted to find the man who had engineered the thefts. So he placed his own daughter in a brothel—I myself don't believe this part—with instructions to receive every man; however, before going to bed with each man she was to compel him to tell her what was the cleverest thing and what was the most unholy thing he had done in his lifetime; and if anyone related the incidents concerning the thief, she was to seize him and not let him leave.

While the girl was doing what her father had ordered, the thief learned the purpose of what she was doing, and decided to outdo the king in trickery. He cut off at the shoulder the arm of a corpse recently slain, and concealing it under his cloak he went to the king's daughter. Asked the same questions as the others, he related that the most unholy thing he had done was to cut off the head of his brother who had been caught in a trap in the king's treasury, and the cleverest thing was to make the guards completely drunk and take down his brother's hanging corpse. When the girl heard this she reached out for him, but in the darkness the thief held out to her the arm of the corpse. She took hold of it and held on in the belief that it was his arm she was holding. But the thief let go and fled through the door.

When this event was reported to the king, he was amazed at the man's cleverness and daring. In the end he dispatched men to every city to announce that he was not only offering amnesty but also making generous promises to him, if the man should come before him. The thief took the king at his word and went to him.

Rhampsinitos marveled greatly and gave him his daughter in marriage on the ground that he was the most intelligent of men, for the Egyptians surpassed other men, but he surpassed the Egyptians.

Herodotos

In this humorous novella the likable thief is appreciated for his cleverness rather than condemned for his immorality, which often happens in tales of tricksters and trickster-like protagonists. As in many wonder tales, the tale ends happily for the hero with his elevation to royal status, the ultimate reward in many tales.

3. THE PHARAOH AND THE COURTESAN

In their stories the Egyptians say that Rhodopis was a very beautiful courtesan. Once while she was bathing, Fortune, which loves to work marvels and surprises, managed events for her that were worthy more of her beauty than of her disposition. While she was bathing and her maidservants were looking after her clothes, an eagle flew down, snatched one of her sandals, and took off. It conveyed the sandal to Memphis, where Psammetichos was sitting in judgment, and threw it onto his lap. Psammetichos, amazed by the form of the sandal and the charm of its workmanship as well as by the action of the bird, ordered a search to be made throughout all Egypt for the woman whose sandal it was. When he found her, he made her his wife.

Aelian

* * *

They relate a fabulous story that while she was bathing, an eagle snatched one of her sandals from her maidservant and conveyed it to Memphis, where the king was administering justice in the open air. When the eagle was above his head, it flung the sandal onto his lap. Stirred both by the form of the sandal and by the strangeness of the event, he dispatched men throughout the land to search for the woman who wore it. She was discovered in the city of Naukratis and brought up to Memphis, where she became the king's wife. When she died she got the tomb mentioned above.

Strabo

The Third Pyramid of Giza, also known as the Tomb of the Courtesan, was popularly supposed to be the tomb of the courtesan Doricha or Rhodopis, built for her by her lovers.

The tale we know as Cinderella is a variant of an international story that is found in different forms over much of the world from China to Europe. It is told sometimes as a legend, as here, and sometimes as a folktale. In the Western branch of the tradition the future husband's interest in the girl is stirred by the sight of the maiden, whereas in the Eastern branch it is initially provoked by her footwear. Accordingly, the Greco-Egyptian legend of Rhodopis belongs to the Eastern branch of the Cinderella tradition.

CHAPTER 2
GODS AND GHOSTS

This chapter brings together stories of the supernatural—gods, nymphs, werewolves, ghosts, magicians, witches, wonder-workers, and religions in conflict.

DIVINE EPIPHANIES

4. THE MUSES APPEAR TO HESIOD

Now, it was the Muses who once taught Hesiod beautiful song
As he pastured his sheep at the foot of holy Mt. Helikon.
The goddesses, Olympian Muses, daughters of aegis-bearing Zeus,
Addressed me in these words first of all,
"You field-dwelling shepherds, miserable reproaches, nothing but bellies,
We know how to speak many lies that resemble the truth, and
When we wish, we know how to utter the truth."
So spoke the glib daughters of great Zeus, and
Gave me a staff, a flourishing shoot of laurel, a marvel, that
They had plucked. And they breathed into me a divine voice
In order that I might celebrate the future and the past, and
Told me to hymn the race of the blessed ones who are eternal, but
Always to sing of the Muses first and last.

Hesiod

In this memorate the Greek shepherd Hesiod tells of a personal experience in which the Muses appeared to him in a desolate place as he tended his sheep, calling him to become a bard by "inspiring" him, literally breathing into him a singer's voice that gave him access to information about the past and the future that otherwise only divinities possess.

In Greek tradition men and women were often said to have acquired their knowledge of, or skill in, this or that art from a deity: a particular bard was taught by Apollon or the Muses, a weaver learned her art from Athena, a skilled rider owed his horsemanship to Poseidon, and so on (Hansen 2005:45). The idea that a person's skill is owed to a supernatural being is still found today. Some Scandinavian and Irish fiddlers, for example, say they got their musicianship from water spirits, and there are Icelandic midwives who attribute their success to the fairies (Almqvist 2008:307–312).

5. THE MUSES APPEAR TO ARCHILOCHOS

They say that when Archilochos was a young man he was sent by his father Telesikles to their farm in the district called Leimones to bring back a cow to sell. He arose when it was night and the moon was still shining, to bring the cow to the city. Reaching the place called Lissides, he saw what he thought was a group of women, and assuming that they were going from their work to town, he went up to joke with them. They responded with playful laughter and asked him if he was bringing the cow in order to sell it, and when he said he was, they said they would give him a fair price. But after they said this, neither they nor the cow was to be seen anymore, while before his feet Archilochos saw a lyre. He was astonished, but when he gradually regained his senses he supposed it was the Muses who had appeared to him and given him a lyre.

He picked up the lyre, went back to town, and explained to his father what had happened. When Telesikles heard this and saw the lyre, he was amazed. First, he instituted a search throughout the entire island for the cow but was unable to find her. After that, the citizens named him a public messenger, together with Lykambes, to go to Delphi to consult the oracle on behalf of the city, and he too wished to inquire about their experience.

After they arrived and entered the oracular precinct, the god gave Telesikles the following response:

That son who is first to address you, Telesikles,
As you leap from your ship onto your native land,
Will be immortal and celebrated in song.

They arrived at Paros during the festival of Artemis, where the first son to meet and address his father was Archilochos.

Mnesiepes

Like Hesiod, Archilochos experiences an unexpected epiphany of the Muses, who summon him to become a poet. Just as Hesiod is handed a branch of laurel as a token of his encounter, Archilochos receives a lyre, in his case in exchange for a cow. Befitting the men's dissimilar poetry and personalities, Hesiod's Muses are serious and critical, whereas Archilochos's Muses are playful.

Archilochos's story is related by a third person, a certain Mnesiepes, who, acting upon oracular instructions from the god Apollon, built an Archilocheion, or hero shrine in honor of Archilochos, on the island of Paros, where the lyric poet had been born four centuries earlier. Mnesiepes records the oracle and his own follow-up in an inscription on marble stone. The text includes this aretalogy telling of Archilochos's life-changing encounter with the goddesses.

6. THAMYRIS COMPETES AGAINST THE MUSES

At the town of Dorion the Muses
Encountered Thamyris the Thracian and put an end to his singing
As he made his way from the town of Oichalia and from Eurytos
of Oichalia.
Thamyris had declared that he could win a competition in song
Even against the Muses themselves, daughters of aegis-bearing Zeus.
They in their anger maimed him, taking away his wondrous voice
And making him forget how to play his instrument.

Homer

***

Thamyris excelled in good looks and in his ability to sing to the lyre. He engaged in a contest of music with the Muses, making the agreement that if he won, he could have sexual intercourse with each of them, whereas if he lost, they could deprive him of whatever they wished. The Muses got the better of him and deprived him of his eyes and of his musicianship.

Apollodoros

What the gods give they can also take away. In Greek mythology humans suffer if they boast they are the equal of, or superior to, a deity in some respect such as hunting, beauty, or happiness, and of course it is worse if they go so far as to engage in an actual contest with a deity, as happens in this legend.

7. STESICHOROS'S *PALINODE*

They say that after Stesichoros blamed Helen in one of his poems, he lost his sight. But as a result of a dream he had, he praised Helen in a second poem, the *Palinode*, and recovered it again.

Suda

The lyric poet Stesichoros composed a poem about Helen, presumably his Helen, *which mentions that she deserted her family, an act that led eventually to the Trojan War. Presently the poet became blind. After learning that his poem was the cause of his blindness, he composed his* Palinode, *or* Recantation, *in which he represented Helen in a better light, whereupon he regained his sight.*

* * *

There is an ancient purification for persons who have done wrong in mythological matters, one unknown to Homer but known to Stesichoros. When Stesichoros was deprived of his sight because he spoke ill of Helen, he was, unlike Homer, aware of the reason and recognized it since he was an educated person. Immediately he composed the following:

> It is not true, this story.
> You did not go on the well-benched ships,
> Nor did you reach Pergamon, Troy's citadel.

After composing his so-called *Palinode*, he immediately recovered his sight.

Plato

8. ASKLEPIOS HEALS PANDAROS

Pandaros, a Thessalian, Who Had Tattoos on His Forehead

While Pandaros slept in the sanctuary, he saw a vision. It seemed to him that the god tied a headband onto his tattoos and ordered him to take off the headband after he had departed from the adytum, and dedicate it as an offering to the temple.

At daybreak he got up, removed the headband, and saw that his forehead was free of tattoos. He dedicated the headband, which had the tattoos from his forehead, as an offering for the temple.

Echedoros Got Pandaros's Tattoos in Addition to Those He Already Had

Echedoros had received money from Pandaros to dedicate an offering to the god in Epidauros on Pandaros's behalf. But he did not pay out the money.

While he slept, he saw a vision. It seemed to him that the god stood above him and asked him if he had gotten any money from Pandaros for dedicating an image of Athena as an offering in the temple. Echedoros said that he had received no such thing from Pandaros, but if the god healed him he would dedicate to him a painted image as an offering. After this, it seemed to him that the god tied Pandaros's headband onto his tattoos and ordered him to take off the headband after he had left the adytum, wash his forehead in the fountain, and look at his reflection in the water.

At daybreak he went out of the adytum and took off the headband, which no longer had its tattoos. But looking closely at the water, he saw that his forehead not only had its own tattoos but had acquired those of Pandaros as well.

anonymous inscription

*This aretalogy is preserved as a testimonial inscription incised on stone in the sanctuary of the healing god Asklepios at Epidauros, displayed for the public to read. It is one of several stone tablets that attest to miraculous cures experienced by persons who sought the god's help. The "tattoos" (*stigmata*) on Pandaros's and Echedoros's foreheads probably indicate the men's previous status as slaves.*

The legend is constructed upon the common folk-narrative device of "unsuccessful repetition," in which a character in the first episode succeeds at something, whereas a character in the following episode fails in his or her attempt to replicate the event.

9. ASKLEPIOS REVEALS SECRETS OF THE GODS

Although many persons have ventured during their lifetime, Caesar Augustus, to transmit a compilation of marvels, no one has been able to fulfill this promise because of the obscurity that clouds Fate's intentions. I am the only person of my generation, I think, to have accomplished something astounding and known to few persons. For I have attempted matters that go beyond the boundaries of human nature, matters involving many ordeals and dangers, and brought them to a fitting end.

I studied the literary arts in regions of Asia, and when I became more proficient than everyone else, I resolved for a while to enjoy the benefits of my knowledge. I sailed to the esteemed city of Alexandria with a lot of money and consorted with the most accomplished men of letters, earning praise for my diligence and intelligence. In addition I regularly attended the lectures of the dialectic physicians, for I was passionate about this kind of knowledge.

When the time came for me to return home, since my medical studies were making good progress, I went around to the libraries in search of the necessary materials. Finding a certain book by Nechepso that featured twenty-four treatments for the body as a whole as well as for individual ailments, by means of stones and plants in accordance with the zodiac, I was astonished by the amazing promises it made. But it was, it seemed, the empty vauntings of a royal fool, for although I assembled the sun disk he admired, as well as his other potent substances, I was unsuccessful in every one of his healing therapies. I regarded this deception as being harsher than death, and I was consumed with grief, for I had trusted rashly in the treatise and had written to my parents about the effectiveness of the treatments as if I had already tried them out, announcing that I was coming home. Now I was unable to remain in Alexandria on account of the laughter of my colleagues, who were envious of my good qualities, but since I was found out as not having lived up to my promises, I felt no enthusiasm for returning home either, so I went around Egypt driven by my tortured soul, seeking to fulfill some part of what I had rashly promised or, failing this, to exit from life. My mind was always divining that I should hold converse with gods, and I constantly stretched out my hands to the sky, beseeching the gods to grant me some such thing through a dream manifestation or a divine inspiration so that I could return to Alexandria and my homeland proudly and cheerfully.

I came to Thebes—I regard it as the most ancient city in Egypt, and it has many temples—and passed my time there. In addition, there were knowledgeable high priests in the city and old men with all kinds of learning. As time went on and my friendship with them grew, I began inquiring whether there was still to be found any magic power. Since most of them put forth promises with the same rashness as I had done, I judged them unfavorably; however, one of them could be trusted on account of his age and lack of pomposity, and I did not shake off his friendship. This man asserted that he had the power of lecanomancy.* I invited him one day to take a walk with me in a very solitary part of the city, not revealing to him what I desired, and when we came to a grove where it was very still, I suddenly fell on my face and wept as I held on to the high priest's feet. He was surprised by the unexpected sight and inquired why I was behaving this way, and I declared that my life lay in his hands, saying, "I must converse with a god. If I don't achieve my desire, I'm going to kill myself." He raised me from the ground and comforted me with gentle words, saying he would gladly do this for me. He told me to purify myself for three days.

My mind was eased at the promises made by the high priest, and I shook his hand and thanked him as tears gushed from me like a fountain, for unexpected joy naturally calls forth more tears than pain does. We came back from the grove and set about my purification, while in my anticipation the days for me seemed like years. In the early morning of the third day I went to the high priest and greeted him humbly.

He had prepared a ritually pure chamber along with the rest of the things pertaining to the encounter. I for my part had the foresight, unknown to the high priest, to have paper and ink in my possession in order to note down whatever I needed to. When the high priest asked me whether I wished to converse with the soul of a dead person or with a god, I said, "With Asklepios," adding that it would be the perfect favor if he would allow me to speak with the god one on one. Although he was not happy about that (his facial expression revealed as much), he gave me his assurance.

Enclosing me in the chamber and bidding me sit down opposite the throne on which the god would be seated, he produced the god through

*A diviner employing lecanomancy reads future events as reflections in a bowl of water.

his secret names, exited, and shut the door. As I sat, my body and mind felt faint from the amazing sight—human speech would not be able to describe either the features of his countenance or the beauty of the clothes he wore. He stretched out his right hand and began to speak: "Blessed Thessalos, receiver of this honor in the presence of a god. As time goes on and your successes become known, human beings will worship you as a god. So ask freely about anything you wish, and I'll gladly answer everything." I hardly heard him, being in a state of amazement, my mind overwhelmed with gazing at the form of the god. Still, I asked the reason why I had been unsuccessful with Nechepso's healing therapies. The god said, "Although King Nechepso was quite sensible and endowed with all ability, he did not succeed in getting his information from the mouth of a god, as you seek to do. With his talents he observed the sympathies of stones and plants, but he did not know the times when and the places where the plants must be gathered. For everything waxes and wanes in due season from the influence of the stars, and that very fine, divine spirit that exists throughout all substance pervades especially those places that the influences of the stars reached during the nativity of the cosmos."

Thessalos

On the Virtues of Plants *is an astrological treatise on the therapeutic uses of plants. In his prologue the author claims that he acquired his medical knowledge in Egypt directly from the god of healing, Asklepios (representing perhaps the Egyptian Imhotep), who in an extraordinary personal interview shared with him occult remedies to which only the gods were privy. The prologue is cast in the form of a letter to the emperor.*

* * *

After the god taught me all this by means of his precepts, I expressed my gratitude for his readily granting my request to learn every kind of treatment.

Then I inquired if there was any plant or stone by means of which a human being could continue living, free of death. The god said there were in fact many kinds of plants and stones on earth that, should they be acquired by humans, would permit them to live forever. "But it's not right for humans to know about them. For although humans have been allotted a short term of life, they neglect the laws, try to destroy one another's lives in mutual treachery, and eagerly strive to sully their hands in great evil, despite the fact that they will live only a short time. If they should get an extension of life, they would not spare god himself."

Thessalos

Thessalos ventures one more question—a big one—but the god declines to answer it.

10. ATHENA SAVES THE LINDIANS

Darius, king of the Persians, once dispatched great forces to enslave Greece. His naval expedition came here first of the islands. Terrified by the assault of the Persians, the inhabitants fled together to all the strongholds, most of them gathering at Lindos. The barbarians settled in and besieged them until the Lindians, suffering from a lack of water, considered handing over the city to the enemy.

At this juncture the goddess stood above one of the city officials as he slept, and urged him to take courage, since she was about to ask her father for the water whose lack was oppressing them. After seeing this vision, he reported to the citizens Athena's encouragement. They estimated that they could hold out for five days, and so asked the barbarians for a truce of that many days, saying that Athena had sent to her father for help. They declared that if help did not come within the stated period of time, they would hand the city over to them.

As soon as Darius's admiral, Datis, heard this, he broke out laughing. But when on the following day a great darkness formed around the acropolis and a substantial thunderstorm unexpectedly burst out in its midst, the besieged had abundant water while the Persian force suffered a scarcity. The barbarian, astonished at this epiphany of the goddess, took off his body ornaments—his cloak, torque, and armlets—and sent these in addition to a tiara and a sword as well as a covered carriage as a dedication. (This last had been preserved previously but was burnt up along with most of the other dedications when the temple burnt at the time when the priest of Helios [= "Sun"] was Eukleus, son of Astyanax.) Datis himself raised the siege because of the aforementioned events, and made a treaty of friendship with the formerly besieged, declaring that these people were protected by the gods.

anonymous inscription

Rising above the town of Lindos on the island of Rhodes is an acropolis with a sanctuary sacred to Athena. This aretalogical text, like that of "Asklepios Heals Pandaros" (8, above), forms part of a larger testimonial inscription displayed for public consumption in a divine sanctuary. Inscribed on stone in 99 BC, the so-called Lindian Chronicle lists gifts that prominent persons have dedicated to the goddess, and describes epiphanies of Athena that have occurred at critical times in the history of Lindos. The goddess's first epiphany, given here, occurred around 490 BC. This religious legend contrasts the simple but well-placed faith of the Lindian folk with the scoffing attitude of the Persian invader. The people of Lindos honor Athena and she in turn looks after them.

This is also the sanctuary in which, according to legend, Helen of Troy dedicated a chalice molded from her breast (see 148 "Helen's Chalice"). However, the Lindian Chronicle does not mention the chalice in its list of the sanctuary's treasures.

11. THE ALTAR OF THE VULTURE GOD

Konon's thirty-fifth narrative introduces two shepherds who were pasturing their sheep at the foot of Mt. Lysson in Ephesia.

They spotted a swarm of bees in a cave that was deep and difficult to descend into. One of them got into a basket, which the other fastened to a rope and lowered into the cave. The man in the cave found the honey and also a large amount of gold. Three times he loaded the basket and told the man outside to draw it up. Finally he yelled that the gold had now all been removed and that he himself was getting into the basket.

But since the suspicion of a plot entered his mind as he spoke, he placed a rock into the basket instead of himself and told the other man to draw it up. When the man above held the basket suspended near the opening of the cave, he suddenly let it go down the throat of the cave in order to do away with the other man. Then he buried the gold in the earth and invented a plausible explanation that he gave to persons who inquired about the missing shepherd.

For the shepherd in the cave there was no means of escape. But Apollon appeared to him in a dream and told him to lacerate his body with a sharp stone and then lie still. He followed this injunction, and vultures, taking him for a corpse, flew to him, fixed their talons partly into his hair and partly into his clothes, lifted him up, and carried him unharmed to their home in a glen at the foot of the mountain. The shepherd went to the chief magistrates and made everything known to them. The Ephesians cross-examined the schemer, forced him to show them the gold he had buried, and punished him. Half of the gold they distributed to the wronged man, and the other half they declared sacred to Artemis and Apollon.

The man who had survived and been awarded the gold joined the ranks of the very wealthy and built an altar to Apollon at the very top of the mountain, calling it the Altar of the Vulture God in commemoration of what had happened.

Konon

This religious legend offers an etiology for the unusual name of an altar near Ephesos.

12. A FORTUNE IN WATER

Why do people on the island of Samos invoke Aphrodite "of Dexikreon"?

Is it because an itinerant man, Dexikreon, purified the Samian women, freeing them from the licentious behavior brought on by their luxury and lewdness?

Or is it because Dexikreon was a shipmaster who sailed to Cyprus to engage in trade, and when he was about to load his ship Aphrodite bade him take on water and nothing else, and set sail as quickly as possible? He complied, putting a large quantity of water aboard the ship before sailing away. After a while it happened that the wind ceased blowing and the sea became still. He sold the water to other merchants and shipmasters, who were thirsty, thereby earning a lot of money. As a result of this, he had an image of the goddess made, which he named after himself.

If the report is really true, the goddess clearly wanted not so much to enrich one man as to save many persons through one man.

Plutarch

The Greek text presents two religious legends that offer different etiologies for the puzzling name of a cult statue of Aphrodite on the island of Samos. The second legend is a variant of an international story in which a person brings something ordinary to a place where it is scarce and much needed, and prospers as a result. Best known, perhaps, is the seventeenth-century English legend of Dick Whittington, which relates how Whittington and his cat come to a land overrun with mice, where he demonstrates to the inhabitants his animal's ability to catch mice, and sells the cat for a good price.

13. THE RESCUE OF SIMONIDES

They say that Simonides was dining at Krannon in Thessaly at the home of a wealthy nobleman named Scopas, and sang for Scopas the song he had composed in his honor, which in accordance with poetic convention he had adorned with many lines about Castor and Pollux. With extreme meanness Scopas told Simonides that he would pay half of the fee agreed upon for the song; if Simonides wished, he could ask the Tyndarids[*] to pay the balance, since he had devoted half of his praise song to them.

---

[*]Tyndarids = sons of Tyndareus = Castor and Pollux.

A little while later, the story goes, a message was conveyed to Simonides to step outside, since two young men were standing at the door and earnestly summoned him to come out. He got up and went outside but saw no one. While he stood there, the room in which Scopas was hosting his banquet collapsed, and the falling debris crushed and killed Scopas and his relations.

When their friends wanted to bury them but were unable to recognize them because of their crushed bodies, Simonides, it is said, remembering where each person had reclined, was able to identify them for individual interment. Prompted by this experience, he discovered that it was an orderly arrangement in particular that best aided memory.

Cicero

The Greek poet Simonides of Keos is hired by a wealthy man to compose an epinikion, *or song in celebration of the man's athletic victory. It was normal in Greek* epinikia *for the poet to include a mythological component of some relevance to the victor or his city, which in the present case takes the form of verses about the divine twins Castor and Pollux (Greek Kastor and Polydeukes). When the patron meanly declares that he will pay only half of the poet's fee, the divine twins appear and pay the balance, as it were, by saving the poet's life.*

Simonides was gifted with an excellent memory and, allegedly inspired by this event, invented a system of mnemonics that became famous in antiquity.

LOWER MYTHOLOGY

Lower mythology refers to the body of narratives that foreground lesser divine beings such as nymphs and satyrs.

14. NARCISSUS

In Thespeia in Boeotia—the town is not far from Mt. Helikon—a boy was born, Narcissus, who was very handsome but also disdainful of Eros and of his would-be lovers. Whereas his other admirers gave up loving

him, a certain Ameinias remained very persistent in beseeching him, but Narcissus not only refused him but even sent him a sword. After earnestly begging the god to be his avenger, Ameinias took his own life at Narcissus's door.

When later Narcissus saw his own face and form reflected in the water of a spring, he became the first and only person to fall strangely in love with himself. In the end, being at a loss what to do and believing that he was suffering justly for his haughty treatment of Ameinias's love, he killed himself. After that the Thespians decided to give more reverence and honor to Eros, sacrificing to him in private in addition to performing their communal sacrifices.

The local people think that the flower called narcissus first emerged from the ground on the place where Narcissus shed his blood.

Konon

***

In the territory of the Thespians there is a place called Donakon. The spring of Narcissus is there. People say that Narcissus looked into this water and, not understanding that he was seeing his own reflection, unwittingly fell in love with himself and died of love at the spring.

But it is completely simpleminded to imagine that a person who was old enough to fall in love could not tell the difference between a human being and a reflection of a human being.

Pausanias

Narcissus (Greek Narkissos) is, according to some authors, the son of Kephisos (a river in Boeotia) and Leiriope (a nymph), and so a partly divine being. He is a handsome youth who scorns both the god of love and also his own would-be lovers, two ways of saying that he is indifferent to passion. Eros exacts his revenge by causing Narcissus to fall in love with himself, an exquisitely ironic punishment that obliges Narcissus in turn to experience erotic feelings that cannot be satisfied.

When the youth meets his end, a narcissus flower springs up, the first narcissus, the ancestor of all narcissi. A seventeenth-century traveler reported seeing the plant growing in great profusion on the banks of a river on Mt. Helikon. So the ancient Boeotian legend was probably localized at a site with a spring and an abundance of narcissus flowers.

15. RHOIKOS AND THE NYMPH

Charon of Lampsakos reports that Rhoikos, seeing an oak tree that was about to fall, ordered his slaves to prop it up. The nymph who would have perished along with the tree appeared to Rhoikos, expressed her gratitude for his saving her, and let Rhoikos ask for anything he wanted. He said he wanted to have sex with her. The nymph said that this would bring loss, but told him notwithstanding that he should avoid the company of other women. A bee served as messenger between them.

Once when Rhoikos was playing a board game and the bee flew around him, he spoke to it very unkindly, turning the nymph's feelings to anger so that she maimed him.

scholiast

*A tree nymph, or dryad or hamadryad, is coeval with a particular tree. She is born at the same time as her tree and her life is bound up with it, so that when the tree dies, she does too (*Homeric Hymn to Aphrodite *256–273).*

Another text of the legend relates that the dryad sends a bee as her messenger to tell Rhoikos when it is time to meet for sex. A messenger is required because the lovers dwell apart, he in a community of humans and she in the wild countryside. When Rhoikos becomes so involved in a mere game that he impatiently drives the bee away, he is rudely rejecting his lover's overture, and as a consequence his supernatural lover punishes him by maiming him in some way.

Because the nymph's initial condition is that Rhoikos be faithful to her, we expect his slight to take the form of his being unfaithful rather than simply dismissive. This seems in fact to be what happens in some forms of the legend.

16. "THE GREAT GOD PAN IS DEAD!"

As for death among such beings, I have heard a story from a man who is neither a fool nor a fraud. Aemilianus the orator, whom some of you have heard, was the son of Epitherses, a fellow citizen of mine as well as my literature teacher. Epitherses had said that once in the course of a voyage to Italy he embarked upon a ship carrying freight and many passengers. In the evening, around the Echinades Islands, the wind abated, and as the ship was passing through, it came near the Paxoi Islands. Most of the passengers were awake; many were drinking, having eaten their dinner.

Suddenly a voice was heard from the Paxoi Islands. Someone was calling out for Thamous, which caused general wonderment. Thamous the Egyptian was our pilot, not a person known by name to many of the passengers. Now, twice he was called and said nothing, but on the third occasion he responded, and the caller, straining his voice, said, "When you reach Palodes, report that the great Pan is dead."

Epitherses said that everyone heard this and was amazed. While they discussed whether it was better to carry out the instruction or not to meddle and let things be, Thamous decided that if there was a wind, he would say nothing as he sailed past the islands, but if there was no wind and the sea was calm, he would report what he had heard. Inasmuch as he reached Palodes without wind or waves, Thamous looked from stern to land and said, just as he had heard, "The great Pan is dead." Before he even finished, there arose a great moaning of many voices, mixed with amazement.

Since many persons were present, the story quickly spread around Rome, and Thamous was summoned by Tiberius Caesar. Tiberius was so convinced of the truth of the story that he made inquiries and questioned people about Pan. The scholars at court, who were numerous, conjectured that he was the Pan who was born of Hermes and Penelope.

Plutarch

The narration is part of a conversation in which several men discuss how the supernatural beings called by the Greeks daimones *differ from gods (*theoi*). Although* daimones *(the source of our "demons") could signify "gods," the word often referred to supernatural beings of lower status. The narrator, Philip, offers this story as evidence that, unlike the gods,* daimones *are subject to death. Since Pan was not a lofty Olympian but a rustic god of the countryside who consorted with nymphs and satyrs, he could be classified as a* daimon.

Philip says he heard the present account from Aemilianus, now an old man, who in turn had heard it from his late father, Epitherses. So Philip is two steps away from the event, which was experienced by a friend of a friend (FOAF), a classic attribution of source in legend transmission.

17. BOGIES

Gello was a maiden. After she died prematurely, the inhabitants of Lesbos say, her ghost haunted children, and they ascribe to her the deaths of persons who die prematurely.

Zenobios

Bogies are usually vaguely conceived supernatural figures with which adults threaten children in order to frighten them into behaving a particular way, such as to eat their meals, not go outside at night, and so on. The principal bogies in ancient Greece were the three ogresses Gello, Mormo (or Mormolyke "Mormo-Wolf"), and Lamia, who were also spoken of generically, especially in the plural, as gelloudes, mormones *(*mormolykeia*), and* lamiai. *Plato (*Republic *2.381e) says that mothers frighten their children by telling them stories about gods going about in strange guises during the night, and Strabo (1.2.8) remarks that adults use pleasant tales to encourage children, and frightening tales of Lamia, Mormolyke, and others to deter them. When the Mantineans fled before enemy peltasts, the Spartans said mockingly that the fleeing men were afraid of peltasts the way children fear* mormones *(Xenophon* Hellenika *4.4.17).*

Such boogiemen and boogiewomen are found in the traditions of many nations. They may have positive or semipositive counterparts, such as Santa Claus, who, children are told, rewards good children with presents—but can also punish bad children by passing them over or bringing them a lump of coal.

* * *

Mormo was a Corinthian woman who ate her own children one evening and then, with some intent or another, flew away. Thereafter, when mothers want to scare their children, they call out to Mormo.

scholiast

* * *

At the base of this mountain there was an immense cave roofed over with ivy and yew, and the story goes that it was the birthplace of Queen Lamia, distinguished for her beauty. They say that because of the savageness of her mind, her looks later became like those of a wild animal, for she had children but they all died. Weighed down with grief and envying women who were blessed with children, she ordered their newborn babies to be snatched out of their arms and straightway put to death. For this reason, down to the present day, reports of this woman continue and her name is very frightening to young children.

Diodoros of Sicily

The narrator represents Lamia as a queen who, in the manner of a monarch, orders others to carry out her wishes, but in the usual tradition it is she herself who acts. In modern Greek folktales lamia *has become a general term for any kind of ogress.*

* * *

Douris, in the second book of his *History of Libya*, reports that Lamia was a beautiful woman, but after Zeus had sex with her, Hera was jealous and caused her children to perish. In her grief Lamia became misshapen, snatches away the children of other women, and destroys them.

scholiast

The Greek bogies are originally human women who have an unsuccessful experience of motherhood and turn into monstrous beings that are not subject to death. Gello dies before giving birth, Lamia has children who perish, and Mormo has children she eats. These females resent motherhood and children, and in ancient folk belief were said to be responsible when a pregnant woman, mother, or child died an untimely death.

* * *

. . . extracting a living child from the belly of a Lamia, after she had eaten her lunch.

Horace

*This passage and the one that follows allude to Lamia stories that are reminiscent of folktales familiar to us today. Horace refers to an unknown tale in which a Lamia swallows a child who is later removed alive from her belly (*neu pransae Lamiae vivum puerum extrahat alvo*). The motif of rescuing a child alive from the belly of an ogre is found in* The Wolf and the Kids *(ATU 123), a tale for children in which a mother goat leaves her kids at home alone, whereupon a wolf pretending to be the mother gains entrance to the house, swallows all but one of the young goats, and falls asleep; when the real mother returns and finds the wolf asleep, she cuts open its belly, releases her children, and fills the wolf's belly with stones. The motif also appears in the Grimm Brothers' version of Little Red Riding Hood (Uther 2008:63–69; Grimm 2014:85–87).*

* * *

. . . will he not recall having heard such things from his nurse when, as a little child, he had trouble sleeping, for example, the Towers of the Lamia and the Combs of the Sun?

Tertullian

Tertullian's mention of the Lamia's Towers has reminded many readers of narratives such as the Grimms' tale of Rapunzel, in which a witch imprisons the long-haired heroine in a tower (ATU 310 The Maiden in the Tower*; Grimm 2014:37–39). But the ancient allusion is too skimpy to confirm a connection with the familiar wonder tale, nor is it clear from Tertullian's allusion whether the Towers of the Lamia (*Lamiae turres*) and the Combs of the Sun (*Pectines Solis*) belong to the same tale.*

SHAPE-CHANGERS

18. THE WEREWOLF

After everyone wished one another happiness and health, Trimalchio looked at Niceros and said, "You used to be better company at the dinner table, but now you're quiet and don't make a sound. Please, I won't be happy unless you tell us about that adventure of yours."

Niceros was delighted at his friend's attention and said, "May I never make another cent if I'm not bursting with joy at your kind words. So let the happiness flow, though I'm afraid these learned men here may laugh at me. Well, that's up to them. I'll tell my story anyway. No loss to me if someone snickers. Better to be laughed with than laughed at." So speaking, he began his tale.

"When I was still a slave, we used to live on a narrow street. Now it's Gavilla's house. There, as the gods would have it, I fell in love with the wife of Terentius the innkeeper. You all know Melissa from Tarentum, the one with the beautiful ass. But, by Hercules, my feelings for her were not for her body alone or for sex but because of her sweet nature. If I asked her for anything, she never refused me. If she made a penny, I got a half-penny. I entrusted my money to her, and she never did me wrong.

"Now, the man she lived with died, and so by hook or crook I did everything in my power to get to her. Well, you know, a friend in need is a friend indeed. It happened that my master had gone to Capua to settle some odds and ends. Since there was an opportunity, I talked one of our guests into walking with me to the fifth milestone. He was a soldier, brave as Orcus. We took off around cockcrow, but the moon was shining like high noon, and we arrived among the roadside tombs. My companion went off to the tombs to relieve himself, while I kept going, singing and counting tombstones. Then as I looked back for my traveling companion, I saw him taking all his clothes off and laying them beside the road. My heart was in my mouth, and I stood there like a corpse. Then he pissed in a circle around his clothes and suddenly became a wolf! I'm not joking. I wouldn't lie about this for anything. But as I was starting to say, he became a wolf and began howling and ran off into the woods.

"At first I didn't know where I was. Then I went to pick up his clothes, but they had turned to stone! If anyone ever died of fright, I did so at that moment. Still, I drew my sword and slashed at shadows until I reached my girlfriend's place. I looked like a ghost when I walked in. I'd all but expired. Sweat was streaming down my crotch, my eyes were glazed, and I pulled myself together with difficulty.

"Melissa was surprised that I'd got there so late, and said, 'If you'd come earlier, you could at least have helped us. A wolf got into the grounds, attacked the flocks, and drained their blood like a butcher. Even though it got away, it didn't get off scot-free. One of the slaves nicked its neck with a spear.'

"When I heard this, I couldn't sleep a wink, and at daybreak I rushed home, dashing like a swindled innkeeper. When I came to the place where the clothes had turned to stone, I didn't find anything except blood. And when I got home, my companion the soldier was lying in bed like an ox, and a doctor was treating his neck. I realized then that he was a werewolf. After that I was unable to eat with him, not on my life.

"What others may think of this is up to them, but if I'm lying, may your guardian spirits attack me."

Everyone was astonished. "I wouldn't doubt a word of it," said Trimalchio. "You can take my word for how my hair stood on end, because I know that Niceros doesn't exaggerate. No, he's reliable and sticks to the truth."

Petronius

The setting of this narration is a banquet, in the course of which the host Trimalchio asks one of his guests, Niceros, to relate an amazing story that, he implies, Niceros is known for. The story proves to be a memorate, or personal narrative about a supernatural experience. Since the events verge on the incredible, much attention is given to the reliability of Niceros's narrative. The narrator is pleased to be asked to tell his story but at the same time is reticent to do so, or pretends to be, since he may be laughed at. He is, he suggests, an ordinary fellow—a slave at the time when he had his supernatural experience, now a freedman—whereas the dinner guests include refined and educated men.

Niceros's werewolf story is a Roman form of a belief legend that is found in many lands: (a) a wild animal makes an attack on a farm, (b) one of the defenders wounds the animal, and presently (c) a neighbor or member of the family is discovered to be suffering from a wound in the same place, (d) which shows that he or she is a shape-changer.

19. THE EMPOUSA

One of the students of Apollonios of Tyana was Menippos of Lykia, twenty-five years old, intelligent, and physically well-built, looking as he did like a handsome and well-bred athlete. Most people thought he had as his lover a foreign woman, and they declared that she was beautiful and quite graceful and wealthy. In fact, she was none of these things at all, but only seemed to be.

He had been walking alone on the road to Kenchreai when he met an apparition in the form of a woman. She took his hand, declaring that she had been in love with him for a long time. She was, she said, a Phoenician and lived in a suburb of Corinth, mentioning a particular suburb. "If you come there this evening," she said, "I'll sing for you and you'll have wine such as you have never tasted before. There will be no rival to bother you, and we'll live as a beautiful couple." The young man was enticed by this offer, for although he was strong in most areas of philosophy, he was weak in matters of love. He went to her place around evening, and after that he visited her frequently as his lover, not understanding that she was an apparition.

Apollonios stared at Menippos as a sculptor might, making a portrait of the youth and observing him. "So you are the attractive youth whom attractive women are chasing. But you are fostering a snake, and a snake is fostering you." When Menippos expressed surprise, Apollonios said, "Your woman is not your wife. But do you think she is in love with you?" "Yes, by Zeus, I do," he said, "since she behaves toward me like a woman in love." "And would you marry her?" he asked. "Yes, it would be lovely to marry a woman who loves me." So Apollonios inquired, "When is the wedding?" "Very soon," Menippos said, "perhaps even tomorrow."

Apollonios watched for the time of the wedding banquet and showed up with the diners. "Where is the pretty woman," he asked, "for whose sake you have come?" "Here," said Menippos, and blushed as he stood up. "And the silver and gold and other valuables decorating the banqueting hall, do they belong to you or your wife?" "To my wife. My own possessions are limited to this," he said, pointing to his threadbare cloak. Apollonios asked, "Do you know of the gardens of Tantalos, which both exist and don't exist?" "Yes, from Homer," he said, "since I haven't been down to Hades's realm." "You should regard these decorations here as being like that. They are not material but have the appearance of material. For you to understand what I mean, the good bride here is an *empousa*, which many people think is the same as a *lamia* or *mormolykeion*. They love sex, but most of all they love human flesh, and they use sex to entrap persons they want to devour."

"Hold your tongue and move on," the bride said, pretending to be disgusted by what she had heard, and she started to make fun of philosophers for always blabbing a lot of nonsense. But then the golden cups and the apparent silver proved to be insubstantial, and everything vanished from sight, as the cupbearers, cooks, and entire serving staff disappeared when they were put to the test by Apollonios. The apparition pretended to weep, begging him not to examine her or force her to confess what she was, but since he persisted and did not let up, she acknowledged she was an empousa and was fattening up Menippos with pleasures in order to eat him. It was usual, she said, to feed on bodies that were young and fit, since their blood was pure.

This is the best known of the stories about Apollonios. I have of necessity related it in some detail, for although most people know the story, since the events took place in central Greece, they have gotten only the short version—that Apollonios once unmasked a lamia in Corinth—and do not know what the lamia was doing and that it was Menippos she was doing it to.

Philostratos

*Merely by observing the external appearance of his new student Menippos, the perceptive Apollonios of Tyana (a historical sage and holy man of the first century AD) is able to discern that the young man's lover is not a human being but an ogress who has assumed the form of an attractive woman in order to seduce her victim sexually with the ultimate aim of eating him. The ancient designations of such an ogress were fluid (*empousa, lamia, *and* mormo *or the variant form* mormolykeion*) as were traditions about their true form (they were snakes, or they had donkey legs, or one leg of bronze and another of dung).*

A lamia (or lamias and empousas as a class) can be a voluptuous, cannibalistic seductress of young men, but she can also be a female who, deprived of her own children, jealously attacks mothers and babies in order to deprive others of what she herself does not have (see 17 "Bogies"). Stories of the former kind of ogress doubtless circulated among adults, while stories of the latter kind were told by adults to children. These same twin aspects of a single female figure, the voluptuous ogress who devours young men and the unhappy ogress who devours young children, have a parallel today in Mexican traditions of La Llorona (Goldstein et al. 2007:92–93).

GHOSTS

Physically speaking, two kinds of ghost are found in Greek and Roman tradition, the disembodied and the embodied. The former are spirit-like specters that are recognizable images of their former selves but have little substance. When, for example, Achilleus tries to embrace the ghost of his companion Patroklos at Troy, he finds to his grief that there is nothing to hold on to (Homer Iliad *23.62–108). In contrast, embodied ghosts, or revenants, are fully corporeal and can be all but impossible to distinguish from ordinary human beings. The amorous revenant Philinnion is this kind of ghost. But some ghosts show inconsistencies with regard to corporality, a specter-type ghost displaying physical strength or a revenant disappearing like smoke, so that they can be said to manifest "incorporeal corporality" (Stramaglia 1999:42–43).*

20. PHILINNION

. . . the nurse went to the door of the guest room, and in the light of the burning lamp she saw the girl sitting beside Machates. Because of the extraordinary nature of the sight, she did not remain there any longer but ran to the girl's mother screaming, "Charito! Demostratos!" She said they should get up and come with her to their daughter, who was alive and by some divine will was with the guest in the guest room.

When Charito heard this astonishing report, the immensity of the message and the nurse's excitement made her frightened and faint. But after a short time the memory of her daughter came to her, and she began to weep. In the end she accused the old woman of being mad and told her to leave her presence immediately. But the nurse replied boldly and reproachfully that she herself was rational and sound of mind, unlike her mistress, who was reluctant to see her own daughter.

With some hesitation Charito went to the door of the guest room, partly coerced by the nurse and partly wanting to know what really had happened. Since considerable time—about two hours—had now passed since the nurse's original message, it was somewhat late when Charito went to the door, and the occupants were already asleep. She peered in and thought she recognized her daughter's clothes and features, but inasmuch as she could not determine the truth of the matter, she decided to do nothing further that night. She planned to get up in the morning and confront the girl, or if she should be too late for that, she intended to question

Machates thoroughly about everything. He would not, she thought, lie if asked about so important a matter. So she said nothing and left.

At dawn, however, it turned out that by divine will or chance the girl had left unnoticed. When Charito came to the room, she was upset with the young man because of the girl's departure. She asked him to relate everything to her from the beginning, telling her the truth and concealing nothing.

The youth was anxious and confused at first, but hesitantly revealed that the girl's name was Philinnion. He told how her visiting began, how great her desire for him was, and that she said she came to him without her parents' knowledge. Wishing to make the matter credible, he opened his coffer and took out the items the girl had left behind—the golden ring he had gotten from her and the breast band she had left the night before.

When Charito saw this evidence she uttered a cry, tore her clothes, cast her headdress from her head, and fell to the ground, throwing herself upon the tokens and beginning her grief anew. As the guest observed what was happening, how all were grieving and wailing as if they were about to lay the girl into her grave, he became upset and called on them to stop, promising to show them the girl if she came again. Charito accepted this and bade him carefully keep his promise to her.

Night came on and now it was the hour when Philinnion was accustomed to come to him. The household kept watch, wanting to know of her arrival. She entered at the usual time and sat down on the bed. Machates pretended that nothing was wrong, since he wished to investigate the whole incredible matter to find out if the girl he was consorting with, who took care to come to him at the same hour, was actually dead. As she ate and drank with him, he simply could not believe what the others had told him, and he supposed that some grave-robbers had dug into the grave and sold the clothes and the gold to her father. But in his wish to learn exactly what the case was, he secretly sent his slaves to summon Demostratos and Charito, who came quickly.

When they first saw her, they were speechless and panic-stricken by the amazing sight, but after that they cried aloud and embraced their daughter. Philinnion then said to them, "Mother and father, how unfairly you have grudged my being with the guest for three days in my father's house, although I have caused no one any pain. For this reason, on account of your meddling, you shall grieve all over again, and I shall return to the place appointed for me. For it was not without divine will that I came here." Immediately after speaking these words she was dead, and her body lay stretched out visibly on the bed. Her father and mother threw themselves upon her, and there were much confusion and wailing in the house because of the calamity. The misfortune was unbearable and the sight incredible.

The event was quickly noised through the city and reported to me. Accordingly, during the night I kept in check the crowds that gathered at the house, for, with news like this going from mouth to mouth, I wanted to make sure there would be no trouble.

By early dawn the theater was full. After the particulars had been explained, it was decided that we should first go to the tomb, open it, and see whether the body lay on its bier or whether we would find the place empty. A half year had not yet passed since the death of the girl. When we opened the chamber into which all deceased members of the family were placed, we saw bodies lying on biers, or bones in the case of those who had died long ago, but on the bier onto which Philinnion had been placed we found only the iron ring that had belonged to the guest, and the gilded wine cup, objects that she had gotten from Machates on the first day.

Astonished and frightened, we proceeded immediately to Demostratos's house to see if the corpse was truly to be seen in the guest room. After we saw the dead girl lying there on the ground, we gathered at the place of assembly, since the events were serious and incredible.

There was considerable confusion in the assembly, and almost no one was able to form a judgment of the events. The first to stand up was Hyllos, who is considered to be not only the best seer among us but also a fine augur and in general has shown remarkable perception in his craft. He said we should burn the girl outside the boundaries of the city, since nothing would be gained by burying her in the ground within its boundaries, and perform an apotropaic sacrifice to Hermes Chthonios and the

Eumenides. Then he prescribed that everyone purify themselves completely, cleanse the temples, and perform all the customary rites to the chthonic deities. (He spoke to me also in private about the king and the events, telling me to sacrifice to Hermes, Zeus Xenios, and Ares, and to perform these rites with care.) When he had made this known to us, we undertook to do what he had instructed.

Machates, the guest whom the ghost had visited, became despondent and killed himself.

If you decide to write about this to the king, send word to me also in order that I may dispatch to you some of the persons who examined the affair in detail.

Farewell.

Phlegon of Tralles

Phlegon's text has the form of a letter from a local official to a higher official elsewhere. Unfortunately, the beginning of the letter is lost, and the name of the writer does not appear at the end because in ancient letters this information is given at the head: "A [the writer] sends greetings to B [the recipient]." The epistle is in any case spurious, a document composed by an unknown person as an exercise or perhaps for amusement. He creates for a traditional ghost story a believable setting by employing as narrator a local person of status whom he makes to be an eyewitness to the events. Although the letter is in effect a piece of short fiction, readers from antiquity to the Renaissance took it as genuine, as does Phlegon, who includes it in his book of marvels, and as Proklos does in the following text, when he summarizes it in his commentary on Plato.

***

The crowning example [that is, of persons dying and coming back to life] is Philinnion, during the reign of Philip. The daughter of the Amphipolitans Demostratos and Charito, she died soon after she was married. Her husband was Krateros.

In the sixth month after her death she returned to life, and for many nights in a row she secretly slept with a youth named Machates because of her love for him. He had come to Demostratos from his native city of

Pella. But when she was detected, she died again, after having proclaimed that what had happened was in accord with the will of the chthonic deities. Her corpse was seen by everyone as it lay in state in her father's house. In their disbelief at what had happened, the members of her family went to the place where they had originally placed her body, dug it up, and found it to be empty.

The events are described in letters written to Philip, some by Hipparchos and others by Arrhidaios, who had been entrusted with affairs in Amphipolis.

Proklos

Although the beginning of the letter that Phlegon transmits is lost, Proklos had access to its full content, which he summarizes here. From it we learn the gist of what happens before the startled servant woman glimpses the recently deceased Philinnion in the guest room, and, further, we can infer that the events are set in the Greek city of Amphipolis on the Strymon during the reign of Philip II of Macedon, father of Alexander the Great, in the mid-fourth century BC.

21. THE LAST PRINCESS AT TROY

It is said that Achilleus once appeared in person to a merchant who frequented the island of Leuke. Achilleus recounted what had happened at Troy, entertained him with drink, and asked him to sail over to Ilium and bring back to him a Trojan maiden, describing such and such a girl who was such and such a person's slave in Ilium. Surprised at the request, the stranger made bold to inquire why he wanted a Trojan slave. Achilleus said, "Stranger, because she was born of the very lineage from which Hektor and those before Hektor derive, and is a descendant of the line of Priam and Dardanos."

So now the merchant, thinking that Achilleus was in love with the girl, purchased her and sailed back to the island, where Achilleus thanked him upon his arrival and instructed him to keep the girl aboard his ship because, I think, the island was not accessible to women. The merchant was to come to Achilleus's shrine in the evening to dine with him and Helen. When the merchant arrived, Achilleus gave him a great deal of money, which merchants are unable to resist, and said he was making the man his guest-friend, rendering his commerce prosperous, and causing his ship to have a good voyage. At daybreak he said, "Take these things and sail, and leave the girl on the beach for me."

The merchant and his crew were not yet a stade distant from land when their ears were assaulted by the girl's cries. Achilleus was mangling her and tearing her apart limb from limb.

Philostratos

The setting of the events in this legend is the mythological island of Leuke, or White Isle, to which Achilleus and Helen were translated after their respective deaths and now dwell together as lovers. They have become heroes *in the Greek cultic sense, mortals who have died but continue to lead an existence as active and supernaturally powerful beings.*

This belief legend brilliantly lulls its audience into expecting a particular conclusion, and surprises, even shocks, by presenting another. The ghost of Achilleus initially plays the hospitable host to a human merchant and makes known his wish for something that the merchant can provide. His motive appears to be ordinary human affection, the wish of a man to be close to a woman he desires or loves. There is, indeed, something unusual about the particular object of his desire, for the girl is a descendant of the Trojan royal house, Achilleus's old enemies. And as soon as Achilleus acquires the object of his apparent affection, he tears her apart limb from limb. We perceive too late that we have been eased into expecting, or even into wanting, human love to motivate a creature that is no longer human, a supernatural being that belongs to a different order of reality.

22. THE GRATEFUL DEAD MAN

Simonides once saw the corpse of an unknown man that had been cast up on shore, and buried it. Later, when he was planning to embark on a ship, he was warned in a dream by the man to whom he had given burial not to do so, for if he sailed, he would perish in a shipwreck. And so Simonides turned back, whereas all those who sailed perished.

Cicero

The "grateful dead man," as folklorists call him, figures in a stable narrative routine in a variety of traditional stories: (a) the protagonist comes upon the corpse of a man he does not know; (b) he kindly arranges for burial at his own expense; subsequently, (c) the dead man's ghost appears to him and helps him in some way. In the present belief legend the grateful dead man serves Simonides as a warning apparition (cf. Felton 1999:30–34).

The American rock band the Grateful Dead took its name from this recurrent figure of folk narrative.

* * *

This man is the savior of Simonides of Keos.
Though dead, he returned a favor to one who was alive.

Simonides

According to tradition, this elegiac couplet was composed by the poet for the tomb of the stranger whom he had buried, and who in turn saved the poet's life.

23. MURDER AT THE INN

Two friends from Arcadia were traveling together and came to Megara, where one of them put up at an inn and the other stayed with an acquaintance in town. Each had his supper and retired to bed.

Early in the night the second traveler had a vision in which the first man begged him to come to his aid since the innkeeper was preparing to murder him. Frightened by the dream, he got up but then, thinking the vision was really nothing to worry about, went back to bed. Later, as he was sleeping, the same man appeared to him and, inasmuch as the other had not come to his aid while he was still alive, asked him at least not to let his death go unavenged. He had been murdered, he said, and his body had been tossed into a cart by the innkeeper and covered over with dung. The murdered man asked his friend to be at the city gate in the morning before the cart left the city. Disturbed by the dream, the friend went to the gate in the morning, came up to the cart driver, and inquired what he had in his cart. The man fled in terror, but the Arcadian dug out the corpse and made the crime known, and the innkeeper was punished.

Cicero

This belief legend features a so-called crisis apparition (Felton 1999:29–34), wherein A appears to B (often a relative or friend) at a moment of crisis for A, such as imminent death.

24. LETTER FROM THE MIDDLE OF THE EARTH

Dionysodoros of Melos was renowned for his knowledge of geometry. When he died of old age in his homeland, his female heirs led his funeral procession. During the days that followed, as the women were completing the customary observances, they are said to have found in Dionysodoros's tomb a letter signed with his name and addressed to those on earth. The letter stated that he had passed from his tomb to the bottom of the earth, which he said lay 42,000 stades away.

Several geometricians interpreted this to mean that the letter had been sent from the middle of the world, which was the longest distance downward from its upper surface and was also the center of the sphere. From the consequent calculation they declared the circumference of the earth to be 252,000 stades.

Pliny the Elder

The identity of Dionysodoros is uncertain, since there were several prominent men of this name. But the calculation of the earth's circumference made on the basis of the information supplied by him after his death agrees exactly with the better-known calculation made in Egypt in the third century BC by the mathematician Eratosthenes. A Greek stade measured six hundred feet.

The best-known letter posted to earth from a different cosmic realm is the so-called Letter from Heaven, or Sunday Letter, allegedly written by Jesus Christ and dropped from heaven or delivered personally by the Archangel Michael (Kr. S. Jensen 1896–1898; Speyer 1970:17). The text of the letter goes back to at least the sixth century AD, and copies in different languages have been in circulation ever since then.

25. THE HAUNTED HOUSE

At this point in our conversation the Pythagorean Arignotos, the man with the long hair and solemn face—you know, the one who is famous for his wisdom, the one they call the holy one—came in. As soon as I saw him, I breathed a sigh of relief, thinking that the very thing I needed had arrived, an ax against lies. "This wise man," I said to myself, "will curb these men from telling tales of monsters and marvels." I supposed that Fortune had rolled him in to me like a deus ex machina, as the saying goes. Kleodemos made room for him, and after he was seated he inquired first about Eukrates's illness and heard from the latter that he was doing better. Then Arignotos asked, "Now what were you discoursing about among yourselves? I overheard you as I came in, and it seemed to me that the conversation was about to turn in a good direction."

"We've just been trying to persuade this adamantine fellow here," said Eukrates, pointing at me, "that supernatural beings exist and that ghosts and souls of the dead go about on the earth, appearing to whom they wish."

I blushed and lowered my head out of respect for Arignotos.

"Eukrates, perhaps Tychiades is just maintaining," he said, "that only the souls of those who died by violence walk—for example, if a person has hanged himself or been decapitated or crucified, or has departed life in some other way like that—whereas the souls of those who died natural deaths do not. If this is what he means, then one need not entirely spurn what he says."

"No, by Zeus," said Deinomachos, "he thinks that such things don't exist at all and are not seen in solid form."

"What is that you say?" said Arignotos, with a sharp glance at me. "Don't you think that any of these things happen? And you maintain this view despite the fact that the whole world, so to speak, sees them?"

"Do make this point in my defense," I said. "If I'm not a believer, it's because I alone of everyone never see these things. If I saw them, I would of course believe just as you do."

"Yes, but if you ever go to Corinth," said Arignotos, "ask where the house of Eubatides is, and when it is pointed out to you beside the Cornel Grove, go in and tell the doorman Tibeios that you wish to see where the Pythagorean Arignotos exhumed the ghost and drove him away, rendering the house habitable from that time forth."

"What was that, Arignotos?" asked Eukrates.

"It had been uninhabited for a long time," he said, "because of terrors, and if a person moved in, he quickly fled in panic, chased away by a frightful and disturbing ghost of some sort. So the house was falling into ruin and the roof was collapsing, and there wasn't a single person who had the courage to enter it.

"When I myself heard about this, I took my books—I have a very large collection of Egyptian books on these matters—and went into the house around bedtime, although my host tried to dissuade me and all but restrained me when he learned where I was going, which he thought was manifestly evil. Taking my lamp, I entered the house alone, and setting down the light in the largest room, I sat on the floor and began peacefully to read.

"The ghost stood by me, thinking that an ordinary person had come and expecting to frighten me like the others. He had long hair and was squalid and darker than gloom. He stood by me and, hoping to overcome me, made trial of me by attacking me from all sides, turning now into a dog and then a bull and a lion. But I took matters into my own hands and, employing the Egyptian language, I charmed him into the corner of a dark room by means of the most horrifying incantation. After I saw where he had sunk into the ground, I slept for the remainder of the night.

"In the morning everyone had given up hope for me, thinking they would find me dead like the others, but to everyone's surprise I emerged. I went to Eubatides with the good news that he could now reside in his house, which had been purified and freed of terrors. Then, taking him and many of the others along with me—they followed because of the surprising turn of events—I led them to the place where I had seen the ghost sink down, and told them to dig with mattocks and hoes. When they had done so, we found, buried around six feet down, a moldering corpse of which only the bones lay together in their proper arrangement. We exhumed it and buried it, and from that time on the house ceased to be troubled by ghosts."

After Arignotos, a man of divine wisdom whom everyone revered, related this event, there was no longer anyone present who did not condemn me for my gross foolishness in doubting these things, and all the more so because Arignotos was the narrator.

Lucian

In antiquity, as today, haunted houses were likely to be inhabited by interactive ghosts, that is, specters that invite rather than discourage attention from humans (Felton 1999:37), and the murder victim or other kind of suffering spirit that calls attention to itself by haunting the site of its interment continues to be a common theme of ghost stories today (J. B. Thomas 2007:81). Underlying this belief legend is the widespread folk idea that dead persons are not at peace if they have not been buried or cremated properly, and so cannot proceed to the next stage in the cosmic cycle of life and death. Stuck as they are between worlds, such ghosts are restless.

Although haunted houses were a well-established theme in Greco-Roman antiquity, they resemble those of modern popular tradition only in being dilapidated as a result of being unoccupied. The stereotypical haunted house of the present day arose later, in nineteenth-century fiction (Grider 2007).

26. THE HAUNTED BATHS

Soon afterward, while Damon was oiling his skin in the steam room, he was slain.

For a long time after that, as our parents tell us, specters appeared in the place and groaning sounds could be heard. For this reason they walled up the doors of the steam room, and up to the present time persons living in the neighborhood think that disturbing sights and sounds issue from it.

Plutarch

Leading up to this event, a young man named Damon is appointed gymnasiarch (official in charge of a gymnasium) in his native city of Chaironeia, in northwest Boeotia. After his murder, the steam room is haunted by ghosts who persist in reenacting the sights and sounds of the event, as though the room cannot be at peace after the violence it experienced. Ghostly phenomena in which supernatural beings theatrically replay earlier violent events are known as "recordings" (Felton 1999:36–37).

27. THE HAUNTED BATTLEFIELD

There is a deme called Marathon, which is equally distant from Athens and from Karystos in Euboea. It was here that the barbarians landed in Attica, were defeated in battle, and lost some of their ships as they were putting out to sea. On the plain is the grave of the Athenians, and on it stand gravestones with the names of the slain listed by tribe. There is another grave for the Plataeans of Boeotia and for the slaves—slaves joined the battle there for the first time. And there is a separate monument for one man, Miltiades son of Kimon, whose death occurred at a later time, after he had failed to capture Paros and was put on trial for it by the Athenians.

Every night on this plain it is possible to hear horses whinnying and men engaged in battle. It has not done anyone any good to try on purpose to get a clear view, though the spirits are not angry at persons who come upon it by chance and in ignorance.

The people of Marathon worship the men who perished in the battle, calling them *heroes*. They also worship Marathon, from whom the deme gets its name, and Herakles, saying that the Marathonians were the first to regard Herakles as a god.

Pausanias

Marathon was the site of the Persian invasion of Greece in 490 BC, and the plain of Marathon was the battlefield on which the invaders and the Greek defenders fought it out. A massive mound of earth, still to be seen, covers the bodies of the slain Athenians and makes a strong impression on the viewer.

"Great battlefields are everywhere believed to be haunted," observes Collison-Morley (1912:24), and Marathon was one of several battlegrounds in Greek and Roman tradition in which the warriors continue to fight their battle as ghosts. Like the baths at Chaironeia, the plain at Marathon experienced violence and so is restless, and like the ghostly activity at the baths, the original battle at Marathon recurs as if it were recorded and being replayed again and again (Felton 1999:36).

Pausanias distinguishes people who come to the plain for the express purpose of experiencing the haunting, from those who come upon the spirits unwittingly. He implies that the former are somehow harmed, whereas the spirits are forgiving of accidental tourists. It appears, then, that some persons came intentionally to the site in the hope of experiencing its reputed haunting, an activity now known as "legend-tripping."

The Marathonians treat the war dead as heroes, *a cultic category signifying mortal persons who have died and receive worship as powerful beings. The worship of the deceased mortal Marathon indicates that he likewise is regarded locally as a hero.*

28. THE HERO OF TEMESA

Euthymos was a renowned athlete, a three-time Olympic victor in boxing. Upon his return to Italy, he fought the Hero. The story about him goes as follows.

In the course of his wanderings after the capture of Ilium, Odysseus was carried, they say, by winds to different cities in Italy and Sicily, and among the places he arrived at with his ships was Temesa. One of his sailors got drunk there and raped a maiden, a crime for which he was stoned by the local people. Treating the loss of the man as of no account, Odysseus sailed away.

But the ghost of the man who had been stoned to death let pass no opportunity to kill inhabitants of Temesa, attacking persons of every age, until the people were preparing to leave Italy entirely. The Pythia, however, forbade them to abandon Temesa, instructing them instead to propitiate the Hero by setting aside for him a sanctuary and constructing a temple in it, and by giving him as wife each year the most beautiful maiden in Temesa. The people of Temesa carried out the god's commands and in other respects were freed of their fear of the ghost.

Now, Euthymos arrived at Temesa at the time when the customary sacrifice was being made to the ghost. He learned the state of affairs and desired to enter the temple in order to look upon the maiden. When he saw her, he felt at first pity and then love for her, and the girl swore that she would marry him if he should save her. So Euthymos equipped himself, awaited the approach of the ghost, won the fight, and drove it out of the land. The Hero plunged into the sea and disappeared. There was a fine wedding for Euthymos, and the local inhabitants were thereafter free of their ghost.

I have also heard something else about Euthymos, that he reached an extremely old age and, once again escaping death, departed from among mankind in some other way.

That Temesa is still inhabited in the present day I heard from a man who had sailed there on business. That much I heard, but I got the following information from a painting I came upon, a copy of an ancient picture. It showed a youth Sybaris, a river Kalabros, and a spring Luka, in addition to the Hero's shrine and the city of Temesa, and among these it showed the ghost that Euthymos drove out. The ghost's flesh was horribly black, his whole appearance was extremely frightening, and he wore wolf's hide for clothing. The words on the painting gave his name as Lykas.

Pausanias

The Hero (Greek Heros*) is a revenant with an appetite for women that predates his death by execution. Physically powerful, he is also violently antisocial, as though acting out his resentment toward the Temesans for bringing his life to a premature end.*

Euthymos, a Greek athlete from Lokris in Italy, was said to be the son either of a mortal father or of a river god. His encounter with the Hero follows closely upon his victory at the seventy-seventh Olympiad (472 BC). The initial event is set, of course, in the heroic age.

* * *

In Temesa a *heros* left behind by Odysseus's ship imposed a tribute on the local residents and their neighbors. They had to bring him a girl of marriageable age as well as a bed, leave them behind, and depart without turning around. In the morning the parents took away, instead of a maiden, a woman. The boxer Euthymos freed them of this tribute. . . .

anonymous

This fragmentary narrative emphasizes the Hero's lust more than his violence.

29. PERIANDER'S WIFE

One day Periander made all the women of Corinth strip off their clothes on account of his wife, Melissa.

Periander had sent messengers to the Oracle of the Dead on the Acheron River in Thesprotia concerning a deposit of money that a guest-friend of his had entrusted to his keeping. Melissa appeared but said she would not tell or disclose the place where the deposit lay, saying that she felt cold and naked inasmuch as she had gotten no benefit from the clothes Periander had buried with her, since he had not burned them. To prove to him that her message was authentic, she said that Periander had put his loaves in a cold oven.

When this was reported back to Periander, he proclaimed straightway that all the women of Corinth should proceed from their houses to the temple of Hera. (Melissa's token convinced him, for he had had sexual intercourse with his wife when she was a corpse.) The women came dressed in their finest attire, supposing there was to be a festival, but Periander had stationed his guards there and made all the women strip, ladies and maidservants alike. Heaping up the clothing in a pit, he burned it with a prayer to Melissa.

After he had done this, he sent messengers a second time, and Melissa's specter revealed the place where she had stowed the deposit of Periander's guest-friend.

Herodotos

Fire is the great transformative agent in Greek myth and cult, converting things of this world into things of the other (Hansen 2005:36). In the present legend, if a man wishes to transmit clothes to the realm of the dead, he must burn them, not bury them.

Periander ruled Corinth in the early sixth century BC. At the time of the incident recounted here, he was a widower in consequence of having killed his wife, Melissa (Herodotos 3.50).

EARLY WONDER-WORKERS

Wondrous themes cluster around several obscure figures active in sixth-century Greece, including Empedokles, Epimenides, and Abaris. Recurrent features include soul travel, bilocation, return from death, astonishing longevity, prescience, and the control of nature. Thus Empedokles, when the etesian winds were blowing so violently that they threatened the crops, ordered donkeys to be flayed and bags made from their hides. He stretched out the bags on hilltops to capture the winds, after which he was called the wind-stiller (Diogenes Laertios 8.60). Epimenides purified the city of Athens in the time of Solon (Aristotle Constitution of the Athenians *1). And Abaris could travel through the air "like a man walking." He was a Hyperborean ("person beyond the north wind"), a people who according to Greek folk tradition lived in paradisiacal conditions in the extreme north, beyond the north wind, and occasionally interacted with peoples to the south.*

30. ABARIS THE HYPERBOREAN

Empedokles of Agrigentum, Epimenides of Crete, and Abaris the Hyperborean performed wonders in many places. Their deeds are manifest above all in the fact that Empedokles is called the wind-stiller, Epimenides the purifier, and Abaris the air-walker.

Abaris was carried on the arrow that had been given to him by Apollon of the Hyperboreans. He crossed rivers and seas and inaccessible places, like a man walking on the air.

Herodotos

* * *

I will not give an account of Abaris the so-called Hyperborean, relating how he carried his arrow around the entire earth, and did so without ever eating anything.

Iamblichos

In the former passage Abaris is conveyed through the air on a mysterious arrow, like a witch riding a broom, whereas in the latter—somewhat illogically—he carries his arrow around.

31. ARISTEAS OF PROKONNESOS

I will relate the story about Aristeas that I heard in Prokonnesos and Kyzikos.

They say that Aristeas, whose family was inferior to none, went into a fuller's shop in Prokonnesos and died there. The fuller closed up his workshop and went to notify the dead man's relatives. The news had already spread through the town that Aristeas was dead when, they say, a man of Kyzikos arrived at Prokonnesos from the town of Artake and disputed the report, saying that he himself had just encountered Aristeas, who was himself on his way to Kyzikos, and had spoken with him. While this man was thus strongly disputing the report, the relatives of the dead man came to the fuller's shop with the things they needed for removing the corpse, but when they opened the room, no Aristeas was there, dead or alive.

In the seventh year after this, Aristeas appeared in Prokonnesos and composed the poem that the Greeks call *Arimaspeia*, and after composing it, he disappeared for the second time.

This is the story told in Prokonnesos and Kyzikos.

Herodotos

In his epic poem Arimaspeia, *known today only in allusion, Aristeas describes how, "possessed by Phoibos Apollon, he went to the Issedones, beyond whom live the one-eyed Arimaspians, beyond them the gold-guarding griffins, and beyond them the Hyperboreans, whose territory reaches the sea" (Herodotos 4.13).*

Prokonnesos (now called Marmara) is the largest island in the Propontis (now the Sea of Marmara), while Kyzikos was a nearby city on the southern coast of the Propontis.

* * *

I know something that happened to the people of Metaponton in Italy two hundred and forty years after the second disappearance of Aristeas, as I myself have discovered by calculating the events that took place in Prokonnesos and Metaponton. The Metapontines say that Aristeas appeared to them in person in their country and bade them establish an altar to Apollon and place beside it a statue named for Aristeas of Prokonnesos. Aristeas told them that they were the only people in Italy to whose country Apollon had come, and that he himself had followed him; he was now Aristeas, but at the time he was following the god, he was a raven. After saying this, he disappeared.

The Metapontines say they sent a delegation to Delphi to ask the god about the man's phantom, and the Pythia told them to obey the phantom, since it would be to their advantage to do so. This was the oracle they received, and they fulfilled the command. So now a statue bearing the name of Aristeas stands beside the image of Apollon, and round about it are laurel trees. The statue is set up in the marketplace.

Herodotos

* * *

It is reported that on the same day and at the same hour that Aristeas of Prokonnesos died in a fuller's shop in Prokonnesos, many persons observed him teaching in Sicily. Since this kind of thing happened to him often and was clearly seen over the course of many years, especially on Sicily, the Sicilians set up a shrine for him and sacrificed to him as a hero.

Apollonios

***

There was a man of Prokonnesos whose body used to lie with the breath of life, but almost indiscernibly and very close to death. His soul used to issue from his body and wander high in the air like a bird, observing everything below—the earth, sea, rivers, cities, nations of men, events, and creatures of every kind, and then enter its body again and rouse it, using it like an instrument. Then the soul would narrate the different things it saw and heard in different places.

Maximus of Tyre

***

We find the tradition that in Prokonnesos Aristeas's soul was seen flying out of his mouth in the form of a raven, along with many other incredible things.

Pliny the Elder

32. HERMOTIMOS OF KLAZOMENAI

About Hermotimos of Klazomenai the following fabulous story is told.

They say that his soul used to leave his body and travel for many years, visiting different places and foretelling future events such as great storms, droughts, earthquakes, plagues, and the like, all while his body lay still. After a certain period of time his soul would reenter his body as though it were a sheath, and awaken it. He did this frequently, and when he was going to depart, he gave his wife orders that no one—neither citizen nor anyone else—was to touch his body.

One time, however, some persons came to his house, and, persuading his wife by their earnest entreaties, observed Hermotimos lying on the floor, naked and motionless. They took fire and completely incinerated him, thinking that if his soul returned but no longer had anything to enter, Hermotimos would be utterly deprived of life, which is in fact what happened.

The people of Klazomenai worship Hermotimos up to the present day and have consecrated to him a temple into which, for the reason I have related above, no woman enters.

Apollonios

Klazomenai was a town on the west coast of Asia Minor near the island of Chios.

33. EPIMENIDES OF CRETE

It is said that Epimenides of Crete was sent to the family farm by his father and uncles to bring a sheep to town. When night overtook him, he left the road and fell asleep for fifty-seven years, as Theopompos says in his history, where he surveys the wonders of different places, and as many others also say. In the meantime the members of Epimenides's family died.

When Epimenides awoke from his sleep, he looked for the sheep he had been sent after and, not finding it, walked back to the farm—he supposed that he had awoken on the same day that he had fallen asleep—and perceiving that it had been sold and that the equipment was different, he set out for town. There he went to his house and learned everything, including what had taken place while he was missing.

The Cretans, according to Theopompos, say that he lived for 157 years before dying. Many other amazing things are told of this man.

Apollonios

* * *

Epimenides, according to Theopompos and many others, was a son of Phaistios (though others say he was a son of Dosiadas or Agesarchos). He was a native of Crete, from Knossos, though he did not look like a Cretan since he wore his hair long.

He was once sent by his father to their farm for a sheep. At noontime he turned aside from the road to a cave, where he slept for fifty-seven years. Afterward he got up and started looking for his sheep, supposing that he had slept for only a little while. Since he could not find the animal, he went back to the farm, where he saw that all the appurtenances had changed and that the property had a different owner.

Utterly perplexed, he went back to town, but when he entered his own house, the people he met there asked him who he was. Finally he found his younger brother, now an old man, and learned the whole truth from him.

He became renowned among the Greeks and was believed to be a special favorite of the gods.

Diogenes Laertios

*Although his soul could leave and return to his body as he wished (*Suda *s.v. Epimenides), much as in the cases of Aristeas, Hermotimos, and others, Epimenides was best known for his long sleep. The two states are not dissimilar, for a man whose soul can leave his body is much like a man in a state of supernatural sleep. Epimenides is said to have grown old in the same number of days as the number of years he had slept. Nevertheless, he lived to an extraordinary age.*

In the Western world the best-known narrative of persons who sleep for many years and wake up to a different reality is the later Christian legend of the Seven Sleepers of Ephesos, in which seven Christians who suffer from persecution during pagan times fall asleep and wake up 360 years later, finding to their surprise that the land has become dominantly Christian. Americans will also think of the long sleep of Rip Van Winkle, recounted by Washington Irving in his short story of the same name (1819).

34. PHEREKYDES OF SYROS

About Pherekydes we have reports of the following sort.

Once, when he was on the island of Syros, he felt thirsty and asked for a drink of water from one of his acquaintances. After he had drunk it, he said that there was going to be an earthquake on the island in four days. When this in fact happened, he acquired a very considerable reputation.

On another occasion, as he was traveling to Samos to see the temple of Hera, he saw a merchant ship coming to harbor, and said to the persons standing with him that it would not enter the harbor. Even as he was speaking, a darkness rushed down and in the end the ship disappeared.

Apollonios

35. PYTHAGORAS

Pythagoras is reputed to have tamed an eagle, stopping it by certain cries as it flew overhead, and bringing it down.

He revealed his golden thigh as he passed among the persons attending the festival at Olympia.

Plutarch

Pythagoras was a philosopher of the late sixth century BC. Indeed he is said to have been the first person to describe himself as a "philosopher."

* * *

Pythagoras taught humankind that he had been born of seed that was superior to that of human nature. On the same day and at the same hour he was seen in Metaponton and in Kroton. In Olympia he let it be seen that one of his thighs was golden.

He reminded Myllias of Kroton that he was Midas the Phrygian, son of Gordias.

He stroked a white eagle, which patiently abided his touch.

As he was crossing the Kosas River, the river addressed him, saying, "Greetings, Pythagoras."

Aelian

Kroton was a city in southern Italy. The Kosas River is probably the same as the Kasas River, near Metaponton in southern Italy. The Nessos River, mentioned below, is unknown.

* * *

Pythagoras is said to have been very dignified, and his disciples were of the opinion that he was Apollon, come from the Hyperboreans.

There is a story that once, when he was partly disrobed, his thigh was seen to be golden.

Many persons declared that the Nessos River addressed him while he was crossing it.

Diogenes Laertios

Pythagoras claimed to be more than human, perhaps even to be Hyperborean Apollon. His superhuman powers were shown in his mastery over wild animals (the eagle), his control of time and space (bilocation), and his ability to identify soul migrations in other beings (the soul of King Midas resident in the body of Myllias). Moreover, the mysterious golden thigh that he occasionally exposed to view implied some sort of divinity. (A later charlatan, Alexander of Abonouteichos, also affected a golden thigh that he sometimes allowed people to glimpse, presumably in imitation of Pythagoras: Lucian Alexander the False Prophet *40.) Even nature, emblematized by the river, or the divine itself in the form of the river god, acknowledged his exceptional status by hailing him in human speech. Walter Burkert (1972:144) observes that "there is always something enigmatic about the meaning of these miracles."*

TRANSMIGRATION OF SOULS

The doctrine of metempsychosis, or transmigration of souls, is first attested in Greece in the sixth century BC in connection with Pythagoras. Although the idea became influential in Greek philosophic circles, it did not become mainstream in Greece as it did in India.

36. PYTHAGORAS REMEMBERS AN EARLIER LIFE

Pythagoras believed in the transmigration of souls and regarded the eating of meat as something to be avoided, saying that after death the souls of all living beings enter into other living beings. He used to declare that in his own case he remembered having been Euphorbos, the son of Panthos, at the time of the Trojan War, and that he had been slain by Menelaos.

They say that Pythagoras once came as a traveler to Argos and, seeing among the spoils from Troy a shield nailed to a wall, began to weep. When the Argives asked him the reason for his grief, he explained that he had carried this very shield at Troy when he was Euphorbos. Since they were incredulous and judged him to be mad, he declared that he would give them verbal proof that this was the case. On the inner side of the shield (he said) there was inscribed, in archaic letters, EUPHORBOS. At this surprising claim everyone called for the shield to be taken down, and, as it happened, this inscription was found on the inner side.

Diodoros of Sicily

If one accepts the notion that a soul resides in one body after another, what is remarkable is not that Pythagoras's soul inhabits a succession of bodies but that he is aware of its migrations. But why is he exceptional in this regard? The answer is that it was a divine gift (Diogenes Laertios 8.4–5). Pythagoras said that he had once been a certain Aithalides, who was in turn a son of Hermes, and when the god told Aithalides that he might choose any gift he wished, except for immortality, Aithalides asked to be able to remember what happened to him as he lived and died. So he recalled everything while he was alive, retained this knowledge after he died, and thereafter remained conscious of his soul's wanderings. The Euphorbos whom Pythagoras recalls having been is a known character. In Homer's Iliad *he is a Trojan warrior who wounds Patroklos (16.806–7) and is later slain by Menelaos (17.9–60).*

37. PYTHAGORAS DISCERNS A FRIEND'S SOUL IN A DOG

Once when Pythagoras was passing by a pup that someone was beating,
He felt pity, they say, and spoke these words,

"Stop, don't strike him! It's the soul of a friend of mine
That I recognized when I heard it yelping."

Xenophanes

Pythagoras is able not only to remember his own incarnations but also to recognize the souls of others.

38. EMPEDOKLES RECALLS HIS EARLIER LIVES

Before now I have been a boy and a girl,
A bush and a bird, and a scaly fish leaping out of the sea.

Empedokles

Like his master Pythagoras, Empedokles can remember his previous incarnations, which in his case include plants and animals.

39. THE WOMAN WHO REMEMBERS TOO MUCH

That human souls pass from one kind of animal to another is shown by a narrative of our own time, or a little before it.

Nestorios, the great practitioner of the sacred, is said to have come to Rome where he encountered a woman, a member of the finer classes, who was scarcely willing even to speak because of her grief at the memory of her previous lives. He heard her relate how in earlier cycles she had been a slave girl in the service of tavern keepers in Adasmaste in Attica, where she had suffered from excessive forgetfulness regarding the orders that her masters would give her. She would weep aloud at her forgetfulness, just as she did later when she spoke of her remembering. Then she had a sexual encounter with an apparition of some sort. She asked to be granted the power of memory, got what she had asked for, and from that point onward remembered everything properly and distinctly.

After that life, she recalled, her soul became that of a dog. She disliked the union and wanted to be released from this bond, so she shoved the dog off a roof. Paying the penalty for her unjust act toward the dog, her soul entered a snake. In her hatred at animating such a creature, she killed it by stretching it out in front of a moving wagon. It was cut to pieces and perished. After that she became a bear, and after cohabiting with this creature for the fated period of time, she entered a human being.

With the help of the gods Nestorios healed her both of her remembering and of her grief at remembering, and caused her to have better expectations for the future.

From these events one is obliged to infer that migrations do take place from one kind of creature to another in accordance with the principle of justice, into fiercer animals in cases of injustice; that justice and injustice exist also among animals; and that justice and law oversee all things.

Proklos

The unnamed woman acquires, as a gift from a supernatural being, the capacity for total recall through life and death, but unlike Pythagoras she experiences it as a painful burden.

MAGICIANS AND WITCHES

40. PASES THE MAGICIAN

There is a proverbial expression: "Pases's half-obol."

This fellow Pases was by nature a gentle person who surpassed all other men in magic. By means of spells he was able to make lavish dinners and servants appear and then completely disappear again.

He owned a half-obol coin that he had fashioned from a single . . . [one or more words are lost here]. When he gave it to merchants from whom he wanted to buy something, it returned to his possession if he wished it to.

Apion the grammarian mentions him in his book, *On Magic.*

Suda

Pases's coin is a so-called hatch-penny, or coin that magically returns to its owner regardless of how often it is spent.

41. ATTACK BY STAR-STROKE

Olympios of Alexandria, who had been a student of Ammonios for a short time, was one of those persons with pretensions to philosophy. He adopted a superior attitude toward Plotinos in his wish to be more highly regarded than he. In his attacks on him Olympios went so far as to attempt an astral assault on him by magical means, but when he perceived that his attempt was recoiling upon himself, he told his intimates that the power of Plotinos's soul was so great that it was able to deflect attacks away from Plotinos and onto the persons who were trying to injure him.

Plotinos used to feel Olympios's attempts as they were happening, saying that his limbs were squeezed against one another, his body contracting like a money bag whose strings were being pulled tight.

Since Olympios himself was more likely to suffer than he was to harm Plotinos, he ceased his attempts.

Porphyry

The philosopher Plotinos (ca. AD 204–ca. AD 270), founder of Neoplatonism, is seen as a rival by Olympios, who tries to crush him via star-power, directing the rays of particular stars against him, but Plotinos is so powerful that he not only is aware of what is happening but can even cause the rays to turn back against his attacker.

Plotinos kept the date of his own birth a secret, ostensibly so that no one would honor it but perhaps also as a defense against astral attack. Olympios may have learned Plotinos's date of birth and used this information malignantly (Edwards 2000:55).

42. A WOMAN DIES FROM SPELLS

Here lies Ennia Fructuosa, most dear wife, a matron of unwavering modesty and praiseworthy for her gracious obedience.

In her fifteenth year she accepted the designation of spouse but was unable to live with it more than thirteen years. She did not receive the fated death that she deserved. She lay in bed for a long time cursed by spells until her spirit was forcibly wrenched out of her and returned to nature. The Manes or the celestial gods will avenge the crime that has been committed.

Aelius Proculinus, her husband, himself set up these words. He was tribune of a mighty legion, the Third Augusta.

Aelius Proculinus

Ennia Fructuosa's semimetrical epitaph takes the form of a personal-experience narrative related by her husband, who attributes her illness and untimely death to sorcery. The Manes that will avenge her are the spirits of the deceased Roman matron in particular or the spirits of the dead in general.

Her tombstone resides among the ruins of Lambaesa, capital of the Roman province of Numidia, in present-day Algeria. The town arose in the early second century AD as a military camp of the Third Legion, in which Aelius was a tribune, and came to be populated mostly by Latin-speaking Berbers.

43. THE SOUL-DRAWING WAND

That the soul is able to leave the body and enter it again is shown by a man described by Klearchos who employed a soul-drawing wand on a sleeping youth. As Klearchos says in his work *On Sleep*, the man persuaded the excellent Aristotle that the soul can separate from the body and enter it again, using it as a sort of hotel.

The man struck the boy with his wand, drawing out his soul, and led it some distance from the body with the wand. He showed how the body remained motionless and unharmed and lacked all feeling even if it was beaten like something lifeless. At that time the soul was at some distance from the body, but after the wand brought it close again and it reentered the body, the youth described the experience in detail.

As a result, Aristotle and the other spectators of the experiment were persuaded that the soul is separable from the body.

Proklos

This scene portrays a demonstration, evidently one at which the philosopher Klearchos (4th century BC) was present along with his teacher Aristotle and other persons. The soul-drawing wand wielded by the unnamed man is reminiscent of the soul-drawing wand employed by the god Hermes in Homer's Odyssey *(24.1–5) when he conducts the souls of Penelope's suitors to their new abode, the realm of the dead.*

44. APOLLONIOS CURES A PLAGUE

When the plague attacked the people of Ephesos and they had no remedy against it, they sent a delegation to Apollonios of Tyana, hoping to make him a physician of their suffering. Thinking he should not put off the journey, he said, "Let's go," and was immediately in Ephesos, replicating the deed of Pythagoras, who was in Thourioi and Metaponton simultaneously.

Apollonios convoked the Ephesians and said, "Take heart, for I will put an end to the plague today." After saying this, he led the entire group to the theater, where the statue of The Averter stands. An old man, it seemed, was begging there and craftily keeping his eyes closed. He carried a pouch with a lump of bread in it, wore ragged clothes, and had a filthy face.

Stationing the Ephesians in a circle around the man, Apollonios said, "Collect as many stones as you can, and cast them at this god-despised

being." The Ephesians were taken aback at his saying this, thinking it terrible to kill a stranger in such a sorry state, while for his part the beggar was supplicating them and asking for pity; but Apollonios persisted in urging the Ephesians to attack him and not to relent. When some of them began to throw stones at the old man, he looked up at them suddenly with his eyes seemingly closed, and showed eyes full of fire. The Ephesians then understood that he was a supernatural being, and they stoned him to death, piling up a heap of stones.

After a while Apollonios instructed them to remove the stones to see what kind of animal they had killed. They uncovered the being they thought they had stoned, but he had vanished, and they saw, crushed by the stones, a dog that looked like a Molossian hound but was as large as a huge lion, and was spewing foam as madmen do. The base of the statue of The Averter (that is, Herakles) stands near the spot where the apparition was stoned.

Philostratos

When the Ephesians call upon the itinerant wonder-worker Apollonios of Tyana to rid them of a plague, he wastes no time, instantly translocating himself to Ephesos merely by saying "Let's go." The sage readily perceives that an apparent beggar is in reality the plague demon, and has him executed. The demon initially keeps his eyes closed in order to conceal the fact that they are fiery, but eventually reveals them.

*As early as the Greek poet Hesiod (*Works and Days *100–104), illnesses were personified as supernatural beings that wander the earth bringing misery to the* *human population. The personification of the plague as a spirit in human or animal form has persisted in later European legendry (e.g., Klintberg 2010:335–340).*

45. THE MAGICIAN'S APPRENTICE

"On the voyage up the Nile it happened that a man from Memphis was sailing with us, one of the temple scribes who was amazing for his wisdom and acquainted with the whole of Egyptian learning. He was said to have lived underground for twenty-three years in a sanctuary being instructed in magic by Isis."

"You mean Pankrates," said Arignotos, "my own teacher, a holy man, clean-shaven, dressed in linen, always in thought, spoke Greek with an accent, a tall man with a snub nose, protruding lips, and thin legs."

"Yes, the very Pankrates," said Eukrates. "At first I didn't know who he was, but after I saw him performing many marvels whenever the boat was at anchor, in particular riding on crocodiles and swimming with wild animals that would fawn on him and wag their tails, I recognized that he was a holy man of some kind. By treating him kindly, I gradually became his companion and associate, and as a result he shared all his secret knowledge with me.

"Finally he talked me into leaving all my servants in Memphis in order to accompany him alone, saying that we would not lack for persons to minister to our needs. Thereafter we lived as follows. Whenever we came to an inn, the man would take the bolt of the door or the broom or even the pestle, put clothes on it, and by saying a certain spell make it walk, and to everyone else it would appear to be a human being. It would go off and fill a vessel with water, buy provisions, and prepare a meal, deftly serving us and ministering to our needs in every respect. When Pankrates had had enough service, he would say another spell and make the broom a broom again or the pestle a pestle.

"I was very enthusiastic to learn this from him, but I didn't know how to go about it. He was grudging about it, despite being most generous with the rest of his knowledge. But one day I secretly overhead the spell—it consisted of three syllables—as I lurked in a dark place. He gave the pestle its orders and left for the marketplace. On the following day, while he was transacting some business in the marketplace, I picked up the pestle, dressed it up in the same way, uttered the syllables, and told it to fetch water. After it had filled the amphora and brought it in, I said, 'Stop, don't fetch water any more. Be a pestle again.' However, it did not obey me but kept continually fetching and pouring water until it had filled the house with water. For my part, I didn't know what to do—I was afraid that Pankrates would return and be angry, which is in fact what did happen—so I took an ax and chopped the pestle in two, but then each of the pieces took an amphora and fetched water, so that now instead of one servant I had two.

"Meanwhile Pankrates showed up. Perceiving what had happened, he turned the servants back into wood again as they were before the spell, whereupon he himself took off without a word and disappeared I don't know where."

"So, now," said Deinomachos, "you do still know how to turn a pestle into a person?"

"Indeed I do, by Zeus," I said. "Well, halfway. Once it's become a water carrier, I'm unable to bring it back to its original state, so we'll have to have a flooded house, with water constantly being poured into it."

Lucian

The international tale of the magician's apprentice is recounted here as a personal narrative, a memorable adventure of Eukrates's youth in exotic Egypt. Lucian's telling of the story inspired Goethe's well-known poem of 1797, "The Sorcerer's Apprentice" (Der Zauberlehrling*), as well as more recent treatments such as that of Walt Disney in his* Fantasia.

46. EVIL LANDLADIES

When I myself was in Italy I would hear such things talked about in a certain region of that country, where people said that landladies who were skilled in evil arts used to give drugged cheese to any travelers they wished, or could, as a result of which the latter were transformed on the spot into pack animals, carried all kinds of goods, and when they had completed their tasks, returned to their original form again. It was said further that their minds did not become those of animals but remained rational and human, just as in the book titled *The Golden Ass* Apuleius wrote happened to him. There he reported or pretended that after taking a potion he became a donkey, except for his retaining his human mind.

These things are either false or so strange that they do not deserve belief.

Augustine

DIVINATION AND SEERS

47. THE LANGUAGE OF BIRDS

A certain companion of ours used to relate that he was fortunate in having a household slave, a boy, who understood everything that birds said, which was all prophetic and announced what was going to happen soon thereafter.

But this understanding was taken away from him. His mother, taking care that the boy should not be sent as a gift to the emperor, urinated into his ears while he was asleep.

Porphyry

The boy's mother deliberately destroys his gift because curiosities and marvels of any sort were liable to be given as gifts to rulers (Hansen 1996:142), or simply taken by them. Although her method is bizarre, it resembles the means employed in other legends in which the ability to prophesy is sabotaged. Thus the god Apollon gives the maiden Kassandra the gift of prophecy, but when she does not in turn honor her part of the bargain (namely, to have sexual intercourse with him), he spits into her mouth, which prevents her prophecies from having conviction, so that no one believes her utterances (Servius on Vergil's Aeneid *2.247). Another legend relates how the seer Polyidos is forced by King Minos to teach the king's son the art of divination, but after the seer instructs him, he tells the boy to spit into his mouth, and when he does so, the boy forgets what he learned (Apollodoros* Library *3.3.2).*

48. THE ACQUISITION OF THE SIBYLLINE ORACLES

It is said that a piece of amazing luck befell the city of Rome during the reign of Tarquin, conferred on it by the favor of some god or lesser divinity. And this luck was not for a short term but saved the city from great evils over and over again throughout its entire life.

A certain woman who was not a native of the country came to the monarch with nine books full of Sibylline oracles that she was willing to sell to him. When Tarquin did not deign to purchase the books at the price she asked, she departed, burning three of the books. A short while later she brought the remaining six books and offered to sell them for the same price. She seemed to be some kind of fool and was laughed at for asking the same price for the smaller number of books that she had failed to get for the larger number of books. She departed and again burned half of the remaining books. She brought the three books that were left, and asked for the same amount of money. Wondering what the woman's purpose was, Tarquin sent for his augurs, explained the matter, and asked what he ought to do. By means of certain signs, they learned that a god-sent blessing had been turned away, and declared that it was a great misfortune that he had not purchased all the books. They told him to pay the woman as much money as she asked, and get the oracles that were left. The woman gave him the books, told him to guard them carefully, and vanished from among human beings.

Tarquin chose two men of distinction from among the citizens, assigned two public slaves to assist them, and entrusted the guardianship of the books to them. When one of them, Marcus Atilius, appeared to have abused his trust in some way and one of the slaves informed on him, Tarquin had him sewn up in a leather bag as a traitor and cast into the sea.

After the expulsion of the kings the city assumed charge of the oracles and appointed as their guardians two men of the highest distinction to hold this commission for life, exempt from military service and civic affairs. The city assigns them public slaves, and the men are not permitted to inspect the oracles without them. In short, there is no possession either sacred or profane that the Romans guard the way they do the Sibylline oracles. They consult them upon the vote of the Senate when there is factional strife in the city or some great misfortune has befallen them in war or some prodigies or great apparitions have appeared to them that are difficult to interpret, as often happens.

Until the time of the so-called Marsian War the oracles remained underground in a stone chest in the temple of Capitoline Jupiter, where they were guarded by ten men, but when the temple burned down after the 173rd Olympiad, the oracles along with the other offerings to the god were destroyed in the fire, either purposely, as some think, or accidentally. The oracles that exist today have been gathered together from many places, some of them brought from cities in Italy and others from Erythrai in Asia, three men having been dispatched there by a resolution of the Senate to make copies. Still others were brought from other cities after they had been transcribed by private individuals. Some interpolations were discovered among the Sibylline oracles, but the latter were proven by means of their so-called acrostics.

Dionysios of Halikarnassos

In this Roman legend an early king of Rome, Tarquin (Tarquinius Priscus), and a mysterious prophetess, the Cumaean Sibyl, confront each other. The theme of the doubled fee, whereby the vendor ironically increases the price after each refusal (or, as here, keeps the fee constant while reducing the quantity of goods), appears in other legends ancient and modern (Hansen 2002a:468–469 n. 16).

A few Sibylline oracles survive today. Considering the protective attitude toward them in antiquity, it is puzzling that we should possess them at all. They are composed in obscure Greek hexameters and display the acrostic feature mentioned by Dionysios (Hansen 1996:40–43, 126–137).

49. WHAT THE SIBYL WANTS

I once saw with my own eyes the Sibyl at Cumae hanging in a bottle. When the children asked, "Sibyl, what do you want?" she would answer, "I want to die."

Petronius

This event, represented as the narrator's personal experience, is puzzling, first, because it is truly strange, and, second, because it is only part of a larger story. In the backstory the god Apollon, wishing to sleep with Sibyl, then a young maiden, offers to grant her any wish. She asks to live as many years as there are grains in a particular pile of sand, but neglects to specify that she should also retain her youth. When Apollon next offers her perpetual youth in return for her love, she still spurns him. In the end she is obliged to live a thousand years, aging all the while, before she can die (Ovid Metamorphoses *14.130–153).*

In the present scene the Cumaean Sibyl, now centuries old but unable to die, has shriveled and shrunk to such an extent that she resides in a mere bottle. The Greek traveler Pausanias says that the Cumaeans pointed out to him an urn containing the bones of the Cumaean Sibyl, kept in a temple of Apollon, and other ancient authors similarly say that the Sibyl or her remains were kept in a little container located in one place or another.

50. BACCHUS FORSAKES ANTONY

That night, it is said, around midnight, while the city was quiet and dejected from the fear and expectation of what was coming, certain harmonious sounds of musical instruments of every kind were suddenly heard as well as the shouting of a throng together with Bacchic cries and the leaping of satyrs, as if some band of revelers was exiting the city with considerable tumult. Its route seemed to be through the middle of the city out toward the gate that faced the enemy, where the commotion became loudest and then faded out. Persons who sought to make sense of the sign thought that the god whom Antony continually most likened himself to and cohabited with, was deserting him.

Plutarch

Mark Antony loses a crucial sea battle against Octavian at Actium in 31 BC. In Alexandria now with his wife and lover Cleopatra, he parties liberally during the night, mentally preparing himself for the possibility of death on the next day. A mysterious sound is heard, as of Bacchic revelers abandoning the city. Local interpreters take the invisible band to be Dionysos and his riotous crew of maenads and satyrs. These are Antony's own supernaturals; indeed, he is even called the New Dionysos (Plutarch Antony *60). But when his gods desert him, it is all over.*

51. CATO EXPLAINS A PORTENT

Cato once put the matter elegantly when a certain man consulted him, saying that mice had gnawed on his shoes. Cato replied that it was not an omen but certainly would have been if the shoes were nibbling on the mice.

Augustine

Augustine relates this apothegm in the context of a discussion about common folk beliefs that he regards as silly and pointless, among them the fear that one's clothing having been nibbled upon by mice portends some future evil. Marcus Porcius Cato, or Cato the Censor, was an important political figure in Rome in the early second century BC.

Cato's remark is much like the modern journalistic aphorism, attributed to several different persons, that if a dog bites a man, that is not news, but if a man bites a dog, that is news.

52. CATO ON SOOTHSAYERS

Cato used to say he was surprised that a soothsayer did not laugh when he saw another soothsayer.

Cicero

Cato means, of course, that as an insider a soothsayer (Latin haruspex*) is fully aware that he and all other soothsayers are frauds.*

FATE

53. POLYKRATES'S RING

Amasis was aware of Polykrates's great prosperity, and it was a concern to him. As Polykrates's good luck grew greater and greater, Amasis wrote this letter and sent it to Samos.

Amasis says to Polykrates:

"Although it is welcome to learn that a friend and ally is doing well, your great good fortune is not pleasing to me, knowing as I do the jealousy of the gods. For myself and those I care about, I wish success in some matters and failure in others, an experience of ups and downs over time, rather than prosperity in everything. I have not heard and do not know of anyone who prospered in everything and did not come to utter ruin in the end. So, then, listen to me and do the following in light of your good luck. Consider what you value most and would feel the most agony of soul to lose. Then throw it away in such a way that it will never again be among men. If after this, you still do not have a mix of good and bad fortune, continue to cure it in the way I have advised you."

Polykrates read this and understood that Amasis was giving him good advice. So he searched among his heirlooms for the one thing that would most agonize his soul to lose, and this is what he decided upon. He had a signet ring with an emerald stone set in gold that he wore, the work of Theodoros, son of Teleklees the Samian.

After determining to throw this ring away, he embarked on a fifty-oared ship with its crew and gave orders to sail out to sea. When he was far away from the island, he removed the signet ring and, while everyone on the ship looked on, cast it into the sea. After he had done this, he sailed back and went home, where he grieved for his loss.

Five or six days later the following thing happened. A fisherman caught a large and fine fish and decided to give it as a gift to Polykrates. He brought it to his door and said he wanted to see Polykrates. When the latter came, the fisherman handed him the fish with these words: "King, although I live by my labor, when I caught this fish I did not think it right to bring it to market. Rather, I decided that it was worthy of you and your position. So I have it here and offer it to you." Delighted with these words, Polykrates responded, "That is very generous of you, and I give you double thanks, for your words and for your gift. Do join me for dinner."

Regarding the invitation as a big honor, the fisherman went off home. Meanwhile, when the servants cleaned the fish they discovered in its belly Polykrates's signet ring. As soon as they saw it and took it out, they brought it joyfully to Polykrates, handing him the ring and explaining how it had been found. He saw that the gods had played a role in this matter, and wrote a letter in which he described all that he had done and what had happened afterward, and dispatched it to Egypt.

When Amasis read the letter from Polykrates, he perceived that no one could save another person from his destiny, and that Polykrates would come to no good end since he was so fortunate in every respect that he even found what he had thrown away. Amasis sent a herald to Samos to say that he was dissolving their guest-friendship, and that he did so in order that, when a great and terrible mishap befell Polykrates, he might not feel agony in his soul for a man who was his guest-friend.

Herodotos

Polykrates, ruler of the island of Samos in the late sixth century BC, and Amasis, king of Egypt, are guest-friends as well as allies. "Guest-friendship" (xenia) *was a form of ritualized friendship between two men, usually upper-class members of different communities.*

Two important themes of Greek culture intertwine in this narrative. One is divine jealousy. The gods are indignant if they perceive a mortal enjoying the sort of unbroken success and happiness that properly characterizes the life of divinities, and so may put an end to the mortal's good fortune. The other is the ineluctability of fate. What must happen will find a way to happen, regardless of human efforts to escape it.

54. "ZEUS, WHY ME?"

Theramenes chanced to be spending some time in a certain house, and when he came out, the house suddenly collapsed. Coming from all directions, the Athenians gathered around him and expressed their happiness at his incredible escape. His reply was not what they expected. "Zeus," he asked, "for what occasion have you preserved me?"

Not long afterward he was put to death by the Thirty, condemned to drink hemlock.

Aelian

The Thirty are a junta of oligarchs who, with the support of Sparta, rule Athens after its defeat in the Peloponnesian War. They execute many politically moderate citizens.

55. THE LAST DAYS OF MYKERINOS

Mykerinos received an oracle from the city of Bouto saying that he was destined to live only six more years and would die in the seventh. Taking this news badly, he sent a message to the oracle, expressing his indignation at the deity and complaining in his reply that although his father and his paternal uncle had closed down temples, not made due remembrance of the gods, and had even murdered persons, they had lived a long time, whereas he himself, a pious person, was thus destined shortly to die.

A second message came to him from the oracle saying that it was for this very reason that his life was being shortened; for he had not done what it was destined for him to do. It was fated that Egypt suffer affliction for a hundred and fifty years, which the two kings who preceded him had understood, whereas he did not.

When Mykerinos heard that his lot had already been decided, he had a large number of lamps made, lighting them at night, and he drank and enjoyed himself without cease day and night. He roamed the marshlands, groves, and any other pleasant place of enjoyment that he came to know. He devised this strategy in order to prove that the oracle was mistaken: by making his nights into days, he had twelve years to live instead of six.

Herodotos

Mykerinos (Menkaure) rules Egypt after his father Chephren, who in turn succeeds his father Cheops. He is interred in what is now known as the Third Pyramid at Giza (the other two belong to Cheops and Chephren), though a legend of the classical period deliciously makes this pyramid the tomb of a renowned courtesan (see 3 "The Pharaoh and the Courtesan").

The meaning of the second oracle is as follows. Egypt is fated to suffer affliction for a hundred and fifty years. The oppressive pharaohs Cheops and Chephren rule for a total of a hundred and six years, leaving forty-four more years that Egypt is to suffer. But Mykerinos, unaware of destiny's decree, rules the land justly and piously, for which reason the gods are obliged to cut his reign short.

56. KLEONYMOS'S NEAR-DEATH EXPERIENCE

Just as there are reports that in earlier times Aristeas of Prokonnesos, Hermotimos of Klazomenai, and Epimenides of Crete appeared among the living after their deaths, so also in our own day some persons have appeared to die, were placed in their tombs, revived, and were seen sitting or standing on their graves. But I say no more, inasmuch as Aristotle's student Klearchos was the first to transmit the following amazing narrative on this topic.

Kleonymos the Athenian, the sort of person who was fond of listening to philosophic discussions, had a friend who died. Kleonymos was deeply pained, became despondent, lost consciousness, and appeared to be dead. On the third day, as was customary, he was laid in state. His mother was embracing him and taking leave of him for the last time, but as she lifted his cloak from his face and tenderly kissed the corpse, she perceived a brief sign of respiration. Filled with joy, she stopped the burial.

Little by little Kleonymos recovered and regained consciousness. He related everything that he had seen and heard while he had been separated from his body, and what it was like. He declared that at the moment of death his soul seemed to be released from his body as it lay there, as though from fetters, and was lifted high into the air. Hovering above the earth, he saw places of every form and color, and river-streams unseen by human beings. Finally he reached a land sacred to Hestia that was tended by divine powers in the form of women of indescribable beauty.

Another person also arrived at that same place. They shared the same language, remained quietly where they were, and observed everything. In particular they saw souls being punished and judged and continually purified, as well as their overseers the Eumenides. Then they were told to withdraw, and when they had done so they asked each other who they were, and they told each other their names and homelands. One was Kleonymos of Athens; the other, Lysias of Syracuse. They exhorted each other by all means to seek out the other if he should come to the other's city.

Not very long afterward Lysias came to Athens. From a distance Kleonymos saw him and cried out that that was Lysias, and in the same way Lysias recognized Kleonymos before he reached him, and told the bystanders that that was Kleonymos.

That is Klearchos's story.

Proklos

*Augustine (*City of God *22.28) relates a similar story, in which two unnamed men die on the same day and meet at a crossroads. After they are told to return to their bodies, they decide to live the rest of their lives as friends, and do so.*

57. EURYNOOS'S NEAR-DEATH EXPERIENCE

A man named Eurynoos, who belonged to the generation that was born shortly before the present, had the same experience in Nikopolis. He was buried outside the city by his kinsmen and returned to life on the fifteenth day of his interment, saying that he had seen and heard many things beneath the earth that were astonishing, but had been instructed not to divulge anything.

He lived a good while after that and seemed a more just person after his return to life than before.

Proklos

The ancients did not distinguish near-death experiences from longer-term returns to life. The Greeks classified both as anabioseis, *"returns to life." Accounts of such experiences interested ancient philosophers and medical doctors for the evidence that they appeared to offer concerning a temporary separation of the soul and the body.*

58. CURMA'S NEAR-DEATH EXPERIENCE

There was a certain man named Curma, who lived in the town of Tullia, very close to Hippo. He was a poor member of the curia with scarcely the property qualification of a municipal magistrate, a simple countryman.

Curma fell sick, lost consciousness, and lay for some days nearly dead. The very faint breathing through his nose that could be detected by a hand held nearby was a meager indication that he was alive, and prevented his being buried as one who had expired. He did not move his limbs or take any nourishment, nor did he perceive anything with his eyes or other senses regardless of any stimulus applied to him.

Still, he did see many things as if he were sleeping, and many days later, as though he had awakened, he narrated what he had seen. The moment he opened his eyes, he said, "Someone go to the house of Curma the blacksmith and see what's happening there." Someone did go, and Curma the blacksmith was found to have died at the very moment that Curma the curia member had regained his senses and come back almost from death. To the persons about him, whose attention was riveted upon him, he explained that when he himself was dismissed, the order was issued to produce the other man. He said that in the place from which he had returned, he heard that the order had been given to bring not Curma the *curialis* but Curma the blacksmith to the land of the dead. In his vision, as if in a dream, he saw deceased persons who were being treated in different ways in accordance with their deserts, and he recognized some persons he had known when they were alive.

Augustine

The story of the wrong man's being taken to and returning from the death realm is a migratory legend that is told of different people in different places. A man dies, or seems to die, and is escorted to the realm of the dead, where it is quickly discovered that a mistake has been made. Sometimes, as here, the intended victim is another person of the same name. Sent back to life, the first man revives just as the other man dies. Curma related the event to Augustine as an experience that he himself actually had.

Hippo Regius was a city in North Africa (in present-day Algeria), where from AD 395 to 430 Augustine served as bishop. Since he met Curma and interviewed him about his experience some two years after the event, Augustine's narration of Curma's story amounts to a vicarious memorate. The bishop struggled to come to terms with Curma's story. He accepted the simple man as a truthful narrator but rejected the reality of his visions.

JEWS, CHRISTIANS, AND PAGANS

59. THE ORIGIN OF THE SEPTUAGINT

Before the Romans ruled their empire and the Macedonians still controlled Asia, Ptolemy the son of Lagos was eager to adorn the library he had founded in Alexandria with the meritorious writings of all peoples. So he asked the inhabitants of Jerusalem for a copy of their scriptures, translated into the Greek language. The people of Jerusalem, still subject to the Macedonians at that time, dispatched to Ptolemy seventy elders—the men most experienced among them in their scriptures and in the two languages—and god's will was done.

Now, Ptolemy wanted secretly to test them, taking care that they might not conspire among themselves to conceal, by means of their translation, the true sense of the scriptures. So he separated them from one another, instructing them each to write out a translation of the same book, and doing the same for all the books.

When the translators came together in the presence of Ptolemy, they compared their translations each to each. God was glorified, and the scriptures were recognized as being truly divine, for each man came up with the same rendering, using the same phrases and words from beginning to end, such that the gentiles present perceived that the scriptures had been translated by god's inspiration.

Irenaeus

The Septuagint is a Greek translation of the Hebrew bible that was made for the use of Greek-speaking Jews in Alexandria and elsewhere. Begun in the reign of Ptolemy II Philadelphos (284–246 BC), it was the bible of common use at the beginning of the Christian era.

The Septuagint gets its title (Latin septuaginta, *"seventy") from the legend, originally Jewish but subsequently taken over by Christians, that the translation of the Hebrew books was made by seventy (or seventy-two) scholars who worked apart in as many rooms over a period, it is sometimes said, of as many days. When the scholars convened and their translations were compared, their renderings were miraculously found to be identical.*

60. MIRACLES OF JESUS

After Jesus crossed over to the other side again in the boat, a large crowd gathered around him.

He was beside the lake, and a president of one of the synagogues, named Iairos, came and, when he saw him, fell at his feet, saying, "My little daughter is at the point of death. Please come and lay your hands upon her to make her well so that she may live." Jesus went away with the man. A large crowd accompanied them and was pressing upon him.

There was a woman who had been experiencing her menstrual period for twelve years. She had been treated by many doctors, had spent all the money she had, and had not been helped but had gotten worse. After hearing about Jesus, she joined the crowd from behind and touched his cloak. For she had said to herself, "If I touch even his cloak, I'll be healed." The source of her blood immediately dried up, and she recognized in her body that she was healed of her illness.

Jesus was immediately aware that his power had gone out of him, and turning around to the crowd, he said, "Who touched my cloak?" His disciples said, "You see how the crowd is pressing you, and yet you ask who touched you?" But he was looking around to see who had done it. In fear and trembling, the woman, who knew what had happened to her, came and fell at his feet and told him the whole truth. He said to her, "Daughter, your faith has made you well. Go in peace and be free of your illness."

As he was speaking, there came persons from the president's house, saying, "Your daughter has died. Why trouble the master further?" But Jesus, overhearing the message, said to the president, "Don't worry. Just have faith." He did not allow anyone to accompany him except for Peter, James, and John, brother of James. Entering the president's house, they saw confusion, crying, and loud wailing. Jesus went in and said to them, "Why are you so distressed and crying? Your child didn't die but is only sleeping." They laughed at him. After sending everyone out except for the child's father and mother and his own companions, he went in where the child was, and taking her by the hand, he said to her, "*Talitha koum*," which means "Get up, child." The child immediately arose and began walking around. She was twelve years old. They were beside themselves with amazement. Jesus gave them strict orders that no one was to know of this, and told them to give the girl something to eat.

Mark

The setting of these events is Galilee. Other kinds of wonders recounted of Jesus in the canonical gospels include exorcism and walking upon water.

61. PAUL AND BARNABAS MISTAKEN FOR PAGAN GODS

At Lystra there sat a crippled man who was lame from birth and had never walked. This man heard Paul speaking, and Paul fastened his eyes on him and, perceiving that he had faith in being healed, said in a loud voice, "Stand up straight on your feet!" And the man leapt up and began to walk.

When the crowd saw what Paul had done, they shouted in the Lykaonian language, "Gods have come down to us in human form!" Barnabas they began calling Zeus, and Paul they called Hermes, since he was their spokesman. The priest of Zeus, whose shrine stood outside the city, brought oxen and garlands to the gate, and he along with a crowd of persons intended to offer sacrifice.

When the apostles Barnabas and Paul heard of this, they tore their cloaks and rushed at the crowd as they cried out, saying, "Men, why are you doing this? We are just human beings with the same nature as your own. We bring you good tidings to turn you away from these empty things to the living god who made the heaven, the earth, the sea, and everything in them. In past generations he allowed all nations to go their own ways, but he has not left himself without witnesses to his beneficence, since he sends you rain from the sky and seasons of harvest, filling your hearts with nourishment and good cheer."

Despite their protests, they barely prevented the crowd from sacrificing to them.

Acts of the Apostles

Setting out into the world to spread the gospel of Jesus, the apostles Paul and Barnabas come to Lystra in ancient Lykaonia, today's south-central Turkey. After Paul heals a cripple, the local inhabitants conclude that the strangers are gods wandering the earth in disguise, and presently a priest and a gathering of pious persons come together and prepare to perform a sacrifice of oxen to them. The horrified apostles explain that they are not gods but Christian missionaries.

Ancient Greek tradition took it for granted that gods tread the earth in the guise of humans in order to observe human behavior. For example, "Gods in the likeness of strangers of all kinds visit cities and observe the insolence and respectful behavior of humankind" (Homer Odyssey *17.485–487). Accordingly, one could never really be sure whether another apparent human being was a human or a deity in disguise. The inhabitants of Lykaonia shared this conviction, and indeed the legend of Philemon and Baucis, set in nearby Phrygia, recounts how Jupiter and Mercury (the Roman equivalents of Zeus and Hermes) tour the neighborhood disguised as mortals (Fontenrose 1945:105).*

62. THE DISCOVERY OF THE TRUE CROSS

The emperor's mother, Helena, after whom the city once known as Drepane was renamed Helenopolis by the emperor, went to Jerusalem after receiving prophetic messages in dreams. Finding Jerusalem to be—in the words of the prophet*—as desolate as a garden-watcher's hut, she assiduously sought the tomb where Christ had been buried and from which he had arisen. Although the task was difficult, with god's help she did find it. I will give a brief account of the source of the difficulty.

Those who were adherents of Christianity after Christ's passion used to hold the tomb in reverence, but those who rejected Christianity concealed the tomb by covering the place over with soil, building a temple of Aphrodite upon it, and erecting a statue of her in order that Christians, seeing the statue, would not make a memorial of the place.

This had happened long before, but now it became evident to the emperor's mother. She took down the statue, and after excavating and clearing out the place, she found three crosses in the tomb, one being the blessed cross on which god had been outstretched, and the other two being the crosses on which the two thieves crucified with him had perished. The

*Isaiah 1.8.

tablet on which Pilate publicly proclaimed in various letters that the crucified Christ was king of the Jews was also found along with the crosses.

Since there was doubt about which cross was the one she was looking for, the emperor's mother was terribly distressed, but not long after that the bishop of Jerusalem, called Makarios, put an end to her grief, solving the uncertainty by means of faith. Asking god for a sign, he got one, as follows. One of the local people, a certain woman, who had been suffering from a chronic illness, had reached death's door. The bishop arranged that each of the crosses be brought to the dying woman, trusting that if the woman should touch the true cross, she would regain her strength. And he was not mistaken, for when the other two crosses were brought to her, the woman's descent into death did not abate, but when the third cross, the true one, was brought to her, the dying woman immediately regained her strength and became well. So this is how the wood of the cross was discovered.

Constantine's mother had a lavish house of prayer constructed in the place where the tomb was located, calling it New Jerusalem and arranging it such that it faced the old Jerusalem she had left behind. Part of the cross she enclosed in a silver chest, leaving it there as a memorial for persons who wished to tell about it, and the rest she sent to the emperor. When he had it in hand, he trusted that it would be completely safe in the city that preserved it, and so he hid it within his own statue, which stands on the great purple column in Constantinople in the Market of Constantine that is named for him.

Everything I have written here I have from oral report, but nearly everyone living in Constantinople declares that it is true.

Sokrates Scholastikos

A portion of the cross that Helena discovered in Palestine was housed as a precious relic in a silver casket in the Church of the Holy Sepulcher in Jerusalem, which the empress built on the supposed site of Jesus's tomb, which was believed also to be the site of his crucifixion (John 19:41–42). A second piece of the cross was placed in the statue of Constantine that stood atop his column in Constantinople, and other pieces were preserved in Rome and elsewhere. Helena came to be venerated as a saint not long after her death, and among her attributes in art is of course the cross.

The cross was in fact a symbol of minor importance during the first centuries of the Christian era but came to be venerated as a symbol of salvation in the early fourth century and in time became the Christian symbol par excellence. Wood believed to be from the cross upon which Jesus had been crucified was displayed in Jerusalem to pilgrims, and soon the present legend arose according to which Helena, mother of the first Christian emperor, Constantine, discovered and identified the cross during her visit to Palestine sometime between AD 325 and 327.

63. THE LAST DELPHIC ORACLE

When Julian became emperor, he began shamelessly to behave as a pagan Greek, washing away holy baptism in the performance of blood sacrifices, and generally doing everything in the service of the lesser gods.

Julian sent Oribasios, his medical doctor and quaestor, to Delphi to revive the temple of Apollon. Oribasios departed, undertook his commission, and got this oracle from the god.

Tell the emperor that my intricate hall has fallen to the ground.
Phoibos no longer has his dwelling, his prophetic laurel, or
His babbling spring. The water's voice has been extinguished.

Kedrenos

As part of his program to restore paganism the emperor Julian sent his friend Oribasios to Delphi to revive the famed oracle of Apollon, but the reported response was in effect paganism's last utterance. The message was related triumphantly by Christian authors, in this case by the Byzantine writer Kedrenos.

When Apollon, called here by his epithet Phoibos, informs the emperor that the prophetic laurel and waters are no more, he refers to the fact that laurel and spring water played a role in the mantic ritual at Delphi. The priestess first bathed in the Castalian spring and perhaps drank from it, then burnt bay leaves and ascended her tripod, wearing a garland of bay leaves and holding a sprig of bay in her hand, and finally drank water from the Kassotis spring (Fontenrose 1978:224).

The famous oracular response was memorably rendered into English by the poet Swinburne, with the title "The Last Oracle":

Tell the king, on earth has fallen the glorious dwelling,
And the water-springs that spake are quenched and dead.
Not a cell is left the god, no roof, no cover,
In his hand the prophet laurel flowers no more.

64. "YOU HAVE WON, GALILEAN!"

The unfortunate Julian took a handful of blood from his wound and cast it at Helios, saying expressly to him, "Sate yourself!" Yes, and he called the other gods evil and murderous.

Philostorgios

After the emperor Julian was wounded in battle, his servants carried him on his shield to his tent. There he blamed the sun god, his own god, for his misfortune. His wound was untreatable, and he died after a couple of days.

During his brief reign (AD 361–363) Julian the Apostate attempted to revive the pagan cults as well as to institutionalize religious toleration for pagans, Jews, and Christians, but was slain in AD 363 on a campaign against Persia. The legend of his deathbed gesture is recounted variously by different Byzantine churchmen.

* * *

When Julian was wounded, it is said that he scooped up blood from his fresh wound and hurled it like a javelin into the air, since he saw an apparition of Christ and blamed him for his slaughter.

But some say that Julian, angry at Helios for assisting the Persians or for not saving his life despite the fact that Helios was the ruler of Julian's birth according to an astrological calculation, took his blood in his hand and, displaying it to him, hurled it like a javelin into the air. If he really saw Christ when he was about to die—the sort of thing that can happen when a soul is already separating from its body and able to see things that are more divine than humans see—I cannot say. For this story is not recounted by many persons.

Sozomenos

* * *

To this day no one knows who delivered the just blow. Some say that one of the invisible ones delivered it, others one of the nomads known as Ishmaelites, and still others a soldier disgusted with the hunger and the desolation. But whether a human being or an angel thrust the sword, he acted as a servant of the divine will.

As soon as Julian received the blow, they say, he filled his hand with his own blood and threw it into the air, declaring, "You have won, Galilean!" With this statement he conceded victory but also ventured to blaspheme, so out of his mind was he.

Theodoretos

In this last version Julian is assassinated, which the Christian narrator views as a divine execution.

All versions of the legend preserve the visually striking scene of the dying emperor's throwing a handful of his own blood into the air and reproaching a deity, though they differ on whether the god was Helios or Christ. "Galileans" was Julian's term for Christians.

65. THE MURDER OF HYPATIA

There was a woman in Alexandria named Hypatia. Daughter of the philosopher Theon, she was so advanced in her learning that she outdistanced the philosophers of her time. Succeeding to the Platonic school of philosophy as restored by Plotinos, she expounded all the principles of philosophy to everyone who wished to hear her, and for this reason would-be philosophers from all over gathered around her. On account of her frank and stately manner of speaking, which was the result of her training, she showed composure when she met face-to-face with magistrates and felt no unease in the company of men. Everyone respected her and was struck by her extraordinary bearing. It was against this woman that envy took up arms.

She was frequently in the company of Orestes, which prompted slander against her among the people of the church, who said that it was she who discouraged Orestes's becoming friends with the bishop. And so a number of men who saw things this way and whose emotions were inflamed—they were led by a certain reader named Petros—maintained a watch as the woman was returning home from somewhere, ejected her from her carriage, dragged her to the church called Kaisarion, ripped off her clothing, pounded her to death with potsherds, and after tearing her apart limb from limb, brought her limbs to the place called Kinaron, and incinerated them.

This act brought no small amount of blame to Cyril and the Alexandrian church, since murders and battles and the like are completely alien to Christian thinking. The event took place in the fourth year of Cyril's term as bishop when Honorius was consul for the tenth time and Theodosius for the sixth time, in the month of March, during Lent.

Sokrates Scholastikos

The principal players in this story, which takes place in Alexandria, are the Neoplatonist philosopher Hypatia, the patriarch Cyril, and the prefect of Egypt,

Orestes—that is to say, a beautiful and popular pagan philosopher, a powerful churchman, and a mighty representative of secular power.

Hypatia presents the romantic figure of a female pagan philosopher renowned for her beauty and her intellect. She combines, as the French poet Charles Leconte de Lisle puts it, "the spirit of Plato and the body of Aphrodite." But in her day she provokes the hatred of Cyril, whose partisans, in the present version of the story, held Hypatia responsible for preventing a close relationship between the prefect and the bishop. A Christian mob brutally murdered her in AD 415, and it appears that no one was ever punished for the crime.

CHAPTER 3
LEGENDS ON VARIOUS THEMES

The supernaturalism of the previous chapter moves on here to legends of the bizarre and continues with a variety of realistic themes from irony to justice.

THE BIZARRE

66. CAPTURE OF A SATYR

Sulla came down to the sea through Thessaly and Macedonia and was making preparations to cross from Dyrrachium to Brundisium with twelve hundred ships. Close by is Apollonia, and near it the Nymphaeum, a sacred place from whose bright-green glen and meadows scattered springs of perpetually flowing fire issue forth.

In that place, they say, a sleeping satyr was caught, a creature such as the sculptors and painters represent in their art, and he was brought to Sulla. He was asked through many interpreters who he was. He uttered nothing intelligible but emitted a sort of hoarse sound, more or less a mix

of the neighing of a horse and the bleating of a goat. Sulla was astonished and had him escorted away.

Plutarch

The Roman general Sulla comes upon a satyr in the course of a military campaign in Greece in 83 BC. Satyrs are two-legged beings having the lower body of a horse and the upper body of a man. Sulla would have known of them from traditional narratives and mythological art.

67. CAPTURE OF A CENTAUR

A hippocentaur was found in Saune, a city in Arabia, on a very high mountain that teems with a deadly drug. The drug bears the same name as the city. Among fatal substances it is extremely quick and effective.

The hippocentaur was captured alive by the king, who sent it to Egypt together with other gifts for the emperor. Its sustenance was meat. But it did not tolerate the change of air, and died, so that the prefect of Egypt had it embalmed and sent to Rome.

At first it was exhibited in the palace. Its face was fiercer than a human face, its arms and fingers were hairy, and its ribs were connected with its front legs and its stomach. It had the firm hooves of a horse, and its mane was tawny, although as a result of the embalming its mane along with its skin was becoming dark. In size it did not match the usual representations, though it was not small either. There were said also to have been other hippocentaurs in the above-mentioned city of Saune.

So far as concerns the one sent to Rome, anyone who is skeptical can examine it for himself, since, as I said above, it has been embalmed, and it is kept in the emperor's storehouse.

Phlegon of Tralles

Like satyrs, centaurs or hippocentaurs (horse-centaurs), are composite beings that are part horse and part human. Centaurs differ from satyrs in being four-legged creatures with the lower body of a horse and the upper body of a man.

*Pliny the Elder (*Natural History *7.35) saw the very creature mentioned by Phlegon, which had been sent to the emperor Claudius from Egypt and was preserved in honey. Since centaurs are fabulous beings, the corpse sent to the emperor and displayed by him was necessarily a fake, assembled possibly, as Adrienne Mayor speculates, "from mummified human and pony parts" (2000:327 n. 12). Phlegon's "corroborative invitation" that skeptics may examine the embalmed centaur for themselves is a common rhetorical strategy in legend narration (Oring 2008:143).*

68. SIGHTINGS OF MERMEN AND MERMAIDS

An embassy from Lisbon was sent to the emperor Tiberius for the purpose of reporting to him that a triton playing on a conch was seen and heard in a certain cave, and was recognized by this configuration.

Nor are reports of Nereids false, except that their bodies bristle with scales even where they are human in shape, for a Nereid was also observed on the same coast, and the inhabitants even heard, at a distance, her mournful song as she was dying. The governor of Gaul wrote to the divine Augustus that many dead Nereids were seen on the shore.

As authorities I have distinguished members of the equestrian order who declare that they saw in the Gulf of Cadiz a merman whose entire body was like that of a human being. He would climb aboard their ships

at nighttime, and immediately the part he sat on was weighed down and, if he had persisted, would even have sunk.

Pliny the Elder

Triton is a deity of the sea, a son of Poseidon and Amphitrite. In addition, we hear generically of tritons as mermen with the body of a human and the tail end of a fish or horse. In ancient art they are often represented as playing on a conch, and it was this combination of merman and shell that led the inhabitants of Lisbon to identify specifically as a triton the being they spotted, a sighting that they deemed worthy of reporting to the emperor.

Nereids ("daughters of Nereus," a sea god) are mermaids. Since they were conventionally imagined as being wholly human in form, the scaly body of the Nereid observed near Lisbon required comment.

69. THE SELF-SUSTAINING BEAST

Greeks and Romans wondered at the vagabond Matreas of Alexandria. He said he was raising an animal that fed on itself.

People still puzzle over what Matreas's animal was.

Athenaios

70. IN LOVE WITH A STATUE

The well-known Cyprian, Pygmalion, conceived a passion for an ivory statue. The statue, which represented Aphrodite, was a nude. Overcome by the statue's shapeliness, Pygmalion engaged in sexual intercourse with it. This is related by Philostephanos.

There was another statue of Aphrodite, in Knidos, a beautiful one made of marble. Another man conceived a passion for it and had sex with the marble, as Poseidippos relates. Philostephanos's account is in his book on Cyprus; Poseidippos's, in his book on Knidos.

So powerfully can art lead amorous persons to their ruin.

Clement of Alexandria

Citing legends of men who were erotically attracted to statues and engaged in sexual intercourse with them, the Christian author Clement concludes that art can be morally dangerous.

* * *

Philostephanos writes in his *Kypriaka* that Pygmalion, king of Cyprus, conceived a passion for a statue of Venus* as if it were a woman, a statue regarded as holy and venerable by the Cyprians from ancient times. Blinded in mind, reason, and judgment, he used to place the deity on a couch and unite with her in embraces and kisses as though they were married, and do other vain things in his fantasy of illusory pleasure.

Similarly Poseidippos, in the book he wrote about Knidos and its history, mentions that a young man of noble birth (he withholds the young man's name) was overcome with love for the Venus for which Knidos is renowned, and that the young man coupled wantonly with the image of the deity, enjoying the matrimonial bed and the pleasures that ensued.

Arnobius

---

*Roman Venus = Greek Aphrodite.

***

With his statue of Aphrodite, Praxiteles made Knidos famous. The shrine in which it stands is entirely open so that the image of the goddess can be viewed from any side, and it is believed to have been made this way with the blessing of the goddess herself. The statue is equally wondrous from any angle.

They say that a certain man once fell in love with it and, by hiding at night, embraced it, and that a stain betrays his lust.

Pliny the Elder

In these scandalous legends a man is erotically attracted to a statue—not just any statue but an image of the goddess of love herself—and acts upon his passion. These are two of many ancient legends about men responding erotically to artistic images.

The Greek island of Cyprus (the site of Aphrodite's birth) and the Greek city of Knidos (the site of her most celebrated statue) had prominent cults of Aphrodite, which included sanctuaries and cult statues. The famous marble statue of Aphrodite sculpted by Praxiteles around 350 BC (Havelock 1995), which perhaps introduced the life-size female nude into Greek statuary art, was the glory of the city of Knidos. Lucian's Loves *gives an account of a visit by three men to Aphrodite's temple on Knidos and the passionate response of one of the men to the beautiful, undraped image. Being painted, the image would have been all the more lifelike. Moreover, the ancients treated cult statues in some ways as though they were alive: they sometimes bathed them, clothed them, addressed them, and married them to other statues. And some statues reportedly behaved as if they were alive: they averted their eyes (at an unpleasant sight), moved their bodies, spoke, bled, wept, and so on.*

Greek narratives of men's sexual attraction to statues arise after sculptors produced life-size nude statues of female deities, and Roman instances are found following the removal of Greek statues to Rome. No new reports appear after the first century AD (Corso 2008:24).

***

Pygmalion saw women leading shameful lives.
Offended by the vices that nature gave in abundance
To the female mind, he lived a celibate life without a wife, and

Long lacked a companion for his bed.
Meanwhile he succeeded with wondrous art in sculpting white ivory,
Giving it beauty such as no woman could be born with, and
Fell in love with his own work.
Its face was that of a real maiden, who you might believe was alive and,
If her modesty did not forbid her, wished to move her body.
To such an extent did his art conceal his artifice. Pygmalion marveled, and
His heart was inflamed for this semblance of flesh.
Often he placed his hands on his work, testing whether it was flesh or ivory,
Unwilling to accept it as mere ivory.
He gave it kisses and thought they were returned. He spoke with it,
Embraced it, and, believing his fingers sunk into the limbs he touched,
Feared he might bruise them.
Sometimes he offered it flattering words, at other times brought it gifts
Such as girls like—shells and smooth stones,
Little birds and flowers of a thousand colors,
Lilies, painted balls, and tears of the Heliades that dripped from trees.*
He adorned its limbs with clothes, put gems on its fingers and
Long necklaces on its neck.
Light pears hung from its ears, ribbons from its breast.
Everything suited it, though in fact it looked no less beautiful unadorned.
Placing it on a coverlet dyed with Sidonian purple,

---

*That is, amber.

He called it the companion of his bed, laying its reclining neck
On soft feather pillows, as if it could feel them.
Then the festival of Venus, most celebrated on all Cyprus,
Arrived. Heifers, their spreading horns covered with gold,
Fell beneath the death-stroke at their white necks, and
Incense was burning. After making his offering, Pygmalion
Stood at the altar and said, timidly,
"Gods, if you can grant anything, let my wife be"—
Not daring to say "the ivory maiden"—"like the ivory maiden."
Golden Venus was of course present at her own festival and
Understood what his prayer meant. As a favorable omen
The flame blazed up and thrice leapt into the air.
When Pygmalion returned home, he went to the image, and,
Leaning over the bed, kissed it. It felt warm.
He moved his mouth to it again and touched its breast with his hands.
The ivory grew soft at contact and its hardness disappeared as it yielded to his fingers,
Just as wax from Mt. Hymettos is softened by the sun and, moulded by a thumb,
Is formed into many shapes, becoming useful by being used.
The lover was dumbstruck but, fearing deception, rejoiced only with reserve.
He touched again and again what he had prayed for.
It was flesh. Veins pulsed at the touch of his thumb.
Then indeed the Paphian hero poured out copious thanks to Venus and
At last pressed his mouth to a real mouth. The maiden felt the kisses and
Blushed. Shyly lifting her eyes to the light,
She saw her lover and the sky at the same moment.
The goddess attended the wedding that she had brought about, and

When the crescent moon had become full nine times,
The girl bore Paphos, from whom the island takes the name.

Ovid

The most familiar version of the Pygmalion narrative today is this religious legend recounted by the Roman poet Ovid in his Metamorphoses, *in which the ivory statue of an ideal woman is miraculously transformed into a living maiden. Nameless in antiquity, she has acquired the name Galatea in modern mythography (Reinhold 1971; Hansen 2014).*

71. ANIMAL OFFSPRING

An extraordinary omen occurred in Rome when the archon at Athens was Deinophilos and the consuls in Rome were Quintus Veranius and Gaius Pompeius Gallus.

A highly respected maidservant belonging to the wife of Raecius Taurus, a man of praetorian rank, brought forth a monkey.

Phlegon of Tralles

For no apparent reason a woman gives birth to an animal.

72. THE UGLY MAN

A certain powerful but unsightly man wanted to beget children. He had a painting of a comely child made on a flat piece of wood. Whenever he had sexual intercourse with his wife, he told her to look at the painted image. She would gaze at it intently, focusing all her attention, as it were, not on the begetter but on the painted image. She gave birth to a child like the image.

Galen

* * *

Need I say that the form of the fetus is affected by the kind of condition the mind is in? Thus, women engaging in sexual intercourse have seen monkeys and conceived monkey-shaped offspring. The ruler of the Cyprians, who was an ugly man, obliged his wife to look at very beautiful statues when they were intimate, and became the father of very comely children. Horse breeders station noble horses in front of mares while they are being impregnated. In order, then, that the offspring not turn out to be ugly when a woman's mind is in a state of drunkenness and subject to strange imaginings, let women be sober when they engage in intimate activities; then the resemblance of the child to its mother is not only physical but also mental.

Soranos

The notion of "maternal impression," according to which an image seen by a female at or around the time she conceives impresses itself on her, causing her fetus to resemble what she saw, was common in antiquity among both ordinary people and intellectuals. A maternal impression might occur unexpectedly as in the case of a woman who chanced to see a monkey around the time she conceived, or it could be arranged on purpose.

73. MALE PARTURITION

The doctor Dorotheus says in his *Reminiscences* that in Egyptian Alexandria a male homosexual gave birth. Because of the marvel, he says, the newborn infant was embalmed and is still preserved.

Phlegon of Tralles

The bearer of the child is described as a kinaidos, *a passive partner in male homosexual relations.*

74. SUDDEN CHANGE OF SEX

It would not be proper to bypass the odd occurrence that took place before the death of Alexander, which on account of its strangeness will perhaps not be believed. A short while earlier, King Alexander was consulting an oracle in Cilicia, where they say there is a temple of Sarpedonian Apollon, and the god, it is said, responded that Alexander should beware of the place that brought forth the biformed one. At the time the oracular response seemed like a riddle, but later, after the death of the king, the meaning of the response was recognized by means of such causes as the following.

A certain man, Diophantos by name and Macedonian by descent, lived in Arabia in a place called Abai. He wed a native Arabian woman and begot a son, named after himself, and a daughter, called Heraïs. His son he lived to see die before the boy's prime, but when his daughter was of marriageable age, he gave her a dowry and arranged a marriage for her with a man named Samiades.

Now the husband, after living together with his wife for a year, went on a journey and was gone for a long time. Heraïs, they say, fell ill with a strange and utterly incredible ailment. A dense tumescence appeared in her lower abdomen, and when the area became more and more swollen and she also developed a high fever, the medical doctors formed the opinion that there was ulceration around the neck of her uterus. They employed treatments that they supposed would reduce the inflammation, when on the seventh day the surface of the swelling burst and from Heraïs's female parts there projected a male genital organ with testicles attached.

At the time that the rupture, and the experience that followed, occurred, no doctors or other persons were present except for Heraïs's mother and two maidservants. Astonished as they were by the strangeness of the event, they took care of her as best they could, and kept quiet about what had happened. After Heraïs had recovered from her illness, she wore female clothes and in other respects preserved a domestic and female mode of life. Those who were aware of the strange occurrence judged that she was a hermaphrodite and, since natural sexual intercourse was inconsistent with this state, they supposed that in her wedded life she had consorted with her husband in the fashion of males.

Her condition was still unknown outside the household when Samiades returned and, as was his due, sought his wife. Since, on account of her shame, she did not have the courage to come into his presence, Samiades became angry. When he persisted ever more insistently in demanding his spouse back and Heraïs's father did not comply but was ashamed to say why, their dispute grew, and the husband brought suit against the father for his own wife, just as in dramas when Fortune leads a strange turn of events into an accusation.

The judges took their seats, the arguments were presented, and the body in dispute was also present for the judgment, but the judges were having difficulty deciding whether the husband should have authority over his wife or the father over his daughter. At last, as the judges were leaning toward the view that the wife must follow her husband, Heraïs revealed the truth. Taking courage, she loosened the clothing that was serving as a costume, displayed her male organ to everyone, and burst into speech, asking with a loud complaint if anyone was going to force a man to live with a man. Struck with astonishment, all expressed their surprise at this marvel.

After the revelation of her shame, Heraïs changed from female attire to the clothing of a young man. For their part the doctors, having been shown the parts that had appeared from her, judged that a male organ had lain hidden within an egg-shaped region of the female organ, and that since the organ had been encased abnormally by skin, an aperture had developed through which excretions were discharged. For this reason they deemed it necessary to lacerate the perforated area to cause it to cicatrize, improving the condition of the male organ and employing a treatment allowed by the circumstances. Heraïs changed her name to Diophantos and was enrolled in the cavalry, and after serving beside the king, withdrew with him to Abai. Thereby the oracle, which previously had not been comprehended, was understood when the king was slain at Abai, the place where the biformed one had been born.

Samiades, they say, remained a slave to his passion and to the relationship he had had. Affected by the shame he felt for his unnatural marriage, he designated Diophantos in his will as heir of his property and then made his departure from life. So she who was born a woman took upon herself a man's reputation and daring, whereas the man turned out to be weaker in mind than a woman.

Diodoros of Sicily

As usual in oracle legends, the oracular response—in this case, "beware of the place that brought forth the biformed one"—is not really helpful to the consulter because of its obscurity, and its sense becomes clear only in retrospect. The legend is set in the second century BC (Alexander Balas died in 145 BC).

Many narratives of sexual transformation are found in ancient authors. The direction of change is always female to male because the stories apparently dramatize the physiological phenomenon of pseudohermaphroditism, in which a male (or predominantly male) child appears at birth to be biologically female so that the parents raise the child as a girl, but in the passage of time the child experiences masculinization with the extrusion of male genital organs, bringing on a crisis in sexual identity.

* * *

There was also a hermaphrodite in Antioch by the Maeander River at the time when Antipater was archon at Athens and Marcus Vinicius and Titus Statilius Taurus, surnamed Corvinus, were consuls in Rome.

A maiden of prominent family, thirteen years of age, was good-looking and had many suitors. She was betrothed to the man whom her parents wished, the day of the wedding was at hand, and she was about to go forth from her house when suddenly she experienced an excruciating pain and cried out. Her relations took charge of her, treating her for stomach pains and colic, but her suffering continued for three days without a break, perplexing everyone with regard to the nature of her illness. Her pains let up neither night or day, and although the doctors in the city tried every kind of treatment, they were unable to discover the cause of her illness. On the fourth day around daybreak her pains became stronger, and she let out a huge scream. Male genitals suddenly burst forth from her, and the girl became a man.

Sometime later this person was brought to the emperor Claudius at Rome. Because of the portent he had an altar built on the Capitoline to Jupiter the Averter of Evil.

Phlegon of Tralles

The dramatic date of the events is around AD 45, as the names of the magistrates indicate.

75. PERIODIC ECSTASY

Aristoxenos the musician says in his *Life of Telestes* that while he was in Italy several calamities took place. One of them, he says, was a strange malady that afflicted the women. They would fall into trances such that sometimes as they sat and ate, they would seem to be hearing someone calling them, and then, leaping up and being past all control, they would rush outside the city.

When the Lokrians and the people of Rhegion consulted the god about relief from this malady, he told them to sing paeans for sixty days in the spring. As a result many persons in Italy became composers of paeans.

Apollonios

Instances of mass hysteria or delusion are found in both mythological and non-mythological narratives, such as when the daughters of Proitos offend Hera, the goddess causes them to roam the land in the belief that they are cows (Akousilaos Argeus *fr. 28 Fowler). Typically these afflictions are one-time events, but the women in the present story suffer from a recurrent malady. The site of their mass hysteria is the southern tip of Italy.*

76. THE LAUGHING TIRYNTHIANS

In his work *On Comedy* Theophrastos says that the Tirynthians, being prone to laughter, were of no use at all in conducting serious business.

Wishing to be rid of their affliction, they resorted to the Delphic oracle. The god told them that if they sacrificed a bull to Poseidon by casting it into the sea, and could do so without laughing, they would be free. Fearing that they would utterly fail to meet the oracle's stipulation, the Tirynthians told their children that they could not be present at the sacrifice. Now, one child learned of the matter and mingled with the crowd. "What's going on?" he said. "Are you afraid I'll upset the offering?" The Tirynthians burst into laughter.

As they learned from actual experience, the god had shown them that, really, curing a habit of many years was all but impossible.

Athenaios

The child's innocent question about the sphagion *("sacrificial victim") can be understood as unintentionally punning on* sphageion *("bowl for catching the victim's blood"): "Are you afraid I'll upset the bull/bowl?" But the Tirynthians probably do not require a pun to burst into laughter.*

77. THE MAN WHO LOSES HIS LAUGH

Parmeniskos of Metaponton, as Semos says in the fifth book of his work *On Delos*, was a man of the first rank in family and wealth. But after he descended to the oracle of Trophonios and emerged again, he was no longer able to laugh. When he consulted the Delphic oracle about his problem, the Pythia said:

You ask me about relenting laughter, relentless one:
Mother will grant it to you at home. Honor her above others.

So he expected he would regain his laugh if he returned to his homeland, and when that did not happen, he thought he had been deceived.

By chance he once came to Delos, and in the course of admiring all the wonders of the island, he came to the temple of Leto, supposing that the statue of the mother of Apollon would be something worth seeing. When he saw that it was only an ill-shaped piece of wood, he burst unexpectedly into laughter. Seeing the point then of the god's oracle and having been freed of his disability, he honored the goddess greatly.

Athenaios

To consult Trophonios's underground oracle, located at Lebadeia in Boeotia, a consulter had to descend into a narrow subterranean space. After his ascent, he was said to be in a state of helpless terror. Priests debriefed him and then turned him over to the care of his relatives. (For a firsthand account of this strange oracle, see Pausanias [9.39.5–14], who himself consulted it.) In Parmeniskos's case, however, the effect of the oracular experience was not a temporary feeling of terror but a permanent loss of his ability to laugh. The challenge of making someone laugh—in international folktales often a melancholy princess—is a widespread folk-narrative motif. Solutions vary but frequently are an absurd and unexpected sight.

78. A STRANGE TOMB

Xerxes, son of Darius, dug through the tomb of Bel of old and found a sarcophagus made of glass, within which the corpse lay in olive oil. Now, the sarcophagus was not full, the oil falling short of reaching the lip by perhaps the palm of a hand. Next to the sarcophagus stood a short stele with an inscription:

> It will not profit anyone to open this tomb if he does not fill the sarcophagus to the top.

When Xerxes read this, he was afraid and gave orders to pour oil in immediately. Still it was not full. He gave orders again to pour in oil. Since he failed to increase the level of the oil, he told his men not to waste any more. He closed the tomb back up and departed in a state of distress.

The stele did not err in what it foretold. Xerxes gathered together 700,000 men against the Greeks and came off badly, and upon his return he died the most shameful of deaths: his own son slit his throat one night in bed.

Aelian

The legend of Bel's tomb features the popular motif of the cursed tomb and the miserable fate of the person who disturbs it. Bel ("Lord") is one of the names of Marduk, patron deity of Babylon, and the reference must be to the immense ziggurat, or temple, of Bel that once dominated that city. The temple was perhaps the material inspiration for the biblical Tower of Babel (Genesis 2:1–9). After the Babylonian revolt of 484 BC, the Persian king Xerxes partially demolished the building.

79. THE LAME MAN AND THE BLIND MAN

A blind beggar carried a man who was lame of foot,
  his payment being the other man's eyes.
Two incomplete persons were joined into one nature,
  making good each other's defect.

Leonidas of Alexandria

* * *

A blind man bore on his back a lame man,
  lending legs, borrowing eyes.

Plato the Younger

The curious idea of two men, each with a different defect, who work together to function as a single whole man is an international narrative theme that finds clever treatment here in light verse. The idea elsewhere underlies a strange episode in the legend of the hero Orion. When Orion is blinded, he places another fellow, Kedalion, upon his shoulders to steer him, and then walks eastward until he meets the sun god Helios, who restores his sight. Kedalion is not said specifically to be lame, although he is a helper of the divine smith Hephaistos, who is famously lame.

IRONY

80. INTAPHRENES'S WIFE

The wife of Intaphrenes came repeatedly to the door of the palace crying and wailing. She persisted in this behavior, making Darius feel pity for her. He sent a courier to her with this message: "Woman, of the members of your family who are being held, King Darius will allow you to save one, whichever you want."

After considering the matter, she responded as follows, "If the king grants me the life of only one out of them all, I choose my brother."

Apprised of her choice and astonished by what she said, he sent her a query. "Woman, the king asks what your reason is for abandoning your husband and children and choosing for your brother to survive, since surely he is more distant from you than your children and less dear to you than your husband?"

She answered, "King, I could get another husband, god willing, as well as other children if I lose these. But since my father and mother are no longer alive, there is no way I could get another brother. This was my thinking when I made my choice."

Deeming that the woman had spoken well, Darius released the brother she had asked for, and also her eldest child, since he was pleased by her, but he had all the others killed.

Herodotos

Fearing that Intaphrenes is plotting against him, King Darius of Persia has him and his entire household arrested, with the intention of putting them all to death, but he relents, allowing Intaphrenes's wife to save her husband or any other member of the family. The woman's choice of her brother is meant to be as surprising to us as it is to King Darius. What is unsettling is her cold reasoning. She treats her husband and offspring as so many slots to be filled rather than as actual living persons with whom she has a relationship and a history.

81. A PARENT'S REQUEST

One of the Persians, Oiobazos, begged Darius to leave behind one of Oiobazos's sons. He had three, all of whom were campaigning with the army. The king replied that inasmuch as Oiobazos was a friend and his request was modest, he would leave him all his children. Oiobazos was thrilled, expecting his sons to be released from military service.

Darius ordered the persons in charge of Oiobazos's sons to kill them, all of them. So the sons were slaughtered and, indeed, left behind for him.

Herodotos

The Persian ruler receives Oiobazos's request as he is setting out with his army to make war. Since the monarch himself is participating in the military campaign, it is surely impolitic to ask that one of his subjects be excused from participation. This logic is explicit in another version of the legend, in which a man asks King Xerxes to allow the eldest of his five sons, all of whom are serving in the army, to be released from service; Xerxes agrees, orders the man's son to be cut in half, and has the army march between the two halves (Herodotos 7.38–39). A similar legend circulated in modern times about Saddam Hussein (Mayor 1991).

82. PLATO'S CHARACTERS

They say that after Socrates heard Plato read his *Lysis*, he said, "Herakles, what a batch of lies the young man has written about me!" For he wrote many things that Socrates had never said.

Diogenes Laertios

***

Others say that when Gorgias read Plato's dialogue, he told bystanders that he had neither said any of it nor heard any of it from Plato. And they say that Phaedo, having read Plato's dialogue *On the Soul*, said the same thing.

Athenaios

Gorgias reads the Gorgias, *and Phaedo reads the* Phaedo, or On the Soul, *and each comments on its inaccuracy. What could be worse than for the very person after whom the dialogue is named to deny its accuracy? These narratives, belonging to the hostile tradition of anecdotes about Plato (see Athenaios 11.504e–509e), illustrate Plato's alleged unreliability.*

A similarly unfriendly tradition contended that Perikles's renowned funeral speech (Thucydides 2.34–46) was actually composed by his mistress, the courtesan Aspasia (Plato Menexenus *236b).*

83. THE UNBREAKABLE GLASS BOWL

There was a craftsman who made a glass bowl that did not break. He got an audience with the emperor and came with his gift. He had the emperor hand it back to him, and purposely let it drop onto the floor. The emperor could not have been more scared, but the man picked the bowl up from the floor. It was dented like a bronze vase. The man then retrieved a small hammer from his pocket and, taking his time, repaired it nicely. When that was done, he thought he had Jupiter by the balls.

The emperor asked him, "Does anyone else know this manufacturing process?" Now see what happens. When the man said no, the emperor had his head cut off, because of course if the method had become known, gold would be dirt cheap.

Petronius

The central theme of a suppressed invention is found in many rumors and legends of the present day. The narrative exemplifies a contemporary, or urban, legend in an ancient setting.

ANIMALS

84. THE DOLPHIN RIDER

I have come upon some material that is true but quite like fiction, something worthy of your very fertile, lofty, and distinctly poetic talent. I

came upon it at the dinner table, as marvelous tales of different sorts were being told, and I myself have great confidence in the credibility of the narrator—though what is that to a poet? Still, the narrator is a person you would trust even if you were going to write history.

There is a colony, Hippo, situated on the coast of Africa. A navigable lagoon lies nearby, and connected with it is a river-like estuary that ebbs and flows with the tide, sometimes flowing into the sea and sometimes back into the lagoon. Persons of every age enjoy fishing, boating, and even swimming here, especially children, drawn by leisure and their love of play. With bravery and a wish to be admired they venture into quite deep water, the winner being the boy who leaves the shore and his fellow swimmers the farthest behind.

In this competition one boy was more daring than the rest and went farther out. A dolphin came to him and swam now in front of him, now behind him, now around him, and finally came up under him and released him and again came up under him, conveying the anxious boy out to the deep but presently turning back to shore and returning the boy to land and his companions.

Word of the event ran through the colony. Everyone flocked to the spot to gaze at the boy like some prodigy, question him, listen to his account, and repeat it. On the following day they besieged the seashore and looked out at the sea and anything like the sea. The children swam, among them the same boy, though more cautiously. The dolphin returned for the occasion and for the boy, who, however, fled along with the rest of the children. But the dolphin, as if inviting and calling him back, jumped and dove and swam in circles around him, first in one direction and then in the other. The same thing happened the next day, the day after that, and the days that followed, until the people began to be ashamed of their fear, since they had after all been reared with the sea. They went up to the dolphin, played with it, called out to it, and even touched and handled it when it offered itself to them. Daring increased with familiarity. In particular the boy who had been the first to interact with it swam to the dolphin as it swam, climbed onto its back, and was borne out to sea and back. He thought it recognized him and loved him, and he himself loved it. Neither was afraid, and neither was feared. The one's trust, and the other's tameness, increased. Some of the other children would swim on their right and left, calling out encouragement and advice. Another dolphin (and this, too, is amazing) used to travel along with the first one, though only as an observer and companion, for it did not do anything or allow anything to be done to it, only accompanying the other dolphin to sea and back to shore, as the other children did the boy. It is hard to believe, but just as true as what I have related above, that the dolphin who carried and played with the children would also let itself be pulled onto land, where it would dry out on the sand and then go back to the sea when it felt hot.

It is generally agreed that, acting on some misguided sense of religiosity, the governor's legate Octavius Avitus anointed the dolphin once with an ointment when it was ashore, and the strange odor made the dolphin take refuge in the deep. Reappearing after many days, it seemed weak and dejected but presently regained its strength and returned to its prior playfulness and familiar tricks.

All the state officials gathered to see the spectacle, and the small town was now burdened with the extra expenses of their arrivals and stays. Finally the place began to lose its peace and quiet, and the folk decided to do away with the dolphin secretly. With what pathos and tears might you elaborate and elevate these events, though there is no need for you to invent or add anything of your own, for it will suffice if what really happened gets its due.

Pliny the Younger

Pliny's narrative is the best-known of numerous ancient accounts of humans and supernatural beings riding dolphins. The theme appears extensively in ancient art and on coins. In modern times dolphin riding by children is attested and has been photographed (Higham 1960).

The Roman colony of Hippo Diarrhytus lay on the north coast of Africa on the site of the present-day city of Bizerte, Tunisia.

85. THE GRATEFUL DOLPHIN

Dolphins are very fond of humans and are also quite intelligent animals that understand how to return a favor. At any rate, Phylarchos reports the following in his twelfth book:

"Koiranos of Miletos saw some fishermen who had caught a dolphin in their net and were about to cut it up. After he entreated them and gave them money, they released it into the sea. Sometime later he was involved in a shipwreck off Mykonos; everyone perished except for Koiranos, who was saved by a dolphin. When he died of old age in his homeland and his funeral procession happened to take place alongside the sea on Miletos, a school of dolphins appeared in the harbor that day at a short distance from the persons who were bearing Koiranos's remains, as though the dolphins were joining in carrying and mourning for him."

Athenaios

86. ANDROKLES AND THE LION

A certain Androkles, whose lot it was to be a house slave, ran away from his master, a member of the Roman senate, though what wrong he had done, or how great it was, I am unable to say. He reached Libya, avoiding the cities, "noting their location by the stars," as the saying goes, and proceeded into the desert. Since he was roasting in the brilliant, fiery sun, he was glad to take refuge and rest under a rock with caves.

Now, this rock was the lair of a lion. Well, it returned from the hunt, pierced by a sharp splinter and suffering from a punishing pain. When the lion came upon the youth, it gave him a gentle look and began to fawn upon him, holding out its paw and imploring him in the hope that he could pull out the splinter. At first the youth recoiled, but when he saw that the lion was gentle, and became aware of what had happened to its paw, he pulled out the source of the distress and so released the animal from its pain. Delighted at being healed, the lion paid its doctor's fee by treating Androkles as its guest and friend, sharing the spoils of its hunting. The one consumed its food raw in the manner of lions, and the other roasted his food for himself. So they enjoyed a common table in accordance with their own natures.

Androkles lived this way for three years, after which, with very long hair and suffering from severe itching, he left the lion and entrusted himself to fortune. While he wandered, men captured him, and after they learned from him whom he belonged to, they bound him and sent him back to his master in Rome. The latter called his house slave to account for the harm he had done, and condemned Androkles to be given to the wild beasts to devour.

The Libyan lion had also been captured, and both the lion and the condemned youth—he who once had shared dwelling and meals with that very lion—were released into the arena. Although the human did not recognize the animal, the latter immediately knew who the human was. Fawning upon him and laying its whole body down, it threw itself at his feet. At last Androkles recognized his host, and embraced the lion and began to greet it like a friend who had returned from abroad.

Since Androkles seemed to be a magician, a leopard was also let loose against him, but as it rushed at Androkles, the lion defended its one-time healer and, mindful of their shared table, tore the leopard to pieces.

As might be expected, the spectators were amazed. The man who was giving the shows summoned Androkles to him and got the whole story from him. Word spread through the crowd, and when the people learned the background, they shouted out to free both the man and the lion.

Aelian

* * *

"Afterward," Apion said, "we used to see Androkles and his lion, attached to a slender leash, making the rounds of the shops throughout the city. People gave him money, and they threw flowers upon the lion. Everyone who encountered them said, 'Here's the lion that was host to a human, and here's the human who was physician to a lion.'"

Aulus Gellius

Gellius tells us that he got his story from the fifth book of Apion's Aigyptiaka *(*Egyptian Topics*), a work about the wonders of Egypt composed in Greek by Apion, a native Egyptian. Apion was fond of representing himself as having actually been present at the wondrous events he describes, and in the present case he declares that he witnessed these events with his own eyes in the city of Rome. He seems to have been an exciting storyteller but an unreliable source, and already in antiquity was regarded as a liar (Pliny the Elder* Natural History *30.5.18; see Dickie 2001:212–216).*

87. HOW OPHITEIA GETS ITS NAME

A certain chieftain, suspecting that his enemies were plotting against his infant son, placed the child in a vessel and concealed it in a place in the land where he knew he had very little to fear. Now a wolf, they say, was about to attack the child, but a serpent coiled itself around the vessel and kept a firm watch. When the child's father arrived, he supposed that the serpent had designs on his child, and hurled his javelin, killing the boy along with the serpent. But after the shepherds informed him that he had killed his child's benefactor and protector, he built a shared pyre for his son and the serpent.

They say that to this day the place is like a burning pyre, and they maintain that the city was named Ophiteia after that serpent.

Pausanias

This etiological legend, recounted about a particular town in Phokis by the local people, purports to explain the origin of its unusual geology as well as of its strange name, Ophiteia (Snaketown).

There is no special significance in the man's placing his child in a clay vessel, which simply serves as a crib.

88. XANTHIPPOS'S DOG

As the whole city sailed away, the sight provoked pity in some, and astonishment at the boldness of the action in others, for men were conducting their families away in one direction, while they themselves, unflinching toward the wailing and tears and embraces of their parents, were crossing over to the island of Salamis. The many citizens who were left behind on account of their old age also stirred feelings of compassion. The sweet disposition of the tame, domestic animals was piteous, as they ran alongside their masters howling as the latter were embarking.

Among the animals, the story goes, was a dog belonging to Perikles's father Xanthippos that could not endure being separated from him. It leapt into the sea and swam alongside the trireme. Cast ashore on Salamis, it passed out and straightway died. They say that the place that is pointed out up to our own day and called the Dog's Mound is its grave.

Plutarch

In the course of the Persian invasion of 480 BC the Athenians dramatically abandoned their city, entrusting it to the protection of its patron goddess, Athena. Women and children were transported for safekeeping to the nearby town of Troizen, while men of military age embarked on ships. The island of Salamis lies about two kilometers from Peiraieus, the port of Athens.

89. THE ACCIDENTAL KILLING OF A CAT

In Egypt whoever kills one of these animals intentionally is put to death—unless it is a cat or an ibis that he kills, for if he kills one of these animals, whether intentionally or not, he is absolutely put to death. The populace assembles and handles the perpetrator most dreadfully, sometimes doing so without any trial. Fearing such treatment, anyone who sees one of these animals dead keeps his distance from it, while shouting loudly, wailing, and calling other persons to witness that he came upon the animal already dead.

Extreme piety toward these animals has so situated itself in the mind of the populace, and the feelings of individual persons are so unalterably oriented toward honoring these animals, that at the time when Ptolemy, their king, had not yet received the appellation of "friend" by the Romans and the populace was making every effort to win over the ambassadors visiting from Italy—and, because of this anxiety, was intent on giving them no cause for complaint or war—a certain Roman killed a cat and a mob gathered at the perpetrator's house. Neither the officials dispatched by the king to intercede for the man nor the people's general fear of Rome sufficed to deliver the man from retribution, despite the fact that his deed had been unintentional.

I record this event not from hearsay, for I saw it with my own eyes on the occasion of my visit to Egypt.

Diodoros of Sicily

Greeks found Egyptians' veneration of certain animals to be curious and fascinating. Sacred animals included cats, mongooses, dogs, hawks, ibises, wolves, and crocodiles, all of which received special treatment such as mummification. The present incident took place around 60 BC.

CHILDREN

90. THE CHILDREN PLAY KING

When Kyros was ten years old, the following event happened to him, revealing who he was.

He was in the village where the ox stalls were, playing in the road with other boys of his age. In their games the boys chose him, nominally the herdsman's son, as their king. He assigned them different tasks, some of them to build houses, some to be his bodyguards, someone to be the King's Eye [= the king's chief inspector], and to one he granted the honor of delivering messages, giving a job to each boy.

Now, one of the boys playing with him was the son of Artembares, who was a distinguished man among the Medes. Since this boy did not perform the task Kyros assigned him, Kyros ordered the other boys to hold him on both sides, and while the boys obeyed this order, Kyros flogged him, treating the boy very harshly. As soon as the boy was released, indignant and chafing at his handling, he returned to the city and complained to his father about the treatment he had encountered at the hands of Kyros—not calling him Kyros, since this was not yet his name, but the son of Astyages's herdsman. Artembares angrily went just as he was to Astyages, bringing his son. He declared that the boy had been handled outrageously. "King," he said, "we have been wantonly insulted by this slave of yours, the herdsman's son," and showed him his son's shoulders.

When Astyages heard and saw this, he wanted to avenge the boy for the sake of Artembares's honor. So he sent for the herdsman and his son. When both were present, Astyages looked at Kyros and said: "How have you, the son of a lowly man, dared to treat so outrageously the son of this man here, who ranks first in my court?" The boy answered as follows: "Master, what I did to him I did justly. In our play the village boys, of whom he is one, picked me to be their king, deciding that I was fittest for the role. Now, whereas the other boys carried out the duties assigned them, he disobeyed me and had no regard for me until he paid the penalty. If I deserve to be punished for this, here I am."

As the boy spoke, a feeling of recognition came over Astyages. The boy's looks, he thought, resembled his own, the way he answered was too free, and the boy's age matched the time since the exposure.

Herodotos

Astyages was ruler of the Medes and Persians. When the Magi divine that his grandson will be king in his stead, Astyages instructs one of his men to take the infant boy away and kill him. The man turns the actual task over to a cowherd, one of Astyages's slaves, but the cowherd and his wife let him live (a motif known as the compassionate executioner) and decide instead to rear the royal child as their own. In this excerpt from the Kyros legend, a children's game proves to be a turning point in the boy's life.

As the story continues, Astyages optimistically concludes that the prophecy of Kyros's becoming king has been fulfilled, and in a trivial and harmless manner at that, by his being chosen king of his playmates. He lets the child live and even reunites him with his biological parents. It proves to be the wrong decision, for Kyros grows up to overthrow Astyages and become ruler of the Medes and Persians.

An underlying assumption in this episode, probably universal in antiquity, was that certain characteristic qualities of free persons and slaves, of rulers and subjects, were inborn rather than acquired. Accordingly, although Kyros is reared by slaves as a slave, his nobility of birth inevitably manifests itself: his playmates deem him fittest among them to be king, and when he addresses a real king, he does so with the boldness of a free man.

91. THE CHILDREN PLAY PRIEST

A man of Mitylene, Makareus by name, a priest of Dionysos, was to all appearances temperate and good, but in most respects he was the most unholy of men.

A visitor came to him and deposited in his keeping an amount of gold, which Makareus buried, after digging a hole in the innermost part of the temple. Sometime later the visitor came and asked for the return of his gold. Makareus led him inside as if to give it back, but cut him down, whereafter he dug up the gold and put the visitor's body in its place. He thought that just as he was escaping detection by humans, he was also escaping detection by god. But things did not happen in that way.

How so? After a short while the time for the triennial festival of the god came around, and Makareus was performing sacrifices on a large scale. While he was thus occupied with Bacchic rites, his children, two in number, were left inside the house. Imitating their father's ritual procedure, they approached the family altar, on which offerings were still burning. When the younger child offered his neck, the elder child, having found a sacrificial knife that was lying around, killed his brother as a sacrificial victim.

The members of the household cried out when they saw this. Hearing the cries, the boys' mother leapt up, and seeing that one boy was dead and the other was still holding the blood-stained knife, she grabbed one of the half-burnt pieces of wood from the altar and killed her son with it. The news reached Makareus, who left the ceremony just as he was, rushed angrily into his house, and killed his wife with the thyrsus he was holding.

When these audacious acts became generally known, Makareus was arrested and confessed under torture to the deed he had done in the temple. In the course of his ordeal he expired. The man who had been criminally cut down was given public honors and burial, as the god directed.

So Makareus paid no contemptible penalty, indeed a poetic penalty, with his own life, that of his wife, and moreover those of his sons.

Aelian

This legend blends the spirit of Greek tragedy with the irony characteristic of contemporary legend. The innocent play of the children, in which they improvise a game of priest and sacrificial victim in imitation of their father's profession (and, unknown to them, also of his secret crime), has the feel of an urban legend, while Makareus's misguided behavior leads with cosmic justice and seeming inevitability to his own tragic downfall along with that of his entire household.

The underlying story is an international tale that is told sometimes as a folktale and sometimes as a legend. The Grimm Brothers included two versions of the story ("The Children Play Butcher") in the first edition (1812) of their collection of fairytales but dropped it in subsequent editions because of its gruesomeness (Grimm 1985:71–72, no. 22; and 267–268).

92. THE CHILDREN PLAY WAR

Among the Samnites a large group of children who were tending sheep on local lands chose two of their number who had well-developed bodies, calling one of them Belisarios and naming the other Wittigis, and urged them to wrestle with each other. The boys engaged in the match with great vigor, and it happened that Wittigis lost. As the band of boys in their play were hanging him from a tree, a wolf chanced to appear. The children all fled, but Wittigis, who was hanging from the tree, continued to suffer his punishment for a while, and died.

When the Samnites learned of these events, they did not punish the children. Not only that, but divining from the events, they also maintained that Belisarios would win a decisive victory.

Prokopios

The children's play is set in the context of the Gothic War, which took place in the sixth century AD between the Eastern Roman Empire ruled by Justinian and the Ostrogothic Kingdom of Italy ruled by Wittigis. Belisarios was Justinian's general.

93. A CHILD STEALS FROM THE GODDESS

Hypereides says that the young child of the priestess at Brauron took one of the offerings that had been given to the goddess.

To test his understanding, a one-drachma coin and a four-drachma coin were placed side by side, and when he chose the four-drachma coin, it was concluded that he could make discriminations of value.

Pollux

***

A young child picked up a golden leaf that had fallen from the garland of a statue of Artemis. But someone had observed the act. So the judges placed toys and knucklebones in front of the child, along with the leaf. Again he went for the gold. For this reason they put him to death for sacrilege, not forgiving him on account of his age but punishing him for his deed.

Aelian

These two texts are perhaps different accounts of the same event. Brauron, on the east coast of Attica, was the site of a well-known sanctuary of Artemis. The knucklebones set before the child were, like the toys, objects of play, since the ancients employed knucklebones as dice.

A recurrent theme in narratives of children's misdemeanors is the question of whether a child should be held responsible for an act that in the adult world is criminal.

FRIENDS

Many sets of devoted friends—always pairs, always males—are celebrated in Greek and Roman tradition, and lists of them were even compiled (Plutarch On Having Many Friends *2; Hyginus* Fabulous Tales *257; cf. Cameron 2004:240–241). Friendship was an important theme of Pythagoreanism, and the relationship of Damon and Phintias, below, crystallized the Pythagorean ideal.*

94. DAMON AND PHINTIAS

Dionysios, who had been driven from power and had come to Corinth, frequently told us about his experience with the Pythagoreans Phintias and Damon. It had to do with surety for a condemned man, and went as follows.

There were, he said, men in his circle who often brought up the subject of the Pythagoreans, whom they disparaged and mocked, calling them boasters and saying that this pomposity of theirs, this pretended good faith, this indifference to suffering would vanish if someone should put them into a state of sufficient fear. However, other persons disputed this claim and an argument arose, so that the following drama was concocted against Phintias and his fellows. Dionysios sent for Phintias, and one of the man's accusers spoke against him, saying that Phintias and others were openly plotting against Dionysios, and all present gave testimony to this effect, which made the charge quite persuasive.

Phintias was astonished at the accusation, but Dionysios expressly declared that he had examined the matter carefully and that Phintias was to be put to death. Since, Phintias said, Dionysios had made up his mind, he asked to be granted the remainder of the day to settle his affairs as well as those of Damon. The two men lived together and held all their possessions in common, and Phintias had assumed responsibility for most of the household management, being the elder of the two. He requested, then, to be released to deal with these matters, naming Damon as his surety. Surprised, Dionysios asked him if a person really existed who would consent to stand surety for a condemned man. Phintias said he did. Damon was sent for, and after he heard what had happened he declared that he would stand surety and remain there until Phintias should return. Dionysios was astonished, whereas the men who had originally proposed the test scoffed at Damon for being about to be left in the lurch. He was, they said mockingly, the deer that had been substituted for the victim.

It was around sundown when Phintias showed up to be executed, which amazed and subdued everyone. Dionysios himself embraced and kissed the men, and asked them to accept him as a third member of their friendship, but for all his persistent entreaties, they would not consent to do so.

Iamblichos

Some versions of this legend ratchet up the tension toward the end by delaying the return of Phintias (or Pythias, as some authors call him), who may be given several days, rather than several hours, to settle his affairs. According to Diodoros of Sicily (10.4), people flocked together in suspense to see if the condemned man would return, and just when they were giving up and Damon was being led away for execution, Phintias came running.

Dionysios the Younger, tyrant of Syracuse (367–357 BC), settled in Corinth following the liberation of Syracuse. There he was fond of telling the present story, in which he had played a part. It is a fine touch that in the end the tyrant asks to be admitted to the friendship of the two Pythagoreans, and it is an even finer touch that they refuse him. He was not, after all, a Pythagorean.

Among later treatments of the legend is the drama Damon and Pythias *by the Irish author John Banim, produced in 1821. Banim's play, with its ideology of fraternal love and friendship, inspired Justus H. Rathbone in 1864 to found a fraternal secret society, the Order of the Knights of Pythias. Created during the American Civil War (1861–1865), the fraternal order was seen as offering a timely message of reconciliation between warring brothers (Carnahan 1892).*

95. FRIENDS UNKNOWN

It is said that the Pythagoreans, even if they did not know each other, strove to do deeds of friendship on behalf of persons they had never set eyes upon if they had evidence that they shared the same doctrines. So one can believe from such actions the story that earnest men, though dwelling very far from one another, are friends with each other before they become known to and meet each other.

In any case they say that a Pythagorean, going on a long and solitary journey by foot, turned in to lodge at a particular inn, and from weariness and various causes he fell into a long and serious illness such that he exhausted his provisions. The innkeeper, whether from pity for the man or from kindness, provided him with everything, sparing neither personal attention nor expense. As the illness became worse and the man was dying, the Pythagorean elected to write a particular symbol on a placard, and instructed the innkeeper, if anything should happen to him, to hang the placard alongside the road and observe whether any of the passersby recognized the symbol. For, he said, this man would compensate the innkeeper for all the expenditures he made on his behalf, and would thank him for the favor shown him.

After the man's death the innkeeper buried him and tended to his body, though he did not nurture any hopes of recouping his expenses, let alone of benefitting from anyone who should recognize the placard. Nevertheless, struck by the man's instructions, he put the matter to the test by displaying the placard in public.

A long time later a Pythagorean who was passing by stopped there, learned who had displayed the symbol, inquired about what had happened, and paid the innkeeper a sum far in excess of what he had expended.

Iamblichos

Part of the fascination of this narrative is the mysterious symbol by means of which Pythagoreans recognized one another. This symbol is the pentagram, which members of the sect understood as being a triple intersecting triangle. Their name for it was "health" (Lucian On a Slip of the Tongue *5).*

96. ABAUCHAS'S CHOICE

This fellow Abauchas once came to the city of the Borysthenites with his wife, whom he loved greatly, and his two children. One of them, a boy, was still breast-feeding, and the other child, a daughter, was seven years old. A companion of his who was also traveling with them, Gyndanes, was suffering from a wound he had gotten when highwaymen attacked them during their journey. As he was fighting with them, he had been pierced in the thigh so that he was unable to stand because of the pain.

During the night as they were sleeping, which happened to be on an upper floor, a great fire broke out that completely cut them off, the flames surrounding them in the house on all sides. At that point Abauchas woke up, left his wailing children, shook off his wife, who was clinging to him, and told her to save herself. Picking up his companion, he managed to break through a place that had not yet been completely burnt away by the fire. His wife came after him carrying the infant and telling their daughter to follow them. Half-burnt, she let the child fall from her arms and with difficulty leapt through the flames, and her daughter with her, who also came close to perishing.

Later when someone reproached Abauchas for abandoning his children and wife and rescuing Gyndanes, he said, "Well, I can easily beget children again, and it's not at all certain whether my present children will turn out well. But I wouldn't find another friend for a long time like Gyndanes, who has given me much proof of his devotion."

Lucian

In the legend of Abauchas the protagonist chooses surprisingly to save his friend rather than his wife or child. In another variant (80 "Intaphrenes's Wife") of this international plot the protagonist chooses to save her brother rather than her husband.

RULERS AND TYRANTS

97. PLATO TEACHES A TYRANT ABOUT DEMOCRACY

They say when the tyrant Dionysios wanted to learn about the government of Athens, Plato sent him the poetry of Aristophanes and advised him to learn about their government by putting Aristophanes's dramas into practice.

Life of Aristophanes

The anecdote attests both to the extremely free speech that is characteristic of Athenian Old Comedy and also to Plato's fondness for the comic poet Aristophanes, whom he portrays genially in his Symposium. *The philosopher is said to have made three visits to the courts of the Syracusan tyrants Dionysios the Elder (ruled 405–367 BC) and Dionysios the Younger (ruled 367–357 BC), father and son, over a period of some twenty-five years, and there are many anecdotes about the supposed conversations of Plato and the two Syracusan tyrants. The encounter of sage and ruler (Solon and Croesus, Diogenes and Alexander, Secundus and Hadrian, etc.), or wisdom and power, was a favorite theme of ancient storytelling.*

98. THE CITY OF FORBIDDEN EXPRESSION

A certain tyrant of Troizen wishing to do away with any conspiracies and plots against himself, issued an order to the local people that no one was to speak to anyone else either publicly or privately.

Since the situation was difficult and all but unmanageable, the people dealt with the tyrant's order craftily. They would nod to one another, employ gestures toward one another, and give looks that were bitter or calm or cheerful. At sad or hopeless matters people knitted their brow into an obvious frown, displaying their feelings to nearby persons by their face.

But these signals also vexed the tyrant, who believed that on account of the intricate gesturing even silence might bring about some sort of harm to him. So he put a stop to this also.

The people, feeling oppressed by and angry at the impossibility of their situation, thirsted to put an end to the monarchy, and one of them went to the marketplace and stood there weeping profusely. People came and crowded around him, and they too were afflicted with lamentation. A message reached the tyrant that no one was employing nods anymore, and tears were now the usual medium.

Eager to stop this, too, and condemning not only the use of the tongue and the use of nods but also the natural freedom of the eyes, he arrived as quickly as he could with his bodyguards to suppress the crying. But the people spotted him and acted first, seizing the bodyguards' weapons and killing the tyrant.

Aelian

This strange tale of paranoia and oppression is more surreal than realistic. The only gesture it makes toward historicity is its vague localization in Troizen, a city-state southeast of Argos.

99. ISMENIAS'S SUBTERFUGE

I wish to mention something done by Ismenias of Thebes that was clever and quite Greek.

Acting as an envoy on behalf of his country, Ismenias went to the king of the Persians and wished to meet personally with the Persian monarch about the business for which he had come. Now, the chiliarch (that is, the man who brought messages to the king and escorted petitioners in) told him, "Theban visitor"—the chiliarch, named Tithraustes, spoke in Persian through an interpreter—"it is a national custom among the Persians that a man coming before the king not engage in speech until he has prostrated himself before the king. So if you wish to meet with him personally, this is the time for you to act according to custom. Otherwise, if you don't prostrate yourself, the same result will be achieved by us on your behalf."

Ismenias responded, "Lead me in." Going on and coming into view of the king, Ismenias removed the ring he happened to be wearing, surreptitiously tossed it at his feet, quickly bent down as if he were prostrating himself, and picked it up again. He thereby gave the Persian king the impression of obeisance, while in fact he did not do anything that would make a Greek feel shameful. So he accomplished all that he wished, and did not fail in getting what he wished from the Persian king.

Aelian

The anecdote crystallizes the Greek view of the Hellene as opposed to the oriental. The Westerner views the Eastern manner of expressing deference to a superior as a humiliation. Ismenias discreetly improvises a deceit such that he satisfies his Persian hosts while maintaining his own sense of dignity.

100. QUEEN FOR A DAY

Different persons praise Semiramis the Assyrian in different ways. She was the loveliest of women, even if she managed her beauty rather artlessly.

She went to the king of Assyria, having been invited by him for her renowned beauty, and when the king met her he fell in love with her. She asked the king if she might have the royal robe and rule Asia for five days, during which time everyone would do what she ordered. Her request was granted.

After the king seated her on his throne and she knew that she had everything in her full control, she commanded the bodyguards to kill the king.

This is how she gained control of the Assyrian Empire.

Aelian

This legend is one of many attached to Queen Semiramis (Sammu-ramat), who ruled Assyria in the ninth century BC. The unfortunate king is Ninos.

101. THE ABSENTMINDED EMPEROR

Among other things people wondered at Claudius's forgetfulness and absentmindedness, or, as they say in Greek, his *meteoria* and *ablepsia* [= forgetfulness and inattentiveness]. Shortly after he had had Messalina put to death, he reclined at table in the dining room and inquired why the empress had not come. He condemned many persons to death and the next morning had them summoned to confer or play dice with him, sending a messenger to reprove them for being sleepyheads, as though they were slow in coming.

Suetonius

Valeria Messalina, the promiscuous wife of the Roman emperor Claudius (ruled AD 41–54), was compelled by him to commit suicide. The forgetful ruler ordered the execution of this or that person and then wondered why he or she was no longer around.

JUSTICE

102. ZEUS'S LEDGER

Zeus ordered Hermes to inscribe
The misdeeds and unjust acts of human beings
On potsherds and pile them up in a chest next to him
In order that, after examining them, he might exact the penalty
From each person. Since the potsherds lie heaped up

One upon another, they come into Zeus's hand
For auditing, some more slowly
And others more quickly.
So no one should be surprised
If some evildoers misbehave early but fare ill late.

Babrios

The text is not so much a myth or tale as a folk idea about a divine process. Stories are wont to reflect contemporary technology, so that after Greeks and Romans adopt writing for record-keeping, they imagine, if only half-seriously, that their gods do so, too. So also today, supernatural judges from god to Santa Claus are popularly thought to keep a ledger in which they record the pluses and minuses of human behavior. Zeus, however, records only misdeeds.

103. THE GOLDEN AX

A man who was cutting wood alongside a river accidentally dropped his ax, and when the stream swept it away, he sat upon the riverbank and wept, until Hermes came along and took pity on him. When the god learned the reason for the man's grief, he descended into the water and brought up first a golden ax, asking the man if it was his. When he said it was not, Hermes descended and the second time brought up a silver ax, again asking if it was the one he had dropped. After the man said that it was not, the third time Hermes fetched the man his own ax. The man acknowledged it, and Hermes, seeing he was an honest man, let him have all the axes.

The man returned with the axes to his companions and related to them what had happened. One of them, casting an envious glance at the axes, wished to have the same success. So, picking up his ax, he went to the same river, and as he was cutting wood he purposely let his ax fall into the eddies. Then he sat down and began to cry. When Hermes appeared and inquired what had happened, he told him about losing his ax. Hermes brought up the golden one and asked if it was the one he had lost, and the man, overcome with greed, declared that it was. The god did not give it to him, and did not restore his own ax either.

anonymous

In traditional narratives, especially in wonder tales, a donor figure may appear out of nowhere, as it were, to a character in need, test the character (for kindness, generosity, honesty, etc.), and, if the character passes, provide him or her with helpful information or a needed object. Here the role of donor is played by the god Hermes, who was inter alia the god of lucky finds, called hermaia *by the Greeks.*

The tale is constructed upon the narrative device of unsuccessful repetition, as in the legend of Pandaros and Echedoros (see 8 "Asklepios Heals Pandaros").

104. THE JUDGE OF THE ANTS

A ship once sank along with everyone onboard, and
A man who saw it declared that the gods decided matters unjustly,
"If one impious man is aboard a ship,
Many innocent persons die along with him."
As he was saying this, the sort of thing that happens—
A swarm of ants came upon him
In their eagerness to nibble on some wheat chaff—
And when one of them bit him, he stomped on most of the others.
Hermes appeared and said, as he struck the man with his staff,
"So, then, won't you let the gods
Be your judges the way you are the judge of the ants?"

Babrios

In this religious tale a deity reveals the justice of an apparently unjust act, or at least affirms the divine prerogative to act in an apparently unjust way. The lesson is that as ants (bees, wasps, etc.) are to humans, so humans are to the gods. Hermes, in his role as mediator between cosmic realms, serves as the divine spokesman.

105. TARPEIA'S REWARD

Another war with the Sabines arose, and it was by far the most serious since the enemy did not act impulsively from anger or greed, nor did they declare war before waging it. And they combined conventional strategy with trickery.

Spurius Tarpeius was in charge of the Roman citadel. His maiden daughter Tarpeia was bribed by Tatius to let armed men into the citadel. She had gone outside the walls, as it happened, to fetch water for use at a sacrifice. Once the men had gotten inside, they killed her by piling their shields on her, either to make it appear that the citadel had been captured by force or as an example of treachery, to illustrate that no trust should ever be given to a traitor.

There is also a story that in exchange for her help she asked for what the men bore on their left hands. For the Sabines commonly wore heavy bracelets made of gold on their left arms as well as exquisite rings with gems. The Sabines gifted her, not with gold, but with their shields, which they heaped upon her.

Livy

In this Roman historic legend, set in the days of Romulus, a maiden betrays her countrymen in general and her father in particular by admitting the enemy Sabines into the Roman citadel on the Capitoline hill. Her motive is greed, or perhaps merely a young girl's weakness for ornament, for she agrees to betray the citadel in return for what the Sabine warriors bear on their left arms, by which she means their jewelry, though the attackers honor their bargain in word only when they instead give her their shields, which they also bear on their left arms, piling them upon her and crushing her.

In some versions Tarpeia's motive is love. In this case she is driven by her passion for the Sabine king, Titus Tatius, who nevertheless spurns her. But there is not much difference between the two motives, both being infatuations that induce the girl to choose personal gratification over the well-being of her community.

106. THE CRANES OF IBYKOS

When Ibykos was seized by robbers in a desolate place, he declared that the cranes which happened to be flying overhead would avenge him. Then he was killed. Later, when one of the robbers was in the city and saw some cranes, he said, "Look, the avengers of Ibykos." Someone heard him and prosecuted him. He confessed, and the robbers were punished.

From this incident there arose a proverbial expression: "The cranes of Ibykos."

Suda

* * *

Weren't the men who killed Ibykos caught in the same way? They were sitting in a theater when some cranes appeared, and they began laughing and whispering to one another that the avengers of Ibykos had come. Persons sitting nearby heard them, and since Ibykos had been missing for a long time and was being sought, they latched on to this remark and reported it to the authorities.

Plutarch

Plutarch, recounting how a certain crime was solved as a consequence of the perpetrator's own talkativeness, is reminded of the legend of Ibykos, a Greek lyric poet of the sixth century BC.

107. THE MURDER OF MITYS OF ARGOS

The tragic is an imitation not only of a complete action but also of events that are fearful and piteous. Events have this quality especially when they are unexpected as well as causally connected, for they are then more surprising than if they occur of themselves or by chance. Of chance events the most astonishing seem to be those that appear to happen by design, as when the statue of Mitys in Argos killed the man responsible for Mitys's death by falling upon him while he was attending a religious festival. Such things do not *seem* to happen randomly.

Aristotle

***

Is it not better for punishments to occur at a fitting time and in a fitting manner rather than swiftly or immediately?

An example is the case of Kallipos, whose friends killed him with the same dagger that he used when he, pretending to be a friend, killed Dion. Another is the case of Mitys the Argive, who had been killed in a factional dispute. During a spectacle in the marketplace the bronze statue of Mitys fell upon the man who had slain Mitys, and killed him.

Plutarch

For Aristotle the interest of these events is that they illustrate the effect a narrative achieves when the incidents combine chance with the appearance *of design, whereas for Plutarch the death of Mitys's murderer does not merely appear to happen by design but does happen by design. He cites the legend to illustrate his contention that although the gods are sometimes slow to punish wrongdoers, they compensate by exacting their punishment at an appropriate time and in an appropriate manner. In this case the manner is the victim's statue as the instrument of punishment, and the occasion is a festival, so that the death of the killer amounts to a public execution (Else 1963:334–335). See also story 172 "Theagenes's Statue."*

The fact that this narrative is felt to be a story *even if its two events—the slaying of Mitys and the subsequent death of his slayer—are not regarded as causally linked, has prompted reflection on the nature of story from Aristotle to the present (e.g., Velleman 2003:5–7; G. Currie 2010:29–32, 38).*

108. AN EYE FOR AN EYE

Zaleukos, the lawgiver of the Lokrians, ordained that persons convicted of adultery should have their eyes put out. But contrary to expectation and hope, fate brought against him what he certainly had not anticipated. His own son was convicted of adultery and was going to suffer the penalty under his father's law.

In order not to undermine a law that had been ratified, Zaleukos himself, its introducer, undertook to give an eye of his own in place of one of his son's eyes so that the young man would not be completely blind.

Aelian

This legend is one of several about Greek lawgivers who introduce a law and ironically are among the first to fall victim to its effects, as when Kleisthenes introduced the idea of legal ostracism into Athens and was the first person whom the Athenians ostracized. The central character in the present story, Zaleukos, was active around the seventh century BC.

109. THE TRIAL OF THE COURTESAN PHRYNE

Phryne was brought to trial by Euthias on a capital charge but was acquitted, and for this reason, Hermippos says, Euthias angrily stated that he would never again plead a case.

Hypereides spoke on behalf of Phryne. When he was not achieving anything with words and the judges seemed likely to convict, he brought her into the open and tore off her shift, baring her breasts and declaiming piteously at the sight of her in his peroration, which caused the judges to feel superstitious fear toward this interpreter and ministrant of Aphrodite, and to indulge their pity and not execute her.

After her acquittal a decree was passed that no one speaking on behalf of a defendant should lament piteously, nor should the defendant, either man or woman, be an object of viewing while being tried.

Athenaios

The hetaera Phryne was so beautiful that she served as model for the painter Apelles when he painted his Aphrodite Rising from the Sea (Anadyomene) *as well as for the sculptor Praxiteles when he sculpted his Aphrodite of Knidos. She was tried on a capital offense around 350 BC.*

***

Hypereides had an intimate relationship with the courtesan Phryne, it is reasonable to suppose, and so became her advocate when she was being tried for impiety. Indeed, he makes this clear at the beginning of his speech.

When she was going to be convicted, he brought her out into the middle of the court and tore off the woman's clothes and displayed her breasts. When the judges saw her beauty, they acquitted her.

Pseudo-Plutarch

***

When Phryne, as they say, was going to be condemned and Hypereides was acting as her advocate, she tore off her shift, and with bare breasts prostrated herself before the judges. She had more power to persuade the judges by means of her beauty than her advocate did by means of his rhetoric.

Sextus Empiricus

The ripping of the defendant's clothing by Hypereides or by Phryne herself was intended to arouse the judges' pity, and the baring of her breasts was meant, one supposes, to astonish the judges with her beauty, as someone who was too lovely to execute. As a courtesan and as a model for artists portraying Aphrodite, Phryne virtually embodied the goddess she served.

*The story has an interesting parallel in heroic legend. At the fall of Troy, Menelaos confronted his unfaithful wife Helen and was about to slay her, but she bared her breasts to him, and he relented (*Little Iliad *fr. 17 Allen; Euripides* Andromache *627–631; Aristophanes* Lysistrata *155; Edmunds 2016: 148–150).*

110. THE PROBLEM OF DREAMT SEX

The compilers of stories tell of a judgment by Bokchoris the Just, as follows.

A young man passionately desired a courtesan and persuaded her to come to him the next day at a price agreed upon in advance. But his desire anticipated the girl in a dream so that he was unexpectedly satisfied, and when she arrived at the appointed time, he turned her away.

After she learned what had happened, she demanded her wage, saying that in any case it was she who had fulfilled his desire. They came before a judge. He instructed the young man to hold out his coin purse with the payment, and to do so in the sunlight, and ordered the courtesan to take hold of its shadow, cleverly instructing the young man to repay the phantom of sexual embrace with a phantom of compensation.

Plutarch

The Egyptian king Bokchoris (ca. 8th century BC), nicknamed the Just, was renowned in tradition for his wise and clever judgments, which were recounted in a cycle of stories: "He was so wise in his judicial decisions," remarks Diodoros of Sicily (1.94.5), "that many of the judgments made by him are remembered for their excellence up to our own time."

* * *

There is in circulation Lamia's response to the well-known judgment given by Bokchoris.

A man in Egypt passionately desired the courtesan Thonis, who demanded a great amount of money. Then he imagined having sexual intercourse with her in his dreams and lost his desire for her.

Thonis sued him in court for her fee. After Bokchoris heard the case, he instructed the man to count out into a container the sum of money that had been asked of him, and move it back and forth in his hand, and he instructed the courtesan to take hold of its shadow on the grounds that something imagined is the shadow of the real thing.

Lamia did not think this judgment was just, since the shadow of the money did not release the courtesan from her desire, whereas the dream did put an end to the passion of the young man.

Clement of Alexandria

The story of quasi sex being answered by quasi payment is an international comic tale that in other forms is also told of nonsexual situations. Normally the story concludes with the judge's clever judgment, but here the plaintiff has the last word. Lamia was a well-known courtesan of the third century BC who figures in a number of anecdotes. "Lamia" was her professional, not her given, name.

III. THE DISPUTED CHILD

. . . so that some judicial decisions that seem to have been uttered on other occasions have been transferred to him. Philiskos of Miletos, for example, wrote that in the case of the two women who were both laying claim to a child, each of them alleging she had given birth to it, he gave orders to cut it in two and give half to each of them.

anonymous

This is of course the legend of the judge who must decide the case of the infant child claimed by two different women. Shockingly, the judge orders that the child be cut in two, and half given to each claimant. When one of the women then withdraws her claim in order to spare the child, the judge recognizes her as the true mother and awards her the child. Although to us the most familiar version of the narrative is that told of the biblical King Solomon (3 Kings 3:16–28), the story is known from Europe to India and is related of many different characters.

The present text comes from a papyrus fragment in which an unknown author discusses how judicial decisions made by different judges have become attributed

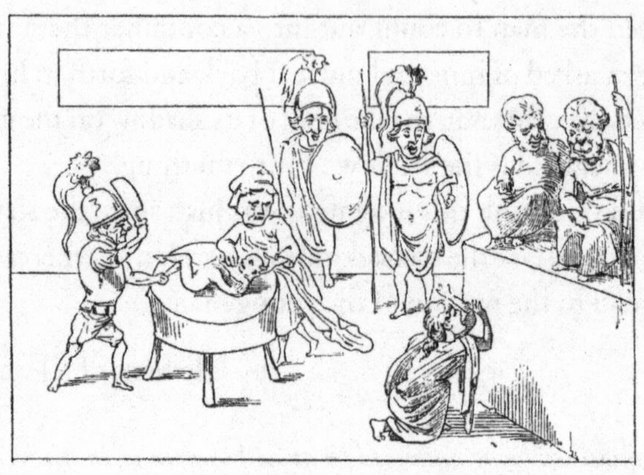

to a single judge, here unnamed. He takes his example from Philiskos of Miletos, a rhetorician of the fourth century BC.

* * *

A remarkable wall painting, which obviously illustrates the story of the disputed child, was discovered in an ancient house in Pompeii in 1882. It portrays the moment at which the judge's order to cut the infant in half is about to be carried out, while the true mother tearfully pleads with the judge. The characters are represented as pygmies, perhaps a comic touch, but they may also serve to locate the events in Egypt, home of the wise king Bokchoris, who was renowned for his judicial decisions (see 110 "The Problem of Dreamt Sex"). The painting was made before AD 79, when Pompeii was destroyed by the eruption of nearby Mt. Vesuvius.

112. ABUSIVE SON OF AN ABUSIVE FATHER

We more readily forgive persons who are acting on natural appetites, since we more readily forgive desires that are common to all persons and to the extent that they are common to all persons. For example, anger or a bad temper is more natural than a desire for extravagant and unnecessary things, as in the case of the man who was defending himself for beating his father, saying, "My father here used to beat his father, and he in turn used to beat his before him, and"—pointing to his son—"when he grows up, he'll beat me. It's inborn in us." And similarly the man who, when he was being dragged by his son, told him to stop at the doorway, saying that he himself had dragged his own father only that far.

Aristotle

Aristotle's second example alludes to an international novella in which a man drags his aged father to the door of his house (or to the gate of the yard). When he himself becomes an old man, his sons likewise drag him, and when they reach the door (or the gate), the old man points out that he dragged his own father no farther than this.

CHAPTER 4

TRICKSTERS AND LOVERS

This chapter brings together legends and novelle on the themes of love, lust, and cleverness.

TRICKERY AND CLEVERNESS

113. TROPHONIOS AND AGAMEDES

In accordance with an oracle King Erginos took to himself a young wife, and Trophonios and Agamedes were born to him. (It is said that Trophonios's father was Apollon and not Erginos. I myself believe it and so does anyone else who goes to consult his oracle.) People say that when these boys grew up they became very skillful at constructing temples for the gods and palaces for men. It was they who built the temple of Apollon at Delphi as well as the treasury of Hyrieus.

This latter building they constructed in such a way that they could remove one of the stones from the outside, and they made a regular practice of taking some of the goods stored there. Hyrieus was speechless, seeing that the lock and the rest of the seals were unmoved, whereas the number of his valuables was continually decreasing. And so above the chests in which his silver and gold were stored he set traps or some other device that would hold fast anyone who entered and laid hold of his valuables. When Agamedes entered, the fetter held him, but Trophonios cut off his head so that his brother might not suffer outrage in the morning and he himself not be denounced as a partner in the enterprise.

Later the earth opened up and received Trophonios in that spot in the grove in Lebadeia where the so-called Pit of Agamedes and the nearby stele are located.

Pausanias

This legend is attached to the site in Boeotia where, according to tradition, the earth swallowed Trophonios, and provides an aition, *or origin story, for his famous underground oracle. The underlying story is migratory. For another realization of the type, see 2 "The Treasury of Rhampsinitos," and for more on the oracle itself see 77 "The Man Who Loses His Laugh."*

114. THE DISHONEST BANKER

A certain man of Miletos, whose homeland was being threatened by Kyros's general, Harpagos, sailed to Tauromenion in Sicily, where he deposited his gold with a banker who was a friend of his. Then he sailed home.

Subsequently Miletos did indeed become subject to Kyros, although it suffered none of the other misfortunes that had been expected. So the Milesian went back to Tauromenion to recover the deposit he had entrusted to the banker. But the latter, while acknowledging that he had received the gold, stoutly maintained that he had returned it. After much quarreling and arguing, the Milesian challenged the wrongdoer to swear an oath.

The banker now devised the following stratagem. He hollowed out a stalk, as when one makes a flute, melted down the deposit, poured it into the stalk, and secured it. Setting out to tender his oath, he held the stalk like a walking stick and leaned upon it on the pretext of a weakness in his legs. As he was about to swear the oath, and the Milesian was standing next to him, he handed the stalk to him with the intention of taking it back again immediately. But when the banker lifted his hands and swore that he had returned the deposit to the depositor, the Milesian was so upset that he threw down the stalk, crying out that Good Faith had disappeared from among mankind. The stalk broke, and at the sight of the gold the perjurious trick became obvious.

So the Milesian had his own property again, and the banker, because of the shame he felt and the abuse he received from everyone else, took his own life with a noose.

Konon

115. THE JOINT DEPOSITORS

Demosthenes's cleverness once came to the aid of a certain old woman in an impressive way. Two guests had deposited an amount of money with her on the condition that she return it to them both at the same time. A while later one of the men, dressed in the filthy clothes of a mourner as though his comrade had died, tricked the woman and made off with all the coins. Subsequently the other man also came and began asking for the deposit. The poor woman, stuck equally between not having the money and not having a defense, was ready to hang herself.

Opportunely Demosthenes appeared as her advocate, and when he came to plead he said, "The woman is prepared to discharge her trust as depositary; however, she cannot do so since, as you yourself have proclaimed, the stated rule was that the money was not to be paid out to one of you without the other."

Valerius Maximus

116. THE TWO THIEVES

A boy sat crying at a well, at the water's edge,
Blubbering with open mouth.
When a sly thief saw him and the tears that had arisen, and
Asked the reason for his present grief,
The boy contrived a story that his rope had broken in two,
Complaining that his crock of gold had fallen to the bottom.
Without delay the man's shameless hand tugged off his clothing,
 and
Now stripped bare, he made his way to the bottom of the well.
The little boy placed the man's cloak around his small neck,
Plunged into some brambles, they say, and hid.
But the man, after facing danger for a deceitful wish,
Sat sadly on the ground, his clothing gone,
Giving vent, it is said, to his complaints and

Disturbing the gods on high with his moans:
"After this, whoever thinks an urn can float upon the clear waters
May suppose there's a good reason why he's lost his cloak."

Avianus

In this humorous tale of thief tricking thief, it is ironically the younger thief who is the trickster's trickster. Avianus does not tell the tale as effectively as he might, for he need not reveal so early in his narration that the boy is only pretending to have lost his gold, and the reference at the end to a floating urn does not jibe with what is said earlier. The narrator casts the tale as a fable, which is why at the conclusion the character who has learned a lesson explains what he has learned.

117. AESOP AND THE FIGS

Aesop's master regarded him as useless for service in town and sent him to one of his properties to do some digging. When Aesop was in the field, a farmhand collected some very fine figs and brought them to Aesop's master, saying, "Master, take these early fruits of your crop." The master was delighted and said, "By my health, these are fine figs." To his household slave he said, "Agathopous, take these and keep them for me. Serve them to me after I've bathed and had my lunch." It happened that at this hour Aesop returned from his work and went to the house in search of his daily bread.

Agathopous took the figs and, hungering after them, ate one or two. He said to one of his fellow slaves, "I wanted to satisfy myself with the figs, but now I'm afraid." The other said to him, "If I eat some along with you, I'll give you an idea of how we can eat them without being whipped." Agathopous said, "How?" The other said, "The two of us will eat the figs, and if the master looks for them, you tell him that Aesop saw an opportunity, came in, and ate all the figs. Since Aesop is handicapped so far as making a defense is concerned, he'll get whipped and we'll satisfy our desire." So they sat down with the figs and began eating them one by one, saying, "Poor Aesop!" Making an agreement between themselves then and

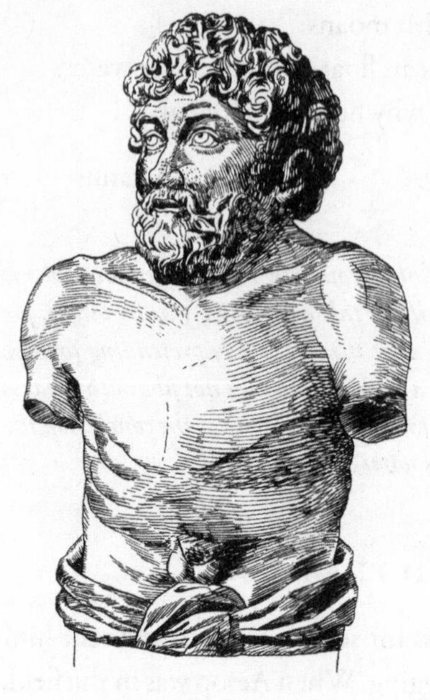

there that if anything ever got broken or spilled they would say that Aesop did it, they ate all the figs.

The master, having had his bath and lunch, said, "Agathopous, give me the figs." Agathopous said, "Master, Aesop saw an opportunity, found the pantry open, and ate all the figs." The master said angrily, "Someone call Aesop for me!" When Aesop appeared, the master said, "Tell me, you piece of crap, are you so disdainful of me that you went to the pantry and ate all the figs that were prepared for me?"

Aesop heard him but was unable to speak because of his defect of speech. Seeing his accusers face to face and finding himself about to be whipped, he fell at the feet of his master and begged him to hold off a bit. Aesop took a pitcher, filled it with warm water, placed a basin on the table, and drank it. Then he stuck his fingers into his mouth, forced himself to vomit, and, since he had not eaten anything, threw up only the water he had drunk. He asked that his accusers do the same, and then the master would know who ate the figs.

Amazed at Aesop's mind, the master ordered the other slaves to do the same. The slaves planned to stick their fingers alongside their jaws and not down their throats, but as soon as they drank the warm water and leaned forward, the figs, which were producing bile, gushed up along with the water. Then the master said, "How could you make false accusations against a person who can't speak?" He ordered them to be stripped and beaten.

They learned the lesson clearly that whoever engineers deceits against another, unwittingly engineers them against himself.

Life of Aesop

In his younger years Aesop was a mute and deformed slave, as here. Subsequently the goddess Isis and the Muses granted him the ability not only to speak but also to devise tales. Eventually Aesop gained his freedom and won renown for his cleverness and wisdom, as illustrated in the following tale.

118. NEVER HEARD BEFORE

King Nektanabo called a meeting of his associates and said, "As you see, on account of this accursed piece of garbage [= Aesop] I'll have to pay tribute to King Lykourgos." But one of his retainers said, "Let's ask him a riddle, saying 'What is it that we've neither seen nor heard?' No matter how cleverly he answers, we'll say that we've heard it and seen it before. Since he'll have no solution for that, he'll lose." The king was overjoyed to hear this plan, thinking that he had found a way to win.

When Aesop came, King Nektanabo said to him, "Solve just one more problem for us, and I'll pay tribute to Lykourgos. Name something that we've never seen or heard."

Aesop said, "Give me three days, and I'll answer you." Leaving the presence of the king, Aesop reasoned to himself, "Whatever I say, they'll assert they've seen it."

But being wily, Aesop sat down and crafted a note of a loan to the effect that Nektanabo had borrowed a thousand talents of gold from Lykourgos, adding that the loan had been given last year. When three days had passed, Aesop went to King Nektanabo and found him in the company of his retainers, awaiting Aesop, whom he expected to have no solution. But Aesop took out the false document and said, "Read this text of ours."

The retainers of King Nektanabo declared falsely, "We've seen and heard this many times."

Aesop said, "I'm happy for your attestation. The money should be repaid immediately, since repayment is now overdue."

But when King Nektanabo heard this he declared, "On what basis are you attesting to a loan that I don't owe?"

Thereupon they said, "We've never seen or heard it before."

So Aesop said, "If that's your response, then the riddle is solved."

Life of Aesop

King Lykourgos of Babylon and King Nektanabo of Egypt engage in contests of wit in which they pose problems to each other. The monarch who fails to solve a problem is required to pay tribute to the other. As the present passage begins, Aesop, representing the Babylonian king, is in Egypt, where the Egyptian ruler fears that, because of Aesop's cleverness, he will lose the current wager.

119. THE SLAVES TAKE OVER

Tyre was founded by Phoenicians, who, troubled by earthquakes, left behind the soil of their own land and established themselves first at the Syrian lake and presently on the shore alongside the sea. They founded a city there, which because of the abundance of fish they named Sidon, which is the Phoenician word for "fish." Many years later they were overcome by the king of Askalon, so they sailed elsewhere and, one year before the fall of Troy, founded the city of Tyre.

There they became worn down by fighting wars over a long period of time and with mixed success against the Persians. Although the Tyrians emerged victorious, their energy was diminished, with the result that they endured humiliation and indignities from their own slaves, who were grown very numerous. Conspiring together, the slaves slew the entire population of freemen including their masters and took possession of the city, seized their masters' houses, usurped their government, wed their wives, and begat what they themselves were not, freemen. Out of the many thousands of slaves there was one who, kindly by nature, was touched by the fate of his aged master and of his little son, and looked upon his masters not with savage fierceness but with pious humanity and compassion. And so he hid them away, as though they had been killed.

Deliberating about what form to give their government, the slaves decided that one of their own number should be made king, and in particular he who should be the first to see the sunrise, as being the person most acceptable to the gods. The slave conveyed this information to Straton (for this was the man's name), his master who lay secretly concealed. When at midnight everyone made their way to the same field and were looking eastward, he alone, having been so directed by his master, was looking toward the western quarter. At first they deemed it folly to look for the rising of the sun in the west, but when, with the approach of day, the rising sun began to shine upon the topmost parts of the city and the others were striving to look upon the sun itself, he was the first to point out to everyone the glow of the sun at the summit of the city.

This sort of intelligence did not seem to be that of a slave. When the other slaves asked him whose idea it was, he confessed about his master. Then they understood how much the natural capacity of freemen exceeded that of slaves, and how much slaves prevail by means of wickedness, not wisdom. The old man and his son were pardoned, and since the two seemed to have been preserved by some deity, Straton was made king. Upon his death the kingdom passed to his son and then to his grandsons.

Justin

Ideologically this historic legend about Tyre, a prosperous city of Phoenicia that lay south of Sidon and north of Galilee, reflects the common view of the ancients that the characteristics of slaves and free persons are not accidents of their status but intrinsic features of their nature. For their part, slaves are incompetent at higher reasoning and therefore fit only to be ruled. The character of the compassionate slave crystallizes the conceit of slave owners that their house slaves love them.

120. THE MILESIANS HOLD A PARTY

The Milesians say that Periander, son of Kypselos, was a very close friend of Thrasyboulos, ruler of Miletos at that time. Periander learned of an oracular response that had been given to Alyattes, and sent a messenger to tell Thrasyboulos everything so that he would know about the matter in advance and could deliberate about the present situation. That is what the Milesians say happened.

When the oracular response was reported to Alyattes, he immediately dispatched a herald to Miletos, since he wanted to make a truce with Thrasyboulos and the Milesians for the length of time that it would take to build a temple. The envoy set out for Miletos, but since Thrasyboulos had been clearly informed of the whole story and knew what Alyattes was going to do, he devised the following plan. He gathered together into the marketplace all the grain that was in the city, both his own and that in private hands, and proclaimed to the Milesians that when he gave the signal, they should all begin drinking and partying with one another. He did all this in order that the herald from Sardis might see a huge mound of grain piled up and the people enjoying themselves, and report this back to Alyattes. And that is what happened. After the herald had seen all this and delivered his message from the Lydian king to Thrasyboulos, he went back to Sardis. The reconciliation between the two rulers, as I learn, came about for no other reason than this.

Although Alyattes was expecting that there would be a severe scarcity of grain in Miletos and that the people would be worn down and in the extremities of misery, he heard the exact opposite from what he had supposed from his herald upon the man's return from Miletos. Following this, the reconciliation between them took place with the agreement that they become friends and allies. Alyattes build two temples to Athena in Assesos instead of one, and he recovered from his illness.

That is the story of Alyattes's war against the Milesians and Thrasyboulos.

Herodotos

The events leading up to this story are as follows. King Alyattes of Lydia was waging war against Miletos. Every year, as soon as the grain was ripe, his army marched into the territory of the Milesians, destroyed their trees and crops, and returned home. This routine continued for eleven years, but in the twelfth year, as the king's army was burning the Milesians' crops, the fire happened also to destroy a temple of

Athena, after which Alyattes fell sick and did not recover. When he sent a delegation to the oracle of Apollon at Delphi to ask the god about his illness, the Pythia declared that she would give the inquirers no oracle until they had rebuilt the temple of Athena. Alyattes intended then to seek a truce for this purpose. In the meantime the townsfolk, in an all-or-nothing gambit, staked their fate on a brave and desperate ruse whereby they gathered together the meager food that remained, pretending theatrically to their enemy that they were all but swimming in supplies. The ruse worked, and Alyattes lifted his siege.

121. SAVING LAMPSAKOS

The preservation of the city of Lampsakos was owed to a single trick. For when Alexander, earnestly intent on destroying it, saw his teacher Anaximenes coming outside the city walls—quite obviously to set his own entreaties against Alexander's anger—he swore an oath that he would not do what the man asked. So Anaximenes said, "I ask you to destroy Lampsakos."

Anaximenes's swift shrewdness rescued a town of ancient renown from the destruction to which it was headed.

Valerius Maximus

Alexander of Macedon was angry at the people of Lampsakos, a city in the northern Troad. The quick-thinking savior of the city is the historian and rhetorician Anaximenes of Lampsakos (ca. 380–320 BC), not the more familiar philosopher, Anaximenes of Miletos. His crafty move seems obvious, even childish, and worked only because Alexander honored his oath, which characters in traditional stories usually do as though they had no other choice.

122. THE SUCKLING DAUGHTER

A praetor found a free-born woman guilty of a capital crime at his tribunal and handed her over to the triumvir for execution in prison. She was received there, but the man in immediate charge of her custody, moved with pity, did not strangle her straightaway. Moreover, he permitted the woman's daughter to have access to her, although he did search the girl thoroughly beforehand to be sure that she did not bring in any food with her, for he was calculating that the woman would die of starvation.

After the passage of many days, however, the man asked himself how it was that his prisoner was holding out for so long. Observing the daughter more closely, he noticed her take out her breast and alleviate her mother's hunger with the help of her own milk. This novel and astonishing scene was reported by the jailer to the triumvir, by him to the praetor, and by him to the board of judges, and a remission of the woman's penalty was granted.

Where does Piety not penetrate, and what does she not devise? In prison she found a new way to save a parent. For is there anything so extraordinary, so unusual, as for a mother to be nourished by her own daughter's breasts? One might think this to be contrary to natural order, if it were not the first law of nature to esteem one's parents.

Valerius Maximus

123. A DONKEY'S SHADOW

Once when Demosthenes was being prevented by the Athenians from speaking in the assembly, he said he wanted to talk to them only briefly.

They became silent, and he said, "A young man hired a donkey in the summertime to go from the city to Megara. When it was midday and the sun was burning fiercely, both the young man and the donkey owner wanted to take refuge in the shadow of the donkey, but each man barred the other's way, one saying he had leased the donkey and not its shadow, and the other that he had hired the donkey and had full rights to it."

After saying this, Demosthenes started walking away. When the Athenians restrained him and asked him to finish the tale, he said, "So you're not willing to listen when I speak about serious matters, but you're willing enough to hear about a donkey's shadow."

Pseudo-Plutarch

Demosthenes's story is a catch tale, in which the narrator sets up the listener by relating an incomplete story, inducing him or her to ask a question for which the teller has a ready answer that makes the questioner appear foolish. "A donkey's shadow" was a proverbial expression for something completely valueless. The present story is one of several in which Greek public speakers express their exasperation at inattentive audiences or the like. Similar stories are told in later times of Christian preachers and their sleepy congregations.

124. THE HOAX

In my opinion, what happened was that some malevolent person inserted statements into the writings of Hippokrates for the purpose of exposing and unmasking these pitiful sophists and bringing their ignorance to light.

Indeed, one of our contemporaries, a man named Lucian, did the same thing. He produced a book in which he wrote down obscure utterances behind which no sense whatsoever lay concealed, and attributed it to Herakleitos. He presented the book to certain persons who in turn brought it to a philosopher whose word carried some weight with the populace and who enjoyed their credence and confidence. They asked him to comment upon it and explain it to them. Since that unfortunate man did not perceive that people wished only to make fun of him, he undertook to provide interpretations of each statement. Since he showed himself to be extremely clever in doing so, he made a fool of himself.

Lucian also produced a collection of apparently allusive expressions that rested upon pure nonsense, and sent them to some literary experts. They interpreted them and commented upon them, making fools of themselves.

Galen

The passage begins with an allusion to an event in which a young medical doctor in Pergamon took seriously the strange advice found in one of the Hippocratic writings for treating barrenness in a woman, which was to feed her a hot, half-cooked octopus. After employing the treatment, the doctor became the laughingstock of the city. Galen, a medical doctor himself, regards the supposedly Hippocratic prescription as nonsense and reproaches the commentators who trouble themselves with trying to understand it, since, in his view, it is a hoax.

This apparent hoax reminds Galen of a hoax whose status was not in doubt. Lucian, an author who took pleasure in exposing the pretensions of the pompous, falsely represented a composition of his own as being the work of the cryptic philosopher Herakleitos (5th century BC). The counterfeit work was taken for the real thing, to the dupe's discomfiture.

These hoaxes are predecessors of such modern-day chicanery as the Sokal Affair, in which physics professor Alan Sokal submitted to Social Text, *a journal specializing in postmodern cultural studies, an article titled "Transgressing the Boundaries: Towards a Transformative Hermeneutics of Quantum Gravity," which he had salted with dense, nonsensical statements about science and mathematics. After the article was published (in 1996), Sokal revealed that his essay was a hoax, prompting much discussion in academic circles.*

LOVERS AND SEDUCERS

125. ZEUS AND HERA WRANGLE OVER SEXUALITY

Among the Thebans there was a seer named Teiresias, son of Eueres and a nymph Chariklo, descended from the family of the Spartan Oudaios. Teiresias lost his sight, and different stories are told about his blinding and his powers as a seer. Some persons say that he was blinded by the gods because he had revealed to human beings matters that the gods wished to keep secret.

Pherekydes, however, says that he was blinded by Athena. For Chariklo was dear to Athena, but [some words have fallen out of the text here, such as "when Teiresias happened to come upon the goddess and"] saw her completely naked, she put her hands over his eyes and disabled his sight.

Chariklo asked Athena to restore his vision, but since Athena was unable to do this, she cleansed his ears, making him understand all the cries of birds, and she gave him a staff of cornel wood by means of which he was able to walk like sighted persons.

But Hesiod says that Teiresias saw snakes copulating on Mt. Kyllene, wounded them, and was transformed from a man into a woman, and that on another occasion he observed the same snakes copulating, and became a man. For this reason, when Hera and Zeus were arguing about whether men or women enjoyed sexual intercourse more, they asked Teiresias. He said that if sexual pleasure had ten parts, men enjoyed one tenth and women nine tenths. Because of this answer Hera blinded him, while Zeus granted him the power of prophecy.

Apollodoros

Two themes appear here. One is how Teiresias acquired his physical blindness as well as his second sight. The other is the relative pleasurability of sex for males and females. In the latter, Teiresias offended Hera by revealing the great secret of women, that their share of sexual pleasure is nine times greater than that of men, whereupon Hera blinded him, and in compensation Zeus endowed him with the insight of a seer.

Athena could not undo her maiming of Teiresias because there is ostensibly a rule that one supernatural being cannot undo something done by another supernatural being. But this supposed cosmic rule is simply a narrative necessity, for if actions could be reversed, stories would fall apart (Hansen 2005:40).

126. THE AFFAIR OF ARES AND APHRODITE

Playing his lyre, the bard began to sing the fine song of
The love of Ares and fair-garlanded Aphrodite,
How they mingled together in love the first time in Hephaistos's house
In secret. He showered her with gifts and shamed the bed and bedding of
Lord Hephaistos. But a messenger came to Hephaistos straightaway,
Helios, who had perceived the two mingling in love.
When Hephaistos had heard the heart-grieving news,

He went to his smithy, brooding on doing harm.
He set the great anvil in its block and began hammering out fetters,
Unbreakable and inescapable, in order that the two might remain fixed in place.
After he had crafted the trap in his anger at Ares,
He went to his bedroom, where there stood his dear bed, and
Around its legs he spread the bonds, in every place all round, and
Many sagged down also from the main roof beam
Like fine spiderwebs that no one could see,
Not even any of the blessed gods, for they had been wrought so artfully.
After he had laid the entire trap around the bed,
He pretended to depart for Lemnos, that well-settled town
Which of all lands was dearest to him.
  Ares of the golden reins kept no blind watch, and
Saw Hephaistos, famed craftsman, going away.
He went to the house of famed Hephaistos,
Desiring the love of fair-garlanded Aphrodite.
She had just come from her father, the powerful son of Kronos,
And sat down. He went into the house,
Clasped her hand, and spoke to her,
"Come here, my dear, and let's go to bed and take our pleasure.
Hephaistos is no longer around but already is
Gone to Lemnos, it seems, to visit the savage-tongued Sintians."
So he spoke, and it was a welcome idea to lie down.
They went to bed and lay down, but around them
The skillfully made bonds of inventive Hephaistos poured down,
And they could neither move any of their limbs nor raise them up.
Then they realized that escape was not possible.
  The famous lame god came near,
Having turned back before reaching the land of Lemnos,

For Helios kept watch for him and informed him.
He went to his house, troubled in his dear heart, and
Stood in the doorway, where a fierce anger seized him.
He uttered a terrible shout and called to all the gods,
"Father Zeus and you other blessed gods who exist forever,
Come here and see this outrageous and intolerable act,
How Zeus's daughter Aphrodite continually dishonors me,
A cripple, and loves destructive Ares
Since he is handsome and sound of foot, whereas I
Was born a weakling. But no one is to blame
Other than my parents, who ought not to have begotten me.
Now see where the two are lying down in love,
Having gone to my bed. I ache when I see them.
I don't expect they'll want to lie in this position for even a little
 while longer,
However much they are lovers. The two of them soon won't want
To sleep together. But my trick and fetters will restrain them
Until my father repays me the bride price,
All that I put into his hands for his bitch of a daughter,
His daughter who is beautiful but unrestrained."
 So he spoke, and the gods gathered at the house with its
 bronze floor.
Poseidon the earthholder came, and the runner
Hermes, and there came lord Apollon the worker-from-afar.
But the female goddesses stayed home from modesty, all of them.
The male gods, givers of good things, stood in the doorway,
And unquenchable laughter arose among the blessed gods
As they looked upon the cunning of inventive Hephaistos.
Thus one of them would say with a glance at another beside him,
"Bad deeds come to no good—the slow overtakes the swift,
Just as now Hephaistos, though slow, has caught Ares by craft,
Though he is swiftest of the gods who dwell on Olympos,

And Hephaistos is lame. Wherefore in fact he must pay the fine
for adultery."
They were talking in this way to one another, but
Lord Apollon, son of Zeus, addressed Hermes,
"Hermes, son of Zeus, guide and giver of good things,
Would you like to be pressed by fetters and
Lie in bed beside golden Aphrodite?" And
The guide and slayer of Argos answered him,
"Indeed I would, lord Apollon, far-shooter.
Though three times as many inescapable bonds confined me on
all sides,
And though you gods and the goddesses all looked on,
Still I would lie beside golden Aphrodite."
So he spoke, and laughter arose among the immortal gods.
But laughter did not grip Poseidon, who kept beseeching
Hephaistos, maker of famous works, to release Ares.
He addressed him, speaking winged words,
"Release him, and I myself promise that, as you bid,
He'll pay all that is fitting in the presence of the immortal gods."
The famous lame god addressed him in turn,
"Earthholder Poseidon, don't ask me to do this.
The pledges of the worthless are worthless.
How might I bind you among the immortal gods
If Ares goes and avoids both fetters and debt?"
Earthshaker Poseidon addressed him in turn,
"Hephaistos, if Ares should flee and
Evade his debt, I myself will pay it."
Then the famous lame god replied,
"It's not possible or proper to reject your word."
After he said this, the mighty Hephaistos unfastened the fetters.
When the two were released from their bond, strong though it was,
They straightaway leapt up, he going to Thrace, and
Laughter-loving Aphrodite, as you might expect, going to

Paphos, where she had a sanctuary and an altar fragrant with
incense.
There the Graces bathed and anointed her with
Ambrosial oil such as they put on the everlasting gods, and
They dressed her all around in lovely garments, amazing to look
upon.

Homer

The union of a lovely and desirable female and an old or deformed male is a virtual guarantee of marital instability of the sort that is exploited in bawdy novelle. This one bears the external trappings of myth in that the characters are assigned the names of gods, but apart from that it is an ordinary ribald novella set in the indefinite past in an anonymous village that operates according to the customs of Greek mortals, not Greek gods: bride price, adulterer's fine, and so on. Even the representation of Aphrodite and Hephaistos as a married couple is probably only a convenience for the sake of the present story. The tradition of Hephaistos's wife was fluid. She is Charis in Homer's Iliad *(18.382–383) and Aglaia in Hesiod's* Theogony *(945). The present novella is the sort that in later times was called Milesian by the Greeks and Romans.*

127. IPHIMEDEIA DESIRES POSEIDON

Aloeus wed Iphimedeia the daughter of Triops. But she, conceiving a passion for Poseidon, went continually to the sea, where she would draw up the waves with her hands and pour them upon her lap.

Poseidon had sexual intercourse with her, begetting two sons, Otos and Ephialtes, who are called the Aloads.

Apollodoros

A similar myth tells of a certain Tyro who conceived a passion for a river, Enipeus, to whose waters she would go and wail. There the god Poseidon, taking the likeness of Enipeus, lay with her (Apollodoros Library *1.9.8).*

128. HIPPOLYTOS AND PHAIDRA

Phaidra conceived a passion for the son whom Theseus had with his Amazon wife, namely, Hippolytos, and begged him to have sex with her. But he hated all women and avoided sexual intercourse.

Phaidra, fearing that Hippolytos would accuse her to his father, smashed the doors of her bedroom, ripped up her clothes, and falsely blamed this violence on Hippolytos. Believing her, Theseus prayed to Poseidon to do away with Hippolytos. As the youth drove his chariot alongside the sea, Poseidon sent up a bull from the waves. Hippolytos's horses were terrified, his chariot was dashed to pieces, and he himself, entangled in the reins, was dragged to death.

Phaidra's passion later became known, and she hanged herself.

Apollodoros

The legend of Phaidra and Hippolytos, set in the heroic age, was so familiar that, according to Pausanias (1.22.1), even a barbarian who learned Greek would know the story. In the backstory the Athenian hero Theseus captured and wed an Amazon maiden, who bore him a son Hippolytos. Later Theseus married Phaidra, a daughter of King Minos of Crete.

The underlying plot, conventionally known as the Potiphar's wife motif, is the most productive erotic plot in Greco-Roman storytelling. The lustful matron, virtuous youth, and gullible husband were also known to the Egyptians ("The Two Brothers"), the Hebrews ("Joseph and Potiphar's Wife"), and other peoples.

129. THE HUSBAND'S UNTIMELY RETURN: I

There was a man who worked in meager poverty and lived on the small wages he earned as a craftsman. He had a wife who likewise was poor but, for all that, notorious for being extremely promiscuous.

One day, right after the man had set out early in the morning for a job he had undertaken, a bold adulterer crept stealthily into the lodging. While the lovers were engaged unconcernedly with the physical struggles of Venus, the husband, who knew nothing of the affair and did not suspect anything, returned home unexpectedly. Finding the door closed and bolted, he praised to himself his wife's temperance and knocked on the door, announcing his presence with a whistle. The crafty wife, who was resourceful in dealing with unsavory situations of this kind, extricated her lover from their close embrace and quietly hid him in a large storage jar that stood half-buried but otherwise empty in a corner of the room. Then she opened the door and, as her husband entered, gave him a harsh reception. "Are you coming home to me empty-handed and idle like this," she said, "and not keeping busy with your usual work, providing for our livelihood and bringing some food? I, poor wretch, work my fingers to the bone spinning wool night and day just to keep an oil lamp burning in our little room. How much happier is our neighbor Daphne who, giddy with wine and breakfast, tumbles around with her adulterers!"

Thus confronted the husband said, "What's this all about? Though the foreman of my workshop has some business in the forum and so has given me the day off, I have in fact made provision for our daily meal. You see that storage jar there that's always empty, takes up space, and doesn't actually serve any purpose except to be in our way? I've sold the thing to someone for six denarii, and he's coming here to pay me and carry it away. So why not cinch up your belt and lend me a hand digging it out so that I can hand it right over to the buyer?"

With a deceit born of circumstance the woman laughed boldly and said, "What a great and masterly businessman I've got in this husband of mine! For what I, a mere woman and housebound at that, sold long ago for seven denarii, he has disposed of for less!"

The husband, delighted at the higher price, asked, "Who's offered that much for it?"

"You fool," she said, "he's already down inside the storage jar checking it for soundness." The woman's words were not wasted on her lover, who swiftly arose, saying, "Do you want to know the truth, lady? This storage jar of yours is too old and is troubled in many places with big cracks." Turning to her husband and pretending not to know who he was, he said, "Fellow, whoever you are, won't you get an oil lamp ready for me so that I can give the inside of the jar a good cleaning and see whether it would be of any use to me, unless you think I throw my money away?"

Without delay or suspicion that keen and excellent husband lit a lamp, saying, "Step out, brother. Stand by and take it easy while I put this pot into proper condition for you." Saying this, he stripped down, took the light, and began scraping out the encrusted deposits from inside the crumbly jug. But the adulterer, fine lad that he was, placed the craftsman's wife face-forward over the storage jar, bent over her, and banged away in safety. Lowering her head into the storage jar, she whimsically managed her husband with the adroitness of a harlot, pointing out to him with her finger this and that place and again another place that needed cleaning, until both tasks were finished, after which she took the seven denarii, while the miserable craftsman was obliged to convey the storage jar on his back to the house of the adulterer.

Apuleius

This tale is one of a group of novelle in which a husband returns home unexpectedly while his wife is entertaining her lover.

130. THE HUSBAND'S UNTIMELY RETURN: 2

Euripides hasn't mentioned this one yet:
how a woman held a garment up to the light

for her husband to see, and so managed to allow
her lover to make his escape from his hiding place.

Aristophanes

The speaker of these lines is listing tricks by means of which unfaithful wives deceive their husbands. Although he merely alludes to the stratagem of the garment, it is recognizable as the central motif of an international folktale and so can be filled out from texts that are complete: a woman is entertaining her lover at home when her husband, who is sometimes represented as having only one good eye, returns unexpectedly; thinking quickly, she calls her husband's attention to a piece of fabric she has recently completed, and while the man examines it, the lover slips out of the room.

131. THE SIGNAL

A man made secret visits to a certain woman during the night and had sex with her. He gave her a signal by which to recognize him. Whenever he came to the door and barked like a little puppy, she was to open the door for him. He did this every night.

Another man observed him walking along the road during the evening, and recognizing the mischief he was up to, secretly followed him one night at a good distance. The lover suspected nothing, went to the door, and behaved as usual. The man who had followed him observed everything and returned to his own house. The next night he got up first, went to the adulteress's house, and barked like a puppy. In the confident belief that it was her paramour, she extinguished her oil lamp so that no one would see him, and opened the door. The man went in and had sex with her.

A little while later the first lover also came and, as usual, barked outside like a puppy. The man inside, recognizing the man who was barking like a puppy outside, stood up inside the house and barked vehemently like a huge dog. The one outside, perceiving that the one inside was bigger than himself, went back home.

anonymous

132. THE WIDOW OF EPHESOS

A certain matron of Ephesos was so famous for her fidelity that she even inspired women from neighboring regions to come and behold her. So when she buried her husband, she was not content to follow the funeral procession in the usual way by letting her hair down or beating her bared breasts in sight of the crowds, but even followed the deceased man into the tomb and in the Greek manner kept watch over the corpse in its subterranean vault, weeping day and night. In her extreme grief neither her parents nor her other relations could induce her to leave, determined as she was to starve herself to death. Finally, the city officials also departed after being turned away. As she spent her fifth day without nourishment, this extraordinary model of womanhood was mourned by everyone. Beside the ailing woman sat her devoted maidservant, who cried along with her and refilled the oil lamp in the tomb whenever it was close to going out. In the entire city there was only one topic of conversation, for persons of every class acknowledged that the woman shone forth as a true and unique instance of conjugal fidelity and love.

Meanwhile the governor of the province gave orders for some robbers to be crucified not far from the little chamber in which the matron was weeping for her recently deceased husband. That night a soldier who was guarding the crosses, to prevent any of the bodies from being taken down for burial, noticed a light shining distinctly among the tombs, and heard the sighs of someone grieving and—prompted by a common human failing—wanted to know who it was and what was going on. And so he went down into the tomb, and when he saw the very attractive woman, at first he stood still, startled as though he were seeing some sort of monster or ghost from the netherworld. Then, seeing the body of the dead man and considering the tears and the cheeks that had been scratched by fingernails, he judged it to be what of course it was, a woman who could not endure her longing for a deceased person. So he brought into the tomb his own little supper and began urging the mourning woman not to persist in hopeless grief or waste her breath in pointless lamentation. He said that everyone must meet the same end and proceed to the same final home, and other such things that restore grief-stricken minds to health. But she ignored his attempts to console her, striking and tearing at her breast all the more vehemently and laying on the body of the dead man the hair she had torn from her head.

Still, the soldier did not retreat but, employing the same exhortations, offered food to the maid, until she, yielding to the fragrance of wine, stretched out her conquered hand to the kind tempter. After the maid was refreshed by food and drink, she herself began to lay siege to the resolution of her mistress. "What good will it do you," she asked, "if you starve yourself to death or bury yourself alive or give up your spirit before the Fates demand it? 'Do you think that ashes or the buried remains of the dead perceive it?' Don't you want to live again? Shouldn't you set aside womanly weakness and enjoy the good things of life as long as possible? The very body of your dead husband should admonish you to live."

None of us dislikes being told that we must eat or that we must live. And so the woman, thirsty after several days of fasting, allowed her resolve to be broken and refreshed herself with food no less avidly than did her maidservant, who had given in first. But you know what temptations often follow upon a full stomach. The same inducements that the soldier employed to make the matron willing to live, he now used to attack her chastity. The young man did seem to the woman, chaste though she was, neither bad-looking nor ill-spoken, in addition to which her maid now tried to win over her favor and said repeatedly, "Will you fight against even a pleasing love?" Why should I draw out my story? The woman did not hold back even this part of her body, and the victorious soldier won her over on both fronts. And so they lay together not only that night, celebrating their nuptials as it were, but also the next day and the third, keeping the door of the tomb shut of course, so that if an acquaintance or stranger came by the tomb, he or she thought that the exceptionally chaste woman had breathed her last over the corpse of her husband. The soldier, delighted with the beautiful woman and with their secret liaison, bought whatever good things to eat that his resources permitted and already on the first night was bringing them into the tomb.

When the parents of one of the crucified men noticed that the watch had been relaxed, they took him down from the cross during the night and gave him his last rites. The soldier was taken advantage of as he sat idle in the tomb, and on the following day when he saw that one of the crosses was missing a corpse, he feared his punishment. Explaining to the woman what had happened, he said he would not wait for the sentence of the judge but would punish his negligence with his own sword. He asked only that she make room for him to die and that she consecrate the tomb to both her husband and him, her significant other.

But the woman, who was no less compassionate than she was virtuous, said, "Heaven forbid my viewing two funerals at the same time for the men I hold dearest. I'd prefer to expend a dead man than to slay a living one." Suiting deed to word, she told him to lift the corpse of her husband out of its coffin and affix it to the vacant cross. The soldier adopted the quite sensible woman's plan, and the next day people wondered how the dead man had clambered up that cross.

Petronius

*The misogynistic humor of this Milesian tale lies in the widow's change of attitude from one extreme to the other in the space of a few days, from initially being determined to follow her late husband in death to finally mutilating her husband's corpse for the sake of her lover. Other humorous touches include the soldier's and maidservant's each citing Vergil (*Aeneid *4.34 and 38, from the tragic story of the seduction of Dido) in the service of their cause.*

133. SLEEPING WITH A GOD

That Kimon, the things he did to us in every city and shore, paying no attention to either custom or law! I had gone to Ilium to view the sights of land and sea. I'll pass over what I saw in the place since there seems to me abundant material to write about and I'm afraid I'll latch onto some poetic nonsense and give the appearance of lacking taste. But as for Kimon's actions and effrontery, even if I had ten tongues I couldn't tell of them adequately.

We were spending many days in Ilium and were not sated with the spectacle of the tombs—I myself had in mind to stay until I had gone through in succession all the verses of the *Iliad* at the site of each event for which verses had come into being—when the day happened to arrive on which most of the inhabitants try to make marriages for their daughters of appropriate age. Many betrothed maidens were present. It is the custom in the Troad for the betrothed maidens to go to the River Scamander, bathe in its waters, and conclude with this line as a sort of sacred offering: "Scamander, take my maidenhood."

Among the others a tall maiden by the name of Kallirhoe, whose father was of no distinguished family, came to the river to bathe. We ourselves, along with the family members of the betrothed maidens and the rest of the spectators, were observing the festival and the baths of the maidens at a distance, where it was proper for nonparticipants to watch. Now, the excellent Kimon had concealed himself in a bush beside the Scamander and had put a wreath of reeds on his head. Clearly this stratagem of his and the daytime ambush of Kallirhoe had been prepared in advance. As she was bathing and (as I learned later) making the customary utterance, "Scamander, take my maidenhood," Scamander-Kimon leapt out from the thicket saying, "I, Scamander, do gladly accept and take Kallirhoe, and I will benefit you in many ways." As he said this, he carried the girl off and disappeared from sight.

His deed, however, did not disappear. Four days later there was a procession in honor of Aphrodite, and the newly married maidens marched in a procession, which we were observing. The new bride saw Kimon, who was standing with me and watching the procession like a complete innocent. Prostrating herself before him, she turned to her nurse and said, "Nurse, do you see Scamander, to whom I gave my maidenhood?" When the nurse heard these words, she shrieked, and the deed became known.

After I got back to the house, I took Kimon aside and did what you might expect, calling him sacrilegious and saying that thanks to him we were in big trouble. He had no fears on this account and felt no shame at what he had done, but began instead to relate long tales in which he listed men from all over who had done deeds worthy of the rack. In fact he said that the same thing had been done at the River Maeander in Magnesia by one of the young men there, and from that day to the present the father believes that his son, the athlete Attalos, is not his own but Maeander's and that it is for this reason that the boy is so well endowed with muscle and strength. After the boy had gotten a beating in a fight and collapsed from exhaustion, the father said that the river was indignant at him because he did not proclaim it publicly as his father. He certainly does not lack an excuse, then, if he loses. And similarly in Epidamnos the musician Karion, because of his credulity, was convinced that the child born to him as a result of adultery was a son of Herakles. "But I myself," Kimon said, "have not begotten any children, though I once had dealings with a girl who was already overripe, whom I spotted bathing in the company of a lone old woman. And besides, it seemed to me," he said, "that in order that the events at Ilium not be all tragic and dreadful, we should experience something novel, doing at the Scamander something of the sort that happens in comedies."

I myself, who was waiting for nothing other than to see where such great shamelessness would come to an end, was petrified with disbelief. Kimon seemed about to bring up a second and third case of adultery—involving Apollon and Dionysos, I think—when I saw a crowd approaching our door, and declared, "This is what I said: they are here to burn us to ashes." I took off through a backroom straight to Melanippides, and from him in the evening to the sea, and then farther. We reached home, thanks to a pushy and inhospitable wind that no one could have endured while sailing if they had not been fleeing a "Kimonian" pollution.

After having these experiences, I thought I should write to you as one who complains even more than I do. You might, I think, get a good laugh.

Pseudo-Aischines

In this fictional letter the writer describes to a friend the highlights of a recent excursion he made to Troy as a tourist in the company of a cheeky friend, Kimon. The story is a novella in which a maiden engaging in her nuptial bath in a local stream is tricked into losing her virginity to a youth who represents himself to her as the river god. It is one of several narratives that recount how a woman is induced to have sexual intercourse with a mortal who pretends to be a god. "Many men pretending to be gods have gained entrance to chaste bedrooms" (Ovid Metamorphoses *3.281–282). In contrast, stories set in mythic and heroic times tell of mortals* really *having sexual intercourse with deities.*

134. THE PERGAMENE BOY

When a quaestor took me with him on his staff to the province of Asia, I was put up at a house in Pergamon. Since I was happy to live there not only on account of the elegance of the residence but also on account of the family's very good-looking son, I devised a plan to be sure that I would not be suspect to the paterfamilias. Whenever the subject of pederasty came up at the dinner table, I acted furious and said in the severest tones that I did not wish my ears to be violated with such obscene talk. Everyone, the youth's mother in particular, thought I must be a philosopher. Presently it was I who escorted the boy to the gymnasium, I who organized his studies, and I who taught him and instructed him not to let any sexual predator into the house.

It chanced one day that we were lying in the dining room since a holiday had curtailed schooling and our extended play had made us too lazy to go to bed. Around midnight I noticed that the boy was awake, and in a very soft voice I uttered a prayer, saying, "Mistress Venus, if I can kiss this boy without his noticing, tomorrow I'll give him a pair of doves." When the boy heard my prayer for pleasure, he started snoring. And so I took the initiative and assaulted the boy with a few little kisses as he pretended to sleep. Satisfied with this beginning, I arose early the next morning and brought a pair of fine doves to the boy, as he expected, and so fulfilled my vow.

When the same opportunity offered itself the next night, I increased the level of my wish, saying, "If my naughty hand caresses this boy and he doesn't notice it, I'll give him two ferocious fighting cocks for enduring me." At this vow the boy moved of his own accord, fearing, I think, that I had fallen asleep. So I relieved him of his worry, gorging myself on his entire body but stopping short of the ultimate pleasure. When day came I brought what I had promised, and he was delighted.

When a third night gave me my opportunity, I got up and said into the boy's ear as he feigned sleep, "Immortal gods, if I'm granted the full and complete satisfaction of my desires with this boy here as he sleeps, tomorrow I'll give him for my bliss a fine Macedonian thoroughbred, though with this proviso, that he doesn't notice what I do." Never did the boy fall into a more profound sleep. And so first I caressed his milky nipples with my hands, next I clung to him with kisses, and then I channeled all my prayers into one.

In the morning he was sitting in the bedroom anticipating my usual behavior. Well, you know it is a lot easier to buy doves and cocks than a thoroughbred, and besides I was afraid that so grand a gift would render my kind attentions suspect. After walking around for a few hours, I went back to the house and gave the boy nothing more than a kiss. Looking around, he put his arms about my neck and said, "Sir, where's my thoroughbred?"

Because of this offense of mine I had closed off the access that I had created, and so I reverted again to my old ways. A few days later a similar occasion placed us again in the same fortunate situation, and when I perceived that his father was snoring, I asked the boy to be friends with me again and let me make it up to him, and said other things that erect passion dictates, but he was still angry with me and said only, "Go to sleep or I'll tell my father."

Nothing, however, is so obstinate that unscrupulous persistence cannot overcome it, and so while he was saying, "I'll wake up my father," I slithered over to him and wrested my pleasure from him as he pretended to fight. But he was not displeased by my wicked behavior, and after complaining for a long time that I had deceived him and exposed him to mockery and ridicule from his fellow pupils, to whom he had boasted of my wealth, he said, "But you'll see, I'm not going to be like you. If you want, you can do it again." So the boy set aside his injured feelings and we made up, and after enjoying his favors, I fell asleep.

The lad, who was fully mature and of an age when one is eager to take it, was not content with a second round, and woke me up from my sleep, saying, "Don't you want to do it again?" His offer was certainly not unwelcome, and so I panted and sweated and banged away, and after he had gotten what he wanted, I fell back to sleep, exhausted with pleasure.

Less than an hour later he poked me with his hand, saying, "Why don't we do it again?" Furious at having been roused from sleep so many times, I answered him in his own words, "Go to sleep or I'll tell your father!"

Petronius

Eumolpus, an older bisexual man, was erotically attracted to the good-looking adolescent male in whose home he was residing and whose teacher he became. He recounts this Milesian tale as a personal-experience narrative.

135. AESOP AND THE MASTER'S WIFE

One day when Aesop was alone, he stripped off his clothing and clapped and shook his hands, adopting the pose of an ungainly shepherd. The wife of Xanthos came upon him suddenly from out of the house and said, "Aesop, what are you doing?" "Mistress," he said, "I'm taking care of myself and helping my stomach." She, however, noticed the length and thickness of his penis and was captured by the sight. Forgetting Aesop's ugliness, she was wounded with desire. She summoned him to her privately and said, "If you please me and don't resist, you will enjoy yourself more than your master does." But he said to her, "You know that if my master learns of this, he'll pay me back terribly in return." But she laughed and said, "If you have sex with me ten times, I'll give you a cloak as a present." He said, "Swear it to me," and, driven by lust, she swore it. Aesop trusted her and also wanted to get back at his master.

Aesop finished his passion the ninth time, and said, "Mistress, I can't do another one." She made a trial of him and said, "If you don't do all ten, you don't get anything." Exerting himself to the utmost, then, he completed the tenth on her thigh, saying, "Give me the cloak, or I'll tell your husband." But the woman declared, "I hired you to dig in my field, but you went beyond the boundary wall and dug in the neighbor's field. Give me what you owe me, and you'll get the cloak."

When Xanthos came back, Aesop went to him and asked him to judge between himself and his mistress. Xanthos asked, "What about?" Aesop replied, "Master, when the mistress and I were taking a walk, she saw a plum tree that was full of fruit. Noticing an especially fruitful branch and desiring it, she said, 'If you can hit ten plums for me with one stone, I'll give you a cloak.' With good aim I threw a stone and got ten for her, but one of them happened to fall onto the manure, and now she's not willing to give me the cloak."

Challenging this account, she said to her husband, "I acknowledge that I got the nine, but I don't count the one in the manure. Let him throw again and knock loose the one plum, and then have the cloak." Aesop said, "My wrist no longer has its vigor."

Xanthos gave as his judgment that Aesop should be given the cloak, and said to him, "Aesop, let's go to the marketplace, since I'm feeling lazy. You can use the occasion to knock down some plums for me that we can take to the mistress." "Husband," she said, "don't start wishing for him to hit any plums for you. I'll give him the cloak, as you've directed."

Life of Aesop

In this story Aesop is a slave, though no longer mute, in the household of the philosopher Xanthos. His master's wife unexpectedly comes upon him in the courtyard as, unclothed, he practices a form of exercise. The lustful matron is a favorite figure of ancient story, but the principal humor of the tale derives from the two adulterers boldly discussing their activities in metaphoric language with the cuckolded husband. Even the plums, which the Greeks called "cuckoo apples," are erotic metaphors. Despite these hints, the obtuse philosopher takes everything literally.

136. THE KING'S TRUSTED FRIEND

Now when Stratonike was married to her former husband, she saw a dream in which Hera instructed her to raise a temple for her in Hierapolis, threatening her with much harm if she disobeyed. At first she disregarded the dream, but later when she was seized by a serious illness, she told her husband about her vision, propitiated Hera, and promised to raise the temple. As soon as she was well again, her husband made preparations to send her to Hierapolis along with money and a considerable army, some of the men to do the actual construction and others for the sake of her safety.

He summoned one of his friends, a very handsome youth whose name was Kombabos. "You are an excellent man, Kombabos," he said, "and of all my friends I love you the most. I praise you greatly for your wisdom and the goodwill you have shown us. Now I have need of your great faithfulness, for I want you to accompany my wife, bring a particular task to completion, perform certain sacrifices, and take charge of my army. When you return, you will be greatly honored by me."

Kombabos begged him persistently and repeatedly not to send him off nor to entrust him with his wife, a sacred task, and an amount of money that was too great for him. He dreaded that at some later time jealous feelings might arise with regard to Stratonike, whom he alone would be escorting. Since Kombabos failed to persuade the king, he begged at least that the monarch grant him a period of seven days, sending him off after he had taken care of a very necessary matter.

Having easily obtained this request, he went home and, falling upon the floor, lamented as follows, "O wretch, what to me is this faithfulness? What to me is this journey, whose end I already see? I'm a young man who'll be accompanying a beautiful woman. It will be a great misfortune for me if I don't remove the entire cause of evil. So I must perform a great deed that will relieve me of all my fear." Saying this, he made himself into an incomplete man by cutting off his genitals, which he then stored in a small vessel with some myrrh and honey and other spices. He sealed it with a signet that he carried, and healed his wound. Later, when he decided he could travel, he went to the king and, in the presence of many persons, gave him the vessel and spoke as follows: "Master, this great heirloom, which I esteem highly, has been kept in store in my house, but now that I am going on a long journey, I deposit it with you. Keep it safe for me, for to me it is better than gold: it is worth my soul. When I return, I'll collect it again from you intact." The king accepted it, sealed it with a different signet, and entrusted it to his treasurers to guard.

After this, Kombabos accomplished his journey safely. When they reached Hierapolis, they began the construction of the temple in earnest. Three years passed in the work. Meanwhile the event happened that Kombabos had dreaded. He spent much time with Stratonike, and she began to feel love and eventually an overpowering passion for him. (The inhabitants of Hierapolis say that Hera was the cause of this, wanting to make Kombabos's goodness manifest and to punish Stratonike for not having readily promised her temple.)

Now, at first she behaved modestly and kept her lovesickness hidden. But when the evil grew too great for her to be calm, she displayed her anguish openly and wept throughout the day, calling for Kombabos to come to her, saying that he was everything to her. Finally, unable to master her affliction, she sought a suitable occasion for making her plea. Although she avoided admitting her love to anyone else, she herself was ashamed to take the first step. So she devised a plan to get herself drunk with wine and then speak to him. For with wine comes also bold speech, and a failure to obtain a wish is not so shameful since actions are blamed on the effects of drinking.

As she had decided, so she did. After dinner she went to the house in which Kombabos passed the night, and there she begged him, taking hold of his knees and confessing her love. But he received her words harshly, rejecting her advances and reproaching her drunkenness. When she threatened to do serious harm to herself, he became fearful and revealed to her his entire story, explaining what he had done to himself and showing her the results of the deed. When Stratonike saw what she had not expected to see, her madness was checked, though she never forgot her love and made the time they spent together a consolation for her impossible passion. This kind of love exists in Hierapolis and occurs even now. Women desire Galli, and Galli are madly in love with women, but no one feels jealous, since they regard the matter as being holy.

The events in Hierapolis touching upon Stratonike did not escape the notice of the king, for many persons came and made accusations, giving an account of what took place. Very pained at these reports, the king sent for Kombabos, whose work was not yet finished. (Other persons give an account that is quite false. They say that Stratonike herself, failing to obtain what she sought, wrote to her husband and accused Kombabos, charging him with making an attempt upon her virtue, so that what the Greeks relate about Stheneboia and about Phaidra of Knossos, the Assyrians tell in legends about Stratonike. But I myself do not believe that Stheneboia or Phaidra acted in that way if Phaidra really loved Hippolytos. But let these things be as they may.)

When the message reached Hierapolis, Kombabos knew the reason, and he went with confidence because his defense had been left at home. The king bound him immediately upon his arrival and held him under guard. After a time, while the same companions of the king were there who were present when Kombabos was being sent forth, the king led him into their midst and began to accuse him, reproaching him for his adultery and licentious behavior. Complaining loudly of his sufferings, he reminded him of his trust and friendship, saying that Kombabos had treated him unjustly in three ways: by committing adultery, by insulting his trust, and by behaving impiously toward the goddess in whose service he acted. Many of the bystanders attested that they had seen the two of them consorting openly. In the end everyone concluded that Kombabos should be executed straightaway for his actions, which merited death.

All this time he stood and said nothing. As he was being led away to execution, he spoke out and asked for his heirloom, saying that the king was executing him not for any insolence or unlawful wedlock but from a desire for what Kombabos had deposited with him when he was departing. The king then summoned his treasurer and bade him bring what he had been given to guard. When the man brought it, Kombabos unsealed it and displayed its contents as well as himself, showing what he had undergone, and said, "King, this is what I was dreading when you dispatched me on that journey, and I went unwillingly. Since I was subject to your mighty constraint, I took this action, good for my master but unfortunate for me. Though I am such as you see, I stand accused of a man's crime."

At this the king cried out, embraced him, and said with tears in his eyes, "Kombabos, what great harm have you done? Why have you, alone of men, brought such ruin upon yourself? I can't approve of this at all. You poor man, enduring this! I wish you hadn't suffered it and I hadn't seen it. There was no need for this defense. But since the deity has so willed it, first of all you shall be avenged by us—death for your false accusers, and then for you, great gifts—abundant gold, an immense amount of silver, Assyrian clothing, royal horses. You shall have the right of approaching me unannounced, and no one shall keep you away from my presence even if I am in bed with my wife." So he spoke and so he did. The accusers were led away to execution, he was gifted with gifts, and the friendship of the two men grew. No Assyrian, it seemed, was the equal of Kombabos in wisdom and prosperity.

After this Kombabos asked to complete the remainder of the temple (for he had left it unfinished) and was sent off again. He completed it and remained there afterward. Because of his virtue and service the king arranged for a bronze statue of him to stand in the temple, and in his honor a bronze Kombabos still stands in the temple, the work of Hermokles of Rhodes. In shape it is like a woman but has the clothes of a man.

Of his friends, it is said, those who were most devoted to him chose to share his misfortune as a solace for his suffering. They castrated themselves and adopted the same manner of life. Others recount a sacred story on this subject, saying that Hera, in her love for Kombabos, put the idea of castrating themselves into the minds of many men in order that Kombabos might not be alone in mourning his manhood. This custom, once adopted, has abided to our own day. Every year many men castrate themselves in the temple and become effeminized in order to console Kombabos or to gratify Hera. In any case they do castrate themselves. They wear male clothing no longer but don female attire and do women's work.

I have heard the cause of this also referred to Kombabos. The following occurrence happened to him. A foreign woman who came for a festival saw that he was handsome and (still at that time) wore male clothing, and she conceived a strong passion for him. When she learned later that he was an incomplete man, she took her own life. In consequence Kombabos, despairing at his incapacity for sexual intercourse, assumed female attire so that in the future no other woman would be similarly deceived. This is the reason for the Galli's female apparel.

Lucian

This legend focuses upon King Seleukos Nikator of Syria, his queen Stratonike, his good friend Kombabos, and a project in the Holy City, Hierapolis, for the Syrian goddess Atargatis, here called Hera. The narrative ends with an etiology attributing the origin of the cult of the Galli to the experience of Kombabos.

137. DREAM-LOVERS

Hystaspes had a younger brother Zariadres, who the natives say was born of Aphrodite and Adonis. Hystaspes was lord of Media and the region below it, while Zariadres was master of the territory above the Caspian Gates as far as the Tanaïs River. Beyond the Tanaïs River Homartes, king of the Marathoi, had a daughter named Odatis. Concerning her it is written in the histories that she saw Zariadres in a dream and fell in love with him, and that the very same experience befell him with regard to her. They continued desiring each other on account of the images in their dreams. Odatis was the most beautiful of the women in Asia, and Zariadres also was good-looking.

Now, earnestly desiring to marry the girl, Zariadres sent a message to Homartes, but the latter would not agree to it because he lacked male children and wished to give her to a member of his own household. Not long afterward Homartes gathered together the princes of the realm as well as his friends and relatives, and began making preparations for the wedding of his daughter without announcing to whom he was going to give her. When the drinking was at its high point, he summoned Odatis to the party and, in the hearing of the guests, said, "My daughter Odatis, we are now celebrating your wedding feast. Take a look around and consider everyone here. Then pick up a bowl, fill it with wine, and give it to whomever you wish to marry, for you will then be the wife of that man." She looked around at everyone and went away in tears, longing for the sight of Zariadres. She had in fact sent a message to him, informing him that her nuptials were about to be celebrated.

For his part, Zariadres was encamped on the Tanaïs River and, unnoticed by his army, crossed it accompanied only by his chariot driver. Setting out by chariot during the night, he passed through a great amount of territory, going some 800 stades.* When he was near the city where the wedding was being celebrated, he left his chariot and driver in a certain place, donned Scythian garb, and went on alone. Entering the court, he saw Odatis standing by the stand for drinking vessels and weeping as she slowly mixed the wine. Stopping beside her, he said, "Odatis, it's Zariadres. I'm here beside you, as you asked." When she saw that there was a stranger there who was both good-looking and like the man she had seen in her sleep, she was overjoyed and offered him the bowl. He snatched her up, brought her to his chariot, and fled with her. Odatis's slaves and maidservants, aware of her love, said nothing, and even when her father ordered them to speak, they said they did not know where she had gone.

This love is preserved in the memory of the barbarians of Asia, who hold it in exceedingly great esteem. Paintings of the story are found in

*About 100 miles.

temples, palaces, and even in private homes, and most of the princes name their daughters Odatis.

Athenaios

One of the charms of this romantic legend is the motif of the reciprocal dreams. Probably we imagine the lovers dreaming their dreams simultaneously, although the text does not expressly say that they do. A similar motif is found in other romantic stories such as Longos's Daphnis and Chloe *(1.7–8), where adoptive fathers have simultaneous identical dreams instructing them to rear their charges as goatherd and shepherd. Since the causes of the dreaming are not explained, we are left with the impression that the lovers are somehow cosmically destined for each other.*

138. THE ASTUTE PHYSICIAN

It seems to me that this is the Stratonike whose own stepson fell in love with her. He was found out through the astuteness of his physician.

When the unfortunate condition took hold of the youth, he was at a loss how to deal with a malady that seemed to him disgraceful, and quietly took sick. He lay in bed with no pain, but his skin color changed and his body wasted away day by day.

The doctor, seeing that the youth's illness had no obvious cause, recognized the sickness as love. The signs of covert love are many: sickly eyes, voice, skin color, and tears. Perceiving these, he did as follows. He placed his right hand on the young man's heart and sent for each member of the household. As each person entered, the youth was wholly at ease, until his stepmother arrived, whereupon he changed hue, began sweating and trembling, and his heart pounded. These symptoms made his love apparent to the physician, who healed the youth in the following way.

He summoned the youth's father, who was in a state of dread, and said, "This illness that the boy is suffering from is not an illness but a wrongful action. He feels no pain but rather is in the grips of love and madness. What he desires is impossible to obtain: he loves my wife, whom I will not give up." This was the physician's clever lie.

The father immediately started beseeching him, "In the name of wisdom and the medical arts, don't let my son perish. He finds himself in this plight not of his own volition, since his illness is involuntary. Don't make the whole kingdom grieve because you are a jealous man, and as a physician don't bring murder to the medical arts." In his ignorance the father entreated him in this manner.

The physician responded, "What you are seeking so eagerly is unholy—using your power against a medical man and depriving me of my marriage. Since you ask this of me, what would you do if the boy were in love with your wife?" To this question the king said he would not make an exception even of his own wife or begrudge his son his life, even if what the young man desired were his own stepmother. For the misfortune of losing a spouse was not the same as losing a son. When the physician heard this, he said, "Why beg me, then? For the fact is that the young man is yearning for your wife. Everything I've been telling you was false."

The father, following the physician's advice, handed over his wife and his kingdom to his son. He himself went to Babylonia, where he founded a city on the Euphrates that he named after himself. There he met his end.

That is how the physician recognized and healed love.

Lucian

The scandalous love of Antiochos for his stepmother Stratonike, wife of King Seleukos I, is based upon historical fact. King Seleukos did yield his wife Stratonike to his son and did divide his kingdom with him, with the result that Seleukos subsequently ruled in the city of Seleukia on the Tigris River while from 324 to 262 BC Antiochos I held sway in Antioch-on-the-Orontes. But the real hero of the story is the astute physician, whose name, Erasistratos, is known from other sources.

139. HERO AND LEANDER

Sestos and Abydos were neighboring cities, separated from each other by a narrow arm of the sea. One of the cities owed its fame to Leander, a very

handsome youth; the other to Hero, a very beautiful woman. When they were apart, the flame of love burnt deep within them.

Unable to endure the fire of love, the youth sought to possess the maiden by any means possible. Finding no way to reach Hero by land, and driven by passion and daring, he entrusted himself to the sea. He swam over to her each night, while from her tower on the opposite side the girl held a lamp to guide his course. But one night an unusually strong wind extinguished her torch, and Leander, losing his way and not knowing where to head, drowned.

The following day, when Hero saw his corpse on the shore, tossed there by the waves, she was overcome with grief and leapt from the top of her tower. And so she bore the bitterness of death with the youth in whose company she had enjoyed some of the pleasure of this world.

First Vatican Mythographer

Leander and Hero, a priestess of Aphrodite, meet at a festival, where he falls in love with her at first sight. She lives with a maidservant in a seaside tower just outside the city of Sestos, while he dwells in the city of Abydos on the opposite side of the Hellespont (today's Dardanelles). In order to meet they agree that Hero will signal him nightly with a lamp from her tower, while Leander, guided by its light, will swim across the strait in order to be with her.

Abydos lay on the Asian side of the Hellespont, in Mysia a bit northeast of Troy, while Sestos lay on the European side, in Thrace, where in antiquity an old tower outside of town was known to travelers as Hero's tower (e.g., Strabo 13.22.591). The strait separating the two sites is about a mile and a quarter wide, and is indeed swimmable. In 1810 Lord Byron swam across it from Sestos to Abydos, which due to the current took him a little more than an hour (Grant 1962:377).

140. XANTHOS, WHO LONGS FOR HIS WIFE

During the time when the Celts overran Ionia and were plundering the cities, the Thesmophoria was being celebrated in Miletos and the women were gathered together in the sanctuary, which lay a short distance from the city. A detachment of the barbarian army entered Milesian territory, made a sudden raid, and carried the women off. Although some of them were gotten back in exchange for a large amount of silver and gold, the barbarians became intimate with others and took them away. Among them was Herippe, the wife of Xanthos, a highly esteemed man in Miletos and a member of a leading family. She also left behind a two-year-old child.

Xanthos yearned greatly for his wife. He converted part of his property to cash and, providing himself with two thousand pieces of gold, first crossed over to Italy, then was conveyed by some private friends to Massalia,* and from there reached the land of the Celts. He came to the house where his wife was living with a man who ranked among the most distinguished of the Celts, and asked to be received. The members of the household readily gave him a hospitable welcome. When he entered, he saw his wife, who threw her arms around him and embraced him with the utmost friendliness. Straightway the Celt appeared, and Herippe told him about her husband's journey and that he had come to pay a ransom for her sake. The Celt, admiring Xanthos's spirit, immediately arranged a gathering of his closest relations and received him as a guest. As the drinking proceeded, he placed the woman next to him and asked through an interpreter how much money he had altogether. When Xanthos said that he had a sum of a thousand pieces of gold, the barbarian instructed him to divide them into four parts, taking out three parts for himself, his wife, and his child, and to leave the fourth part as ransom for his wife.

---

*Massalia is the later Marseilles.

When they went to bed, his wife began to criticize Xanthos for having promised the barbarian a large amount of gold that he did not have, saying that he would be endangering himself if did not make good on his promise. But he said that another thousand pieces of gold were hidden in the slaves' boots on account of the fact that he had not expected to encounter so fair-minded a barbarian, and had thought he would need a larger ransom.

The next day the woman revealed the amount of gold to the Celt and encouraged him to kill Xanthos, declaring that she much preferred him to her own country and child, and utterly detested Xanthos. The Celt was not pleased, however, with what she said, and planned to punish her.

When Xanthos was hastening to depart, the Celt personally escorted him with the utmost friendliness, bringing along Herippe as well. When they reached the borders of the Celtic country, the barbarian said that he wished to perform a sacrifice before they separated. When a victim was brought, he told Herippe to hold it, and she did so, as she had been accustomed to do at other times. Holding up his sword, he brought it down and cut off her head. He urged Xanthos not to bear him ill, reporting to him his wife's plot and allowing him to take all the gold back with him.

Parthenios

In this unusual triangle tale of male nobility and female duplicity, male solidarity is affirmed in the end when the Celtic chieftain converts sacrifice into execution (Lightfoot 1999:418).

The reference to Celtic incursions into Ionia indicates that the dramatic date of the events is ca. 278 BC.

141. ARISTON AND HIS FRIEND'S WIFE

Ariston was a Spartan king. Although he had married twice, he had no children, and since he was not willing to acknowledge the fault as his own, he married a third wife, which he did as follows.

He had a friend among the Spartans to whom, of all his fellow townsmen, he was most attached. As it happened, this man's wife was by far the most beautiful woman in Sparta; moreover, she had gone from being the most ugly to being the most beautiful. Her nurse, seeing that she was an unattractive child, that she was the daughter of prosperous parents but was so ill-favored, and that her parents deemed her looks a misfortune, had considered all this and had come up with an idea. She brought her every day to the shrine of Helen, the one in the place called Therapne, above the temple of Phoibos. When the nurse brought the child there, she would set her before the image and beseech the goddess to free the child of her ugliness. One day as the nurse was leaving the shrine, it is said, a woman appeared to her and asked what she bore in her arms. She said she was carrying a child. The woman asked her to show her the child, but she refused, since the parents had forbidden her to show the child to anyone. The woman insisted that she show her the child. Seeing that it was important to the woman to see the child, the nurse showed her. Stroking the child's head, the woman said that the child would become the most beautiful woman in Sparta. From that day onward her looks changed, and when she reached marriageable age, Agetos the son of Alkeidas married her. This was Ariston's friend.

Now, Ariston was stung by love for this woman, and devised a plan. He promised his friend, whose wife she was, to give as a gift any possession of his that the man should choose, and he bade his friend do the same. Agetos did not fear for his wife, seeing that Ariston also had a wife, and so consented. They bound themselves to these conditions with oaths. Ariston gave from his treasured possessions the one that Agetos chose, and then, taking his own turn, Ariston attempted to lead away his friend's wife. The man consented to give up any of his possessions except for this one. Constrained, however, by his oath and by the deception, he let Ariston lead her away.

That is how Ariston wed his third wife, after divorcing the second.

Herodotos

Two interconnected stories, set in Sparta in the sixth century BC, are linked by the character of the woman who is wife first of Agetos and then of Ariston. In the former story she acquires her extraordinary beauty miraculously by the supernatural intervention of the divinity Helen, in her own day the world's most beautiful woman. In time she becomes a second Helen, a superlative beauty who is wed to one man and carried off by another.

The latter story relates how Ariston tricks his best friend out of his wife. The story turns on the theme of "Laconic swearing," in which a Spartan cleverly and/or duplicitously honors the letter rather than the spirit of his oath. It depends upon the principle of narrative irreversibility, according to which a character cannot be permitted to change his or her mind if it would force the story to move backward (Hansen 2005:50–51): if Agetos should declare that he regards the deceptive oath as nonbinding, the story would fall apart.

142. OLYMPIANS IN THE BEDROOM

The pancratiast Leontiskos once loved
Mania, reserving her for himself
Like a wedded wife. But
Later he was quite upset to learn that
She was committing adultery
With Antenor. "Don't let it bother you,
My dear," she said. "I just wanted to learn
And feel what two athletes, Olympic victors,
Could do, stroke for stroke, in a single night."

Machon

This witty poem about the courtesan Mania and two Olympic athletes comes from a compilation of comic anecdotes in verse, mostly about courtesans.

CHAPTER 5

ARTISTS AND ATHLETES

This chapter brings together stories about two kinds of performers, artists and athletes, who present their talents for public evaluation and frequently attain the status of celebrity.

ARTISTS AND THE ARTS

143. HERAKLES FOOLED

At Pisa Daidalos made a statue of Herakles, and Herakles, mistaking it during the night for a living being, pelted it with a stone.

Apollodoros

The point of the legend may be less the realism of Daidalos's statue than the novelty of statues as such. Although the first maker of life-size figures was the divine craftsman Hephaistos (see 288 "The Origin of Human Miseries"), the first sculptor among mortals was Daidalos, a character of the heroic age (Apollodoros Library *3.15.8). Pisa was a town or district near Olympia, its name sometimes used synonymously with Olympia.*

144. NATURE FOOLED

A bull once mounted the bronze bull at Peirene. And a painted bitch, pigeon, and goose were once approached and leapt upon, respectively, by a dog, a pigeon, and a gander.

Athenaios

* * *

There is, or was, a picture of a horse made by Apelles, painted for a competition in which he turned from the judgment of humans to appeal to that of dumb quadrupeds themselves. When he perceived that his rivals were prevailing by intrigue, he had some horses brought and showed them the pictures one by one, and the horses neighed only at the horse painted by Apelles.

This same thing always happened on subsequent occasions, showing it to be a sound test of art.

Pliny the Elder

Realism as a criterion of artistic quality is a recurrent theme in ancient art criticism, especially in popular criticism, from the late fifth century BC onward, according to which the most admirable works of art are those in which the boundary between life and art is the least (Pollitt 1974:63).

145. PAINTER FOOLED

The story is told that Parrhasios and Zeuxis entered into a competition.

Zeuxis exhibited a painting of grapes that he had represented so successfully that birds flew to the wall. Then Parrhasios exhibited a painting of a linen curtain that he had represented with such realism that Zeuxis, who was priding himself on the verdict of the birds, insisted that the curtain should now be drawn and the painting displayed. When he perceived his mistake, he conceded the prize with honor and modesty, saying that whereas he himself had fooled birds, Parrhasios had fooled him, an artist.

Pliny the Elder

Apparently the two painters exhibited their entries in an open-air theater, hanging them on the front wall of the stage building.

146. THE SCULPTOR POLYKLEITOS

Polykleitos sculpted two images of the same subject, one that gratified the populace and the other made in accordance with the principles of art. He gratified the populace in the following way. Following the guidance that each visitor gave him, he changed or transformed a feature. Then he exhibited both pieces.

One of them won praise from everyone, and the other was ridiculed. Polykleitos responded to the public, saying, "But you yourselves made the one you are criticizing, and I the one you admire."

Aelian

The anecdote addresses the tension between the artist's vision and the public's taste. A later instance—one of many—is provided by the two different conclusions that Charles Dickens penned for his novel Great Expectations *(1860–1861): the original, less happy ending, which is found in Dickens's manuscript, and the altered ending, which came to be published. The former presumably satisfied Dickens, whereas the latter appealed to Dickens's friend, Edward Bulwer-Lytton, who, after reading the proofs, urged the author to make the change (Dickens 2008:xxxii–xxxvii).*

147. MODELS FOR HELEN OF TROY

There was a painter named Zeuxis, whom the inhabitants of Kroton regarded as a wonder. When he was doing a painting of a nude Helen, the Krotoniates allowed him to see their own maidens unclothed. It was not because they all were beautiful, though it is unlikely that they were altogether ugly. But Zeuxis brought together into a single bodily image the feature possessed by each maiden that was worthy of portrayal, so that out of a compilation of many parts his art synthesized one figure of perfect beauty.

Dionysios of Halikarnassos

*In another version of the legend Cicero relates how the wealthy citizens of Kroton commissioned Zeuxis to make a number of paintings to ornament their temple of Hera. The painter wished to include a picture of Helen, famous for her beauty. Asking the citizens to send him their most beautiful maidens, he selected as his models the five most attractive girls, for the qualities he sought could not be found in a single person (*On Invention *2.1.1–3). Cicero's narrative was influential in Renaissance art circles as an exemplification of the artistic process.*

Probably few people are aware that a similar story lies behind the familiar visage of the cook and food expert Betty Crocker. An artist created a face for Betty Crocker in 1936 by blending features of the women in General Mills's Home Service Department into a single portrait. Since that time Betty Crocker's image has been updated many times in response to changing social attitudes, such that over the years she has become younger and more professional-looking, and recently has acquired a slightly ethnic look (Panati 1987:409).

148. HELEN'S CHALICE

At Lindos on the island of Rhodes there is a temple of Athena in which Helen dedicated a chalice made of electrum. Tradition relates that the shape of the cup is that of her breast.

Pliny the Elder

Helen's chalice is the earliest written reference to an association between drinking vessels and women's breasts (Mayor 1994). Modern tradition, for example, links the coupe (a stemmed glass for champagne or dessert) with cups molded from the breasts of Marie Antoinette.

Greek temples and sanctuaries were replete with offerings associated with figures of myth and legend such as the stone swallowed by Kronos, Agamemnon's scepter, Marsyas's flute, and Meleager's spear (Rouse 1902:318–321). Updated, the practice has continued into Christian and Muslim times. Thus the Column of Constantine in Constantinople used to hold such relics as the hatchet employed by Noah to build the ark as well as wood from the cross upon which Jesus was crucified, and present-day visitors to the Palace of Topkapi in Istanbul can view Islamic holy relics known as the Sacred Trusts, which include Abraham's cooking pot and Moses's staff.

149. ARCHILOCHOS: LETHAL IAMBICS

Lykambes had a daughter, Neoboule. When Archilochos sought her hand in marriage, her father promised her but did not give her to him. In his anger at this, Archilochos wrote an abusive poem against Lykambes, who was so overcome with anguish that he hanged himself along with his daughter.

Pseudo-Acron

Archilochos of Paros (7th century BC) was famed for his iambic verse, a poetic form that frequently served as a vehicle for insult and obscenity. The legend of his employing his iambs as a weapon against Lykambes and his daughters is mentioned by many ancient authors. In some versions Lykambes's three daughters all hang themselves, and sometimes his wife does, too. Unhappily, the caustic poem has not survived.

* * *

This tomb beside the sea belongs to Archilochos, who
    Was the first to dip his bitter Muse into the gall of Echidna,
Staining mild Helikon with blood. Lykambes knows it,
    As he weeps for the nooses his three daughters used.
Wayfarer, pass by softly, lest
    You stir up the wasps that sit on this tomb.

Gaitoulikos

This is an imaginary epitaph for Archilochos's tomb. For the ancients, as for us, wasps were reputed to be quick-tempered, attacking and stinging with little provocation. Ancient epitaphs were often in verse, and poets were fond of composing epitaphs for well-known persons of the past.

150. HIPPONAX: MORE LETHAL IAMBICS

Boupalos was a painter in Klazomenai, a city in Asia. To raise a laugh he painted a picture of a certain poet, Hipponax, representing him as deformed. Incensed by this, Hipponax assailed Boupalos with such a poem that he hanged himself.

Pseudo-Acron

Hipponax (6th century BC) was another iambic poet known for his biting verse.

151. THE CICADA

The River Halex separates Rhegion and Lokris, exiting through a deep ravine. A peculiar thing about the cicadas there is that those on the Lokrian bank make a sound, whereas those on the opposite bank are mute. The reason for this, people conjecture, is that the habitat of the one is so thickly shaded that the cicadas are moist with dew and cannot expand their membranes, while the other cicadas, basking in the sun, have dry and hornlike membranes.

A statue of Eunomos the singer and kithara player, with a cicada sitting on his kithara, used to be displayed in Lokris. Timaios says that this man and Ariston of Rhegion were once competing at the Pythian Games and got into a dispute about their respective lots. Ariston beseeched the Delphians to support him, seeing as his ancestors had belonged to the god and their colony had been dispatched from Delphi. But Eunomos declared that persons in whose land the cicadas, most sweet-voiced of animals, were mute had no business even participating in a voice competition. Ariston was nonetheless held in high regard and hoped for victory. But it was Eunomos who won and dedicated in his homeland the statue I mentioned. For during the contest, when one of his strings broke, a cicada perched on his kithara and supplied the missing note.

Strabo

The Pythian Games, held in Delphi in honor of the god Apollon, featured both athletic and artistic contests.

152. A SINGER'S COMPENSATION

At an event in which a well-known musician was performing, Dionysios promised the man substantial compensation. But later he gave him nothing at all, on the grounds that he had already paid him his boon. "While we were delighting in your singing," he said, "you were taking pleasure in your expectations."

Plutarch

The Sicilian ruler Dionysios ungenerously claims that the transient pleasure an audience experiences in hearing music performed is balanced by the transient pleasure the musician experiences in anticipation of being paid. For a similar idea set in the realm of sexual pleasure, see 110 "The Problem of Dreamt Sex."

153. PINDAR'S SACRIFICE

When Pindar came to Delphi and was asked what he had come to sacrifice, he said, "A paean."

Apothegms of Pindar

Being a poet, Pindar offered the god a poem. A paean was a song such as a hymn, victory song, or war song addressed to Apollon.

In a similar spirit the Seven Sages each dedicated a wise statement; these were inscribed on Apollon's temple at Delphi: "Know yourself," "Nothing overmuch," and so on (e.g., Plato Protagoras *343a–b).*

154. PINDAR'S HOUSE

When the Spartan king Pausanias was burning Thebes, someone wrote on Pindar's house:

> Do not burn the dwelling of Pindar the poet.

And so his house alone remained unravaged. Today it is used in Thebes as a town hall.

Ambrosian Life of Pindar

* * *

When Alexander was sacking Thebes, he ordered that the house and household of the poet Pindar be spared.

Pliny the Elder

The Theban poet Pindar (6th–5th centuries BC) was very highly esteemed by the Greeks. When the Spartan king Pausanias was ravaging Thebes, he spared the poet's house, and subsequently Alexander of Macedon did the same when he leveled the city in 335 BC. Some six hundred years after the poet's death the Greek traveler Pausanias (9.25.3) mentions that the ruins of Pindar's house at Thebes could still be seen.

155. PHRYNICHOS FINED

The Athenians made clear how deeply grieved they were for the capture of Miletos in many ways. In particular, when Phrynichos wrote and directed his play *The Capture of Miletos*, the spectators at the theater burst into tears. They fined Phrynichos a thousand drachmas for reminding them of their calamities, and forbade any future production of the play.

Herodotos

The Capture of Miletos *was a pioneering attempt by a Greek tragic poet to treat a contemporary event as opposed to a heroic legend or myth set in the remote past. Phrynichos's subject, a Greek defeat, differed from that of his younger contemporary Aeschylus, who in his* Persians *portrays a Greek victory. Not surprisingly, perhaps, Phrynichos's play does not survive.*

156. THE CHORUS OF AESCHYLUS'S *EUMENIDES*

Some say that in the performance of his *Eumenides* Aeschylus had members of the chorus enter one by one and so frightened the spectators that children fainted and women had miscarriages.

Life of Aeschylus

This anecdote about the original production of Aeschylus's Eumenides, *with its terrifying chorus of Furies, is meant to illustrate the power of Aeschylus's drama. The anecdote is frequently cited as evidence that playgoers at Greek tragedies included women and children.*

157. SOPHOCLES ON HIMSELF AND EURIPIDES

Sophocles said that Euripides portrayed persons as they are, whereas he portrayed them as they ought to be.

Aristotle

158. "I SEE A WEASEL"

Take courage: we're doing fine.
It's possible for us to say, as Hegelochos did,
"After the storm I again see a weasel."

Aristophanes

This anecdote, alluded to in a scene of a comedy by Aristophanes, refers to the unfortunate tragic actor Hegelochos, who played Orestes in the initial production of Euripides's Orestes *at the Great Dionysia of 408 BC. One of his lines was "After the storm I again see the calm"* (Orestes *279), but unhappily he mispronounced the accent of a word, saying* galen *("weasel, ferret") instead of* galén *("calm"). The result was not only ludicrous but also incongruous, since in Greek lore encountering a weasel was not a good omen, as the scene requires, but a bad one. The slip did not escape the notice of the Athenian audience, and the Greeks did not let Hegelochos forget his lapse, as here in a comedy produced three years after the event. Twenty-five centuries later we still talk about it.*

159. "MOTHER, I CALL TO YOU"

A fool would pay no more heed than Fufius did on that occasion when, drunk,
He slept through the part of Iliona, while not one Catienus but twelve hundred of them
Shouted, "Mother, I call to you!"

Horace

***

This Fufius was a tragic actor. Once, he was drunk while acting in the tragedy *Iliona*, in which he was supposed to represent Iliona sleeping. Under the influence of wine he fell into a real sleep. So just as a fool does not hear his mother or wife or father asking for help, Iliona, played by the drunken Fufius, could not hear a thousand Catieni taking the role of her son.

Porphyrio

Iliona, *a lost drama by the Roman tragedian Pacuvius, opens with the heroine Iiona sleeping while the ghost of the murdered Polydorus, a youth whom Iliona has brought up as her son, calls to her and implores her to bury him: "Mother, I call to you, who suspend your cares and relieve them in sleep and/Pity me not. Rise and give burial to your son!" The mournful scene had a powerful effect on Roman audiences. On one occasion, however, Fufius, the actor playing Iliona, got drunk, really did fall asleep, and so failed to hear the pleas of Catienus, the actor playing the ghost of Polydorus. Presumably Catienus kept repeating his lines in an attempt to get a response from Fufius, and finally the audience of over a thousand spectators joined together to help him by shouting, "Mother, I call to you" (*Mater, te appello*).*

160. SAVED BY EURIPIDES

Most of the Athenians perished in the stone quarries from illness and the terrible living conditions in which they received a daily ration of a pint of barley and a half pint of water, but some were sold after they were stolen away by stealth or taken for house slaves. And when these men were sold as house slaves, a horse was tattooed on their forehead, so that the Athenians had to endure this in addition to enslavement. But even these men were helped by their respectful and orderly demeanor, being set free or remaining with their owners in positions of honor.

Some were even saved on account of Euripides. For the Sicilians, it seems, more than any other Greeks outside their homeland, have a yearning for his poetry. They would learn by heart little specimens and morsels whenever visitors brought them, and cheerfully share them with one another. In the present situation, at least, they say that many of the Athenians who reached home safely greeted Euripides warmly, some of them recounting how they had been set free from slavery after teaching the verses of his that they remembered, and others recounting how, as they wandered around after the battle, they got food and water in exchange for singing parts of his choral hymns.

So one need not wonder that when, they say, a Kaunian ship, pursued by pirates, was putting into the harbor of Syracuse, it was not admitted at first but prevented from entering, but when the Kaunians were asked if they knew any songs by Euripides and said that they did, they were permitted to bring their ship to land.

Plutarch

A phase in the Peloponnesian War between Athens and Sparta and their allies was Athens's disastrous naval expedition to Sicily (413 BC). Most of the Athenian combatants who were not killed were enslaved, many of them being sent to work the stone quarries at Syracuse.

* * *

Some say that a motion was actually made among the allies to sell the Athenians into slavery, and the Theban, Erianthos, also proposed that they raze the city and let the land revert to pasturage for sheep. Presently, however, when the leaders assembled at their drinks and a certain Phocian sang the *parodos* of Euripides's *Elektra*, which begins

O daughter of Agamemnon,
I have come, Elektra, to your rustic courtyard,

their resolve was shaken. It seemed to them a cruel deed to destroy and put an end to a city that was so glorious and had produced such men.

Plutarch

Having taken control of Athens, the Spartan general Lysander discusses with his allies what to do with the city and its inhabitants.

The lines come from Euripides's Elektra *(167–168). The* parodos, *the first song sung by the chorus after it makes its entrance, is customarily sung in the Doric dialect, which the Spartans spoke.*

161. HOW MENANDER COMPOSES HIS PLAYS

They say that one of Menander's friends said to him, "Menander, it's almost time for the Dionysian Festival, and you haven't composed your comedy."

He replied, "But, by the gods, indeed I have. The plot is all worked out. I just need to add the verses."

Plutarch

*According to Aristotle, a tragedy has six parts: plot, character, diction, thought, spectacle, and song, of which plot is the most important. He observes that a fault of novices is that they attempt to master diction and character before they master plot construction (*Poetics *6.1450a). A poet, he goes on, should be a maker of plots more than of verses (9.1451b). Applying these principles to comedy, we find that for the naïve viewer, represented in the anecdote by Menander's friend, the versified lines of the play are its substance, whereas for the accomplished poet it is the arrangement of the incidents.*

Menander (4th–3rd centuries BC) was a popular playwright of New Comedy.

162. THE FIRST LINE OF PLATO'S *REPUBLIC*

We cannot make words fit together better by trimming or polishing them but have to use them such as they are, and choose places for them. The only thing that can make our discourse rhythmical is an appropriate change of word order. That is why the four memorable words with which Plato, in his finest work, signifies that he "went down to Peiraieus," were found written on his wax tablets in many different ways: in order that he might try out which word order would be most effective.

Quintilian

According to this anecdote, manuscripts found after Plato's death show the first four words of the Republic *written in different arrangements. These words are* katebèn chthes eis Peiraia *("I-went-down yesterday to Peiraieus"). In normal Greek six different arrangements of the words are possible. The anecdote offers a supposed glimpse into Plato's workshop, illustrating the philosopher's close attention to style and suggesting that his artistry is the product of hard work.*

163. OVID'S WORST LINES

Ovid did not use words with excessive freedom except in his poems, where he was not ignorant of his faults but loved them.

This can be plainly seen from the fact that his friends once asked him to delete three lines of his verse, and he asked in turn to be able to make an exception of three lines over which they should have no say. His condition seemed fair enough. So his friends wrote down in private the lines they wanted removed, while he wrote down the ones he wanted preserved. Each tablet had the same verses.

Albinovanus Pedo, one of those present, reported that the first line was

> semi-bull man and semi-man bull

and that the second was

> and cold Boreas and uncold Notus.

From this it appears that the gifted man did not lack the judgment to restrain poetic license, but the will. He used to say sometimes that a face is the better looking for a mole.

Seneca the Elder

The verses illustrate Ovid's willingness to be playfully repetitive. The first line (semibovemque virum semivirumque bovem), *alluding to the Minotaur, appears in Ovid's* Art of Love *(2.24), while the second* (et gelidum Borean egelidumque Notum*), describing the North and South Winds, is in his* Amores *(2.11.10). The narrator does not give the third line, or perhaps it has fallen out of the manuscript.*

ATHLETES

164. THE ORIGIN OF THE STADIUM

Since it was generally agreed that Herakles paced off the racecourse for the stadium in Pisa near the temple of Olympian Zeus, making it six hundred feet in length, and since other stadia in Greece constructed later by other men were also six hundred feet in length but a bit shorter, Pythagoras easily calculated that the length of Herakles's foot was greater than that of other men by as much, proportionally, as the Olympic stadium was longer than other stadia.

Aulus Gellius

A Greek stadium was six hundred feet long, but since the length of a foot was not standardized in ancient Greece, actual stadia varied in length. The longest was at Olympia (192.28 meters, or about 631 feet); the shortest, at Corinth (165 meters, or about 541 feet). According to the present legend, the original racecourse at Pisa, or Olympia, was established in the heroic era by Herakles, who ran six hundred steps, and the course was longer than those elsewhere because Herakles, being a hero, was larger in stature than the men who stepped out the later courses. For all that, the focus of the narrative itself is not actually the origin of the stadium racecourse but the cleverness of the philosopher Pythagoras, who managed to calculate Herakles's height and foot size by comparing the lengths of the different stadia.

*Herakles is the athlete among the gods—the first wrestler, the first pancratiast—and was treated by Greek athletes more or less as their patron deity. His heroic feats included not only subduing monsters in the wild but also founding, or cofounding, the great cultural institution of the Olympic Games. The first Olympic event to be established, and for many years perhaps the only athletic event at the festival, was the stadium race, a sprint for runners on a course (*dromos*) the length of the stadium (*stadion*). Even after the introduction of other events the men's stadium-long footrace remained the most important event at the ancient Olympic festival.*

165. THE FIRST MARATHON

According to Herakleides of Pontos it was Thersippos of Eroiadai who brought back news of the battle at Marathon, although most sources say that it was Eukles who, running in full armor and hot from the battle, burst in at the doors of the leading men, said only, "Rejoice, we are victorious!" and straightway expired.

Plutarch

The Battle of Marathon (490 BC), one of the decisive battles of world history, was fought between Greek defenders and Persian invaders in the Attic deme of Marathon, situated on the coast northeast of Athens. Despite being outnumbered, the Greeks carried the day. The legend recounts how news of the outcome of the battle was brought back to Athens, where the populace awaited word of its fate.

* * *

The first person to say *xairete* [= "rejoice"] was the ultra-long-distance runner Philippides, it is said, when he came from Marathon bringing news of the victory to the magistrates, who were sitting in session and anxious about the outcome of the battle. "Rejoice, we are victorious!" he said, dying along with his utterance, breathing his last breath with his greeting.

Lucian

The interest of the narrator lies in the origin of the Greek salutation xairete, *which means literally "rejoice" but is also commonly employed to signify "greetings" and "farewell." According to the legend, the use of the word as a salutation sprang from its employment by the Marathon messenger.*

The messenger ran the approximately twenty-four miles from Marathon to Athens, informed the magistrates of the Greek victory in a memorable utterance, and expired. The runner's name varies in different versions: Philippides (or Pheidippides) or Thersippos or Eukles. Sometimes he is called a hemerodromos *(literally "day-runner," but, in effect, "ultra-long-distance runner"), meaning that he was a professional courier.*

There was no marathon race in ancient athletics and so no legend of its origin as such. Rather, it was introduced in 1896 at the first modern Olympic Games, where the course retraced the route of the ancient Marathon messenger, proceeding from the tomb of the ancient warriors, a massive mound that covers the bodies of the fallen Greek fighters, to the modern Panathenaic Stadium in Athens. This first race was won by the Greek shepherd Spyridon Louis with a time of 2:58:50. Marathon courses are now fixed at 26.2 miles.

166. THE ORIGIN OF NUDE ATHLETES

Among the ancients it had been customary to wear loincloths around the genitals and engage in athletic contests in this manner. But at the thirty-second Olympiad, when Orsippos of Sparta was competing, his loincloth came undone, as a result of which he won. Since that time the custom has been to run nude.

Etymologicum Magnum

Greek male athletes engaged in athletic exercises and contests completely nude. The Greeks were aware that they were peculiar in this respect, differing from other peoples such as Asians and Romans; indeed, they knew that they differed from their own earlier selves. Since athletes in Homer's Iliad *and* Odyssey *wear loincloths, a change in custom took place sometime after the heroic era, in historical times. Thucydides (1.6.5) asserts that until recently athletes at the Olympic Games wore loincloths and that the Spartans were the first people to disrobe completely in athletic competitions.*

***

At the fourteenth Olympiad, when Hippomenes was archon at Athens, it happened that while runners were running the stadium race in their loincloths, one of them, Orsippos, was impeded by his loincloth, tripped, and died. As a result an oracle instructed competitors to contend nude.

scholiast

* * *

Near the grave of Koroibos is that of Orsippos, who, when athletes wore loincloths in the contests in accordance with ancient practice, ran the stadium race nude and won an Olympic victory. (They also say that later when Orsippos served as a general he annexed some neighboring territory.) It is my own opinion that he intentionally let his loincloth slip off at Olympia, knowing that a nude man runs more easily than a man wearing a loincloth.

Pausanias

* * *

In Rome the practice of wearing loincloths has persisted down to my own time, as was originally the case among the Greeks, but the Spartans put an end to it. The first person who disrobed and ran nude at Olympia was Akanthos the Spartan in the fifteenth Olympiad. Before this, all Greeks felt ashamed to display their bodies nude in athletic exercise, as is evidenced by Homer, the most trustworthy and ancient of witnesses, who represents the heroes as wearing loincloths.

Dionysios of Halikarnassos

During the stadium race Orsippos's loincloth came undone, or he intentionally discarded it, and unhampered by clothing he won the race; once the advantage of running naked was apparent, it became customary to do so. Or, his loincloth came undone such that he stumbled and was killed, whereupon an oracle instructed athletes henceforth to compete unclothed. The epitaph on Orsippos's gravestone states: "He was the first to be crowned at Olympia/nude, for previously the competitors in the stadium race wore loincloths."

The legend of Akanthos offers a competing account of the origin of nudity in Greek athletics, with a story that is similar to that of Orsippos. Whereas Orsippos ran the stadium race, Akanthos ran the "long race" (dolichos)*, which consisted of running multiple lengths of the stadium.*

167. THE ORIGIN OF NUDE TRAINERS

As you go from Skillous along the road to Olympia, before you cross the River Alpheios, there is a precipitous mountain with high cliffs. It is called Typaion. The custom among the Eleans is to cast down from it any women who are caught at the Olympic Games or who even cross the Alpheios on days when women are prohibited. They say, however, that no woman has been caught—with the sole exception of Kallipateira. (Some authors call her Pherenike rather than Kallipateira.)

Kallipateira's husband had predeceased her, and so after disguising herself to look in all respects like a male gymnastic trainer, she brought her son to Olympia to compete. When Peisirodos won, Kallipateira leapt over the wall that kept the trainers separate and, in so doing, exposed herself. Although she was detected as a woman, she was released without penalty out of respect for her father, brothers, and son, all of whom had been Olympic victors. But a law was passed requiring trainers in the future to enter the arena nude.

Pausanias

The prohibition against females as spectators at the Olympic Games applied only to married women, and the law requiring trainers to be unclothed existed only at Olympia; elsewhere trainers wore a simple cloak.

In the usual manner of traditional story the change of practice from wearing clothes to being nude is represented as the result not of a succession of gradual changes but of a single occurrence.

168. POLYMESTOR THE SPRINTER

The winner of the boys' stadium race at the forty-sixth Olympic festival—the competition was first introduced at that time—was a handsome boy, Polymestor of Miletos. In the rush of his legs he could overtake hares.

Philostratos

The folk-narrative motif of the impossibly fast runner is found in different genres from heroic legend to tall tale. The hero Iphiklos was faster than the wind and so

light in the swiftness of his feet that he could run over the top of a wheat field without bending the ears of wheat (Hesiod fr. 62 MW); the hero Euphemos could run upon the sea so swiftly that his feet did not get wet (Apollonios of Rhodes Voyage of the Argonauts *1.179–184); and the warrior maid Camilla was capable of both feats (Vergil* Aeneid *7.803–811). Legends and anecdotes about athletes often illustrate in a concrete and striking way their exceptional ability in one form of athleticism. Here the boy Polymestor can outrun a hare.*

169. AGEUS THE LONG-DISTANCE RUNNER

Ageus of Argos won the long race and brought news of his victory back to Argos on the same day.

Eusebios

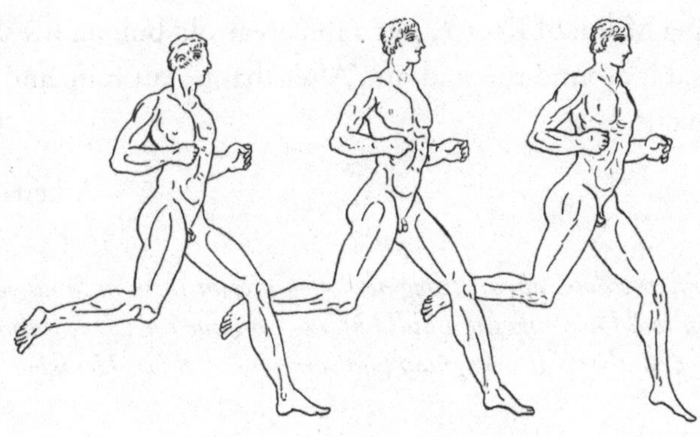

Ageus won the long race in the 113th Olympiad (328 BC), got his olive crown, and ran back home to Argos the same day to report his victory, a distance of some sixty-eight miles. On another occasion Drymos, presumably another long-distance runner, did the same, except that his home-city of Epidauros was even farther, 140 miles away. The long race varied from seven to twenty-four lengths of the stadium.

170. MILON THE WRESTLER

Milo carried a bull that he had accustomed himself to pick up since it was a calf.

Quintilian

Milon (Milo is the Latin form of his name) won six victories in wrestling at Olympia, beginning when he was a boy, and seven at the Pythian Games. Nevertheless, the legends about him focus upon his strength rather than upon his wrestling skills. Perhaps wrestling was perceived mostly as a game of strength.

In the present legend, so well known that it became proverbial, Milon lifted a calf each day, so that when it grew into a mature bull, he was still able to carry it. Similar incremental feats are told of other persons, ancient and modern. For example, the nineteenth-century Irish strongman Doney O'Donnell picked up a particular foal every day and so was still able to lift it when it was a grown horse (Cashman 2008:110–111).

* * *

In Olympia Milon of Kroton put a four-year-old bull on his shoulders and carried it around the stadium. After that he cut it up and ate it by himself in one day.

Athenaios

Legends and anecdotes about strongmen often present them as prodigious eaters. Thus Milon could not only lift a bull but also consume the whole animal. In the Greek heroic era the great strongman and voracious eater was Herakles.

* * *

When the men of Sybaris took the field with three hundred thousand, the men of Kroton were ranged against them with one hundred thousand. They were led by the athlete Milon, who because of his exceedingly great bodily strength was the first to put to flight the men ranged opposite him. This man, a six-time Olympic victor with prowess that matched his stature, is said to have presented himself in battle crowned with his Olympic garlands and equipped with a lion skin and club in the manner of Herakles.

Diodoros of Sicily

The outstanding strongman of his time identified himself with his heroic predecessor, Herakles.

* * *

Milon's death, they say, came about from wild animals. In a place near Kroton he chanced upon a tree trunk that was drying out. Wedges had been inserted into it, separating the trunk in two. In his pride Milon inserted his hands into the trunk, the wedges slipped, and he was held fast by the wood, becoming a prize for the wolves.

Pausanias

171. EUMASTAS THE STRONGMAN

Eumastas, son of Kritoboulos, lifted me from the earth.

anonymous inscription

A black, oval-shaped, volcanic boulder weighing 1,056 pounds (480 kg) is represented as speaking and declaring its own story. Found in a vineyard on the island of Thera (modern Santorini), the stone features a circular inscription incised in the sixth century

BC. A similarly circular inscription on a sandstone block weighing 315 pounds (143 kg) found at Olympia states: "Bybon, son of Pholas, threw me over his head with one hand."

172. THEAGENES'S STATUE

The Thasians say that Theagenes was not the son of Timosthenes, but that Timosthenes was a priest of Thasian Herakles and that a phantom of Herakles in the likeness of Timosthenes had sexual intercourse with Theagenes's mother.

When the boy was nine years old, they say, he was walking home from school and wrenched up the bronze statue of some god or other that was standing in the marketplace—he liked the statue—and put it on his shoulders and carried it home. The citizens were enraged at him for what he had done, but one of them, an old and respectable man, would not let them put the boy to death, but instead ordered him to bring the statue from his house back to the marketplace. When he had carried it back, the boy became very famous for his strength, and his feat was talked about throughout all Greece.

Pausanias

Local tradition accounted for the boy's astonishing strength by representing his biological father not as the mortal Timosthenes but as the hero-god Herakles, the great strongman of the heroic era, who is said to have assumed the form of Timosthenes and impregnated Theagenes's mother.

* * *

Theagenes won a total of one thousand four hundred crowns. After he had departed from this life, one of the men who were hateful to him while he lived used to come every night to his statue and flog it, abusing the bronze statue as though it were Theagenes himself. But the statue fell upon the man, which put an end to his outrageous behavior.

The dead man's children prosecuted the image for murder. The people of Thasos dropped the image into the sea, following the thinking of Drakon, who, when he wrote laws regarding homicide for the Athenians, decreed banishment even for nonliving objects if they fell upon a human being and killed him.

Pausanias

173. POULYDAMAS THE PANCRATIAST

Whereas other men have won notable victories in the pankration, Poulydamas not only won crowns for the pankration but also distinguished himself in other feats.

In the mountainous parts of Thrace, on this side of the River Nestos that runs through Abdera, wild animals of various kinds are found, including lions. These lions once attacked the army of Xerxes, mauling the camels that were carrying the food supplies. They often roam into the region around Mt. Olympos (one side of this mountain faces Macedonia, and the other side turns toward Thessaly and the River Peneios). It was there on Mt. Olympos that Poulydamas killed a lion, a huge and powerful beast, without the use of any weapon. He was drawn to this exploit from a desire to emulate the labors of Herakles, since legend has it that Herakles had subdued the Nemean lion.

Another amazing exploit by Poulydamas has entered tradition. He went into a herd of cattle and took hold of the largest and fiercest bull, holding it by the hoof of one of its hind legs and not letting go despite the animal's leaping and hurling, until at last the bull exerted all its strength and got loose, leaving its hoof behind with Poulydamas.

It is said, too, that he stopped a charioteer who was driving his chariot at a fast speed. Poulydamas grabbed the back of the chariot with one hand, constraining the horses and holding back the charioteer at the same time.

Darius—the illegitimate son of Artaxerxes, who with the help of the Persian common people dethroned Artaxerxes's legitimate son Sogdios and became ruler in his stead—learned of Poulydamas's feats, dispatched messengers promising him gifts, and persuaded him to come into his presence at Susa. There Poulydamas challenged three of the Persians called Immortals to fight him all at once, and slew them.

Some of the feats I have listed are represented on the pedestal of Poulydamas's statue in Olympia, and some are set forth in the inscription.

But, in the end, Homer's prophecy about persons who have a high opinion of their strength was destined to apply to Poulydamas as also to other men. He was fated to perish by his own strength. It was summertime, and Poulydamas and some of his close companions went into a cave, when by an unkind fate the roof began cracking and was obviously about to fall on them and would not hold out for long. Perceiving the imminent disaster, Poulydamas's companions turned to flight, while he chose to stay where he was. He lifted up his hands to hold out against the collapsing cave and not be crushed by the mountain. That was how he met his end.

Pausanias

The pankration ("total mastery") was a combat sport that mixed boxing, wrestling, kicking, and the like.

174. KLEOMEDES RUNS AMOK

At the previous Olympic festival, they say, Kleomedes of Astypalaia killed Ikkos of Epidauros in a boxing match. Charged with foul play by the judges and deprived of his victory, he went out of his mind from grief.

Returning to Astypalaia, he stopped at a school of some sixty children, where he overturned the column that held up the roof so that it collapsed upon the children. The citizens began to stone him, and he took refuge in a temple of Athena. He climbed inside a wooden chest that was standing in the temple, and drew down the lid. Although the Astypalaians tried to open the chest, their efforts were in vain, and when finally they broke the boards of the chest, they found no Kleomedes, neither dead nor alive.

So they dispatched men to Delphi to inquire what happened to Kleomedes. The Pythia, they say, gave them the following oracular response:

Last of the heroes is Kleomedes of Astypalaia.
Honor him with sacrifices since he is no longer a mortal.

And so from this time onward the Astypalaians have honored Kleomedes as a hero.

Pausanias

Kleomedes was strong by nature but inclined to violence. Deprived of his Olympic victory, he expressed his rage by destroying a schoolroom of children, perhaps the entire population of young boys in Astypalaia. Then he mysteriously disappeared within a chest in a temple. An oracle explained that Kleomedes had become a hero, a Greek cultic category designating a mortal who, instead of dying, is transformed into a powerful supernatural being.

175. ASTYLOS ANGERS HIS HOMETOWN

The statue of Astylos of Kroton is the work of Pythagoras. Astylos won three victories at Olympia in a row, in the stadium race and in the double flute. But on the second and third occasions, in order to please Hieron the son of Deinomenes, he publicly proclaimed himself a Syracusan, and for this reason the citizens of Kroton condemned his house to be a prison and pulled down the statue of him that had stood beside the temple of Lacinian Hera.

Pausanias

Different cities might lay claim to celebrity athletes for the sake of prestige, as here Astylos was claimed as a citizen by his hometown of Kroton and also by the city of Syracuse, which in the early fifth century was ruled by Hieron I.

*The "double flute" (*diaulos*) was a footrace twice the length of the stadium race, the competitors running the length of the stadium and back again.*

176. EXAINETOS PLEASES HIS HOMETOWN

In the previous Olympiad, the ninety-second, when Exainetos of Akragas won, they brought him back home to the city on a chariot, and three hundred chariots with white horses escorted him, all of them from the Akragantines themselves, in addition to other escorts.

Diodoros of Sicily

The runner Exainetos won the stadium race twice in the late fifth century. Upon his second victory he received a hero's welcome from his hometown of Akragas, Sicily.

177. GLAUKOS THE BOXER

Glaukos of Karystos, they say, was from Anthedon in Boeotia, a descendant of Glaukos the sea deity. The father of this man of Karystos was Demylos, and they say that initially he worked the land.

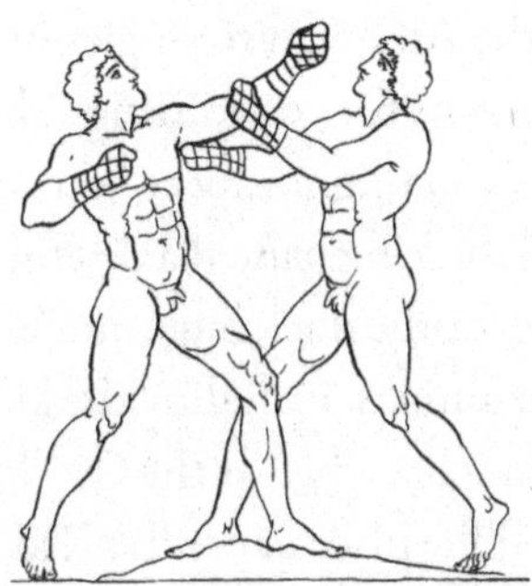

Once when the plowshare fell out of his plow, he fitted it back into place using his hand instead of a hammer. Demylos happened to observe what his son was doing, and for this reason took the boy to Olympia to box. There Glaukos, owing to his inexperience in fighting, suffered injuries from his opponents, and when he was boxing against the last of them, he appeared to be fading from the large number of blows. His father, they say, yelled at him, "Son, the one from the plow!" So he dealt his opponent a more violent blow and straightway had the victory.

They say Glaukos won other crowns, twice in the Pythian Games and eight times each in the Nemean and Isthmian Games. A statue of Glaukos, made by Glaukias of Aigina, was set up by his son. The statue represents a figure sparring, because of the men of his time Glaukos was the most fit at using his hands. When he died, they say, the people of Karystos buried him on an island that still to this day is called Glaukos's Island.

Pausanias

178. THE RELUCTANT DUELER

In the course of drinking, an unusual thing happened that is worth mentioning.

Included among the king's companions was a certain Macedonian named Koragos, who surpassed other men in physical strength and had performed many deeds of bravery in battle. Spurred on by the drink, he challenged Dioxippos the Athenian to single combat. Dioxippos was an athlete who had won crowns for very distinguished victories. The guests at the drinking party, as you might expect, joined in egging him on, and after Dioxippos agreed, the king named a day for the fight.

When the time came for the duel, huge numbers of men convened for the spectacle. The Macedonians, including the king, favored Koragos because of their shared ethnicity, whereas the Greeks sided with Dioxippos. The Macedonian entered the place of contest clad in expensive armor, and the Athenian entered unclothed, his body oiled, carrying a club of suitable size. Both men were looked at with wonder for their physical strength and preeminence in prowess, as though the spectators expected a battle of gods. The Macedonian, causing amazement because of his physical stature and the brilliance of his arms, was thought to look somewhat like Ares, while Dioxippos excelled in strength and athletic training, and because of the peculiarity of his club bore a resemblance to Herakles.

As they came at each other, the Macedonian cast his javelin from a suitable distance, but the other man turned aside slightly and avoided the oncoming strike. Then the one charged holding his Macedonian pike leveled, but as he got close, the other struck the pike with his club and broke it. Experiencing two setbacks, the Macedonian was forced to have recourse to his sword. As he was about to draw it, the Greek sprung on him and with his left hand seized the man's swordhand, while with his other hand he knocked his opponent off balance and caused him to lose his footing. When the Macedonian fell to the ground, the Greek placed his foot on the man's throat, lifted his club aloft, and looked up at the spectators.

The crowd roared on account of the unexpected course of events and the superiority of the man's skill. The king ordered that Koragos be let go, dissolved the gathering, and left, feeling upset at the defeat of the Macedonian. Dioxippos released his fallen opponent and, having won a resounding victory, departed, crowned with a headband by his compatriots, as having brought credit upon all Greeks. But Fortune did not allow the man to boast of his victory for long.

The king became more and more unfavorably disposed toward him. Alexander's friends and all the Macedonians at court, who were jealous of the man's prowess, persuaded one of the servants to place a golden drinking cup under his banqueting cushion, and at the next drinking party they pretended to find the cup, and accused Dioxippos of theft, bringing shame and disgrace upon him.

Perceiving the coordinated action of the Macedonians against him, Dioxippos left the drinking party and came shortly to his own quarters, where he wrote a letter to Alexander about what had been contrived against him. After instructing his servants to give it to the king, he took his own life.

Although he was ill-advised to agree to the single combat, taking his own life was far more senseless, and for this reason many of the persons who found fault with him and rebuked him for his foolishness declared that it was a hard thing to have great strength of body but a weak mind.

Reading the letter, the king was upset at the man's death. He often missed the man's excellence, which he had not made use of while the man was around, and he yearned for him now that he was gone, perceiving that the excellence of the man was of no use to him after the cowardice of his accusers.

Diodoros of Sicily

The initial scene of the narrative is a feast hosted by Alexander the Great.

The legend confronts two kinds of men, the flashy and brash warrior Koragos and the modest and agile athlete Dioxippos. The latter was drawn into a match that he did not seek and did not want, and in the absence of fair play (although the narrator deems him to have overreacted) it led tragically to his doom. The trick by which he was brought down, the planted cup, is well known from the Hebrew legend of Joseph (Genesis 44) but is found in Greek tradition and elsewhere as well.

CHAPTER 6

MEMORABLE WORDS, NOTABLE ACTIONS

This chapter consists of legends and anecdotes about well-known persons, ranging from portents of future greatness, through characterization by means of words or deeds or experiences, to exit lines and gestures at life's end.

PORTENTS

An event in the early life of a future celebrity often foreshadows his or her subsequent nature.

179. THE INFANT PINDAR ON MT. HELIKON

When Pindar was a boy, as Chamaileon and Istros write, he was hunting in the area of Mt. Helikon and, feeling very tired, drifted off into sleep. As he lay asleep a bee settled on his mouth and made a honeycomb.

Ambrosian Life of Pindar

A honeybee landed on the mouth of the future poet Pindar and proceeded to produce honey, portending the youth's future eloquence as a favorite of the Muses, whose agents bees are. The scene, Mt. Helikon, was sacred to the Muses, the very place where earlier the Boeotian shepherd Hesiod encountered these goddesses, who made him a singer (Hesiod Theogony *22–35).*

180. THE INFANT PLATO ON MT. HYMETTOS

Periktione was carrying Plato in her arms, and Ariston was sacrificing to the Muses or nymphs. While some members of their party were occupied with the ritual, she put Plato down in the dense and thick myrtle that lay nearby. As Plato slept, a swarm of humming bees laid honey from Hymettos on his lips, presaging in this way his eloquence.

Aelian

Plato's parents made an excursion to nearby Mt. Hymettos, southeast of Athens, to perform a sacrifice, fittingly enough to the Muses or nymphs, who appeared to reciprocate by bestowing the gift of future eloquence upon the infant child. Or the bees portended what was already fated to happen. Hymettos was renowned for its honey.

181. YOUNG DEMOSTHENES IN COURT

When Demosthenes came of age, he received from his guardians less than he should have gotten, and as their ward he took them to court. This occurred during the archonship of Timokrates. There were three of them: Aphobos, Therippides, and Demophon (or Demeas), and Demosthenes especially accused the last named because the man was his mother's brother. He claimed damages of ten talents in each suit, and obtained convictions. He did not, however, exact any part of the penalty but let them go, some for money and some as a favor.

Pseudo-Plutarch

When young Demosthenes was seven years old, his father died, after which he and his sister were raised by their mother, Kleoboule, and the family together with its monetary resources came under the control of male guardians, including a maternal uncle. Demosthenes's future career as a brilliant speaker was portended when as a youth he successfully sued his guardians for cheating him of his inheritance.

CHARACTERIZATIONS

182. A STATUE OF HOMER

A Pierian bee wandered about his divine mouth,
Working industriously to produce wax dripping with honey.

Christodoros of Egyptian Thebes

Describing statues in a public gymnasium, a poet includes this detail about a bronze statue of Homer.

As usual, honey in the mouth signifies eloquence, but here it is a sign of respect celebrating the poet's mellifluous verse rather than a portent of his future accomplishment.

183. THEMISTOKLES AND THE MAN FROM SERIPHOS

When a man from Seriphos was disparaging Themistokles, saying that his distinction was owed not to himself but to his city, he replied, "I would not be a man of note if I were from Seriphos, nor would you if you were from Athens."

Plato

The anecdote wittily distinguishes contributing cause from sufficient cause. Seriphos is a small and, relatively speaking, insignificant Cycladic island in the Aegean Sea.

184. ARISTEIDES THE JUST

As voters were inscribing their *ostraka*, it is said, one of the illiterate, very rustic voters held up his *ostrakon* to Aristeides as if he were any chance person, and asked him to write ARISTEIDES on it. Surprised, Aristeides asked him whether Aristeides had done him some wrong. "Not at all," said the man. "I don't even know the fellow, but I'm tired of hearing him called 'the Just' everywhere."

On hearing this, Aristeides made no reply but inscribed his own name on the ostrakon and gave it back to the man.

Plutarch

In the peculiar Athenian institution of ostracism, citizens scratched upon an ostrakon, *or potsherd, the name of a citizen they thought should be banished from the city for ten (later, five) years. The idea was to expel persons whose prestige or power seemed to be a threat to the democracy as an institution. After the ostraka were tallied, the man who received the most votes had to withdraw from Athens. The statesman Aristeides, son of Lysimachos, was ostracized in 482 BC. One hundred and twenty-one sherds incised with his name have been found. They survive because old ostraka were sometimes used as fill.*

185. TIMON THE MISANTHROPE

Antony left the city and the company of his friends, and constructing a mole that extended out into the sea, prepared a dwelling for himself by the sea near Pharos. There he lived as an exile from mankind, declaring that he was content to imitate the life of Timon on the ground that their experiences were similar. Like Timon, he said, he had been treated poorly and thanklessly by his friends, and for this reason distrusted and disliked everyone.

This Timon was an Athenian who lived around the time of the Peloponnesian War, as can be inferred from plays by Aristophanes and Platon in which he is lampooned as being hostile and misanthropic.

Although he avoided and repulsed every human interaction, he used to greet Alkibiades, who at that time was young and spirited, and kiss him enthusiastically. When Apemantos expressed surprise at his behavior and asked the reason for it, Timon said he loved the youth because he knew he would be the cause of much suffering for the Athenians.

The only person Timon sometimes admitted to his company was Apemantos, because Apemantos imitated Timon's mode of life and was like him. Once during the Festival of the Pitchers the two men were feasting by themselves, and Apemantos said, "Timon, what a nice dinner party we are having." "Yes, it would be," he replied, "if you weren't here."

One time when the Athenians were gathered in assembly, it is said, Timon walked up to the speaker's platform, an action so incredible that it caused everyone to fall silent and to expect something important. "Athenians," he said, "I own a small piece of land, and there is a fig tree growing on it. From this tree many of our fellow citizens have hanged themselves. Since I am now planning to build a house on the place, I wanted to proclaim my intention publicly so that if any of you wish to do so, you may hang yourselves before the tree is cut down."

When he died and was buried at Halai beside the sea, the shore in front of his grave eroded away, and the waves surrounded it, making the grave inaccessible and unapproachable. His epitaph reads:

Here I lie, having broken off my oppressive life.
You won't learn my name, and to Hades with you.

They say he composed it when he was still alive. But the epitaph in current oral circulation was composed by Kallimachos:

I who dwell herein am Timon the misanthrope. But pass by.
Curse me all you want, just pass by.

These are a few of the many anecdotes told about Timon.

Plutarch

After Mark Antony (Marcus Antonius), the Roman statesman, general, and lover of Cleopatra, was defeated by Octavian at Actium in 31 BC, he made his way to Alexandria, Egypt, where he withdrew to a solitary dwelling in the harbor near Pharos, the lighthouse. There he likened himself to the famed misanthrope Timon and even named his residence the Timoneion.

Like the Cynic philosopher Diogenes, Timon was a familiar type in Greek popular tradition. "He's a real Timon!" remarks one character about another in a Greek comedy (Aristophanes Birds *1549). According to Lucian's dialogue* Timon, or the Misanthrope, *Timon was once a wealthy man whose friends exploited his wealth but deserted him in his poverty. In the present passage Antony has this backstory in mind when he complains that his friends have treated him thanklessly. Lucian's* Timon *was the principal inspiration for Shakespeare's* Life of Timon of Athens *and Molière's* Misanthrope.

186. THE ARREST OF THERAMENES

The herald of the Thirty ordered the Eleven to go to Theramenes. As they entered with their servants, led by Satyros, the boldest and most shameless of them, Kritias said, "We hand over this man here, Theramenes, who has been condemned according to the law. You, the Eleven, take him and lead him away to the proper place and take care of the next steps."

As he said this, Satyros began dragging him away from the altar, and his servants did likewise. Theramenes, as you would expect, called upon gods and men to witness what was happening. The members of the Council remained silent, perceiving that the men at the railing within the council chamber were of the same sort as Satyros and that the front of the council house was full of guards, who, they were also well aware, had come armed with daggers.

They led Theramenes away through the agora as he shouted out in a loud voice what was happening to him. One of his reported utterances is the following. When Satyros said he would be sorry if he didn't keep quiet, Theramenes asked, "And if I do keep quiet, then I won't be sorry?" And they say that subsequently, when he was being compelled to die by drinking hemlock, he tossed out the last drops as though he were playing *kottabos*, and said, "Let this one be for the handsome Kritias!"

Now, I am well aware that such apothegms are not worthy of mention, but I deem it admirable in the man that although death stood beside him, he kept both his presence of mind and his sense of humor.

Xenophon

Toward the end of the fifth century BC Athens was ruled by a junta of conservative oligarchs called the Thirty, whose leader was Kritias. A board of citizens in charge of condemned persons was known as the Eleven.

The story of the arrest and execution of the politician Theramenes in 404 BC illustrates the statesman's wit and composure in the face of flagrant injustice. Although Xenophon apologizes for reporting mere apothegms (the word appears in this passage for the first time), it is Theramenes's retort in the first instance and his ironic toast in the second that capture the man's character and make the events memorable.

Kottabos *was a Greek drinking game played by men at symposia, or drinking parties. A lover toasted his beloved, usually a younger male, while attempting to toss the dregs of his wine goblet accurately into a bowl some distance away. Theramenes treats the gesture mockingly, toasting his enemy rather than his lover and using poison instead of wine (Russo 1997:61–62).*

187. SOCRATES'S HARDIHOOD

Later on we [= Alkibiades and Socrates] participated in the military campaign against Potidaia together and were messmates there. Now, first, with regard to the hardships Socrates surpassed not only me but also everyone else—whenever we were cut off and forced to go without eating, as happens on a campaign, we others lacked all ability to endure—but when there was abundant food, he was singularly able to enjoy it. And when he was obliged to drink against his will, he outdrank everyone, and, most amazing of all, no one has ever seen Socrates drunk. And this next seems to me the real test of this. So far as enduring the winters there—and they are really severe—he was amazing, including a time when there was a bad frost and no one ventured outside, or if he did, he wrapped himself in a mound of clothing and wore footwear, wrapping his feet in felt and sheepskin. Socrates went outdoors in these conditions wearing only the sort of cloak that he otherwise was accustomed to wear, and he made his way over the ice barefoot more easily than the other men did with footwear. The soldiers gave him dirty looks as though he were disdaining them.

Plato

Alkibiades, a young admirer of Socrates, describes his experience of him as a fellow soldier during the Athenian siege of Potidaia (432–430 BC).

188. SOCRATES PONDERS A PROBLEM

After reflecting on some matter, Socrates arose early in the morning pondering it, and when a solution did not come to him, he did not give it up but stood there trying to find an answer. Presently it was midday, and people began noticing him and saying to one another in astonishment that Socrates had been standing there since early morning thinking about something. Finally in the evening some of the Ionians ate their supper and—it was summertime when this happened—brought their bedding outside to lie down in the coolness and also to keep an eye on Socrates to see if he was going to stand there all night. He stood there until dawn and sunrise. Then, with a prayer to the sun, he went away.

Plato

After describing Socrates's hardihood, Alkibiades goes on to relate this anecdote about Socrates's working through a problem.

189. DEMOSTHENES'S HANDICAPS

They say that when Demosthenes was still a young man he withdrew to a cave and studied there, having shaved half of his head to keep himself from going out. In order to get up quickly he slept on a narrow bed. He worked moreover on the sound of "r," which he was unable to pronounce. Since his shoulder made an awkward movement when he practiced speaking, he put a stop to it by hanging a small spit, or as some say a dagger, from the ceiling to frighten himself into remaining at rest. As he progressed in the force of his speaking, he equipped himself with a full-length mirror and looked at it while he practiced so as to correct his faults. And they say he used to go down to the seashore at Phaleron and broadcast his thoughts to the breakers in order that if people should sometime make a commotion, he would not be distracted. As he was short of breath, he paid the actor Neoptolemos ten thousand drachmas to teach him to speak whole periods without taking a breath.

Pseudo-Plutarch

* * *

To his physical defects Demosthenes applied the following regimen, as Demetrios of Phaleron reports, saying that he heard about it from Demosthenes himself when the latter was an old man. Demosthenes got rid of his indistinctness of speech and corrected his lisp by reciting speeches with pebbles in his mouth. His voice he exercised by running or by climbing a steep slope while conversing, and by reciting speeches or lines of verse without taking a breath. He had a large mirror at home and went through his exercises standing in front of it.

Plutarch

When the young Demosthenes is not presented as a prodigy who successfully sued his guardians (181 "Young Demosthenes in Court"), he is characterized as the contrary, an unpromising hero, an orphan who aspired to be an orator but suffered from handicaps such as shortness of breath and a speech defect. The handicapped youth dealt determinedly with his shortcomings by means of an extraordinary self-imposed program of training and discipline. Doubtless the most remembered feature of his regimen today is his declaiming with pebbles in his mouth.

190. "DELIVERY!"

Once, Demosthenes left the assembly and was walking home feeling low. Eunomos the Thriasian, already an old man, chanced to meet him and gave him encouragement. But the person who encouraged him the most was the actor Andronikos, who told him that his speeches were fine but his manner of delivery was deficient, whereupon Andronikos recited from memory the words spoken by Demosthenes in the assembly. Convinced, Demosthenes entrusted himself to Andronikos. And so when someone asked Demosthenes what the first thing in oratory was, he said, "Delivery." And what was the second? "Delivery." And the third? "Delivery."

Pseudo-Plutarch

191. ONLY HUMAN

When Philip overcame the Athenians at Chaironeia, he was elated by his success. Still, he kept his senses and did not become arrogant. For this reason, he thought he ought to be reminded by one of his slaves each morning that he was a human being, and assigned this task to his slave. And so, they say, he did not go out nor did any petitioner come in before his slave had shouted out to him three times, "Philip, you are a human being."

Aelian

The success referred to is the resounding victory of Philip II of Macedon over Athens and her allies at Chaironeia in 338 BC.

In the same spirit as Philip's routine, it is commonly supposed that during Roman triumphal processions a slave stood behind the triumphator *in his chariot and repeatedly whispered, "Look behind you. Remember you are a man."*

The anecdote about Philip's handling of his victory makes a fine contrast with that concerning his son Alexander, who upon his own successes desired to be proclaimed a divinity (203 "Alexander the Great Becomes a God").

192. WHAT ALEXANDER SLEEPS UPON

Alexander was by nature a lover of learning as well as a lover of reading. Since he deemed and called the *Iliad* a viaticum of the art of war, he carried with him Aristotle's edition, the one called the *Iliad of the Chest*. He always kept it under his pillow along with his dagger.

Plutarch

The narrative illustrates a recurrent theme of ancient anecdotes, that this or that famous man sleeps upon a particular book, suggesting that he deems it personally significant. Thus Plato not only brought the mimes of Sophron to Athens but also slept with them beneath his head (Diogenes Laertios 3.18). Here, in an interesting variation on the theme, the warrior Alexander the Great kept under his pillow a copy of Homer's Iliad *and a dagger.*

193. CLEOPATRA'S WAGER

There were two pearls, the largest in all history. They were the possessions of Cleopatra, last of the queens of Egypt, and had been handed down to her from the kings of the East.

Now, when Antony was gorging himself daily with exquisite banquets, Cleopatra, with bold and haughty pride, like the whorish queen she was, spoke disparagingly of all their splendor and display. When Antony asked her what addition could increase the magnificence of his feasting, Cleopatra replied that she herself would expend ten million sesterces on a single meal. Although Antony was eager to learn how this could be done, he doubted it was possible.

So they made a wager, and on the following day, when the matter was to be decided, Cleopatra had a banquet set before Antony that was indeed magnificent—in order that the day not be wasted—but no more extravagant than usual. Antony made fun of it and belittled the expense. But Cleopatra said that the banquet itself was merely an extra, affirming that it would round off her account and indeed that her meal alone would cost ten million sesterces, whereupon she gave orders for a second course to be served.

As instructed, her servants placed before her a single vessel of vinegar, the strength and harshness of which were sufficient to turn pearls into slush. She was wearing in her ears that singular and truly unique work of nature that pearls are. As Antony waited to see what she was going to do, she took off one of her earrings, dropped it into the vinegar, and when it was liquefied, swallowed it. Then she reached for the other earring, preparing to consume it too in the same way, but Lucius Plancus, who was umpire of the wager, declared that Antony had been defeated, an ominous remark that was subsequently confirmed.*

A story is also told about the mate of that celebrated pearl. After the queen who had won the grand wager was herself captured, it was cut in two, and half of Antony and Cleopatra's banquet was put on each ear of the Venus in the Pantheon at Rome.

Pliny the Elder

The anecdote illustrates oriental luxury and in particular the extravagant private life of Cleopatra and the Egyptian court, as seen from a European perspective. Of two magnificent pearls, handed down from monarch to monarch in the East and too precious for ordinary mortals, one was consumed by the queen, and the other was cut in two to make earrings for the statue of a goddess.

As usual, scholars focus their energies almost exclusively upon the question of the anecdote's historicity. They disagree about whether pearls do actually dissolve in vinegar, and some commentators suspect that the wily Cleopatra swallowed her

---

*In 31 BC Mark Antony was defeated in a naval battle at Actium by Octavian.

pearl whole and recovered it later. But consuming pearls was not unique to Cleopatra, for ancient authors mention other persons who consumed a pearl dissolved in vinegar or wine, such as the emperor Caligula (Suetonius Gaius *37). It was a quirky and extravagant but not outrageous gesture. Noteworthy in Cleopatra's case was the extraordinary value of the pearl she consumes, as indicated by its royal pedigree, the wager, and the intervention of the umpire to prevent the destruction of its mate.*

194. THE LAMPREY POOLS

That was the year Vedius Pollio died, a man who in other respects had accomplished nothing worthy of remembrance—he was descended from freedmen, was reckoned among the knights, and had performed no splendid deed—but became famous on account of his wealth and his cruelty, and as such entered the historical record. Most of his doings it would be tedious to relate, but he had pools in which he raised lampreys that had been trained to eat human beings. Any slave he condemned to death he threw into these pools.

On one occasion when Pollio was entertaining Augustus, his cupbearer broke a crystal chalice. Without any consideration for his dinner guest, Pollio ordered the slave to be thrown into the lamprey tanks. The slave cast himself at the feet of Augustus and supplicated him, whereupon Augustus tried to persuade Pollio not to do such a thing. When Pollio did not comply with his request, Augustus said, "Bring out all the rest of the drinking cups you have like this one and any other special cups you own, so that I can use them." After they were brought out, he ordered them to be broken. When Pollio saw this, he was distressed, since for one thing he was angry more about the large number of other chalices that had been destroyed than about the one chalice, and for another thing he could not punish his servant for Augustus's actions. Much against his will, he said nothing.

That was the sort of man Pollio was, who died at that time.

Cassius Dio

This anecdotal legend is one of several that illustrate the evils of slavery as an institution in which one person has absolute, or virtually absolute, power over another. On the practices of Roman slaveholders and the lives of their slaves see Joshel (2010:111–160).

195. A PRINCIPLED MAN

It was for Titus Labienus that a new punishment was first devised. His enemies brought it about that all his books were burnt. It was an unheard-of novelty that punishment should be exacted from literature.

* * *

Labienus could not bear this affront, nor did he wish to outlive his own talent. He had himself carried to the tomb of his ancestors and shut in, fearing, I suppose, that his body might be denied the flames to which his authorship had been subjected. So he not only put an end to his own life but even buried himself.

* * *

A fine quip by Cassius Severus, a person much disliked by Labienus, was in circulation at the time when by the decree of the senate Labienus's books were burnt. "Now *I* ought to be burnt alive," he said, "since I know his books by heart."

Seneca the Elder

Since the orator Titus Labienus did not wish to survive the books he had written, he had himself immured in the family mausoleum, and died there. But Cassius Severus knew the man's works by heart, and said so publicly. So in AD 8 the Roman Senate also sentenced Cassius's writings to the fire, and Cassius himself to exile in Crete. Once there, he was given the opportunity to repent, which he declined to do. Later the senate made his punishment even harsher, banishing him to the little island of Seriphos, where he eventually died.

196. NERO FIDDLES

A disaster followed, though it is uncertain whether it was due to chance or to the guile of the emperor (each version has its backers), a more serious and terrible conflagration than all the others that had befallen Rome.

It arose in the part of the Circus that borders the Palatine and Caelian Hills. The fire started and gained strength in shops stocked with flammable goods, and stirred by the wind it hastened along the entire length of the Circus, where there were no houses with boundary walls or temples with surrounding walls or anything else to slow it down. In their fury the flames first overran the level districts, then rose up to the heights, and then again ravaged the lower areas. The fire kept ahead of all measures to temper it because of its speed and because of the narrow, winding, and irregular streets that were typical of old Rome.

Add to these difficulties terrified and wailing women, weak persons, and young children, some of them seeing to themselves, some of them to others, as they dragged along the infirm or waited for them, impeding everything by their slowness or their haste. Often, if they looked behind them, they found they were surrounded by fire on the sides or in front, or if they made their way to neighboring districts, they found those areas also attacked, and even distant districts were discovered to be in the same plight. At last, uncertain about where to go and where not to go, they filled the roads and lay down in fields. Some who had lost all their means, even their daily food, chose to die despite there being a means of escape open to them, as did others also, out of love for relatives whom they were unable to rescue.

No one dared to fight the fire, since there were persons who with repeated threats prevented others from extinguishing the flames, while some openly threw firebrands, shouting that they were authorized to do so, either because they really were acting under orders or the more freely to loot.

At this time Nero was staying in Antium and did not return to the city until the fire was nearing his own house, which connected the

Palatine with the Gardens of Maecenas. Still, it was not possible to prevent the Palatine, his house, and all the surroundings from being destroyed. As a relief for the homeless and fugitive populace, Nero opened up the Campus Martius, the buildings of Agrippa, and even his own gardens, and had some shelters hastily constructed to accommodate the destitute multitude. The necessities of life were conveyed up from Ostia and nearby towns, and the price of grain was lowered to three sesterces.

All these popular measures lost their effect, however, when a rumor went around that at the very time when Rome was in flames, Nero mounted his private stage and sang the *Fall of Troy*, likening the present disaster to a calamity of olden times.

Tacitus

The Great Fire of Rome ravaged the city for around a week in the summer of AD 64. Ancient opinion was divided as to whether the emperor himself bore some responsibility for it, since he may have wished to clear out part of the city for his own use. Be that as it may, several ancient historians report that Nero donned his performance clothes, mounted his private stage (or watched the conflagration from the nearby Tower of Maecenas), and, as the fire raged, sang of the destruction of Troy. Nero is known to have composed a Troica, *or* Song of Troy *(Juvenal* Satires *8.211–230).*

The emperor was in fact an enthusiastic musician and often performed in public competitions. He played the Greek kithara, *a stringed instrument (and ultimate source of our word "guitar") that the player, usually a professional musician, strummed or plucked.*

Although the legend of Nero's singing inspired the English-language saying "Nero fiddled while Rome burned," the precise origin of the expression is not known. It is not ancient and must have arisen no earlier than the 1500s, when the noun "fiddle" (from Latin fidula, *signifying any stringed instrument) came into use in English and the verb "fiddle" developed the secondary sense of aimless activity, as in "fiddle around." Both meanings seem to be present in this expression, for Nero literally plays a stringed instrument and, in doing so, indulges himself in an activity that does not make a helpful contribution toward the crisis in the city.*

197. "WHERE WOULD HE BE NOW?"

Mauricus, you will say, spoke with firmness and courage on that occasion. Well, of course. It was nothing new for him. He acted no less courageously in the company of the emperor Nerva.

Nerva was once dining with a few others. Reclining next to him and even leaning on his chest was Veiento. Merely to name that creature is to say it all. The conversation turned to Catullus Messalinus, whose loss of sight had only added to his cruel nature. The man felt no fear or shame or pity, for which reason Domitian quite often dispatched him like an arrow that traveled blindly and thoughtlessly against some upright man. The diners were all talking about Messalinus's depravity and murderous decisions, when the emperor asked, "What do you think would have happened to him if he were still alive?" "Why, he would be dining with us," said Mauricus.

Pliny the Younger

Pliny's anecdote excellently illustrates the outspokenness of Junius Mauricus, who expressed himself freely even in the presence of powerful and dangerous people. Fabricius Veiento, present at the table, and Catullus Messalinus, the topic of conversation, were notorious and much-feared informers.

198. A SLAVE'S EYE

I saw someone in anger stick a reed pen into his slave's eye. And the emperor Hadrian, they say, stuck his pen into the eye of one of his attendants. After realizing that in stabbing him, he had destroyed the slave's eye, Hadrian summoned the man and told him to choose a gift to compensate for his injury. When the injured man remained silent, Hadrian again bade him ask for whatever he wanted. The slave said that he only wanted his eye back.

And indeed what gift could be worth the loss of an eye?

Galen

Although the physician Galen was not himself present at the event with Hadrian, which preceded his employment at court, he says he personally witnesses another instance of a person's angrily poking his pen into a slave's eye.

199. THE PEOPLE OF AKRAGAS

When he saw the people of Akragas building lavish houses and dining with equal extravagance, Plato said, "The Akragantines build houses as if they are going to live forever, but they dine as if they are going to die tomorrow."

Aelian

Akragas (Latin Agrigentum) lay on the southwest coast of Sicily. Its inhabitants, like the Sybarites, were represented in tradition as living lives of astonishing luxury. The Akragantines reputedly used oil flasks of silver and reclined on couches of solid ivory (Aelian Historical Miscellany *12.29). However, the present anecdote is also told of other Greek cities and the utterance attributed to other philosophers.*

LACONIC SPARTANS

Spartans were famous for their brachylogia, *or terseness, although their words could hit the mark. Plato's Protagoras observes that "if a man converses with a very ordinary Spartan, he'll find his conversation to be ordinary for the most part, and then at some chance point in the conversation the Spartan, like a fine spear-thrower, will toss in a notable phrase, brief and taut, making the person he's talking with appear like a child"* (Protagoras *342d–e; see further Bayliss [2009:236–240]).*

200. TOO MANY WORDS

When Samians who had been banished by Polykrates arrived at Sparta, they stood before the authorities and gave a long speech, one in proportion to their great need. At this first meeting the Spartans responded that they had forgotten the first words and did not understand the rest.

After this the Samians stood before the authorities a second time and, carrying a sack, said nothing but that the sack needed meal. The Spartans responded that the word "sack" was superfluous. But they did decide to help the Samians.

Herodotos

In their dislike of wordiness the Spartans explained that it would have been enough for the Samians to have pointed to the sack and said, "Needs meal."

201. A SPARTAN MOTHER

A Spartan woman, handing her son his shield, exhorted him, "Son, either with this or on this."

Plutarch

*The force of this famous apothegm, spoken in the Spartan dialect, comes from its terseness and its sentiment. For the first, the utterance is elliptical. With Laconic brevity the Spartan mother tells her son, as he departs for military service, that when he returns he should either be carrying his shield or be carried on it. A soldier who wanted to beat as quick a retreat as possible might cast aside his shield in order not to be encumbered by it. Such a person was a "toss-shield" (*rhipsaspis*). For the second, she makes clear that she cares more about honor than her son's life, preferring a dead son to a cowardly one.*

*The anecdote probably circulated mostly among non-Spartans, expressing an image of Spartans that fascinated outsiders, though perhaps Spartans would have approved. Laconic apothegms were a recognized subgenre of the Greek apothegm tradition. Aristotle (*Rhetoric *2.21.8) refers to them, and Plutarch published two collections of them,* Laconic Apothegms (Apophthegmata Lakonika) *and* Apothegms of Spartan Women (Lakainon Apophthegmata).

202. DISCUSSION AT THERMOPYLAE

When Xerxes wrote Leonidas a message, telling him to hand over his weapons, Leonidas wrote back, "Come take them."

Plutarch

*The Persian king Xerxes invaded Greece in 480 BC and was confronted at the pass of Thermopylae by the Spartan king Leonidas with a small group of Greek defenders. The Spartan king's famous response to Xerxes's demand is even more succinct in Greek (*molon labe*) than in English.*

203. ALEXANDER THE GREAT BECOMES A GOD

After Alexander overcame Darius and gained control of the Persian Empire, he had a very high opinion of himself and felt that because of the success that embraced him, he was becoming a god. So he sent word to the Greeks to vote that he was a god.

How laughable! What he did not possess by nature, he was not going to gain by asking it of human beings. So while different communities voted one thing or another, the Spartans voted as follows: "Since Alexander wants to be a god, so be it."

In their native Laconic manner the Spartans treated Alexander's stupidity with contempt.

Aelian

204. ON SPARTAN ADULTERY

People recall the argument put forth by a certain Geradas, a Spartan of the old sort. When he was asked by a stranger what the punishment for adulterers was among them, Geradas said, "Stranger, there is no adulterer among us."

The man replied, "Well, if there were one."

"His penalty is to provide a bull so large that it will span Mount Taygetos as it drinks from the Eurotas River."

The man was astounded and said, "But how could there be so huge a bull?"

Geradas said with a laugh, "How could there be an adulterer in Sparta?"

Plutarch

Sparta is situated in the valley of the Eurotas River. To its west lies the Taygetos range, which runs in a southerly direction. So the imaginary bull would face east as it stands astride the mountain range and drinks from the stream. In the idealized Sparta of the past, Spartan women were so virtuous that adultery was unthinkable. The anecdote begins as a classic apothegm and continues with additional probing and responses. Its logic is much like that in 239 "Thales on Life and Death."

DELUSION

205. MENEKRATES, WHO CALLS HIMSELF ZEUS

Menekrates. A physician of Syracuse.

Although he did not charge any fees for his treatments (he treated the sacred disease), he demanded that persons who had been treated successfully by him agree to be his slaves. He called himself Zeus, and the persons healed by him he called gods, giving each one a name, one man being Hermes, another Apollon.

Suda

Menekrates (4th century BC) was a Sicilian physician whose specialty was the treatment of epilepsy, known also as the sacred disease. Enjoying much success, he referred to himself as Menekrates-Zeus, dressed like the god Zeus, and went about with a following of people who regarded themselves as deities and dressed accordingly.

The counterpart to Menekrates in the mythological tradition was King Salmoneus, who called himself Zeus, ordered his subjects to sacrifice to him, and drove around in his chariot flinging torches into the sky as though they were lightning. In the end, Zeus destroyed him and the inhabitants of his city with a real thunderbolt.

***

By Athena, not even Menekrates of Syracuse, the one who added Zeus to his name, would have prided himself in this [= bringing the dead back to life], although he did pride himself through his medical skill as being the sole cause of life for humankind. In any case he treated a number of persons afflicted with the so-called sacred disease, making them draw up a contract according to which if they should be saved, they would obey him as his slaves.

One of his followers was a person with a Herakles outfit who was called Herakles. (This man, Nikostratos of Argos, had been cured of the sacred disease.) He is mentioned by Ephippos in *The Peltast*, who says,

> Didn't Menekrates used to say that he was the god Zeus?
> And Nikostratos the Argive, that he was another Herakles?

Another man had a cloak, caduceus, and wings like Hermes, as Nikagoras of Zeleia says. He became a ruler of his native city, according to the historian Batos in his work *On the Tyrants of Ephesos*. Hegesandros says that Astykreon was cured by Menekrates and called Apollon. Another man cured by him adopted the attire of Asklepios and went around with him to his own ruin. Zeus himself was dressed in purple, had a golden crown on his head, wielded a scepter, and shod in boots went around with his band of divinities.

Athenaios

Menekrates's following included the sun god Helios, whose given name was Alexarchos. He founded a city, Ouranopolis (Heaven City), on the peninsula of Athos. Ouranopolis had its own coins and its own dialect, a special form of speech characterized by the use of kennings (Athenaios 3.98e; Squillace 2012:162–165), presumably in imitation of the old idea that the gods spoke a peculiar language of their own.

206. MENEKRATES-ZEUS WRITES TO KING PHILIP

Menekrates once sent a letter to King Philip, writing as follows:

> Menekrates-Zeus to Philip: greetings!
>
> You are king of Macedonia, and I of the art of medicine. You can destroy healthy persons when you wish, whereas I can heal the

> sick and keep vigorous persons who obey me free from sickness and alive until old age. Macedonian bodyguards attend you, but all posterity attends me, for as Zeus I give them life.

Philip sent him a letter back, treating him as a madman:

> Philip to Menekrates: get well!

In a similar way Menekrates sent letters to King Archidamos of Sparta and to others, always using the name Zeus.

Athenaios

*In his response Philip plays upon Greek conventions for greeting someone in live social interaction and written letters. The most common salutation was "rejoice" (see 165 "The First Marathon"). Thus letters customarily began with the salutation "A bids B rejoice (*xairein*)," meaning in effect "A sends greetings to B" and corresponding to our "Dear B." Whereas Menekrates's salutation to Philip is unremarkable ("Menekrates bids Philip rejoice"), Philip's countersalutation is ironic: "Philip bids Menekrates get well (*hygiainein*)."*

207. PHILIP HOSTS MENEKRATES

Philip once invited Menekrates and his personal gods to dinner. He had them all recline together on a couch situated in the middle and decorated in a very stately and reverend manner. Alongside it he had a table placed upon which there was an altar together with the first fruits of all kinds of produce of the earth.

Whenever dishes of food were brought in and placed beside the other guests, the slaves burnt incense and poured libations for Menekrates and his followers. Eventually, as Hegesandros records, the novel Zeus along with his obedient gods departed from the mockery of the symposium.

Athenaios

The ordinary humans got normal banquet food, but the Macedonian monarch served the would-be divinities the sort of fare that the ancients offered gods when they performed sacrifices to them.

208. HANNON'S BIRDS

Because of his delicacy Hannon the Carthaginian deemed that he deserved better than to continue to be bound by humanness. He decided to spread reports of himself in which he represented himself as being superior to the nature that was in fact his lot. So he bought an immense number of songbirds and raised them in a dark place, teaching them to say one thing: "Hannon is a god."

The birds heard only this single sentence, and after they had mastered it, he released them in different directions, thinking that the birdsong about himself would spread everywhere.

But once the birds loosened their wings, got their freedom, and went to their accustomed abodes, they sang their own compositions—birdsongs—and completely dismissed from their minds Hannon and the lessons they learned in captivity.

Aelian

209. THE WOMAN WHO HOLDS UP THE WORLD WITH HER FINGER

We know that such a humor can bring on countless other strange and varied fantasies. Some persons have thought that they were a clay pot or a leather hide, or that they were a rooster and wanted to mimic its voice, while others thought they were a nightingale and mourned the loss of Itys, and still others that they were supporting the sky like Atlas and were afraid it would fall and crush not only themselves but everyone else as well.

I have myself observed a woman with this fantasy. She kept the middle finger of her hand bound in the belief that she was supporting the whole world on it, and she wept in fear that she might bend her finger with the result that the whole world would collapse, destroying everything at once.

Alexander of Tralles

The physician Alexander of Tralles (6th century AD) describes a number of delusional persons suffering from melancholia, which was an imbalance of humors in the blood. Some of these people identified with characters of Greek mythology. Nightingale (Aedon) is a woman whom the gods transform into a bird, in which form she unceasingly mourns the loss of her son Itys. Atlas is of course the Titan god who supports the sky.

210. THE HOUSE CALLED TRIREME

Timaios of Tauromenion says that there is a house in Akragas called the Trireme. Here is the reason.

Some young men in the house were drinking liberally and, flush with drink, became so deluded that they believed they were sailing on a trireme and were being driven by a terrible storm at sea. They got so far out of their senses that they began hurling all the furniture and bedding out of the house, as though they were casting it into the sea, imagining that the pilot was telling them to discharge the cargo because of the storm. Many persons were now gathering around the house and appropriating the goods that had been hurled out, but even so the youths did not cease from their delusion.

On the following day the authorities came to the house and brought charges against the young men, who were still suffering from seasickness. To the inquiries of the magistrates they replied that they had been caught in a storm and were forced to discharge their superfluous cargo into the sea. While the authorities were marveling at their madness, one of the youths, although he seemed to be the eldest of the group, said, "Fellow Tritons, out of fear I cast myself into the lowest possible part of the hold and lay there." So the magistrates made allowance for their delirium, sentenced them to moderation in their use of wine, and released them.

The youths confessed their gratitude. "If we reach harbor," one said, "and escape so rough a sea, we will establish your cult in our country as manifest Saviors together with the sea gods, since you have manifested yourselves to us so auspiciously."

From this incident the house was called the Trireme.

Athenaios

211. THE HAPPY SHIPOWNER

Thrasyllos, son of Pythodoros, of the deme Aixone, was once afflicted by a form of madness in which he supposed that all the ships putting in at Peiraieus belonged to him. He would register them in his accounts, dispatch them, and generally manage their business, and as they returned from a trip he would receive them with the sort of pleasure that one would feel if one were the person in charge of so many goods. Although he did not pursue inquiries into ships that had been lost, he would rejoice at those that were safe, and carried on with the greatest pleasure.

When his brother Kriton came to town from Sicily, he took charge of Thrasyllos, handing him over to a doctor, and his madness ceased. But Thrasyllos often spoke of the way he had lived when he was mad, declaring that in his entire life he had never enjoyed himself more, for he had felt no pain whatsoever, whereas the amount of pleasure he had felt was overwhelming.

Athenaios

212. THE HAPPY PLAYGOER

It is said that a certain man in Abydos became deranged in mind and used to go to the theater and observe for many days as though there were persons acting, and signify his approval with applause. When he recovered from his mental affliction, he said that that had been the most pleasant time of his life.

Pseudo-Aristotle

MEMORABLE WORDS

213. ARS LONGA, VITA BREVIS

"I think we shouldn't waste time, knowing as we do the truth of what the physician from Kos said, that 'Life is short, but art long.' He was talking about medicine, of course, something easier to learn, whereas philosophy is unconquerable even after a long time unless one stays intently awake and stares at it grimly. And the stakes are not small—either to perish as a miserable wretch in the midst of the common herd or to experience happiness as a philosopher."

Lucian

Describing the conditions of a practicing physician, Hippokrates writes, "Life is short, art long, opportunity fleeting, experiment hazardous, and judgment difficult" (Aphorisms *1.1). By art's being long, Hippokrates has in mind the art* (techne*) of medicine and the long time that is required for one to become competent in it.*

Over time Hippokrates's original aphorism has come to be even more aphoristic and has taken on additional meanings. In the present passage the speaker cites only its initial words, and this has continued to characterize the tradition. Moreover, he transfers their application to another realm, in this case from medicine to philosophy. In modern usage the order of the clauses, frequently cited in Latin or in English translation, is usually reversed, and the meaning is again different. Now "art" refers to the fine arts, and the point of the now-proverbial saying is that while human life is brief, art endures. The old aphorism continues to inspire variation, as in the case of the French playwright Georges Feydeau (1862–1921), who was fond of saying, "Life is short, but we get bored just the same" (Pronko 1975:12).

214. WHICH CAME FIRST?

Next there was dragged into our conversation the problem of whether the hen or the egg came first, a problem that causes investigators much difficulty.

Plutarch

Since an egg cannot come into existence without a bird and a bird cannot come into existence without an egg, it is difficult to imagine how the cycle of chicken and egg began. The question of which came first, the hen or the egg, crystallized for ancient philosophers a difficult problem of causality, and different thinkers offered different solutions. According to some, including Aristotle (Censorinus On the Birthday *4.3–4), the answer to the dilemma is that the cycle did not have a beginning: although individuals come into being and pass away, species are uncreated and indestructible, and so have no beginning.*

215. ALTER EGO

Asked what a friend is, Zenon replied, "Another I."

Diogenes Laertios

*The basic idea of this apothegm, that a friend is another instance of oneself, found expression among the Greeks and Romans in two forms. The philosopher Zenon (335–263 BC), founder of Stoicism, says that a friend is "another I" (*allos ego*), while the philosopher Aristotle (*Nicomachean Ethics *9.9–10 [1166a.31–32]) remarks that "A friend is another self (*allos autos*)," or "second self." Equivalent expressions are found in Latin authors. "You are a second brother to me, a second I (*alter ego*) to whom I can tell everything," writes the statesman Cicero in a letter to his friend Atticus (*Epistulae ad Atticum *8.14.2), while elsewhere he says, "A true friend will never be found; he is a person who is, as it were, another self (*alter idem*)" (*Epistulae ad Familiares *7.5.1).*

Today the expression "alter ego" has these meanings but has also taken on additional ones. For example, in Robert Louis Stevenson's novel The Strange Case of Dr. Jekyll and Mr. Hyde, *Edward Hyde can be said to be Dr. Jekyll's alter ego, just as in the comic-book series Clark Kent is Superman's second self.*

216. "GIVE ME A PLACE TO STAND, AND I'LL MOVE THE WORLD!"

Archimedes, a kinsman and friend of King Hieron, wrote to him that it was possible with any given force to move any given weight. And, they say, he boldly stated on the strength of his proposition that if he had another world, he would go there and move this world.

Amazed, Hieron begged him to put his proposition into action, exhibiting a great weight being moved by a small force. Now, there was a three-masted trading vessel belonging to the royal fleet that had been hauled up onto land with great effort by many men. Archimedes put many persons on board as well as the ship's customary load of freight, and then sat down at some distance from the ship. With little effort, only a gentle back-and-forth motion of his hand at the end of a compound pulley, he drew the ship toward himself smoothly and evenly, as though she were gliding on the sea.

Plutarch

The brilliant Syracusan mathematician and inventor Archimedes boasted that he could move a given weight with a given force. He had in mind employing the mechanical principle of the lever. Asked by the ruler of Syracuse for a demonstration, Archimedes used a system of pulleys to draw a fully laden merchantman effortlessly down to the sea.

* * *

Moving any given weight by means of any given force belongs to the same theory. This was a mechanical discovery made by Archimedes, concerning which he is said to have stated, "Give me a place to stand, and I'll move the world."

Pappos of Alexandria

Archimedes's famous statement comes down to us in different forms. According to the biographer Plutarch, he said, "If I had another world, I would go there and move this one." The mathematician Pappos reports the words in the form that is most familiar to us: "Give me a place to stand, and I'll move the world." The philosopher Simplicius quotes Archimedes with Laconic succinctness in his native Doric dialect: "A place to stand, and I'll move the world."

217. LIFE IS LIKE THE OLYMPIC GAMES

They say that Pythagoras—as Herakleides of Pontos, a pupil of Plato's and a learned man of the first rank, writes—came to Phleious and there discussed certain subjects learnedly and extensively with Leon, ruler of the Phleiasians. When Leon marveled at his intelligence and eloquence and asked him what body of knowledge he relied on the most, Pythagoras said he possessed no particular body of knowledge but was a "philosopher." Leon wondered at this novel term and asked him what philosophers were and how they differed from the rest of mankind.

Pythagoras replied that human life seemed to him to be like that festival that was attended by crowds from all over Greece and was celebrated with a huge display of games.* Just as some persons trained their bodies and went there in search of glory and the distinction of a garland, and others were drawn to it to buy and sell for the sake of gain and profit, so too was there another kind of person, predominately freeborn, who was not seeking applause or profit but came to observe and examine closely what was happening and how it happened.

In the same way we ourselves entered this life from another life and nature, some as slaves to glory and others as slaves to money, as though setting out from some city to a sort of festival with many people. But there were certain people, few in number, who regarded these gains as valueless and closely gazed at the nature of things. These individuals called themselves fond of wisdom, that is, philosophers. Just as at the festival it was noblest to observe, without seeking to acquire something for oneself, so also in life the contemplation and understanding of things surpassed all other pursuits by far.

Cicero

---

*Pythagoras has in mind the great festival celebrated every fourth year at Olympia, the Olympic Games.

According to tradition, Pythagoras was the first person to call himself a philosopher. Explaining the novel term, Pythagoras compared life to an athletic festival. Just as a grand sports event is frequented by athletes, vendors, and spectators, so also in human life some people compete for glory or money, while others—the few and the finest—are there to observe and understand. Pythagoras assigned athletes and merchants a lower status because of their motivation for gain, and spectators a higher status because of their disinterested attitude.

Pythagoras's much-cited metaphor is one of many "life is like x" statements. My own favorite is a somewhat cryptic instance that I recall from an elementary book on philosophy that I read as an adolescent: "Life is like a glass of beer," a man remarked. "Why is that?" his companion asked. "I don't know. I'm not a philosopher."

218. "THE DIE IS CAST"

Caesar rejoined his cohorts at the Rubicon River, which was the boundary of his province. He stopped for a while as he considered the magnitude of what he was undertaking, turned to those around him, and said, "We can still withdraw, but if we cross over this little bridge, everything will be decided by weapons."

As he hesitated, a prodigy occurred. A being of exceptional stature and beauty suddenly appeared nearby. It sat and played a reed pipe. The shepherds flocked around to hear him, and also many soldiers left their posts, among them some of the trumpeters. The apparition snatched a trumpet from one of them, rushed to the river, sounded the call to battle with a great blast, and continued to the opposite bank. Caesar then said, "Let's go, then, to where the gods' portents and our enemies' injustices are summoning us. The die has been cast."

And so after he had crossed his army over and met with the tribunes of the plebs, who came to him after being driven from Rome, he assembled the soldiers and, weeping and tearing his clothing from his chest, asked them for their loyalty.

Suetonius

When Julius Caesar led an army across the Rubicon into Italy, he was implicitly declaring war. The River Rubicon flowed in northeast Italy, running from the Apennine Mountains to the Adriatic Sea. It separated the Roman province of Cisalpine Gaul to the north from Italy to the south. The Rubicon may be the stream that is known today as Fiumicino.

The legend has three moments: uncertainty, divine encouragement, and commitment. For all the drama of the action, it is Caesar's brief remark about the die (= singular of dice) being cast that is most remembered. The comment is attributed to Caesar by later historians; in his own account of the events he does not record any pointed remark.

***

Coming to the River Rubicon, which bounded the province allotted him, Caesar stood in silence and held off acting, thinking to himself about the magnitude of so daring a deed. Then, like people throwing themselves off some cliff into a yawning abyss, with his eyes shut to reason and veiling himself against danger, he shouted out only this to his companions, in Greek, "Let the die be cast!" Then he had his army cross the river.

Plutarch

Suetonius, writing in Latin, reports Caesar's words as "Iacta alea est," *or "The die has been cast" (traditionally rendered in English as "The die is cast"). It is actually a Greek proverbial expression, and Plutarch, writing in Greek, gives it in its proper form:* "Anerriphtho kubos," *or "Let the die be cast." Some scholars suppose that Suetonius actually wrote* "Iacta alea esto" *("Let the die be cast") and the final letter of* esto *fell out of the manuscript. The point of the proverb is, of course, that once a player makes his or her cast, it cannot be undone. In Caesar's case, once he and his army should cross the Rubicon, there could be no turning back.*

Like many other Romans, Caesar was bilingual and fond of speaking Greek, so that, whether he cited the Greek proverb on this occasion or not, his choosing to comment in Greek was not in itself remarkable.

219. "ET TU, BRUTE?"

As Caesar was sitting down, the conspirators gathered around him under the pretense of paying their respects, whereupon Cimber Tillius, who had assumed the lead, came closer as if he intended to ask Caesar something, and when Caesar by a nod of his head and a gesture of his hand was putting him off to another time, Tillius took hold of his toga at both shoulders. Then, as Caesar cried out, "This is violence!" and turned away, one of the two Cascas stabbed him just below the throat. Caesar grabbed his arm and jabbed it with his stylus, but as Caesar tried to spring up, he was hindered by another wound. Perceiving that his assailants had him surrounded with drawn daggers, he pulled his toga over his head, while with his left hand he drew its hanging fold down to his feet in order to perish the more decently, with the lower part of his body covered. In this way he was pierced twenty-three times, sighing softly at the first strike. Some persons relate that as Marcus Brutus was rushing at him, he said, "You, too, my son?"

The conspirators fled in different directions, and Caesar lay lifeless for some time until three young slaves placed him on a litter and carried him home, one arm hanging down. Of so many wounds no single one was found to be fatal, in the opinion of the physician Antistius, except for the second wound in his chest.

Suetonius

Caesar was assassinated by a group of senators as he was taking his seat in the Curia, or senate-house, in Rome. Two traditions circulated about his dying words. According to one, he uttered nothing more than a sigh; according to the other, when Caesar saw that Marcus Junius Brutus was one of his assassins, he addressed him in Greek: "Kai su, teknon?" *("You, too, my son?" or, literally, "You, too, child?"). The Latin phrase so familiar to English-speakers—* "Et tu, Brute?" *("You, too, Brutus?")— is found in no ancient author and derives rather from Shakespeare's* Julius Caesar *(act 3, scene 1, line 77).*

Three simple words, but then not so simple. For one thing, Caesar's utterance is normally punctuated as a question: he expressed surprise that Brutus was one of his assailants. That is, for example, how Shakespeare treats the equivalent phrase in *his play: "*Et tu, Brute?*—Then fall Caesar!" He means that if even Brutus wished him dead, he had no hope at all. However, one could imagine (though with less likelihood) that the utterance is rather an exclamation, a prophetic warning that Brutus's own turn will come: "You, too, my son!"*

The word teknon *("child, son") was commonly employed metaphorically by Greek-speaking adults from Homeric times onward as an affectionate form of address to a younger person who was not biologically related. However, Caesar did in fact have a long-term affair with Brutus's mother, Servilia, one that lasted until his death, leading some historians to suspect that in addressing Brutus as "son," Caesar was making a literal reference to, or acknowledgment of, his paternity of Brutus. If they were father and son, Brutus was both a tyrannicide and a parricide.*

220. IN HOC SIGNO VINCES

Constantine called upon this god in his prayers, entreating him and crying aloud to him to declare who he was and to extend to Constantine his right hand for the undertaking that lay ahead. As the emperor uttered these prayers and persisted in his supplications, a most strange divine sign appeared to him, one that it would not be easy to accept if another person were telling it, but since the victorious emperor himself narrated the story to the present writer a long time after the event when I was deemed worthy of his acquaintance and company, and confirmed it with an oath, who would hesitate to believe his report, and especially since the passage of time has provided evidence of its truth?

He said that around the midday hours, when the day was turning, he saw with his own eyes, in the sky and resting above the sun, a trophy made of light and having the form of a cross with a text attached that said WITH THIS CONQUER. Amazement at the spectacle gripped both him and his army, which was accompanying him on a campaign that he was then setting out for, and also observed the marvel.

Constantine was very much at a loss as to what the apparition was. He pondered and reasoned about it for a long time until night came on and overtook him. Then, as he slept, he said he saw god's Christ along with the sign that had appeared in the sky, and Christ instructed him to make a copy of the sign that he had seen, and to use it as protection in battles with his enemies.

In the morning when he arose, he made known the secret to his friends. After that he summoned goldsmiths and jewelers, sat down among them, and explained the image of the sign, instructing them to copy it in gold and precious stones.

Eusebios

The emperor Constantine the Great (3rd–4th centuries AD), anticipating a military confrontation with his enemies, who included the emperor Maxentius, agonized over which god or gods he should ask to support him. He decided to pray to a single god, whose identity was unknown to him. In a daytime vision Constantine and his army saw a cross of light above the sun and the Greek words EN TOUTOI NIKA. That evening Constantine, now by himself, had a second vision, a dream in which Christ instructed him to use this sign (that is, the cross) in battle. So Constantine ordered a material copy of the heavenly emblem to be fashioned in the form of a military standard, a cross surmounted by the intertwined letters XP, the first two letters of the word "Christ" in Greek. Once Constantine learned the identity of the god who had appeared to him, he converted to Christianity.

Although the words en toutoi nika *appear to say "in this conquer," the clause really means "with this (or by this) conquer," reflecting the instrumental use of the preposition* en *in Byzantine Greek. The conventional Latin translation* in hoc signo vinces *("in this sign you will conquer") renders the Greek prepositional phrase literally and converts the verb into a future indicative. In its Latin form the clause has become a widely adopted motto for schools, military units, sports teams, and other groups.*

Following his military victory over Maxentius at the Battle of the Milvian Bridge (AD 312), Constantine became sole emperor in the west as well as the first Christian emperor of Rome. His fostering of Christianity led to the Christianization of the Roman Empire, then to the Christianization of Europe, and so to the Christianization of much of the world.

MEMORABLE EXPERIENCES

221. TOXIC HONEY

After the Greeks made their ascent, they encamped in numerous villages that had abundant provisions.

Nothing seemed strange to them other than the presence in the area of many swarms of bees. But all the soldiers who ate any honey lost their senses and suffered from vomiting and diarrhea, and not a single man could stand up. Those who had eaten a little were like really drunk men, and those who had eaten a lot were like madmen, some of them like men who were dying. Many lay down as though they had been routed in battle, and there was a widespread sense of despondency. Still, on the following day no one died, and around the same hour as they had eaten the honey they began to regain their senses, one after the other. On the third and fourth days they got up, as if having been drugged.

Xenophon

*The Athenian aristocrat Xenophon was traveling with an army of Greek mercenaries who were making their way to the sea after a failed military adventure in Persia. The event he describes took place near Colchis, along the east coast of the Euxine Sea (Black Sea). That the local honey was toxic was of course known to the natives but not to the visitors. It was produced by bees from nectar of the poisonous blossoms of the rhododendron (*Azalea pontica*). Toxic honey is still found today in the Caucasus, northern Turkey, and elsewhere, where in very small amounts it sometimes serves as an intoxicant.*

The stance of Xenophon's personal narrative is entirely objective. Although he is a participant in the events, he nowhere mentions his own presence or feelings.

222. A NARROW ESCAPE

When Alexander learned that I had come to the city and that I was *that* Lucian (I had also brought two soldiers, a spearman and a pikeman, whom I had gotten from the governor of Cappadocia, then a friend of mine, to escort me to the sea), he straightaway sent for me very courteously and with much friendliness.

When I went, I found him with many men, but by some good fortune I had also brought along with me the two soldiers. He extended his right hand for me to kiss, as he was accustomed to do for the multitude, and I held it as though intending to kiss it but instead gave it a proper bite that very nearly crippled it. The men with him tried to strangle and pound me for my sacrilege, already being indignant at my having addressed him as "Alexander" and not as "prophet." But he bore it quite nobly and patiently and restrained the men, promising that he would easily tame me and demonstrate how Glykon's power transforms even angry persons into friends.

After sending all the others away, Alexander began to make his case, saying that he knew me quite well and knew the advice I was giving to Rutilianus. "What has provoked you to do this to me," he asked, "seeing that it is possible for me to promote you greatly in his favor?" I for my part gladly accepted the friendship he proffered, considering the dangerous situation I found myself in, and shortly thereafter emerged as his friend. It caused no little wonder in the onlookers that my change of attitude had come about so easily.

When I made the decision to sail, Alexander sent me many gifts and presents (I happened now to be in town only with Xenophon, having sent my father and my other family members on to Amastris) and said that he would personally provide me with a boat and rowers to take me away, which I thought was sincere and courteous. But when I was in midjourney and saw the pilot tearfully arguing with the sailors, I began to make pessimistic estimations of my prospects. They had been ordered by Alexander to pick us up and heave us into the sea, and if that had happened, Alexander would have brought the war against me to a conclusion. But the pilot, weeping, persuaded his fellow sailors not to do us any harm, saying to me, "As you see, I've lived a devout and blameless life for sixty years, and I wouldn't wish to defile my hands with murder at this age and with wife and children," and explaining the purpose for which he had taken us aboard and the orders that Alexander had given. The pilot set us ashore in Aigialoi, which noble Homer mentions, and they went back.

There I happened upon some men from the Bosporos who were sailing along the coast. They were envoys going to Bithynia with the annual contribution from King Eupator. When I explained to them the danger we were in, I found them to be courteous, was taken aboard their ship, and, after having come so close to being killed, was conveyed safely to Amastris.

Lucian

Lucian despised the popular sage and prophet Alexander of Abonouteichos, regarding him as an ambitious charlatan. He harassed Alexander in different ways such as by submitting to Alexander's oracle the same question multiple times under different names. Then one day Lucian showed up in Alexander's city, and the two men met. Unlike Xenophon, above, Lucian presents his experience subjectively.

Two characters require explanation. Glykon was the name of an artificial, human-headed snake that Alexander represented as being a manifestation of the god Asklepios, whose prophet Alexander was. Rutilianus was a prominent Roman official who, despite Lucian's urging to the contrary, married Alexander's daughter, who Alexander said was his offspring with the goddess Selene, or Moon.

223. THE GREAT FISH

King Alexander sends his greetings to Aristotle.

I must relate a strange thing that happened to us in India. We came to the city of Prasiake, which seems to be the capital of India, and occupied a splendid promontory of the sea that lies alongside it.

I set out with a few of my companions to the aforesaid promontory. After making close observations, we found that it was inhabited by fish-eating humans who had the form of females. I hailed some of them and found that they spoke a non-Greek language. When I asked about the region, they pointed out an island to us, which we all could see in the middle of the sea. They said it was the tomb of an ancient king to whom a great quantity of gold had been consecrated. . . . The natives vanished, leaving behind their small boats, twelve in number.

Now my truest friend Pheidon along with Hephaistion, Krateros, and the rest of them would not allow me to cross over. "Let me sail there instead of you," Pheidon said, "so that if there's any problem, it will be I who is endangered, not you, and if there's no problem, I'll send the ship for you later. If I perish, you'll find other friends, but if you perish, it would be a misfortune for the entire inhabited world." They persuaded me, and I let them cross over.

The men disembarked upon the supposed island, but an hour later the creature suddenly descended into the deep. We cried out as the creature vanished and the men perished, including my truest friend. I was extremely upset. I looked for the natives but did not find them.

We remained on the promontory for some days and on the seventh saw the creature, which had elephants on it. Having passed sufficient time there, we went back to the city of Prasiake.

Pseudo-Kallisthenes

The text is the first part of a letter allegedly written by Alexander the Great to his teacher Aristotle, wherein Alexander describes some of the wonders he encountered in his exotic travels.

224. THE DISCOVERY OF ARCHIMEDES'S TOMB

When I was quaestor I searched for and found the tomb of Archimedes, which was unknown to the inhabitants of Syracuse, who even denied it existed. It was surrounded on all sides with thornbushes and a thicket, and covered over.

I had in mind certain little lines of verse that I had learned were inscribed on his monument, stating that the tomb was surmounted with a sphere along with a cylinder. As I was looking over things—there were very many tombs at the Agrigentine Gate—I noticed a small column sticking up a little from a thicket, and on it was the figure of a sphere and cylinder. Immediately I said to the Syracusans—some of their leading men were with me—that I thought this was the very thing I was searching for. Slaves with sickles were dispatched to clear and open the space up, and when it was accessible, we approached the base that faced us. The inscription was visible, though the latter halves of the verses were worn away.

So this very famous Greek city, once indeed a very learned city, would have been ignorant of the sepulchral monument of its single most brilliant citizen if a man from Arpinum had not pointed it out.

Cicero

Cicero, a native of Arpinum in Latium, recalls this event from some thirty years earlier (75 BC), when at the beginning of his political career he served as quaestor in Sicily. The forgotten gravesite of the great Archimedes was over a century and a quarter old by that time. Although Archimedes had been unjustly slain by an ignorant Roman soldier (see 237 "Archimedes"), his tomb at least was rescued from unjust oblivion at a later period by a cultivated Roman.

Archimedes was particularly proud of his work on cylinders and spheres, and asked his kinsmen and friends to place over his eventual grave a representation of a sphere enclosed within a cylinder, along with an inscription giving the formula he had discovered for the ratio of their respective volumes (Plutarch Marcellus *17.7). He treats the mathematics of these two kinds of solids in his magnum opus,* On the Sphere and the Cylinder.

SUMMING UP AND LAST WORDS

225. COUNTING ONE'S BLESSINGS

It is said that Thales used to say that he thanked fortune for three things: first, that he was born a human being and not an animal; next, that he was born a man and not a woman; and, third, that he was born a Greek and not a barbarian.

Diogenes Laertios

* * *

Socrates used to deem himself blessed for many reasons, among them that he was a rational animal and that he was an Athenian.

Favorinos

***

Plato, when he was close to death, used to praise his fate and fortune, first, that he was by nature a human being and not an irrational animal; then, that he was born a Greek and not a barbarian; and, in addition to these, that his birth happened in the time of Socrates.

Plutarch

Catalogs of blessings, usually three in number, have enjoyed a long life. Very similar to the Greek lists is one found in the ancient liturgy of the Jewish synagogue: "Rabbi Judah says, 'Three praises one must say daily: praised be you, who did not make me a gentile, did not make me a woman, did not make me uncultivated'" (Holtzmann 1912:94–95, translating Tosefta Berakot *7.18, a Hebrew work dating to around the 3rd century AD).*

Similar lists continue to be generated. A saying in the American South is, or used to be, "You can't be too thin or too rich," or more fully, "You can't be too thin or too rich or too white." By way of contrast, To Be Young, Gifted, and Black *is the name of a play assembled posthumously from the unpublished works of Lorraine Hansberry (1968–1969), the title of which went on to inspire a song by Nina Simone (1970) as well as an album,* Young, Gifted, and Black, *by Aretha Franklin (1972). Around the same time, Ralph Ellison asks in his essay "Homage to Duke Ellington on His Birthday" (1969): "And to how many thousands has he defined what it should mean to be young and alive and American?" (Ellison 1995:681).*

226. SOCRATES

The man who had given Socrates the drug put his hands on him, and after a while he examined Socrates's feet and legs, and then, putting considerable pressure on his foot, asked him if he felt anything. He said he did not. After that he did the same to his shins. And making his way upward in this manner, he showed us that Socrates was becoming cold and rigid.

Again he put his hands on him, saying that when it reached his heart, he would be gone. At that moment it was his abdominal region that was cold. Socrates uncovered his face—it had been covered—and speaking the words that were the last he uttered, he said, "Kriton, I owe a rooster to Asklepios. Repay him and don't neglect it."

"It will be done," said Kriton. "But see now, do you have anything else to say?" Kriton asked this and received no answer, but a little while later Socrates moved. The man uncovered Socrates's face, and his eyes were fixed. When Kriton saw this, he closed his mouth and eyes.

This was the end, Echekrates, of our companion, who was, we might say, of the men of that time whom we knew, the best and wisest and most righteous.

Plato

In 399 BC Socrates was executed in a cell by being given hemlock to drink. He was attended by several of his close friends. His last words are notable for their ordinariness: attention to a pious debt.

The final words of Socrates, as reported in Plato's Phaedo, *were well known in antiquity, and the scene of Socrates's death became an ancient classic. On his last night the Roman statesman Cato chose to read the* Phaedo *(Plutarch* Cato the Younger *68), and the philosopher Seneca even modeled his own death on the scene in the* Phaedo *(Tacitus* Annals *15.64); in contrast, the Sybaritic Petronius deliberately devised an un-Socratic exit (see 236 "Petronius Arbiter").*

227. THEOPHRASTOS'S LAMENT

Aristotle found fault with the philosophers of old who, according to him, judged that, thanks to their mental gifts, philosophy had been perfected; they were, he says, either very foolish or very boastful. Still, he himself saw that since great advances had been made in the space of a few years, philosophy would be absolutely complete within a short time.

As he lay dying, however, Theophrastos is said to have found fault with nature for having given a long life to crows and stags, to which it made no difference, and so brief a life to humans, to whom it made the greatest difference. For if the lifespan of humans could have been longer, he said, all systems of knowledge would be brought to completion and human life refined by every kind of learning. So he complained that just when he had begun to glimpse these things, his own life was passing out of existence.

Cicero

Theophrastos of Eresos (4th–3rd centuries BC), one of Aristotle's students, plaintively contrasts the brief lifespan of humans to that of crows and stags because a crow was reputed to live for nine human generations, and a stag four times as long as a crow (Hesiod fr. 304 MW). For other comments on the brevity of human life see 213 "Ars Longa, Vita Brevis" and 252 "Protagoras's Books Burned."

228. VESPASIAN'S LAST WORDS

As Vespasian drew near to death, he said, "Oh dear, I think I'm becoming a god."

Suetonius

The Roman emperor Vespasian (ruled AD 69–79) enjoyed a reputation for having a good sense of humor (Suetonius Vespasian *22–23). A sample of his wit can be glimpsed in this utterance, in which, as he was dying, he claimed to be consciously experiencing his transformation from a mortal to a divine being (*Vae, puto deus fio*). He was referring to the Roman habit of deifying emperors upon their death; and in fact he was deified after his death.*

Vespasian's remark displays the same witty spirit as that in memorable exit lines preserved in modern compilations of deathbed utterances such as Lytton Strachey's "If this is dying, I don't think much of it" and Heinrich Heine's "God will pardon me. It's his trade." On such collections see Guthke (1992). Most exit lines reported from modern times are witty, whereas ancient ultima verba *usually are not. Ancient anecdotes focus more often upon the kind of death experienced by notable persons than upon their last words.*

* * *

Although Vespasian was oppressed by illness and had also contracted a bowel problem as a result of using the cold waters too frequently, he nonetheless continued to perform his customary duties as emperor, even receiving delegations as he lay in bed. Upon experiencing a sudden attack of diarrhea, he declared, "An emperor should die on his feet," and while he was trying to rise, he expired in the arms of those helping him up, on the ninth day before the Kalends of July, at the age of sixty-nine years, one month, and seven days.

Suetonius

*On 23 June, AD 79, as Vespasian lay on his deathbed, he uttered the proud sentiment that an emperor should die standing (*Imperatorem stantem mori oportet*), and attempted to rise from his bed.*

DEATHS

*Many prominent persons died unusual deaths, at least in legend. Several ancient authors, including Hyginus (*Fabulous Tales *246–248) and Valerius Maximus (9.12), compiled accounts of memorable deaths.*

229. PYTHAGORAS

Pythagoras died in the following way.

While he was deliberating with his associates in the house of Milon, the house was set afire out of envy by a person who had not been deemed worthy of admission into the society of Pythagoreans. Some people, however, say that it was the inhabitants of Kroton themselves who did it, since they were worried that Pythagoras might be establishing a tyranny. They seized Pythagoras as he was fleeing, for when he came to a field of beans, he stopped in order not to pass through the field, saying he would rather be captured than trample on the beans, and that it was better to be slain than to speak. His throat was cut by his pursuers. In this way also most of his companions, some forty in number, were slain.

Diogenes Laertios

Although he was a vegetarian, Pythagoras avoided beans and forbade his disciples from eating them (Diogenes Laertios 19); indeed, his attitude toward beans seems of a kind with his reverence toward animals. Once when the philosopher saw an ox feeding on beans in a field, he advised the herdsman to tell the ox to abstain from beans. When the man responded that he did not speak the language of oxen, Pythagoras went up to the animal and whispered something in its ear, after which the ox never again ate beans (Porphyry Life of Pythagoras *24). The legend of Pythagoras's death is one of several ancient stories in which an idiosyncrasy or doctrine associated with a person rebounds upon him, contributing to his death (Fairweather 1973:235).*

230. AESCHYLUS

Aeschylus was greatly honored by Hieron and the inhabitants of Gela, and after living three more years, he died an old man in the following way.

An eagle snatched up a tortoise and, unable to hold on to it, dropped it onto the rocks to break its shell, but the tortoise landed upon the poet, killing him. The event had been foretold in an oracle:

> A heavenly missile will slay you.

After his death the inhabitants of Gela interred him lavishly in the city's cemetery and honored him magnificently, with this inscription:

> This monument covers Aeschylus the Athenian, son of
> Euphorion,
> Who perished in wheat-bearing Gela.

The grove of Marathon can speak of his distinguished valor
As can the thick-haired Mede, who knows it well.

Life of Aeschylus

The tragic poet Aeschylus died circa 455 BC during an extended visit to Sicily, where he was a guest of Hieron I.

Aeschylus's epitaph makes no mention of his accomplishments as a playwright, only of his military service, and of that only his participation in the Battle of Marathon (490 BC), in which the greatly outnumbered Athenians and their allies defeated the invading Persians, or Medes.

* * *

Eagles seize dryland tortoises and dash them against rocks from on high, and after they have smashed the tortoise in this way, they extract its flesh and eat it. This is how, I hear, the tragic poet Aeschylus of Eleusis lost his life.

Aeschylus had sat down on a rock, doubtless musing and writing on his usual topics. Being bald, he had no hair on his head. An eagle thought his head was a rock and let fall down upon it the tortoise he was holding. The missile struck Aeschylus and killed him.

Aelian

The bizarre manner of Aeschylus's death was foretold in an oracle, but as usual in such cases the prophecy was of no practical use, its true sense being apparent only after the event.

231. EURIPIDES

Euripides left Athens and went to the court of King Archelaos of Macedonia, where he lived and enjoyed the highest honor. He died through the plotting of Arrhibaios of Macedonia and Krateuas of Thessaly, poets who were jealous of him. They persuaded the king's house slave, Lysimachos by name, who had been purchased for ten minas, to let loose on Euripides the king's dogs, which Lysimachos himself was tending.

Other persons, however, report that Euripides was torn apart, not by dogs, but by women as he made his way during the dead of night to Krateros, the beloved of Archelaos (for they say that Euripides also engaged in loves of this sort), or, as other persons say, to Arethousia, the wife of Nikodikos.

He had lived seventy-five years. The king had his bones conveyed to Pella.

Suda

The legends attached to the tragedian Euripides agree that he died violently, as characters in tragedies often do. His end was much like those of the mythological Aktaion (torn apart by dogs), Orpheus (torn apart by women), and Pentheus (torn apart by Maenads); these last appear prominently in Euripides's final drama, The Bacchae. *Deserved or not, Euripides had a reputation for being a misogynist, although his fellow tragedian Sophocles declared that "Euripides hated women in his tragedies but loved them in his bed" (Athenaios 13.557e).*

232. PHILEMON

The comic poet Philemon, who like Kratinos lived to be ninety-seven years old, was once reclining quietly on his couch when he saw a donkey devouring the figs that had been prepared for him. Bursting into laughter, he called to his servant and, laughing heartily and incessantly, told him to give the donkey some wine as well to gulp down. Suffocating from laughter, Philemon died.

Lucian

Philemon (4th–3rd centuries BC) was a writer of New Comedy. If it is appropriate for a tragic poet to die a tragic death, it seems fitting for a comic poet to die laughing.

* * *

Philemon lived 101 years. He was whole in body and blessed in having all his senses intact. People agree about the following event.

During the war between the Athenians and Antigonos, when Philemon was living in Peiraieus, he had a dream in which he saw nine maidens departing from his house. He asked them, as it seemed to him, why they were leaving, and they said they were going outside because it was not right that they hear anything. And then the dream came to an end.

When he awoke, he recounted to his servant what he had seen, heard, and said. Then he finished writing the play for the competition that was on his mind, and having discharged that task, lay down quietly. Next, he was softly snoring. The people indoors thought he was sleeping, but after this continued for a long time, they uncovered him and saw that he was dead.

And so, Epicurus, the nine Muses also kept company with Philemon, and when he was about to set out on his final, funereal journey, they went away. For it is not right for gods to see corpses, even if they are very dear, nor to defile their eyes with mortal expirations. You fool, who say they have no concern for us.

Suda

This alternate legend of Philemon's last day has nothing in common with the story of his dying laughing. There the emphasis is upon the comic poet's good-natured sense of humor, whereas here it is on the fact that the Muses blessed the playwright with their presence, leaving him only when they knew he was about to die. Compare 50 "Bacchus Forsakes Antony."

233. DIOGENES THE CYNIC

Diogenes of Sinope, when at the end he was sick and dying, brought himself with difficulty to a bridge and cast himself down on it. The bridge lay near a gymnasium, and Diogenes told the gymnasium guard that when he could see that Diogenes had breathed his last, he should cast him into the Ilissos.

So little did Diogenes care about death and burial.

Aelian

Living his life like an ownerless dog, the Cynic wished to be treated like one in death. The stream of the Ilissos used to flow outside of Athens.

234. ZENON

Zenon died in the following way. As he was leaving his school, he stumbled and broke a finger. Striking the ground with his hand, he said that line of Niobe's,

"I'm coming. Why are you calling me?"

and straightway held his breath and died.

Diogenes Laertios

Zenon of Kition (4th–3rd centuries BC), founder of Stoicism, taught in the Stoa Poikile *(whence the name of his school), or Painted Colonnade, in Athens. He interpreted his fall and minor physical injury as a preliminary summons from Hades, lord of the dead. Beating one's hands on the ground and calling out was an old way of attracting the attention of the rulers of the death realm in order to say something to them (Homer* Iliad *9.566–572).*

235. CLEOPATRA

After lamenting, Cleopatra placed a garland on Antony's coffin and embraced it.* She ordered a bath to be prepared for herself, and when she had

*She is in the tomb of her late lover and husband, Antony.

bathed, she reclined at table and began dining upon a fine meal. A man came from the country carrying a basket. When the guards asked what he was carrying, he opened it, lifted the leaves, and showed them that the jar inside was full of figs. The guards admired the size and beauty of the figs, and the man invited them to take some. Feeling no mistrust, the guards told him to proceed on in with them. After dining, Cleopatra took a tablet that she had written on and sealed, and sent it to Octavian. Then she dismissed everyone in the room except for her two female attendants, and closed the door.

Octavian opened the tablet, and when he found in it prayers and lamentations along with a request that she be buried with Antony, he grasped the situation immediately. At first he himself started to go to her aid but instead dispatched other persons to go and investigate with all speed. The incident went swiftly. His men went there at a run and reached the guards, who had perceived nothing, but when they opened the doors, they found her lying dead upon a couch of gold, dressed in royal attire. Of her female attendants the one called Eiras was dying at Cleopatra's feet, while Charmion, already tottering and scarcely able to hold up her head, was arranging the diadem on the queen's head. Someone said in anger, "A fine deed this is, Charmion!" "Yes, very fine," she responded, "and one befitting the descendant of so many kings." She said no more but fell there beside the couch.

They say that the asp had been brought in with those figs and lay concealed beneath the leaves, and that Cleopatra had ordered it that way in order that the serpent might attack her body without her knowing it in advance. She picked up one of the figs and said, "So here it was all along," and bared her arm, presenting it to be bitten. Other persons, however, are sure that the asp was confined in a water jar and that, as Cleopatra tried provoking it with a golden distaff in an effort to get it to come out, it attacked her and fastened itself upon her arm. But no one knows what really happened.

It was also said that she wore a hollow hairpin filled with poison that she kept concealed in her hair, although no ulcerated spot or other sign of poison was found on her body. Nor was any creature seen in her room, though people said that they saw signs of serpents alongside the sea from the windows in her room. Some say that on Cleopatra's arm two slight and indistinct punctures could be seen. Octavian believed as much, for in his triumph there was borne an image of Cleopatra with an asp fastened upon her.

These then are the various accounts of her death.

Plutarch

Cleopatra, more precisely Cleopatra VII Philopator (1st century BC), is the most famous of the Ptolemies. After the defeat of Antony by Octavian, the fall of Alexandria, and the death of Antony, Cleopatra was held captive in her palace. Octavian's presumed plan, which she here foiled, was to bring her to Rome and display her as part of his triumphal procession. Instead, he was able to parade only an image of the Egyptian queen.

Two versions of Cleopatra's suicide were in circulation, one that she died of poison and the other that she died of the bite of an asp ("asp" derives from Greek aspis *"shield," referring to the hood of the hooded cobra). A stylized cobra, or uraeus, rearing up as if about to strike, formed part of the royal headdress of the Egyptian pharaohs.*

The vividness of Plutarch's narration is owed in part to the presence of dramatic details such as the conversational exchange between the countryman and the guards and Cleopatra's comment as she uncovers the hidden asp, which could be known only to an omniscient observer.

236. PETRONIUS ARBITER

Petronius spent his days in sleep, and his nights on the business and delights of life. Whereas others attained fame through diligence, he did so through idleness. He was not regarded as a glutton or spendthrift like most of those who squander their resources, but as a person of refined luxury. The more unrestrained his talk and doings were and the more they displayed a certain carelessness, the more they were received in the spirit of candor. Still, as proconsul of Bithynia and presently as consul he showed himself to be both vigorous and competent.

But then he lapsed into vice, or an affectation of it, and was adopted into the small circle of Nero's intimates as his Arbiter of Elegance.[*] Nero thought no luxury to be charming and agreeable unless Petronius had given his approval to it. As a result Tigellinus[†] was jealous of him as though he were a rival who possessed a greater knowledge of pleasure. Tigellinus worked on the emperor's cruelty, his dominant passion, accusing Petronius of having had a friendship with Scaevinus,[‡] and suborning a slave to play the informer. The accused was given no opportunity to put up a defense, and most of his household was arrested.

At that time, as it happened, the emperor was in Campania, and Petronius got as far as Cumae, where he was detained. He did not put things off from fear or hope, but neither did he rush headlong to take his life. Instead, he severed his veins, then bound them up, then opened them again according to his whim, and he conversed with his friends, but not about serious matters or about topics that might gain for him a reputation for courage. He listened to his friends, who did not speak about the immortality of the soul or the tenets of philosophers, but recited trivial songs and light verse. He bestowed gifts on some of his slaves, and beatings on others. And he dined and he napped, so that his death, although involuntary, might seem natural. He wrote no codicil to his will in which, as many dying persons do, he flattered Nero or Tigellinus or some other powerful man, but instead wrote out a full description of the emperor's outrageous conduct grouped under the names of the men and women involved, as well as the novel features of their debaucheries, and sent it

---

[*]That is, *elegantiae arbiter*, presumably playing on Petronius's *cognomen* Arbiter, if it truly is his surname. There is some uncertainty regarding his *praenomen*, or given name (Gaius?), and *cognomen* (Arbiter?). Petronius is his *nomen*, or family name.

[†]Ofonius Tigellinus rose to be the head of the Praetorian Guards under Nero, in which capacity he recommended the execution of many persons.

[‡]Flavius Scaevinus had been involved in a failed conspiracy against Nero.

under seal to Nero. Then he broke his signet ring in order that it not be used to endanger anyone later.

Tacitus

Nero's Arbiter of Elegance, forced to commit suicide, chose a pointedly un-Socratic exit. He drew out the process of dying, passing the time with his friends in discussion on light topics. In contrast, his contemporary, Seneca, who one year earlier was obliged to take his own life, modeled his death scene closely upon that of Socrates (Tacitus Annals *15.62–64; Ker 2009).*

237. ARCHIMEDES

Marcellus, at the capture of Syracuse, perceived that his victory had been much and long delayed by Archimedes's engines of war, but since Marcellus had a high regard for so gifted a man and anticipated that almost as much glory would accrue to himself for preserving Archimedes as for crushing Syracuse, he decreed that the man's life should be spared.

While Archimedes's mind and eyes were fixed upon the diagrams he was drawing in the soil, a soldier in search of booty burst into his house, held a drawn sword over Archimedes's head, and asked who he was. Archimedes was too absorbed in his investigation to give his name and, covering the dust with his hands, said only, "Please, don't ruin this." The soldier cut him down for ignoring his conqueror's order.

Valerius Maximus

During the Roman siege of the Sicilian city of Syracuse, in 212 BC, the Roman general Marcellus, admiring the Greek city's famous native son, ordered the life of the brilliant inventor and mathematician Archimedes to be spared.

There are numerous versions of the manner of Archimedes's death. In most of them Archimedes was at home working on a problem when a Roman soldier broke into his house. Archimedes pled with the soldier not to disturb his diagrams or to wait until Archimedes had completed the proof he was working on, or the like, but the soldier cut him down, not knowing who he was. The event took place indoors, for ancient mathematicians and geometers made their drawings on a dust-covered table called an abacus, *somewhat like today's children's toy Etch-a-Sketch. Many modern commentators wrongly imagine Archimedes to be outdoors drawing in the ground.*

Like Thales, Archimedes is presented sometimes as the self-absorbed and sometimes as the worldly wise intellectual.

CHAPTER 7
SAGES AND PHILOSOPHERS

This chapter focuses upon themes of wisdom and intelligence, from the Seven Sages of early Greece, through the brilliant and eccentric philosophers and scientists of later times, to the fables associated with Aesop.

TRUTH AND WISDOM

238. THE SEVEN SAGES AND THE PRIZE OF WISDOM

What especially established the sages' honor and reputation was the way the tripod went around, cycling through them all as each man in his turn declined it with generous goodwill.

The story goes that while men from the island of Kos were lowering a dragnet, some strangers from Miletos purchased the catch in advance. A golden tripod appeared, dragged along in the net. Helen, they say, had thrown it overboard in the course of her voyage home from Troy, mindful of some old oracle. Initially the strangers and the fishermen quarreled over the tripod, and eventually, as their cities took up the dispute, it came to the point of war. At this juncture the Pythia told both parties in an oracle to give the tripod to the wisest man.

First it was sent off to Thales in Miletos. For although the people of Kos had waged war against all the Milesians as a group, they were willing to bestow it on that man individually. But Thales, declaring that Bias was wiser than he, sent it to him. And from him in turn it was sent off to another as being wiser than he. Making the rounds and being continually forwarded, the tripod came to Thales a second time. Finally it was conveyed from Miletos to Thebes and dedicated to Ismenian Apollon.

Theophrastos, however, says that the tripod was sent first to Bias in Priene and secondly to Thales in Miletos, having been sent on by Bias. After cycling through all the sages back to Bias, it was sent off to Delos.

These are the versions of the story commonly repeated by most persons, except that instead of a tripod some say that the gift was a bowl that had been sent there by Croesus, and others that it was a wine cup left there by Bathykles.

Plutarch

In this curious legend a mysterious object emerged from the sea, and a disagreement arose over who should possess it. The dispute was referred to the oracle of Delphic Apollon, whose priestess said that the object should be given "to the wisest man," whereupon the prize was presented to one of the Seven Sages. But he sent it on to another sage, and he in turn to another, until the prize passed through the hands of all seven and came full circle back into the possession of the first sage, who thereupon dedicated it to Apollon.

The historical legend of the Tripod of Wisdom can be thought of as a male counterpart to the mythological tradition of the Apple of Discord (Snell 1971:115), the former awarded to the wisest male, the latter to the most beautiful female. The female contest took the form of earnest efforts by the goddesses Hera, Athena, and Aphrodite to win the prize for beauty, whereas the men's contest took the form of a competition in modesty, "as befits wise men," remarks John Dillon (2004:189–190), who nicely labels the golden apple and the golden tripod the motif of the contentious gift.

The Seven Sages are, according to tradition, wise men from different parts of Greece who were active in the sixth century BC. Lists of them vary but often include Thales of Miletos, Bias of Priene, Pittakos of Mytilene, Kleoboulos of Lindos, Solon of Athens, Chilon the Lacedaemonian, and Periander of Corinth; sometimes Aesop is one of the seven. Many sayings of practical wisdom such as "know yourself" and "nothing in excess" are credited to them. They engaged individually as statesmen in local politics or toured the courts of prominent rulers, as when Solon of Athens visited the court of King Croesus of Lydia (Herodotos 1.29–33). Occasionally they convened to talk with one another.

239. THALES ON LIFE AND DEATH

Thales said that there was no difference between life and death.

"So then," someone said, "why don't you die?"

"Because there's no difference," he said.

Diogenes Laertios

240. A QUESTION OF RESPONSIBILITY

The young Xanthippos, angry at his father Perikles's treatment of him, began making fun of him, first by exposing to laughter Perikles's domestic pastimes and the discourses he had with sophists. For example, a certain pentathlete had accidentally struck Epitimos the Pharsalian with a javelin, killing him. Perikles lavished an entire day with Protagoras puzzling over whether the javelin, the person who had thrown it, or the directors of the games should, in the strictest sense, be held responsible for the misfortune.

Plutarch

241. A PROBLEM OF IDENTITY

The ship on which Theseus had sailed with the youths and then returned safely home, a thirty-oared galley, was preserved by the Athenians down to the time of Demetrios of Phaleron. The Athenians would take out old planks and replace them with sturdier ones, engineering it in such a way that for the philosophers the ship became an example of the contentious problem of becoming. Some persons held that it was still the same ship, whereas others said it was not.

Plutarch

In heroic legend the Athenians dispatched young Theseus as one of seven youths and seven maidens as tribute to King Minos of Crete, in whose Labyrinth they were to perish as victims of the monstrous Minotaur. But Minos's daughter Ariadne fell in love with Theseus, and with her help he slew the Minotaur and returned safely to Athens. In the centuries that followed, the Athenians maintained the old ship, replacing decaying wood as necessary, such that in classical times the vessel became for philosophers the standing example of the problem of identity: is it the same ship? If not, which piece of timber made the difference?

242. SECUNDUS THE SILENT PHILOSOPHER

Secundus was a philosopher. During the entire time that he professed philosophy, he observed a practice of silence, having chosen a Pythagorean way of life. The reason for his silence is as follows.

When he was a little boy, he was sent by his parents to be educated. In the course of his education it happened that his father died. He used to hear this saying: "Every woman is a whore. A chaste woman is one who has not been noticed."

When he was full-grown, he returned to his homeland as an adherent of the Cynic way of life. He carried around a staff and a leather pouch and let his hair and beard grow. He took lodging in his own house, but no one in the household recognized him, including his mother.

Wishing to evaluate whether the saying about women was true, he summoned one of the maidservants and, pretending to love her mistress, his own mother, promised to give her six gold pieces. She took the money and was able to persuade her mistress with a promise of fifty gold pieces. The mistress made an agreement with the maidservant, saying, "In the evening I'll arrange for him to enter secretly, and sleep with him." The philosopher, having this promise from the maidservant, sent provisions for dinner. After they had dined and it was time for sleep, she expected to have carnal intercourse with him, but he embraced her as one would one's mother, and focusing his eyes upon the breasts that had suckled him, he slept until morning.

At daybreak Secundus got up and wanted to go, but she took hold of him, saying, "Did you do this to condemn me?" He said, "Not at all, mother, but it isn't right to defile the place from which I was born. May such a thing not happen!" She asked him who he was, and he told her, "I am Secundus, your son." Condemning herself and unable to endure the shame, she hanged herself.

Secundus, recognizing that his tongue was the cause of his mother's death, forbade himself ever to speak again, and observed a practice of silence until his death.

Life of Secundus

Unselfconsciously misogynistic, the story of Secundus condemns the entrapped woman but not the philosopher who used her as an unwitting subject in a private experiment.

CONVERTING TO PHILOSOPHY

Just as Hesiod experienced a call to become a bard, so also were some summoned to philosophy.

243. PLATO

Plato, son of Ariston, turned initially to poetry, composing heroic verse. Then he felt contempt for his work and burned it, seeing that it was much inferior in comparison to the work of Homer. So he attempted tragedy, and indeed composed a tetralogy and was about to contend for the prize, having already given the actors their parts. But before the festival of Dionysos he went and heard Socrates, and being instantly captivated by that Siren, he not only withdrew from the competition but also entirely renounced the writing of tragedies, committing himself to philosophy.

Aelian

*According to this anecdote Plato devoted himself to writing different kinds of verse before his conversion to philosophy. His early love of drama may suggest a reason why his philosophic works took the form of dialogues. But the story may also be Platonic doctrine transformed into biography: the superiority of philosophy to poetry (*Republic *10.597e).*

244. AXIOTHEA

After Axiothea read one of Plato's works on government, she left Arcadia and went to Athens, where she heard Plato lecturing. She concealed the fact thereafter that she was a woman, just as Achilleus had done at the court of Lykomedes.

Themistios

Among Plato's many students were two women, Axiothea of Phleious and Lasthenia of Mantinea, who wore male clothing (Diogenes Laertios 3.46). Drawn to philosophy after reading a work by Plato, Axiothea entered Plato's Academy disguised as a man.

245. EPICURUS

Apollodoros the Epicurean, in the first book of his work *On the Life of Epicurus*, declares that Epicurus came to philosophy after finding fault with his teachers, who were unable to explain to him what Hesiod says about Chaos.

Diogenes Laertios

*In his mythic cosmogony the early Greek poet Hesiod says that in the beginning Chaos was born, followed by Earth, Tartaros, and Eros (*Theogony *116–122).*

* * *

When Epicurus was just a boy and his teacher was reading aloud to him,

> "Now, indeed, first of all Chaos was born,"

Epicurus asked him who Chaos was born from, if it really was born first. After the teacher replied that it was not his job to teach such things but that of the so-called philosophers, Epicurus said, "Well, then, if they know the nature of reality, I've got to make my way to them."

Sextus Empiricus

BENEFITS AND PERILS OF PHILOSOPHY

One of the questions frequently put to philosophers was what benefit one gets from philosophy. These exchanges often take the form of apothegms.

246. ARISTIPPOS ON THE PHILOSOPHER'S ADVANTAGE

When someone asked Aristippos what advantage philosophers had, he said, "If all laws are annulled, we'll live the same as we do now."

Diogenes Laertios

Aristippos of Cyrene (5th–4th centuries BC), an associate of Socrates, founded the Cyrenaic school of philosophy.

247. ARISTIPPOS ON THE BENEFITS OF PHILOSOPHY

When someone asked Aristippos what benefit he had gotten from philosophy, he said, "Being able to associate confidently with anyone."

Diogenes Laertios

248. ANTISTHENES ON THE BENEFITS OF PHILOSOPHY

When someone asked Antisthenes what benefit he had gotten from philosophy, he said, "Being able to associate with myself."

Diogenes Laertios

Antisthenes (5th–4th centuries BC) was a precursor to the first Cynic, Diogenes.

249. DIOGENES ON THE BENEFITS OF PHILOSOPHY

When someone asked Diogenes what benefit he had gotten from philosophy, he said, "If nothing else, being prepared for any kind of fortune."

Diogenes Laertios

Diogenes of Sinope (5th–4th centuries BC) was the first and best-known of the Cynic philosophers.

250. KRATES ON THE BENEFITS OF PHILOSOPHY

Krates said that the benefit he had gotten from philosophy was "a cup of beans and freedom from care."

Diogenes Laertios

Krates of Thebes (4th–3rd centuries BC), a disciple of Diogenes, had been a wealthy man, but after becoming a Cynic he disposed of his wealth and traveled about with his common-law wife (see 268 "Krates and Hipparchia"). The beans he refers to are lupines, the cheap staple of the Cynic diet.

251. THE MOST USEFUL MAN IN EPHESOS

Herakleitos assailed the Ephesians in these words for banishing his companion Hermodoros: "All Ephesians from youth on up should be hanged and leave their city to their children. They have banished Hermodoros, their most useful man, saying: 'Let there be no most-useful-man among us. Or let him be most-useful-man somewhere else for someone else.'"

Strabo

The pre-Socratic philosopher Herakleitos (flourished ca. 500 BC) and his friend the lawgiver Hermodoros were both natives of Ephesos.

252. PROTAGORAS'S BOOKS BURNED

In another of his books Protagoras begins this way: "Concerning the gods I am unable to say whether they exist or not. There are many obstacles to knowing this, both the obscurity of the subject and the shortness of human life."

On account of this beginning in his work he was expelled by the Athenians, and after a herald went around collecting his writings from each person who had acquired them, they burnt his books in the marketplace.

Diogenes Laertios

Protagoras of Abdera (5th century BC) was a prominent sophist. The particular sentence that offended the Athenians appeared in his book On the Gods, *which he is said to have read in public in Athens. His numerous works have not survived.*

The public burning of Protagoras's books in the Athenian agora was perhaps the first of many instances of book-burning in antiquity. Frequent victims were books on philosophic topics, books on magic and divination, and in Christian times books by religious authors who were out of favor with the currently dominant Christian authorities. In Rome book-burning began with works composed by the orator Titus Labienus (see 195 "A Principled Man").

253. SINNING AGAINST PHILOSOPHY

When someone asked Aristotle why he was leaving Athens, he replied that he did not want the Athenians twice to commit an offense against philosophy, whereby he alluded to the experience of Socrates and to the danger he himself was in.

Aelian

Aristotle had been the tutor of Alexander of Macedon, and after Alexander's death in 323 BC, the philosopher deemed it wise to leave Athens. He moved to Chalkis

on the island of Euboea. Earlier, Plato and other Socratics are said to have fled to Megara for fear of experiencing the same fate as Socrates.

THE PHILOSOPHIC LIFE

254. THALES IN THE WELL

It is said, Theodoros, that Thales, while studying the stars and gazing upward, fell into a well, and a certain witty and charming Thracian slave girl made fun of him, saying he was eager to know about things in the sky but did not notice things that were right behind him or alongside his feet.

The same piece of mockery suffices for everyone who leads a philosophic life. Really, such a person not only does not notice what his neighbor or the person next to him is doing, but scarcely notices even whether the person is human or some other kind of creature. Rather, he seeks and troubles himself with investigating just what a human being is and how human nature differs in action and experience from that of other beings.

Plato

255. THALES AND THE OLIVE PRESSES

They say that people taunted Thales for his poverty, alleging that philosophy was useless.

But Thales, though it was still winter, perceived from observing the stars that there would be a large crop of olives, and with a small amount of money he made deposits on all the oil presses in Miletos and Chios, leasing them cheaply since no one bid against him.

When the season came and suddenly many persons were seeking presses at the same time, Thales leased them out on his own terms and made a considerable amount of money, showing that it is easy for philosophers to be rich if they wish, but this is not what they care about.

Aristotle

*Like contradictory proverbs, some anecdotes spar with each other, taking opposite stances. In the former narrative the philosopher is represented as a distracted intellectual, perhaps the earliest instance of the popular stereotype of the absent-minded professor. Indeed, for the Greeks, Thales was the type of the genius: "He's a real Thales," declares a character in a play by Aristophanes (*Birds *1009), the equivalent of "He's a real Einstein," as Americans used to say. In contrast, a positive intellectual trait, in this case practical cleverness, emerges in the latter story.*

WEALTH VS. WISDOM

256. SIMONIDES'S VIEW

Many people need what the rich possess. This is the reason for Simonides's comment about wise people and wealthy people, after the wife of Hieron asked him whether it was better to be wealthy or wise. "Wealthy," he said, "for I see the wise spending their time at the doors of the wealthy."

Aristotle

The poet Simonides of Keos visited Hieron, tyrant of Syracuse, around 470 BC.

257. ARISTIPPOS'S VIEW

When asked by Dionysios why philosophers go to the doors of the wealthy, whereas the wealthy no longer go to the doors of philosophers, Aristippos said, "Because philosophers know what they need, whereas the wealthy do not."

Diogenes Laertios

Dionysios was one of the tyrants of Sicily of that name, most likely Dionysios I.

THE CYNICS

*More anecdotes were told about the Cynic philosophers than about any other group of people, and most of them feature Diogenes, the original Cynic and the most outrageous of the lot. Centuries after Diogenes's death, Dion Chrysostomos remarks on the continuing popularity of Diogenes anecdotes (*Oration *72.11), which circulated like local-character anecdotes or jokes. Even today the number of anecdotes preserved about Diogenes exceeds five hundred.*

*Diogenes grew up in Sinope, a town on the Black Sea, and moved to Athens, where he developed a minimalist mode of living based upon voluntary poverty. His possessions consisted of his cloak, his leather knapsack, and his staff. He lived outdoors and therefore publicly, eating such food as people gave him and doing in public such activities as his fellow townsmen did in private. He slept in porticoes or in a large storage jar (*pithos*) that lay on its side. This unselfconscious behavior earned him the appellation Diogenes the Dog, or simply The Dog, and accordingly he and other sages who adopted this mode of living were called Cynics, from the Greek adjective* kynikos *"canine."*

258. DIOGENES ON BEING LAUGHED AT

When someone said to Diogenes, "Most people laugh at you," he replied, "And donkeys probably laugh at them. But they don't pay any attention to the donkeys, and I don't pay any attention to them."

Diogenes Laertios

259. DIOGENES AND THE LANTERN

Diogenes lit a lantern in broad daylight, saying, "I'm searching for a human being."

Diogenes Laertios

* * *

He once lit a lantern during the day and walked around with it. When people asked him why he was doing so, he said he was looking for a human being.

Arsenios

The anecdotal Diogenes typically acted out his convictions, performing them as philosophic theater, rather than discussing them in the Socratic manner. So his lantern was in effect a prop. Diogenes explained his quest by saying that he was searching for a "human being" (anthropos)*. Although translators often render the object of Diogenes's quest as a "man" or an "honest man," such a rendering is misleading. What Diogenes sought was not a man (as opposed to a woman or a god or an animal) or a truth-telling man (as opposed to a liar), but a person who was truly and fully human, a* mensch*, as it were. He believed that just as a person must have a knowledge of music to be a musician, so must a person have an understanding of humanness to be human* (Codex Patmos *263, no. 55). Accordingly, when Diogenes once came out of the public baths and someone asked him if there were many people* (anthropoi *"human beings") bathing, he said there were not; but when another person asked him if there was a big crowd inside, he said there was (Diogenes Laertios 6.40).*

260. THE MEETING OF DIOGENES AND ALEXANDER

Alexander once stood before him and said, "I am Alexander, the Great King."

"And I," he said, "am Diogenes the Dog."

Diogenes Laertios

261. ALEXANDER'S OFFER

Diogenes was sunning himself in the Cypress Grove when Alexander stood before him and said, "Ask me for anything you would like."

"Stand out of my light," he replied.

Diogenes Laertios

In this famous anecdote the Macedonian conqueror, whose thirst for acquisition seemed unquenchable, met the Cynic philosopher, who prefered poverty. The setting was the Kraneion, "a cypress grove just outside Corinth containing a gymnasium, where Diogenes was supposed to have set up home when he was in Corinth" (Hard 2012:207).

* * *

Does Diogenes—a man whom Alexander saw sitting in the sun, stood before, and asked if he wanted anything—lack fame? When Diogenes bade him only stand aside a little from the sun, Alexander was struck by his spirit and said to his friends, "If I were not Alexander, I should like to be Diogenes."

Plutarch

In the shorter form of the anecdote Diogenes has the last word, but in the longer one Alexander caps Diogenes's response with his own surprising remark. Alexander can be imagined to see in Diogenes a person who, unlike him, is content with little, or to admire him as one who, like him, acknowledges no one else as his sovereign.

262. DIOGENES ON PERSONAL ATTIRE

When Diogenes went to Olympia and saw at the festival some young men from Rhodes attired in luxurious clothing, he laughed and said, "Such vanity."

When next he came upon some Spartans wearing mean and filthy tunics, he said, "Another kind of vanity."

Aelian

263. DIOGENES ON TEMPLE THEFT

Once when Diogenes saw the custodians of temple treasures leading away a man who had filched a bowl, he said, "The big thieves are leading away the little thief."

Diogenes Laertios

264. DIOGENES ON A PUBLIC READING

When someone giving a long public reading pointed to the white space at the end of his scroll, Diogenes said, "Courage, men, I see land ahead!"

Diogenes Laertios

Several anecdotes show that Diogenes's wit does not always have a philosophic purpose, or perhaps storytellers happily attached to him, as one who famously spoke his mind, humorous anecdotes with forthright speech that were little more than humorous stories.

265. DIOGENES VISITS A BROTHEL

When someone was chiding Diogenes the Cynic philosopher, saying that he saw Diogenes coming out of a brothel, Diogenes said, "Why, should I have been coming out of your house instead?"

Favorinos

266. DIOGENES ON THE CITY OF MYNDOS

Diogenes came to Myndos and, seeing that the gates were large but the city was small, declared, "Men of Myndos, close your gates or your city will get out!"

Diogenes Laertios

267. "WATCH OUT!"

When a man carrying a beam of wood collided with Diogenes and said, "Watch out!" he said, "Why, are you going to hit me again?"

Diogenes Laertios

268. KRATES AND HIPPARCHIA

After hearing various arguments from Diogenes and adding others of his own, Krates rushed to the forum, renounced his possessions as being a pile of dung that was more burden than benefit, and then, when a crowd had gathered, shouted out at the top of his voice, "Krates sets Krates free!" After that, as long as he lived, he lived happily not only in solitude but also naked and free of possessions.

Apuleius

When Krates of Thebes decided to commit himself to the life of a Cynic philosopher, he announced his conversion in public. His proclamation took the form of a statement of manumission of himself, in which Krates the master manumitted Krates the slave from a life of servitude to convention and material wealth.

* * *

Hipparchia, sister of Metrokles, was also captured by Cynic teachings. She and her brother were both born at Maroneia.

Hipparchia fell in love with the discourses and life of Krates and paid no attention to any of her suitors, regardless of their wealth or high birth or good looks. For her, Krates was everything. She repeatedly threatened her parents that she would kill herself if she were not given to him in marriage. The parents urged Krates to dissuade the girl, and he, trying everything and failing to persuade her, finally stood up, removed his gear in front of her, and said, "This is the bridegroom, and these are his possessions. Give the matter some thought, since you can't be a companion of mine unless you share my way of life."

The girl made her choice. Adopting the same attire, she went around with her husband, had sexual relations with him in public, and went with him to dinners.

Diogenes Laertios

Just as Krates was converted to Cynic philosophy by Diogenes, so Hipparchia was converted by Krates, in addition to which she fell in love with him and would have no other man.

*Although it may seem surprising that Krates and Hipparchia dined in people's homes, Cynics were popular dinner guests, and Krates was even nicknamed the Door-Opener (*Thyrepanoiktes*).*

269. MONIMOS ON WEALTH

Monimos said that wealth was Fortune's vomit.

Stobaios

Monimos was a Cynic philosopher, a disciple of Diogenes.

PHILOSOPHERS CRITICIZE ONE ANOTHER

270. DIOGENES CRITICIZES PLATO

When someone was praising Plato, Diogenes remarked, "What is so august about Plato, a man who, though he has practiced philosophy for a long time, has never caused anyone any pain?"

Plutarch

Diogenes criticized Plato for his dialectical approach to philosophy, as opposed to the bluntness of the Cynics, who spoke frankly and without fear of hurting another's feelings if it served a philosophic purpose.

271. PLATO CRITICIZES DIOGENES

When Diogenes invited Plato to eat with him in the marketplace, Plato said, "How charming your unaffectedness would be if it weren't affected."

Gnomonologium Vaticanum

Diogenes's alleged affectation was his living his life as public theater.

272. PLATO CHARACTERIZES DIOGENES

Plato often said of Diogenes that he was Socrates gone mad.

Aelian

273. DIOGENES ON PLATO'S THEORY OF IDEAS

When Plato was conversing about his Ideas, using the terms "tableness" and "cupness," Diogenes said, "Plato, I see a table and a cup but no tableness and cupness."

"Of course not," he responded. "For you have eyes with which to perceive a table and a cup, but not the mind with which to see tableness and cupness."

Diogenes Laertios

Diogenes made the mistake, perhaps, of engaging Plato in debate. When he objected to Plato's theory of the existence of abstract entities by saying that he could not see them, he set up Plato's comeback.

274. DIOGENES ON A DEFINITION OF PLATO'S

When Plato defined a human being as "a bipedal creature without feathers" and gained general approval for it, Diogenes plucked the feathers off a rooster and brought it into the philosophic school, saying, "Here is Plato's human being."

As a consequence Plato added to his definition, "And having flat nails."

Diogenes Laertios

This anecdote mocks Plato's preoccupation with definitions, which Cynics regarded as a waste of time. As often, Diogenes makes his point theatrically.

Although this definition does not occur in Plato's genuine works, it is found in the pseudo-Platonic Definitions *(415a).*

275. DIOGENES ON THE IMPOSSIBILITY OF MOTION

When someone said that motion was impossible, Diogenes stood up and walked around.

Diogenes Laertios

The unnamed person probably had in mind the four arguments against motion developed by the pre-Socratic philosopher Zeno of Elea ("Zeno's paradoxes"). Diogenes's refutation characteristically took the form of a demonstration.

EDUCATION AND LEARNING

276. A SONG BEFORE DYING

Solon of Athens, son of Exekestides, delighted in a song of Sappho's that had been sung by his nephew over wine, and told the boy to teach it to him.

When someone asked him why he was so earnest about it, he said, "So that I may learn it and die."

Aelian

Solon (7th–6th centuries BC), an Athenian statesman and a contemporary of the poetess Sappho, was one of the Seven Sages of early Greece.

277. THE ENTRANCE TO PLATO'S CLASSROOM

In front of Plato's school of philosophy there stood this inscription: "Let no one enter who is unlearned in geometry," that is to say, who is unequal and unjust. For geometry seeks equality and justice.

scholiast

Ancient schools of philosophy were said to have mottos above their entranceways; however, this is the only one that has come down to us. It resembles the notices sometimes posted at Greek sanctuaries that forbade entrance to a certain category of people such as women, men, slaves, or profane persons. This motto gives geometry a moral interpretation in accordance with Platonic thought, in which geometry is viewed as propaedeutic to philosophy.

278. THE DELIAN PROBLEM

After an oracle was given with instructions to double the volume of the altar at Delos, a task requiring the highest skill in geometry, Plato said that the god was not so much prescribing a task as he was directing the Greeks to practice geometry.

Plutarch

Fuller versions of this anecdote go approximately as follows. The inhabitants of the tiny island of Delos suffered from a plague, consulted Apollon, and received a strange oracle telling them that if they doubled the volume of their altar, their troubles would come to an end. Since the altar was a cube, the challenge was to double the cube while maintaining its cubic shape. The Delians failed in their attempt, for they doubled the width and length of the cube and thereby produced a solid that was greater than double the volume of the original. They asked Plato to solve the problem, and, as it happened, he alone understood the true intent of the oracle, which really was an encouragement to the Greeks to study geometry—a pursuit that, in the god's view, they had been neglecting. Eventually the geometrical problem of doubling the cube was solved by two Greek mathematicians.

279. THE WORST PUNISHMENT

When the Mitylenaeans ruled the sea, they imposed the following punishment upon allies who revolted: their children should neither learn literature nor be taught music. Of all punishments they regarded this as the most grievous, to live one's life without knowledge or the arts.

Aelian

DISCOVERIES AND INVENTIONS

In Greek popular thought each element of human culture had a discrete beginning, which it owed to a particular inventor or discoverer, whom the Greeks called its "first finder" (protos heuretes)*. Thus, kingship came from Zeus, weaving from Athena, musicianship from Apollon and the Muses, thievery from Hermes, and so on.*

280. THE INVENTION OF HUNTING

Hunting and hounds are an invention of gods, of Apollon and Artemis. They bestowed them on Cheiron, honoring him with them because of his righteousness. He gladly accepted the gift and made use of it, and had as students of hunting and other excellent things Kephalos, Asklepios, Meilanion, Nestor, Amphiaraos, Peleus, Telamon, Meleager, Theseus, Hippolytos, Palamedes, Odysseus, Menestheus, Diomedes, Kastor, Polydeukes, Machaon, Podaleirios, Antilochos, Aineias, and Achilleus.

Xenophon

The legend of the origin of hunting illustrates the notion that individual deities invented different arts and skills, which they had taught (and continued to teach) to others, whence these arts became part of human culture. In the present story the archer siblings Apollon and Artemis devised the art of hunting, which they passed on to the centaur Cheiron, who in turn taught it to different men of the heroic age. From them hunting became a feature of human culture.

281. THE INVENTION OF BOARD GAMES

The oldest game is the throwing of dice. Palamedes invented the game of dice and the game of pebbles at Ilium as a diversion for the army when it was afflicted by famine.

Suetonius

* * *

At Ilium people point out a stone on which, according to Polemon's report, the Achaians played pebbles, and in Argos they point out the so-called game board of Palamedes.

Suetonius

Just as individual gods devised the major arts of civilization, so individual human beings contributed the smaller details. In this legend the culture hero Palamedes was credited with the invention of dice games and pebble games. The Greek game of "pebbles" (pessoi) *was a board game; although its rules are unknown, it was probably a war game. After a day of battle, the warriors pass their leisure time in symbolic warfare.*

* * *

The Lydians declare that the games currently in use among themselves and the Greeks were an invention of theirs. They say these games were invented among themselves at the same time as they colonized Etruria. They give the following account. During the reign of Atys, son of Manes, all Lydia experienced a terrible famine. The Lydians carried on and persisted for a while, but when the famine did not come to an end, they sought some relief, different persons devising different remedies. It was at that time, then, that dice games, knucklebone games, ball games, and all other kinds of games were invented, except for pebbles. This last the Lydians do not claim as their own invention.

After they invented them, the Lydians did as follows regarding the famine. Every other day they spent entirely playing games, in order not to go looking for food, and the other days they spent eating, taking a break from their games. They lived this way for eighteen years.

Herodotos

This historic legend ascribes the origin of certain games to a time of prolonged famine, calling attention to their ludic function as distractions.

282. THE ORIGINAL LANGUAGE

Before the rule of Psammetichos, the Egyptians considered themselves to be the oldest of mankind. But Psammetichos became king and wanted to know who the oldest were, and after that they considered the Phrygians to be older than themselves but they themselves to be older than other peoples.

Since Psammetichos was unable to discover by inquiry any way to determine who the first people were, he devised the following plan. He gave two newborn infants of ordinary parents to a shepherd to bring up among his flocks. The manner of their upbringing was to be this: no one who came face to face with the children was to utter any word; the children were to lie by themselves in an isolated hut; at appropriate times the shepherd was to bring goats to them, give them their fill of milk, and tend to their other needs. Psammetichos put this into effect and gave these instructions because he wished to hear what language the little children would first speak once they were past the stage of meaningless sounds. And that is what happened.

The second year had passed, and the shepherd was performing his tasks. He opened the door and entered the room. The children both fell down before him and said, "Bekos," as they held out their hands to him. Now, at first the shepherd remained silent, but after he heard this utterance frequently in the course of his visits and caregiving, he notified his master and, at the latter's bidding, brought the children into his presence. When Psammetichos himself had heard them, he inquired what people called something "bekos." From his inquiries he found that it was the Phrygian word for "bread." So the Egyptians formed their judgment from this test, acknowledging that the Phrygians were older than they themselves.

This is the version that I heard from the priests of Hephaistos at Memphis. But the Greeks relate a lot of other nonsense such as that Psammetichos had the children live with women whose tongues he had cut out.

Herodotos

Psammetichos may have assumed that if one placed human infants in conditions like those of the first humans, they would produce the same language as the original humans did (Lloyd [1975–1988] 2:5), or perhaps he thought that the original language of mankind was innate. Psammetichos I (Psametik) was a ruler of the Twenty-sixth Dynasty in the seventh century BC.

Similar language-deprivation experiments were reportedly carried out in later times by the Holy Roman Emperor Frederick II (13th century), James IV of Scotland (16th century), and Akbar the Great, ruler of Moghul India (16th century). In Frederick's case the children perished from lack of human contact; in James's, they spoke "goode hebrew"; and in Akbar's, they failed to speak any language at all.

283. THALES INSCRIBES A TRIANGLE IN A CIRCLE

Pamphile says that Thales, having learnt geometry from the Egyptians, was the first to inscribe a right triangle in a circle, after which he sacrificed an ox.

Diogenes Laertios

Making an important geometrical discovery, the philosopher Thales thanked the gods by performing a sacrifice.

284. THALES MEASURES THE HEIGHT OF THE PYRAMIDS

Thales had no teacher, except that he went to Egypt and spent time with the priests there. Hieronymos says he measured the pyramids from their shadows after observing the moment when a person's shadow was equal to his height.

Diogenes Laertios

Thales discovered how to measure the height of the pyramids at Giza by observing that when the sun was at a certain angle (45 degrees), a person's height and shadow were equal in length, and inferring that this relationship must hold true for other objects. (The legend ignores the complication that a pyramid, unlike a person or a stick, is not perpendicular to the ground but has a base that extends outward.) Three centuries later, similar close observation of the sun's shadows in an Egyptian setting underlay Eratosthenes's calculation of the circumference of the earth (Nicastro 2008).

285. THALES PREDICTS AN ECLIPSE

According to some authorities Thales was the first to study the stars and to foretell solar eclipses and solstices, as Eudemos says in his work *On the History of Astronomers.*

Diogenes Laertios

* * *

The Medes and the Lydians were waging war against each other with equal success. In the sixth year an engagement took place, and while the battle was in progress day suddenly became night. Thales of Miletos had predicted to the Ionians that this eclipse would occur, setting that year as the time by which the eclipse would happen.

Herodotos

This eclipse of the sun took place shortly before sunset on May 28, 585 BC.

286. THE PYTHAGOREAN THEOREM

It is possible to hear the historians of antiquities trace this theorem back to Pythagoras, saying that he discovered it and, upon doing so, sacrificed an ox.

Proklos

Pythagoras, like Thales before him, sacrificed an ox to the gods upon making a geometrical discovery, although in this case the slaying and consumption of an ox were inconsistent with the sacrificer's vegetarianism. The Pythagorean theorem states that in a right triangle the square of the hypotenuse is equal to the sum of the squares of the other two sides.

287. "EUREKA!"

Although Archimedes made many different and wonderful discoveries, of them all, the following, which I shall describe, he seems to have worked out with infinite ingenuity.

After gaining royal power in Syracuse and enjoying other successes, Hieron decided to place in a certain temple a golden garland as a votive offering to the immortal gods. He contracted to have it fashioned at a particular price, and weighed out the exact amount of gold to the contractor. At the appointed time the man showed the finely crafted work to the king for his approval, presenting a garland whose weight appeared to correspond to that of the gold.

Subsequently, however, when information was laid that in making the garland the man had withheld some of the gold and mixed in an equal amount of silver, Hieron was indignant at being treated so contemptibly. But since he found no way to detect the theft, he asked Archimedes to take up the matter and give it some thought. It chanced that while Archimedes was considering the problem, he went to the public baths, and as he was lowering himself into a tub, he noticed that the amount of water overflowing from the tub was equal to the amount of his body that was immersed. As this showed a way of solving his problem, he waited no longer but leapt joyfully out of the tub and went home naked shouting aloud that he had found exactly what he was looking for. As he ran, he repeatedly cried out in Greek, "I've got it! I've got it!" (*Heureka! Heureka!*).

Proceeding from that first insight Archimedes, it is said, fashioned two lumps of the same weight as the garland, one of gold and the other of silver. After that, he filled a large vessel with water up to its brim and

lowered the lump of silver into it. The amount of water that overflowed corresponded to the magnitude of the lump that had sunk in the vessel. Then he removed the lump and replaced the water, using a pint measure, until it was level with the brim as before. In this way he discovered that the weight of the silver corresponded to a particular measure of water.

After he had put this to the test, he similarly lowered the lump of gold into the vessel, removed it, measured the water back into it in the same way, and found that not so much water was lost. This corresponded to the smaller quantity of the gold compared with the same weight of silver. Now, refilling the vessel and lowering the garland itself into the same water, he found that more water ran over for the garland than for the lump of gold of the same weight. Reasoning from the fact that more water was displaced in the case of the garland than in the case of the lump of gold, he detected that the gold had been mixed with silver, thereby revealing the contractor's thievery.

Vitruvius

Vitruvius says he tells this story in illustration of one of Archimedes's ingenious discoveries, although what most persons today remember is not Archimedes's discovery of the law of buoyancy, also called the Archimedes principle, but the central scene in which he comically ran naked through the streets shouting, "Eureka!" (more correctly, Heureka *= "I have found"). They likely envision the bathing scene as taking* *place in Archimedes's house, but the narrative represents him being in the public baths, from which he ran home, doubtless to record his discovery or to work out its implications. Although the text is in Latin, the narrator gives Archimedes's exclamation in Greek, indicating that for the Romans the Greek words were part of the color of the legend, as they are for us today.*

Archimedes's famous exclamation has been transferred to many other contexts. One is to the story of the discovery of gold in California, which led to the famous gold rush of the mid-nineteenth century and gave the state of California its motto, "Eureka." Another is a term for the experience of sudden insight into a problem, the "Eureka effect" or "Eureka moment."

Archimedes, a native of Syracuse, and Hieron II, ruler of Syracuse, lived in the third century BC.

HAPPINESS AND CONTENTMENT

288. THE ORIGIN OF HUMAN MISERIES

Zeus the cloud-gatherer angrily said to Prometheus,
"Son of Iapetos, you who know counsel beyond all others,
You rejoice for having stolen fire and deceived my mind—
A great woe to you yourself and to human beings hereafter.
In exchange for fire I will give an evil to humans
For them all to enjoy in their heart as they embrace their own evil."
So he spoke, and the father of men and gods laughed.
Zeus ordered famous Hephaistos as swiftly as possible
To mix earth with water and to put in it a human voice
And strength, making it like the immortal goddesses in face,
A beautiful, lovely maiden's image. He ordered Athena
To teach her crafts, to weave the intricate web.
He ordered golden Aphrodite to pour charm over her head
And painful longing and limb-consuming cares.
And he ordered the messenger, Hermes Argeiphontes,
To put in her the mind of a dog and deceitful behavior.
So he spoke, and they obeyed lord Zeus, Kronos's son.

Immediately the famous Lame One [= Hephaistos] formed from
earth
The likeness of a modest virgin in accordance with the plan of
Kronos's son.
Owl-eyed Athena girded her and adorned her.
The divine Graces and mistress Persuasion put
Golden necklaces on her skin, and on her head
The lovely-haired Hours put a garland of spring flowers.
Pallas Athena arranged each adornment on her skin.
And in her chest the messenger Argeiphontes [= Hermes]
Wrought lies and sly stories and deceitful behavior
In accordance with the plan of deep-sounding Zeus. The herald
Of the gods put a voice in the woman and named her
Pandora [= All-Gift], since all who have Olympian homes
Had given her a gift, a woe to barley-consuming men.
When he had finished the sheer, irresistible deception,
The father sent famed Argeiphontes, swift messenger of the gods,
To take the gift to Epimetheus, and Epimetheus
Did not think about how Prometheus had told him
Never to accept a gift from Olympian Zeus, but to send it
Back lest it turn out to be some evil for mortals.
For earlier the tribes of humans used to live on the earth
Apart from and without evils and without toil
And harsh diseases, which bring death to men.
Now mortals straightway grow old in misery.
The woman removed with her hands the great lid of the
storage jar,
And scattered these, devising sad cares for humans.
Hope alone, there in the unbreakable home,
Remained within under the rim of the storage jar and did not
Fly out, for before this she replaced the lid of the storage jar
In accordance with the plan of aegis-holder, cloud-gatherer Zeus.

But the rest, uncounted miseries, wander among humans.
The earth is full of evils, the sea is full.
By day and by night diseases of their own accord
Visit humans, bringing evils to mortals
Silently, since crafty Zeus took away their voice.
So there is no way to evade the mind of Zeus.

Hesiod

The myth of Pandora tells of the advent of human miseries, which are a divine punishment not for human misbehavior but for an offense committed by the god Prometheus acting on behalf of humans.

The first woman, Pandora, was manufactured by a committee of Olympian gods, who made her attractive on the outside so that human males would accept her, but unattractive on the inside so that they would suffer. The gods offered her to Epimetheus because he was too slow-witted to decline their gift. Pandora presently took the lid off a jar, releasing miseries into the world in the form of spirits of illness, including fatal illnesses and so death. The narrator is silent about the origin of the jar and what her motive was for opening it.

In its misogynism the Greek myth of the first woman is a match for the Hebrew myth of Eve. Pandora and Eve each bore immediate responsibility for the entry of miseries into human life.

289. THE ROCK OF TANTALOS

The poets say that Tantalos of old was a lover of pleasures.

In any case the composer of the *Return of the Atreidai* says that after Tantalos came to the gods and passed some time in their company, Zeus allowed him to ask for anything he desired. Since Tantalos was insatiably devoted to sensual pleasures, he specified sensual pleasures and living a life like that of the gods.

Zeus was angry at what he wished for, but granted it because of the promise he had made. But in order that Tantalos might have no enjoyment of the things before him, but be in a constant state of anxiety, Zeus hung a rock over his head that made it impossible for him to reach any of the things in front of him.

Athenaios

Tantalos lived in the mythic era, when the relations of gods and mortals were closer than in later times. He enjoyed the gods' favor and hospitality but hubristically abused his privilege by asking to become like the gods themselves. The boulder that Zeus placed above his head was positioned so delicately that any movement on his part might cause it to tumble down, or so he feared.

According to a different version (Homer Odyssey *11.582–592), Tantalos was punished not with a rock over his head but by being teased with delectable foods that were always just out of his reach, a punishment that has given the world the word "tantalize."*

290. THE SWORD OF DAMOCLES

One of Dionysios's toadies, Damocles, kept bringing up in conversation the ruler's troops, his wealth, the splendor of his rule, the abundance of his possessions, and the magnificence of his royal palace, saying that no one had ever been happier. So Dionysios said, "Well, since this life of mine pleases you so much, Damocles, would you like to have a taste of it and experience my good fortune yourself?"

When he said he certainly would, Dionysios had the fellow placed on a golden couch strewn with a beautiful woven blanket with splendid embroidery, and set it off with several side tables chased with silver and gold. Then he ordered boys selected for their outstanding attractiveness to stand by the table, watch for any nod Damocles might make, and wait upon him attentively. There were perfumes and garlands; there was incense burning; there were tables spread with sumptuous meals. Damocles thought himself a lucky man.

In the midst of this display Dionysios ordered that a gleaming sword be suspended from the paneled ceiling by a horse hair in such a way that it hung over the neck of that happy man. And so Damocles did not notice those good-looking attendants or the artfully crafted silver, nor did he reach for anything on the table, and presently even his garlands slipped down. Finally he prevailed upon the tyrant to let him go, because he no longer wished to be happy.

So Dionysios showed quite well, did he not, that there was no happiness for a person who was always menaced by some terror?

Cicero

The legend of Damocles and the ruler of Syracuse is a counterpart to the myth of Tantalos and the ruler of the cosmos. Each monarch gave his guest what he desired, while ensuring that he could not enjoy it. "The rock of Tantalos" was a proverbial expression among the Greeks (Otto 1890:340, no. 1742), just as "the sword of Damocles" is among us.

291. KING MIDAS

In return for a kindness, Father Liber granted Midas the opportunity to ask for anything he wanted. Midas asked that everything he touched turn into gold. He got his request, returned to his palace, and whatever he touched turned to gold.

But when he became tormented by hunger, he asked Liber to take away this fine-sounding gift. Liber told him to bathe in the River Pactolus, and when Midas's body touched the water, it turned the color of gold. This stream is now called Chrysorrhoas ["Goldenflow"] in Lydia.

Hyginus

Midas, a king of Phrygia in the latter part of the eighth century BC, was proverbial among the Greeks and Romans for his power and wealth. This legend foregrounds his wealth and alleged poor judgment. When Liber (that is, Bacchus) offered to grant him any wish, Midas shortsightedly asked for a golden touch. In this version the monarch was allowed to learn his lesson and get on with his life, but in less-happy forms of the story he starved to death. The theme of the unwise wish was a favorite in ancient storytelling.

292. WEALTH AND HAPPINESS

Pheraulas invited the Sacian, the one who had given him his horse, to his house and entertained him, providing for him generously and, after they had dined, Pheraulas filled the drinking cups he had gotten from Kyros, offered a toast to his guest, and gave him the cups as a gift.

The Sacian, seeing the abundance of beautiful coverlets, the abundance of beautiful furniture, and the many servants, said, "Tell me, Pheraulas, was your family at home also rich?"

Pheraulas said, "Rich? No, we plainly lived by the work of our hands. My father gave me a child's scant education while he worked and supported me, and when I became a young man, he brought me out to the farm and told me to go to work, since he couldn't support an idler. And there I supported him in turn as long as he lived, digging and sowing a plot of land that was very small, not poor really but quite just. For whatever seed it received, it returned fairly and justly along with a little interest, and sometimes in its nobility it returned what it had received twofold. That, then, was my life at home. Everything that you see now has been given to me by Kyros."

The Sacian said, "How blessed you are both for the obvious reasons and because you used to be poor and have become rich. I imagine that it's much more enjoyable for you to be rich because you became rich after hungering for wealth."

Pheraulas said, "So you suppose, my Sacian friend, that the more I possess, the more enjoyable my life is? You aren't aware," he said, "that I eat, drink, and sleep not the slightest bit more enjoyably now than when I was poor. From possessing a lot I gain only this: I have more to guard, I have more to distribute to others, and I have more to take the trouble of managing. Now it is I to whom many servants look for their food, many servants for their drink, many servants for their clothing. Some of them need doctors. One comes reporting that sheep have been torn apart by wolves or cattle have fallen over a ledge, or saying that the herds are beset by an illness. So it seems to me," said Pheraulas, "that I have more grief nowadays from having much than I did before when I had little."

The Sacian responded, "But still, by Zeus, when it's safe and sound, the sight of your abundance makes you many times happier than I am."

Pheraulas said, "My Sacian friend, it's not so enjoyable to possess wealth, you know, as it is distressing to lose it. You'll recognize that what I say is true: a rich person is not forced to lie awake because of joy, whereas you won't see a person who is losing something being able to sleep because of grief."

"No, by Zeus," said the Sacian, "but neither would you see a person who is gaining something nodding off from joy."

"That's right. For if possessing were as enjoyable as acquiring, the rich would differ greatly from the poor in their happiness. And, you know, the man who has a lot has also to spend a lot on the gods, on friends, and on guests. Be aware, then, that whoever mightily enjoys having money is also mightily distressed spending it."

"Yes, by Zeus," said the Sacian, "but I myself am not one of those. I think happiness would be to have a lot and spend a lot."

"Then, by the gods," Pheraulas said, "why don't you become happy at once and make me happy? Take all this, possess it, and use it as you wish. Support me as simply a guest or even more sparingly than a guest. It will be enough for me to share what you have."

"You're joking," said the Sacian.

But Pheraulas swore that he was speaking in earnest. "And, my Sacian friend, I'll obtain other favors for you from Kyros—exemption from attending Kyros's court and from military service. For your part, just stay at home being wealthy, and I myself will perform these functions on behalf of you and me. And if I receive some additional good from attending on Kyros or from some campaign, I'll bring it to you so that you'll have even more to rule over. Only," he said, "free me from this care. If I am liberated from these concerns, I think you'll be very useful to both me and Kyros."

Following this conversation they agreed to these terms and put them into effect. The one man deemed himself to have become happy because he commanded much wealth, while the other regarded himself as very blessed because he would have an administrator who would give him the leisure to do whatever he enjoyed doing.

Xenophon

293. WATER AND A LOAF OF BREAD

Epicurus, a member of the deme of Gargettos, used to proclaim that a man who is not satisfied with a little is not satisfied with anything. He said he was prepared to contend in happiness against Zeus himself if he had a barley cake and some water.

Aelian

294. GOLD VS. FIGS

If a person should lock up a pile of gold in a house,
A few figs, and two or three people,
He would perceive how much better figs are than gold.

Ananios

295. UNTOUCHED BY GRIEF

They say that when Darius was distressed at the death of his beautiful wife, Demokritos of Abdera could not say anything that sufficed to console him. So Demokritos promised to bring his departed wife back to life if Darius would undertake to supply him with what was needed. Darius bade him spare no expense but confirm his promise by taking whatever was needed.

Demokritos let a little time pass and then told him that everything else had been gotten together for carrying out the task, and only one thing was lacking, which he himself did not know how to procure but which Darius, being king of all Asia, would perhaps find without difficulty. When he asked what this great thing was that only a king might know about, Demokritos answered that if they inscribed on his wife's tomb the names of three persons who have been untouched by grief, she would straightaway return to life, obliged by the law of the rite. Darius was at a loss and, as you might expect, could not find anyone who had not experienced sorrow of some kind, whereupon Demokritos burst into his usual laughter and said, "You silly man, why do you mourn without end as though you were the only person to have experienced so great a grief—you who can't find even a single person out of all those who have ever lived who was without a share of personal sorrow?"

Julian the Apostate

This legend appears within a letter of consolation attributed to the emperor Julian the Apostate and addressed to his friend Himerios upon the death of the latter's wife. Darius is presumably Darius II of Persia (5th century BC), and Demokritos is the Greek atomist, known as the Laughing Philosopher.

* * *

Alexander instructed his amanuensis to write to his mother as follows.

> King Alexander sends greetings to his dearest mother.
>
> When you have received this last letter of mine, make arrangements for a lavish banquet in requital of Providence above for having provided you with such a son. But if you want to honor me, go out and gather everyone together, both small and large, both rich and poor, to the banquet, saying to them, "Look, the banquet is ready. Come and feast! But let no one enter who has a past or present sorrow, because I made the banquet not for sorrow but for joy."
>
> Take care, mother.

Olympias did this, but no one came to the banquet, for no one was found, small or large, rich or poor, who was without a sorrow.

Immediately she recognized Alexander's wisdom, that he had departed from among the living and had written the letter as a consolation, since what had happened to him was not something unusual but rather something that has happened and happens to everyone.

Pseudo-Kallisthenes

Alexander the Great dictated the letter as he lay on his deathbed.

296. THE HAPPY MUTE

They say that Demaratos, a disciple of Timaios the Lokrian, fell ill and was mute for ten days. On the eleventh day he slowly recovered from his disorder and said that it had been the most pleasant time of his life.

Pseudo-Aristotle

297. PYRRHOS AND KINEAS

Seeing that Pyrrhos was making preparations to set out against Italy, Kineas caught him at a moment of leisure, and engaged him in the following conversation.

"Pyrrhos, the Romans are said to be warriors as well as rulers of many warlike nations. If god should grant a victory over these men, how will we use our victory?"

"Kineas," he said, "you are asking something obvious. Once the Romans have been overcome, no barbarian or Greek city there is a match for us in battle, and we'll straightaway possess all Italy, whose size and excellence and strength ought to be better known to you than to anyone else."

Kineas paused for a little while and said, "After we have taken Italy, what will we do?"

Pyrrhos, not yet perceiving his intent, said, "Sicily, a prosperous and populous island and one easy to capture, reaches out its arms nearby. Everything there is in disorder with lawless cities and demogogues, now that Agathokles is gone."

"You're probably right," said Kineas. "But would our expedition stop with this, then, the taking of Sicily?"

"May god keep granting us victory and success! We'll treat these conquests as the preliminaries of a great enterprise. For who could keep his hands off Libya, or Carthage when it has gotten within his reach, a city that Agathokles came very close to taking after he stealthily escaped from Syracuse and crossed the sea with only a few ships? And once we have overcome them, none of our enemies who now behave arrogantly toward us will offer us any resistance—that goes without saying."

"Yes, it does," said Kineas. "For it's clear that, relying on such great power, it will be possible for us to retake Macedonia and to rule Greece with firmness. But after these places have become subject to us, what will we do?"

And Pyrrhos said with a kindly laugh, "Why, we'll have lots of time, my dear friend, and there'll be goblets of wine every day, and we'll delight each other with our company and conversation."

Stopping Pyrrhos at this point, Kineas said, "Then what's standing in our way if we want to drink goblets of wine and pass the time with each other now, since we have all these things already at hand without any trouble—all those things that we have in mind to attain by bloodshed, great toil, and danger after doing much harm to others and suffering much harm ourselves?"

By this reasoning Kineas troubled Pyrrhos more than he relieved his mind. Pyrrhos thought of how much happiness he was leaving behind him, since he was not able to give up the hopes for the things he yearned for.

Plutarch

Kineas, a Thessalian with a reputation for wisdom, served King Pyrrhos of Epirus as an ambassador and military man.

This excellent story is still told today, adapted to modern circumstances. In one version the man who does not have enough is an American businessman with an MBA from Harvard, while the man who is content with what he has is a Mexican fisherman in a small coastal village.

ON DRINKING

A limit of two (or three, depending upon the source) cups of wine was proverbial among Greeks and Romans for temperate drinking.

298. THE THIRD CUP OF WINE

Xanthos entered and reclined on a couch. After the drinking had gone on for a while and Xanthos had become a little tipsy, the company began to pose problems and questions, as philosophical men do. When a struggle arose around the posing of problems, Xanthos began to join in the discussion, but in the spirit of a lecturer rather than of a symposiast.

Aesop, recognizing that Xanthos was on his way to creating a battle, said, "When Dionysos invented wine, he mixed three cups of wine and showed human beings how they ought to make use of drinking. The first one, he said, was for pleasure, the second for good cheer, and the third for carelessness. For this reason, master, drink the cup of pleasure and that of good cheer, but yield the cup of carelessness to the young. You have lecture halls for your expositions."

But Xanthos, who by now was drunk, said, "Shut up, won't you?"

Life of Aesop

Trying to induce his master, the philosopher Xanthos, to moderate his drinking at a party with his students, the slave Aesop cites a story in which the god Dionysos, after inventing wine, instructed human beings in its proper use.

* * *

Three bowls of wine only do I mix
For the temperate—one for health,
Which they empty first; the second
For sexual passion and pleasure; and the third for sleep,
Which wise men drink up
And go home.

The fourth is no longer
Mine; it's for abusive words. The fifth is for shouting;
The sixth, for roving bands of revelers; the seventh, for black eyes;
The eighth, for a court summons; the ninth, for a dark mood; and
The tenth, for madness and throwing stones.

Euboulos

The speaker is the god of wine, Dionysos. Although the context is lost, it is likely that Dionysos had just invented wine and was instructing humans in the prudent consumption of the beverage at symposia, or drinking parties.

ON BEHAVING LIKE ANIMALS

The likening of humans and animals has a long history. As an insult we encounter it as early as Homer's Iliad, *where the angry Achilleus tells Agamemnon that he has the eyes of a dog and the heart of a deer (1.159, 225), that is, he is shameless like a dog and fainthearted like a deer. Helen calls herself a bitch (e.g.,* Iliad *6.344). Earlier, the gods had given the first woman, Pandora, the mind of a dog (Hesiod* Works and Days *67).*

299. THE DIFFERENT STAGES OF LIFE

A horse, an ox, and a dog, suffering
From the cold, came to a man's house.
He opened his doors to them,
Led them inside, warmed them by the hearth
With its abundant fire, and set out something for them to eat—
Barley for the horse and grass pea for the hard-working ox,
While the dog stood beside the man as a fellow diner.
In return for his hospitality the animals gave the man
Shares of the years they were going to live.
The horse went first, wherefore in our early years
We are overconfident in our thoughts.

The ox followed, wherefore coming to middle age
A man toils, enjoying work and accumulating wealth.
The dog, they say, granted the final years, which is why,
Branchos, old men are so grouchy.
They fawn only on the persons who feed them,
They are always barking, and they do not care for strangers.

Babrios

*The division of human life into stages is a common notion from antiquity to the present day. In a well-known passage Shakespeare mentions seven stages of life (*As You Like It*, act 2, scene 7). In Babrios's tale the different stages of life are correlated with different kinds of animals.*

300. THE DIFFERENT KINDS OF PEOPLE

On Zeus's orders Prometheus fashioned humans and animals. When Zeus saw that the nonrational animals were much greater in number, he instructed Prometheus to destroy some of the animals and convert them into humans. Prometheus did as he was ordered, and it turned out that the ones who had not been fashioned as humans from the beginning had the form of humans but the mind of animals.

anonymous

In this tale, as in the following one, the connection between animal nature and human behavior manifests itself, not diachronically in different stages of life, but synchronically in different human types.

301. THE DIFFERENT KINDS OF WOMEN

This too is by Phokylides. From these four
The tribes of women have come: one from a bitch, one from a bee,
One from a bristling sow, one from a long-maned mare.
This last is manageable, quick, roams, has fine form.

The one from the bristling sow is neither good nor bad.
The one from the bitch is difficult and fierce, but the one from
the bee is
A good manager and understands how to work.
With this last one, dear friend, pray to obtain a lovely marriage as
your lot.

Phokylides

In folktales deriving different kinds of women from different kinds of animals, much is found to blame in women and little to praise. This is especially true of a poem by Semonides of Amorgos (fr. 7), who says that Zeus created a messy woman from a sow, a moody one from a vixen, an ill-tempered one from a bitch, and so on from the earth, the sea, a donkey, a weasel, a mare, a monkey, and finally a bee, this last being the only good kind of woman and wife.

AESOPIC FABLES

Just as humans can be likened to animals, so also animals can stand in for humans. Most fables feature animals, which serve as metaphors for different kinds of human beings.

302. THE FOX AND THE CRANE

Just as the wine should be common to all, so too should the conversation be one in which everybody participates. Persons who propose abstruse topics appear to be no more suitable for fellowship than Aesop's crane and fox.

The fox had the crane over for dinner, pouring a thin broth onto a flat stone. The crane got no meal from it and looked ridiculous as well, since the broth, being liquid, escaped from its bill. So the crane in turn invited the fox, serving dinner in a flask with a long, thin neck, into which the crane easily inserted its bill and enjoyed the meal, whereas the fox, being unable to do so, got the dinner it deserved.

And so when philosophers at drinking parties plunge into subtle and disputatious problems, they irritate most of the guests, who cannot follow

them and throw themselves into singing songs, relating silly tales, and talking shop. Gone then is the symposium's goal of fellowship, and Dionysos is insulted.

Plutarch

Plutarch decrees that conversational topics at dinner parties should be those in which all the guests can participate. Inconsiderate sympotic behavior is an insult to the god Dionysos inasmuch as it amounts to a misuse of wine, Dionysos's gift to humans.

The fable shows a high degree of analogism, in that the fox and crane behave more like human beings than like animals, hosting dinner parties for each other.

303. THE DOG WITH A PIECE OF MEAT

A dog carrying a piece of meat was crossing over a river. When it saw its own reflection in the water, the dog thought it was another dog with a bigger piece of meat. So it dropped its own piece and sprang at the other dog to take its piece away. The result was that the dog lost both. It did not get the other piece because it did not exist, and its own was swept away by the river.

This tale can well be applied to a greedy man.

anonymous

This tale is a realistic animal fable. Unlike the fable of the fox and the crane, the animal character displays no peculiarly human traits.

304. THE RAVEN WITH A PIECE OF MEAT

A raven seized a piece of meat and perched on a tree. A fox spied it and, wanting to get hold of the meat, began to praise the raven for its size and beauty, saying that it would be quite fitting for the raven to be king of the birds and that if only it had a voice, it would by all means be so. The raven, wishing to show the fox that it did have a voice, dropped the piece of meat and uttered a loud screech. The fox dashed up, seized the piece of meat, and said, "Raven, if you had any sense, you'd be equipped to be the king of everyone."

This tale is appropriate for a foolish person.

anonymous

305. THE KING OF THE APES

Two men, one deceitful and the other truthful, were making a journey together. In the course of their walking they came to the land of the apes.

When one of the crowd of apes caught sight of them, he who appeared to be their chief ordered the men to be detained in order that he might question them about what people were saying about him. He ordered all his fellow apes to stand in front of him in a long line to his right and left, and to bring him a throne. He had them stand this way because he had once seen the emperor do it. Then he ordered the men to be brought forth.

The chief asked, "Who am I?"

The deceitful man said, "You are the emperor."

Again he asked, "And these whom you see before me?"

He responded, "They are your attendants, your chancellors, your field marshals, and your military officials."

Since he and his crowd had been praised with these lies, he ordered the man to be given a reward. The man had flattered them all, and so had deceived them.

Now, the truthful man thought to himself, "If this deceitful man, who lies about everything, is so well accepted, I shall receive a greater reward for telling the truth."

Then the chief of the apes said, "You, too, tell me. Who am I, and who are these whom you see before me?"

The man, who always loved the truth and was accustomed to speak truthfully, answered, "You are in fact an ape, and all these like you are apes and always will be."

Immediately the chief ape ordered the man to be torn to pieces by teeth and claws for telling the truth.

This tale is for wicked men who love deceit and malice, and who tear honesty and truth to shreds.

Phaedrus

306. THE APE WITH IMPORTANT ANCESTORS

A fox and an ape that were journeying together were disputing about the nobility of their families. As they were going through each point in detail, they came upon some tombs, and the ape moaned upon seeing them. When the fox asked the reason for this, the ape showed it the monuments and said, "Well, why shouldn't I cry when I see the grave markers of my family's freedmen and slaves?" The fox responded, "You can lie all you want, since none of these are going to arise from the grave to refute you."

So also among human beings, liars are most given to boasting when there is no one around to refute them.

anonymous

307. THE SOUR GRAPES

Spying some clusters of grapes hanging from a vine that had grown up a tree, a hungry fox wanted to get hold of them but could not. As it departed, it said to itself, "They're sour."

So also some persons, when they fail to reach a goal on account of their own weakness, blame circumstances.

anonymous

Strictly speaking, the epimythium of this well-known fable misses the point, since the fox did not blame anything for its failure; rather, when it found the goal to be unattainable, the animal depreciated it. The fabulist sees correctly that the fox reacts dishonestly to its failure, but he misapprehends the nature of the animal's dishonesty.

308. THE ANT AND THE CICADA

Cold and wintry weather came down from Olympos. The ant had collected a lot of food during harvest time, storing it in its house, but the cicada went into its hole and was panting from hunger, gripped by starvation and the considerable cold.

The cicada asked the ant to share its food in order that the cicada too might eat some wheat and be saved from starvation. But the ant asked, "Where were you in summer? Why didn't you collect food during harvest time?" The cicada answered, "I was singing and giving pleasure to the wayfarers." The ant showered it with laughter, saying, "Then, in winter, dance."

The tale teaches us that nothing is more important than to give thought to the necessary provisions, and not to devote one's leisure time to pleasure and revelry.

anonymous

Ants were proverbial for their industry and providence, storing away grain in the summer for use in the winter, while cicadas were beloved by the Greeks (less so by the Romans) for their singing, which delighted farmers and wayfarers during hot summer days. The present fable confronts the two creatures, the hardworking ant and the music-making cicada, presenting the latter as a carefree and improvident musician.

309. THE LION'S SHARE

A wild ass and a lion were partners in a hunt,
The lion being superior in strength, the ass in swiftness of foot.
When they had gotten an abundance of prey,
The lion divided it, laying out three portions.
"I myself," he said, "will take the first portion,
Inasmuch as I am king. I'll take that portion, too,
Since I'm an equal partner. And this third one here
Will cause you trouble if you're not willing to run off."
Measure yourself. Do not involve yourself in a business or
Partnership with a person more powerful than yourself.

Babrios

This fable is known in several forms, but the proverbial phrase it inspired is now more familiar than the tale itself.

310. THE RACE OF THE TORTOISE AND THE HARE

A tortoise and a hare were arguing with each other about their speed. And so they set a date and parted. Now the hare, because it was naturally speedy, paid little attention to the race, lay down beside the road, and fell asleep, whereas the tortoise, knowing how slow it was, did not stop running and so ran past the sleeping hare and got the prize of victory.

The story shows that hard work often trumps a careless nature.

anonymous

In addition to being one of the best-known Aesopic fables and a special favorite of children, the tale of the tortoise and the hare presumably suggested the imagery underlying Zeno of Elea's second paradox, that of Achilleus and the tortoise, which Greeks called "the Achilleus argument." If the swift Greek hero Achilleus (or, in another version, a swift horse) and a tortoise have a race, if the tortoise has a head start, and if each runner proceeds at a constant speed, the swifter will never overtake the slower, for by the time that Achilleus (or the horse) reaches the point at which the tortoise began, the tortoise will have moved some distance ahead, and so on until the end of the race (Aristotle Physics *6.9 [239b15]; Ross 1955:71–85).*

311. THE LION AND THE MOUSE

A mouse ran over the body of a sleeping lion. The lion woke up, seized the mouse, and was about to devour it. The mouse begged the lion to let it go, saying that if it should be spared, it would repay the favor. The lion laughed and released it.

Not long afterward it happened that, thanks to the mouse, the lion was saved from death. For when the lion had been captured by some hunters and tied with a rope to a tree, the mouse heard it moaning, came to his aid, gnawed the rope, and set the lion free, saying, "You laughed at me at the time, since you didn't expect to get a return for your favor, but now you realize that even mice know gratitude."

The story shows that in changes of circumstance even the powerful come to have a need for the weak.

anonymous

312. THE PLUMP DOG

A very plump dog met a wolf,
Who questioned him, asking where he was raised
Becoming so large and fat a dog.
"A generous man," he said, "feeds me."
"But your neck," the wolf said, "how did it become bare?"
"It's rubbed by the iron dog-collar that

My keeper forged and put on me."
The wolf laughed at him, saying,
"Well, for my part, I say no to this luxury,
For the sake of which iron would rub my neck."

Babrios

The tale of the plump dog and the lean wolf is an instance of a "choice fable," in which a character evaluates two options.

313. THE TRANSFORMED WEASEL

A weasel fell in love with a handsome youth and prayed to Aphrodite to change her into a woman. Taking pity on her plight, the goddess transformed her into a beautiful girl. And so when the youth saw her, he fell in love with her and took her home with him.

As they sat together in their bedroom, Aphrodite, wanting to learn whether in changing her body the weasel also changed her character, released a mouse in the middle of the room. The girl forgot her present circumstances, got up from the bed, and chased the mouse in her desire to eat it. Discontented with her, the goddess restored her to her original form.

So also people who are evil by nature, even if they change their outward form, do not alter their character.

anonymous

Weasels, which are good mousers, played a role in ancient Greek households similar to that of modern-day housecats. That one's basic nature does not change is a common theme of ancient fables.

314. THE GOOSE THAT LAYS GOLDEN EGGS

Hermes was the object of extraordinary religious devotion by a man, and gave him a goose that lay golden eggs. Not waiting for the benefits in small amounts, the man did not hesitate to sacrifice it, since he supposed that the goose was solid gold inside. As it happened, he not only was disappointed in this expectation but also lost the eggs, for he found that the goose was all flesh inside.

So greedy persons, in their desire for more, often lose what they have already in hand.

anonymous

315. THE TORTOISE THAT WISHES TO FLY

After a tortoise observed an eagle flying, it wanted to fly, too. It went to the eagle and asked what payment it would take to teach the tortoise. Although the eagle replied that it was not possible, the tortoise kept asking and pressing. So the eagle lifted it up, rose high into the air, and released the tortoise above a rock, where it landed, burst, and died.

The tale shows that because of their ambition many people take no heed of prudent persons and harm themselves greatly.

anonymous

316. THE KING OF THE FROGS

The frogs, distressed at not having a ruler of their own, sent a delegation to Zeus, asking him to provide them with a king. Aware of their simple nature, Zeus dropped a log onto their pond. At first the frogs were so frightened by the sound that they descended to the depths of the pond, but later, since the log did not move, they came back up again and were so scornful of it that they even tread and sat on it.

Indignant at having been given so unworthy a king, they came a second time to Zeus and asked him for a change of rulers, saying that the first one was too sluggish. And Zeus, in his irritation at them, sent them a water snake, which would catch and eat them.

The story shows that it is better to have slothful rulers than chaotic ones.

anonymous

317. THE ASTRONOMER

An astronomer had the habit of going out each evening to gaze at the stars. Once he was walking around in the outskirts of the town with his mind entirely upon the heavens, and fell into a well before he realized it. He groaned and shouted, and a passerby who heard him moaning came to the place. On learning what had happened, the man said to him, "Fellow, when you try to see what's in the heavens, don't you pay any attention to what's on the earth?"

This tale could be applied to people who swagger about their good repute but cannot even discharge ordinary human activities.

anonymous

The fable of the astronomer features only human characters. As often, the final speaker sums up the point of the tale.

318. THE SHEPHERD WHO CRIES "WOLF!"

A shepherd who drove his flock a good distance from a certain village repeatedly played the following trick. He shouted to the villagers for help, saying that wolves were attacking his sheep. The villagers panicked and dashed out two or three times, and the shepherd laughed at them as they returned. Finally it happened that a wolf really did make an attack. The shepherd's flock was cut off and he shouted for help, but the villagers supposed that he was joking as usual, and paid him little attention. And so it happened that he lost his sheep.

The story shows that what a liar gains is that he is not believed when he is telling the truth.

anonymous

The shepherd's folly is of a different sort from that of, for example, the raven with the piece of meat. The bird behaves foolishly from a lack of intelligence, whereas the shepherd acts like an immature child, and indeed some texts represent him as a young boy.

319. "HERE IS RHODES!"

A pentathlete was constantly criticized by his fellow citizens for his lack of manliness. He once went abroad, returned after a while, and began boasting about the many manly deeds he accomplished in different cities, and in particular how in Rhodes he made a jump that none of the Olympic victors could approach. He declared, moreover, that if any of the persons who were there ever came to town, he would present them as witnesses of his feat. One of the bystanders interrupted him and said, "But, fellow, if this is true, you don't need witnesses. Here is Rhodes and a chance to jump!"

The story shows that words are superfluous about actions for which a test is at hand.

anonymous

This tale is an example of a fine fable that is rarely anthologized, probably because it speaks less to children than to adults. But it was well known to the ancients and gave rise to a proverb: "Lo, Rhodes and a chance to jump!" (Apostolios 8.100).

The pentathlon was an athletic contest consisting of a sequence of five events: long jump, run, discus throw, javelin throw, and wrestling.

320. THE BELLY AND THE FEET

The belly and the feet were wrangling about their respective might. When the feet kept saying that they were much stronger in that they also carried the stomach around, the stomach replied, "Yes, you do, fellows, but if I didn't take in nourishment, you couldn't carry anything."

So also in armies, numerical superiority does not matter if the generals do not use excellent judgment.

anonymous

To judge from the number of authors who mention it, including the apostle Paul, the fable of the belly and the feet, or, in other versions, the belly and the members, was an ancient favorite. It is a so-called strife fable, in which two characters debate their relative superiority or importance.

*The fable of the belly and the members is memorably employed in a Roman legend set in the early fifth century when, amid growing tensions and conflict between the patricians and the plebs—that is, the senatorial class and the populace—the latter withdrew from society in what came to be known as a plebeian secession (*secessio plebis*), the first of several such secessions in Roman tradition. The populace encamped on the Sacred Mount, several miles from the city. The alarmed patricians dispatched Menenius Agrippa, a man of consular rank but of plebeian origin, to talk sense to them. In his address, Menenius recounted the fable, according to which the members of the body once grew resentful of providing food for the belly, since it did nothing, and so ceased bringing it anything to eat. Presently, however, the members found that the body was wasting away, and so it became apparent to them that the belly too made a contribution, since it returned nourishment to the rest of the body. When Menenius pointed out the parallel with the governing class and the governed, the common people agreed to negotiate, which resulted in the creation of a new kind of official, tribunes of the plebs, whose function was to protect the common people from the power of the consuls (Livy 2.32.9–12).*

321. THE OAK AND THE REED

An oak tree and a reed were disputing about their strength. When a powerful wind arose, the reed, bending and moving to and fro with its blasts, escaped being uprooted, whereas the oak made a stand and was toppled roots and all.

The tale shows that one ought not dispute with those who are more powerful.

anonymous

Plant fables are relatively few in number compared to animal fables. Most often they are structured as disputes. Oddly, the fable's epimythium ignores the strife of the oak and the reed, focusing instead upon the relative strength of the oak and wind.

SHORT FABLES

Short fables, or fable-proverbs, are ultrashort narratives that are treated sometimes as fables, sometimes as proverbs.

322. THE MOUNTAIN IN LABOR

A mountain was in labor and then gave birth to a mouse.

Diogeneianos

The tiny narrative refers of course to disappointed expectations. One uses it, explains Diogeneianos, "when a person expects something major but instead encounters a thing of small importance." So in his Art of Poetry *Horace advises poets not to announce a grand theme such as the entire Trojan War, for how likely is it that their work will live up to their promise? "Mountains will be in labor," he says, "and a ridiculous mouse will be born."*

323. THE ATTENTIVE DONKEY

Someone told a story to a donkey, and it wiggled its ears.

Zenobios

A fool thinks that since the donkey moves its ears, it is listening to him.

CHAPTER 8
NUMSKULLS AND SYBARITES

The anthology concludes with a sampling of comic tales starring foolish numskulls, quick wits, delicate Sybarites, and others.

TRADITIONAL NUMSKULLS

324. MARGITES

Margites was a fool who did not know about sex with a woman. His wife encouraged him by telling him that a scorpion had bitten her and that he needed to mount her in order to heal her.

Hesychios

***

When Margites got married, he did not have sexual congress with his bride until, at her mother's suggestion, she pretended to be wounded in her lower region, and said that no medicine would help her except if his male member should be fitted to the place. So he consorted with her in order to heal her.

Eustathios

In bawdy narratives seducers sometimes represent sexual intercourse as being something else—in this case, treatment for a spider bite.

The simpleton Margites is the principal character of an early comic epic poem, Margites *(7th century BC?). Unfortunately the poem has not come down to us, and our knowledge of its content is owed largely to prose paraphrases such as those above. Among the few actual lines that are preserved is "He knew many things, but he knew them all badly" (*Margites *fr. 3 West).*

325. MELETIDES

They say that Meletides did not know how to count past five and was unaware which of his parents he was born from. He did not touch his bride for fear that she would tell her mother.

Suetonius

Meletides, like Margites, was an adult with a child's understanding of number and sexuality.

326. KOROIBOS

Some people say that Koroibos was such a blockhead that he would count the waves of the sea.

Zenobios

Counting the waves was proverbial among the Greeks as an impossible, and therefore useless, activity. "Sillier than Koroibos" became a proverbial expression.

327. MORYCHOS

You are more stupid than Morychos, who got rid of his furniture and now has to sit outside his house.

Zenobios

"More stupid than Morychos" was a Greek proverbial expression.

328. AKKO

Akko was a woman well known for her stupidity. They say that when she looked in a mirror, she conversed with her image as though it were another woman.

Zenobios

***

They say that Akko took down a half-finished cloak from her loom and put it on, and also that she looked in her mirror and spoke to herself as though to another woman.

Suetonius

329. THE FOOLISH KYMAIANS

The city of Kyme is ridiculed for its stupidity, because of its reputation, as some say, that not until three hundred years after the founding of the city did the people of Kyme farm out public taxes for the harbor, and did not reap this revenue earlier. They got the reputation of having taken a rather long time to notice that they dwelled in a seaside city.

There is also another story, according to which the citizens borrowed money for public use, pledging their porticoes as security for the loan. When they did not repay the loan on the appointed day, they were prohibited from using their porticoes. Whenever it rained, however, the creditors, feeling a sort of shame, would make an announcement, telling the people to go under the porticoes. Now, since the herald would cry out, "Go under the porticoes," the report went around that the Kymaians did not perceive that one should go under the porticoes when it was raining unless someone made an announcement instructing them to do so.

Strabo

The Aeolic Greek city of Kyme lay on the seaboard of Asia Minor, near the islands of Lesbos and Chios. Many jokes were told about the supposedly simpleminded Kymaians. Two examples follow.

***

At a funeral for a distinguished man in Kyme a man came up and asked the members of the funeral procession, "Who is the deceased?" One of the Kymaians, turning and pointing, said, "The fellow lying on the bier there."

Philogelos

* * *

Two Kymaians bought two jars of dried figs. Surreptitiously each began to devour the figs from the other's jar, not from his own. When they had eaten up each other's figs, they turned their attention to their own jars, which they found to be empty. And so each laid hold of the other and brought him before the magistrate.

Giving his judgment, the magistrate instructed them to exchange their empty vessels with each other and thereby compensate each other for the cost of the figs.

Philogelos

330. THE FOOLISH ABDERITES

They say, my dear Philon, that during the reign of Lysimachos a sickness of the following sort befell the Abderites. At first the entire population got a fever that right from the start was strong and persistent. Around the seventh day some of them experienced a copious flow of blood from their nostrils and others heavy sweating, which broke the fever.

The sickness brought their minds into a ridiculous state. Everyone became crazy with tragedy, uttering iambs and shouting loudly. Mostly they sang solos from Euripides's *Andromeda*, rendering Perseus's speech in song. The city was full of seventh-day tragic actors, all of them pale and thin, crying out,

> "O Eros, you tyrant over gods and humans!"

and so on in loud voices and continuing to do so for a long time, until indeed winter and cold weather put an end to their folly.

Lucian

*The proverbially silly inhabitants of Abdera, a community in northeast Greece, became afflicted with the delusion that they were all tragic actors, and shouted lines of tragedy for days on end. The poet Juvenal calls Abdera "the land of blockheads" (*Satire *10.50).*

***

An Abderite dreamt he was offering a piglet for sale and wanted one hundred denarii for it. He woke up just as he was rejecting an offer of fifty denarii. So he closed his eyes again, stuck out his hand, and said, "All right, give me the fifty."

Philogelos

OTHER NUMSKULLS

331. CARRYING THE LOAD

X: Thrice unfortunate is this neck of mine here,
Since it's being pressed down and can't joke.
D: Now isn't this an example of outrageous softness!
I, Dionysos, son of Wine Jar,
Do all the toil of walking on foot, and let him ride
So he won't have to be miserable or carry a load.
X: You mean I'm not carrying anything?
D: How can you carry something when you're being carried?
X: Well, by carrying this load here.
D: How are you carrying something?
X: With a lot of difficulty.

D: Isn't the donkey carrying the load that you're carrying?
X: No, by Zeus, absolutely not the load that I'm holding and carrying.
D: How can you be carrying anything when you yourself are being carried by something else?
X: I don't know, but my shoulder here is under a lot of pressure.

Aristophanes

In this scene from Aristophanes's comedy The Frogs, *the god Dionysos and his slave Xanthias are traveling together. While Dionysos walks, his servant rides a donkey and carries a load on his shoulder. The comic routine revolves around the logical quibble of whether a person who is being carried can be said to carry anything.*

332. ACQUIRING SENSE

A certain woman had a simpleminded daughter. She prayed to all the gods for her daughter to get some sense, and her daughter often heard her praying.

One day they went to the countryside. Leaving her mother, the maiden went outside the farmhouse, saw a man having sexual intercourse with a donkey, and asked him, "What are you doing?" He replied, "I'm putting some sense into her." Recalling her mother's prayer, the simpleminded girl said, "Put some sense into me, too." He declined to copulate with her, saying, "There's nothing less grateful than a woman." She responded, "Don't worry about that, sir. Even my mother will thank you and pay you whatever you wish. She prays for me to get some sense." So he deflowered her.

The girl ran joyfully to her mother, saying, "I have gotten sense, mother." The mother said, "The gods have heard my prayers." "Yes, mother," said the girl. She asked, "How did you get sense, child?" The simpleminded girl explained, "A man put a long, red, hard thing in me that ran in and out." When the mother heard her daughter's explanation, she said, "Child, you've lost whatever sense you once had."

Life of Aesop

In this obscene joke the naïve maiden, like simpleminded Margites (see 324 "Margites"), does not understand what sexuality is. She engages in sexual intercourse under the impression that she is improving herself.

333. SEEING THE DOCTOR

A numskull saw his doctor coming and hid himself. When a companion asked him why he did so, he answered, "I feel ashamed that I haven't been sick for a long time."

Philogelos

334. THE TRAINED DONKEY

A numskull wanted to train his donkey not to eat, and so gave it no food. When the ass died of starvation, he said, "What a loss! Just when it learned not to eat, it died."

Philogelos

335. THE BOOKS

A numskull received a letter from a friend who was away on a trip, asking him to purchase some books for him. But the numskull neglected to do so.

When he encountered his friend upon the latter's return, he said, "I never got the letter you sent about the books."

Philogelos

336. THE SLAVE

A man encountered a numskull and said, "The slave you sent me died."

"By the gods," he replied, "he never did anything like that when he was with me."

Philogelos

337. A CALL OF NATURE

A merchant from Sidon with traveling with another man. A bodily necessity obliged him to remain a bit behind, so his fellow traveler went on ahead after writing on the column of a milestone: "Hurry up and catch up with me." When the other man read this, he inscribed beneath it: "Wait for me."

Philogelos

338. THE TWINS

There were twin brothers, and one of them died. When a numskull encountered the survivor, he asked, "Was it you who died, or your brother?"

Philogelos

339. THE FUNERAL

A numskull lost his little son. When he saw that because of his own high position, many people were present for the funeral, he said, "I feel ashamed that with such a large gathering I am burying only a little child."

Philogelos

340. THE BALL IN THE WELL

The son of a numskull was playing with a ball. When the ball fell into a well, the boy bent over the edge and, seeing his own reflection, asked for the ball. Then he complained to his father that he had not gotten it back.

So his father bent over the edge and, seeing his own reflection, said, "Sir, give the boy back his ball."

Philogelos

341. THE EDUCATED SON

A numskull wrote a letter from Athens to his father, and, full of conceit from his education, added, "I pray that I find you on trial for a capital offense so that I can show you my skill as a speaker."

Philogelos

342. THE TRAVELERS

A numskull, a bald man, and a barber were traveling together and, having stopped to pass the night in a desolate place, agreed that each of them should stay awake for four hours to guard their belongings.

The first watch fell to the barber. Wanting to have some fun with the numskull, the barber shaved the man's head while he slept, and then roused him since his own hours were now over. As he awoke, the numskull stroked his head, found that he had no hair, and said, "That worthless barber. He got mixed up and woke up the bald guy instead of me."

Philogelos

343. THE GRATEFUL FATHER

A numskull encountered a friend of his who said, "Congratulations on your new child." "Yes," he replied, "I have you my friends to thank for that."

Philogelos

344. A PAIR OF TWINS

A numskull saw twin brothers. When some persons were marveling at their similarity, he said, "This one doesn't look as much like that one as that one looks like this one."

Philogelos

345. THE FUGITIVES

There were two cowardly numskulls, one of whom hid himself in a well, the other in a reed bed.

When soldiers lowered a helmet down into the well to draw water up for themselves, the numskull who was in the well, imagining that a soldier was coming down, begged for mercy and was captured. When the soldiers said that if he had said nothing, they would have passed him by, the numskull hidden in the reed bed said, "Then pass me by. I'm not saying anything."

Philogelos

346. THE PILLOW

Polydoros put an empty water jug at his head when he was going to sleep, but its hardness made him uncomfortable. So he stuffed it with chaff, filling the vessel up in order that, one might suppose, his pillow would be soft.

Suetonius

***

A numskull, wanting to go to sleep but not having a pillow, told his slave to set a clay jar under his head. When the slave said that the jug was hard, the man told him to fill it with feathers.

Philogelos

This is one of several ancient jokes that is still in oral circulation. In a modern Irish version a beggar named McCall plans to use a drainpipe as a pillow. When his companion Linehan points out that a drainpipe will make a hard pillow, McCall explains that he plans to stuff it with straw first (Wilde 1983:9).

WITS

347. TOO HEALTHY

When a sick man was asked by his doctor how he was doing, he said he was sweating more than he should. The doctor said that this was a good symptom. On another occasion when he was asked how he was, the man said that he was overcome with shivering. The doctor said that this too was good. When the doctor came a third time and asked him about his illness, he said that he was suffering from dropsy. The doctor said that this also was good.

After a member of the household came into his room and inquired how he was, he said, “I’m dying of good symptoms.”

anonymous

348. WHAT DOES IT TASTE LIKE?

Someone saw an ape hanging in a butcher shop
Among the other goods and victuals, and
Asked what it tasted like. Responding humorously,
The butcher said, "It tastes like it looks."

Phaedrus

More exactly, the butcher replied that its flavor was like its head; that is, the meat tasted as bad as the head looked.

349. ALL IN THE FAMILY

A numbskull got into bed with his grandmother one night. Beaten by his father for doing so, he said, "You've been riding my mother for a long time without any grief from me. And now you're angry at finding me just once on your mother?"

Philogelos

350. THE STRONGEST THING

Diphilos, in his comedy *Theseus*, says that three Samian girls were once riddling as they drank at the festival of Adonis. Someone posed to them the riddle: "What is the strongest of all things?"

One of them said, "Iron," and she offered as proof of this that people dig and cut everything with it and use it against all substances.

She was complimented, and the second girl proceeded, declaring that the blacksmith had much greater strength, for he works the iron, and despite its strength he bends and softens it to make whatever he desires.

But the third girl declared that a penis is the strongest thing of all, explaining that the rump of the groaning smith is pierced with it.

Athenaios

This chain tale is built on a sequence of strong and stronger things.

351. CAESAR'S SOLDIERS SING

During Caesar's triumphal procession following his victory in Gaul, his soldiers escorted his chariot while singing humorous songs, including the notorious one that went:

> Caesar subdued Gaul, but Nikomedes subdued Caesar.
> Behold, this is the triumph of Caesar, who subdued Gaul,
> But there's no triumph for Nikomedes, who subdued Caesar.

Suetonius

The soldiers' ditty is another variation on the chain of strong, stronger, strongest. Gaul, Caesar, Nikomedes; or, more abstractly: nation, general, penis. The chain has the same ironic conclusion as that in the foregoing tale: iron, blacksmith, penis. Unusual for a chain tale, the narrative refers to a supposedly historical event.

A triumph was a ritual parade in Rome honoring a victorious general. The procession included civic officials, prominent captives, spoils, sacrificial animals, the honoree himself riding in a chariot, and his army. Custom allowed the soldiers to sing ribald songs. The present one alluded to an infamous affair that Julius Caesar was supposed to have had with King Nikomedes of Bithynia (1st century BC). Caesar had a reputation not only as a seducer of women but also as a man fond of passive homosexual relations. So the soldiers' triumphal song alluded to Caesar's affair with Nikomedes, in which the monarch was represented as playing the active role.

MISCELLANEOUS

352. NOT AT HOME

A person came to visit a grouchy man. The grouch called out, "I'm not in."

The visitor laughed and replied, "Well, of course you are. I recognize your voice."

"You piece of crap, if my slave had said I wasn't in, you'd believe him. Don't you find me more credible than a slave?"

Philogelos

*The grouch (*dyskolos*) is a recurrent character in ancient jokes and comedies.*

* * *

Nasica was calling upon the poet Ennius, and when he inquired about him at his front door, he was told by the maidservant that Ennius was not at home. Nasica, however, perceived that the maidservant said this on the orders of her master and that he was in fact inside.

A few days later Ennius called at Nasica's house and asked for him at the door, whereupon Nasica called out that he was not at home.

"What?" said Ennius, "Don't I know your voice?"

To this Nasica replied, "What impudence! When I asked for you, I believed your maid saying that you were not at home. Don't you believe me when I tell you *myself*?"

Cicero

Whereas the former version has the form of a joke, the latter is cast as a comic anecdote. Scipio Nasica and Ennius lived in the second century BC.

353. THE PORTENT

After this a servant came round and said, "Periander asks you and Thales to come along with your friend here to inspect something that has just now been brought to him, to see whether its birth is some kind of sign and portent or something else. He himself seems very upset, thinking it's a defilement and stain on his sacrifice." He led us right away to one of the rooms off the garden.

There was a youth there, a herdsman apparently, beardless and good-looking, who unfolded a piece of leather and showed us a creature newly born, as he said, from a mare. The upper part of its body, as far down as its neck and arms, was human in form, and it was crying like a newborn infant, but the rest of its body was that of a horse.

"Preserve us from evil," said Neiloxenos and averted his gaze. But Thales stared at the youth for a long time before smiling and saying (he was always teasing me about my profession), "You no doubt have in mind to set in motion a rite of purification and bother the deities who protect us from evil, on the supposition that something big and terrible has happened."

"And why shouldn't I?" I said. "The sign is one of strife and discord, and I'm afraid it may affect marriage and family before we propitiate the first cause of wrath, since as you see the goddess is bringing to light a second one."

Making no answer to this, Thales left the room laughing. When Periander ran into us at the door and inquired about what we had seen, Thales left me, took Periander's hand, and said, "Whatever Diokles tells you to do you will carry out at your leisure, but as for myself I advise you not to employ such young men as grooms for your horses—or give them wives."

Periander very much liked what he heard, it seemed to me, because he burst out laughing and put his arms around Thales and embraced him.

Plutarch

Thales implied that the composite offspring was not a portent signifying divine wrath for an offense that must be expiated, but rather the consequence of the adolescent groom's engaging in sexual intercourse with the mare.

354. THE DEAF JUDGE

Two hard-of-hearing men were at trial, one accusing the other,
But the judge was deafer than the two of them.
One man contended that the other owed him five months' rent,
While the other said that he ground grain during the night.
The judge, looking them both in the eye, asked, "Why are you
quarreling?
She is your mother, and you both must maintain her."

Nikarchos

The humor of this comic epigram arises from three hearing-challenged people interacting with one another, each of them—plaintiff, defendant, and judge—making a fervent statement that had nothing to do with what the others said.

355. THE SCYTHIAN

Once during a snowfall the king of Persia asked a certain Scythian if he did not feel cold, seeing as the man was enduring the cold lightly clad. The Scythian in turn asked the king if his forehead was cold. When the king said it wasn't, the Scythian said, "I'm not either. I'm all forehead."

Aelian

This narrative is an international comic tale that confronts a "civilized" man (Persian, Englishman, Frenchman, American) with a lightly clad "natural" man (Scythian, ancient Briton, beggar, Native American). The civilized man is weak, but the natural man is inured to the challenges of climate.

356. THE COLD READING

Upon returning from a trip, a man asked an incompetent seer how his family was. "They are all well," he said, "including your father."

"But my father died ten years ago!" said the man.

"You do not know your real father," replied the seer.

Philogelos

The seer ventured what he regarded as a safe statement, but when it proved to be off the mark, he was obliged to improvise in order to save face. Incompetent seers were a staple of the ancient comic tradition. In modern versions of this joke the role of the seer is played by a computer.

357. THE COVETOUS MAN AND THE ENVIOUS MAN

Jupiter sent Phoebus to earth from the citadel of the sky
To learn about the uncertain minds of human beings.
Just then two men were imploring the gods with opposite wishes,
One man being covetous, the other envious.
The Titan looked them over and offered to mediate.
When the men entreated him with their prayers, he said,

"The gods, being kind, grant fulfillment: whatever one of you
asks for,
The other will instantly get the same, but doubled."
Since far-reaching greed cannot be satisfied,
The one man—to his own eventual loss—put off making a prayer,
Confident that he would gain from the other man's wish and
Calculating that he would carry off two divine gifts by himself.
But the other, seeing his companion grasping for his own prize,
Triumphantly wished that a punishment be inflicted on his own
body,
Asking to live his life with the loss of one eye, on the condition that
The other, getting double, should lose both.
Then Apollon, now the wiser, laughed at the human lot, and
From personal experience reported back to Jove about the curse
of jealousy.
It rejoices in others' disappointments, and in its exultation
Is unhappy enough to desire its own harm.

Avianus

Apollon attempted to mediate between two men, one greedy and the other jealous, who were praying for opposite things. The god promised to grant one man's request but give the other man double. The envious man phrased his wish in such a way that the other man would lose, rather than gain, twice as much.

Variations on this international comic tale can still be heard. For example: "A Jew in heaven is told that whatever he asks for, Hitler will get double. He asks that one of his testicles be removed" (Legman 1975:611).

THE DELICATE SYBARITES

The Greek city of Sybaris, founded on the Gulf of Taranto in southern Italy, prospered for around two hundred years until it was destroyed in 510 BC. It was famous for its wealth, prompting a cycle of tales on the theme of the extreme luxury and personal delicacy of the Sybarites, and the term "sybarite" became a synonym for "voluptuary."

358. UNCOMFORTABLE SLEEP

Smindyrides the Sybarite ran aground onto an extremity of delicacy. Of course, it was the business of all Sybarites to live luxuriously and softly, but Smindyrides outdid the rest. Once he lay down and slept on some rose petals. When he got up, he said his bed had given him blisters.

Aelian

So-and-so "ran aground onto delicacy" is the rather odd introductory formula that often signals a Sybarite tale. The defining trait of the Sybarites, truphe, *signifies "delicacy" or "luxury" or both. "To run aground" is a navigational term.*

* * *

He complained that he did not feel at all well because the rose petals he lay upon were curled up.

Seneca the Younger

359. THE SUITOR

Smindyrides the Sybarite, they say, ran aground onto such an extremity of luxury that when he came to Sicyon to sue for the hand of Kleisthenes's daughter Agariste, he brought with him a thousand cooks, an equal number of fowlers, and another thousand fishermen.

Aelian

Kleisthenes, ruler of Sicyon, wanting to give his daughter Agariste in marriage to the best man in Greece, made a public proclamation at the Olympic Games in which he invited young men who deemed themselves worthy of being his son-in-law to come to Sicyon, where he would make his choice among them within the year. Smindyrides came as one of Agariste's suitors (Herodotos 6.126–130).

360. NOISE POLICY

The Sybarites were the first people to forbid tradesmen who make noise, such as smiths and carpenters and the like, from being located in the city, in order that the Sybarites' sleep not be disturbed in any way. It was not even allowed to raise a rooster in the city.

Athenaios

361. THE AFFLICTION OF WORK

Timaios relates, on the subject of Sybarites, that a man of Sybaris went to the country one day and said he got a fracture from seeing the farmers digging.

To this one of his listeners replied, "Hearing you tell of your experience has given me a side ache."

Athenaios

A similar instance of studied indolence in our own day is the comment made by the French playwright Georges Feydeau (1862–1921) when a cloakroom attendant was helping him put on his coat: "Don't bother. This is my only form of exercise" (Pronko 1975:7).

362. EXCURSIONS TO THE COUNTRY

When wealthy Sybarites went to the country for a vacation, they took three days to make the one-day trip, even though they traveled in carriages. And some of the roads leading to their country estates were roofed.

Athenaios

363. CHAMBER POTS

They were the first to invent chamber pots, which they brought to their drinking parties.

Athenaios

364. PIPED WINE

Most of them have wine cellars near the sea, the wine being conveyed there from their country estates by means of pipes.

Athenaios

365. POLICY ON PARTIES

After the Sybarites had run aground onto luxury, says Phylarchos, they passed a law that women should be invited to festivals and that persons issuing invitations to sacrifices should send them a year in advance in order that the women might make proper preparations of dress and other ornament in the interval beforehand, and proceed thus prepared to the events.

Athenaios

366. DANCING HORSES

The Sybarites went so far in their luxury that they had even trained their horses to dance to the flute at their feasts.

Now, the men of Kroton knew this, and when they were at war with the Sybarites, as Aristotle relates in his account of their constitution, the men of Kroton performed the dance tune for the Sybarite horses, for the men had with them flute players in military dress. As soon as the horses heard the flute music, they not only danced away but even deserted to the men of Kroton, taking their riders with them.

Athenaios

The citizens of Kroton were neighbors and sometime enemies of the Sybarites.

TALL TALES

367. TOPSY-TURVY LAND

I think it is better to leave such stories and tales to nurses to tell to little children who need to go to sleep—of a certain sea that is sweet, of river horses, of the sea that flows into a river, and other such soporifics.

Aristeides

* * *

Ptolemy mentions the nonsense talk of children according to which fruits grow in the sea and fish in trees.

Tertullian

In topsy-turvy land, evidently a favorite of children, the sea was not salty, horses lived in water (cf. hippous potamious *"river horses" = hippopotami), water flowed upstream, apples grew in the sea, and fishes grew on trees.*

368. FROZEN SPEECH

Antiphanes said jokingly that in a certain city words froze from the cold as soon as they were uttered, and then later, as the words thawed out, people heard in summer what they had conversed about in winter.

Plutarch

*Antiphanes of Berge was a renowned liar who lived in the fourth century BC. He even inspired a verb, "to bergize" (*bergaizein*), which signified "to say nothing truthful." He wrote a fabulous account of a journey he made to the north, which would have been a suitable context for his lie about frozen words.*

369. THIN MEN

The poet Philitas of Kos was rather thin. Because of his leanness he wore leaden balls around his feet to keep the wind from knocking him over.

Athenaios

The poet and scholar Philitas (4th–3rd centuries BC) was the butt of jokes about ridiculously extreme thinness.

* * *

Epicurus wrote, Alkimos, that the entire world consisted of atoms,
Thinking that an atom was the slightest thing there was.
But if Diophantos had existed at that time, he would have written
that it consisted of Diophantos,
Who is slighter even than atoms.
Or he would have written that other things consisted of atoms,
But the atoms themselves of Diophantos.

Loukillios

This epigram humorously mocks a certain Diophantos in the spirit of a tall tale.

APPENDIX

ACROSS THE GENRES: ANCIENT TERMS, BELIEF, AND RELATIVE NUMBERS

ANCIENT TERMS

The ancients used mostly general words when referring to complex kinds of story such as myth, heroic legend, historic legend, novella, and the personal narrative. In Greek these terms include *logos* ("tale, story," connected with *legein* "to speak, tell"), *mythos* and *mythologema* ("tale, story," connected with the denominative verb *mytheisthai* "to speak"), and *historia* (originally "inquiry," then also "history, story," whence the modern English terms), as well as *diegema* ("narrative, tale") and *diegesis* ("narration"). Latin has *fabula* and its diminutive *fabella* ("tale, story," connected with *fari* "to speak, tell"), *narratio* ("narrative"), and, borrowed from Greek, *historia*. Most of these terms are neutral so far as historicity is concerned, being used of both credence narratives and non-credence narratives, "true things" and "false things." But tradition bearers rarely announce the precise genre of a story that they are about to relate, and, like us, ancient narrators usually did not do so. The most common lead into the telling of a credence story was a form of vague attribution: "they say," "the Corinthians declare," "it is said," "the story is told," and so on.

For the simpler genres, however, the ancient languages were rich in terms. Greek words that could refer to a joke include *geloion* ("something amusing," from *gelos* "laughter"), *asteion* ("something witty, urbane," from *astu* "town"), and *khleue* ("joke, jest," cognate with English "glee"), while

Latin has *ridiculum* ("something funny," from *ridere* "to laugh"), *iocus* ("joke, jest"), *facetiae* ("something amusing, joke"), *sales* ("witticisms," plural of *sal* "salt"), and others.[1] For the anecdote the Greeks used mostly *chreia*, a word whose principal meaning was "use, service," and the Romans borrowed it as *chria*. Our word "apothegm" derives from Greek *apophthegma* ("pointed utterance"), for which the corresponding term in Latin is *dictum*. Greek nouns that could refer to the fable include *ainos* ("tale with a hidden meaning," connected with *ainigma* "riddle," whence our "enigma"), *logos*, and *mythos*. The usual words in Latin for the fable are *apologus* ("story, tale, fable," a borrowing from Greek), *fabula* ("tale, story," the word adopted in many modern languages to refer to the fable), and *fabella*.[2]

Most of these terms were polysemous in that they did not refer unambiguously to a particular genre of story. Thus, Hesiod in his *Works and Days* introduces his narration of the Myth of the Ages by saying: "But if you wish, I will sum up another story for you," where he uses the noun *logos*.[3] In Homer's *Odyssey*, Helen proposes to the diners that they pass the time telling stories: "Now sit in the hall and feast, and take pleasure in stories" (4.238–239); she uses the plural of *mythos*. She herself begins, and it turns out that she has personal-experience narratives in mind. A *logos* or *mythos* or *fabula* might refer to a myth, a legend, a novella, a fable, or almost any other kind of story. Similarly, a joke might be a *geloion*, but so could a humorous anecdote or an Aesopic fable, all of which the ancients regarded as amusing narratives. In the case of the fable one could reduce the polysemy by referring to the fabulist Aesop, as when the orator Demades offers to tell an "Aesopic tale" (*Aisopeios mythos*),[4] but few genres offered such an option.

In emic classification, then, narratives of all sorts—long and short, complex and simple, historical and fictional—were "stories." Some of them could be more closely specified as "fabulous" or "humorous" or "indecent" or "Aesopic," but for the most part they were not. The categories were fuzzy, overlapped with one another, and did not accord a label to every kind of story the Greeks and Romans told. Overall, narrators cared more about the point and content of a particular story than they did about its generic affiliation.

To complicate matters, not only did native genre terminology lack precision, but it also changed over time. Some terms drifted in sense. *Mythos* acquired a coloration of fictitiousness, so that although *logos* and *mythos* were often used interchangeably in the classical period, *mythos* was more likely to connote an invented tale if an author employed the two words contrastively.[5] The preferred word for a particular genre could shift, as happened in the case of the fable. Among Greek speakers during the archaic period the dominant term was *ainos*; in the classical period, *logos*; and from Hellenistic times onward, *mythos*.[6] New genre terms came into use. Greek *apophthegma* is first attested in Xenophon's *Hellenika*, composed in the early fourth century BC. The term *Milesia* (sc. *fabula*), or Milesian tale, entered the Latin language around the first century BC as an appellation for the ribald novella. Another term that is first attested after the classical period is aretalogy (*aretalogia*), a narration of a miracle performed by a deity. One could not speak of apothegms or Milesian tales or aretalogies as such before the fourth century. The lack of a term, however, did not necessarily mean the lack of a genre, for one does not have to have a term for ribald novella in order to tell one, and the Greeks surely related apothegms before they settled upon a word to denote them. The existence of many compilations of stories by genre—myths, legends, novelle, anecdotes, apothegms, fables, jokes, and so on—shows that narrative categories were often felt and recognized even if specific terms were not available for them.

BELIEF

The criterion of credence versus noncredence, based in turn upon the supposed historicity or nonhistoricity of particular narratives, determines the assignment of most narratives to one or the other of two great groups of story: legend and folktale. An exception is myth, which despite its being a credence narrative I treat as a category of its own, since mythic narratives take place back when the cosmos was in the process of formation, whereas all other stories are set in the familiar world. Alternatively, one could fold myth into a bipartite system of legend and folktale, in which case myth would become a species of legend, "mythic legend."[7]

Traditional credence stories and traditional fiction differ in their poetics. The former typically feature devices to enhance credibility, representing themselves as factual reports: the characters may be named, the events may be set at a definite time in the past and in a specific locale, and the narratives may be attributed to a trustworthy source.[8] In contrast, folktale characters and locales are usually generic ("a woodcutter," "a beautiful princess," "a fox," "a distant kingdom") or bear general folktale names, and the temporal setting is usually the vague past. In addition, their status as invented narratives may be signaled by such formulaic elements as a conventional introduction ("back when animals could speak"), a conventional close ("the tale has been saved"), and formulistic numbers such as trebling (three brothers, three attempts, etc.) and round numerals.[9] So far as genre assignment is concerned, the crucial point is not whether a particular narrative is historically true or not, nor even whether it is believed or not, but whether its poetics are one characteristic of historical reports or of fiction.

Since our sources are written texts rather than living informants, we cannot probe the narrators' attitudes concerning belief directly and must fall back on inference. To make things more difficult, belief itself is more complicated than a simple either/or, since there are different sorts and grades of belief, not to mention a plurality of belief wherein a person displays an attitude of belief toward something in one context and an attitude of nonbelief in another.[10] Let us sample some different stances regarding the credibility of particular oral narratives.

In his mythological poems the Greek poet Hesiod draws upon the high, dignified genres of myth and heroic legend. He displays calm, unquestioning belief in his material. He tells, for example, how Prometheus stole fire from the gods and gave it to men, provoking Zeus to punish men as well as Prometheus. "So there is no way to escape the mind and intention of Zeus," he comments, "not even for Prometheus."[11] One never doubts that Hesiod believes and expects to be believed, confident in the verity and value of the traditions he relates, regardless of how unrealistic or extreme the events may be, as when the god Kronos castrates his father Ouranos (Sky) with a sickle. Paul Veyne goes so far as to assert that Hesiod "is the first to believe everything that enters his head" (1988:28), and surely it is hard to be lukewarm about stories as outrageous as that of Kronos and Ouranos. One either accepts them or rejects them.

At the other end of the spectrum is the attitude expressed by, say, Socrates in Plato's *Republic*. The philosopher describes Hesiod's stories of Ouranos, Kronos, and Zeus as lies. Even if the stories are true, he goes on to say, they are unsuitable for young persons, and the same can be said of unseemly stories of the gods, the giants, and the heroes whom Homer represents as misbehaving and acting in conflict with one another (*Republic* II.378). That is, myths in which the gods behave immorally must be untrue because gods do not do that. Several centuries later the Roman author of the rhetorical treatise *Rhetorica ad Herennium* (early 1st century BC) goes further when he defines *fabula* categorically as a story "consisting of matter that is neither true nor probable, such as that which is transmitted in tragedies."[12] Here there is no moral condemnation; mythological narratives are simply untrue.

These positions, the confident acceptance or the confident rejection of the veracity of myth, are alike in that they both take the inherited traditions literally. The stories say what they appear to say, and so either they are historically true or they are not. In between these extreme attitudes there arose in Greece two interpretive strategies that staked out a middle way, allegorism and rationalism. Allegorical interpreters held that myths and legends had two levels of meaning, an apparent, literal meaning and an unobvious, metaphorical meaning. The true sense of the narrative, the message that its deviser wished to communicate to those who could understand him, was the latter. For example, the Neoplatonist philosopher Proklos decodes the legend of the Trojan War as follows: Helen represents worldly beauty, and the Greeks who do battle for her at Troy are really souls that, enticed by worldly beauty, leave their true home and engage in a different form of existence for a period of time before returning to their own realm.[13]

Whereas allegorists interpreted narratives symbolically, rationalists took them as a mix of literal truth and distortion, as unreliable history.[14] Thus the view of the historian Thucydides is that poets exaggerate and elaborate their subject matter, and that prose chroniclers are more concerned with entertaining their readers than with informing them, while ordinary persons for their part are uncritical in their acceptance of traditional accounts (1.20–21). His own position regarding the historicity of heroic legend is that it contains a core of truth.[15] He treats the Trojan War, an event of the heroic era, as a historical event, and he discusses figures of that age such as Minos, Pelops, Achilleus, and Agamemnon as historical persons. According to Thucydides, Agamemnon led the campaign against Troy, although he did so not because the suitors of Helen were obliged by their oaths to her father Tyndareus to defend her, as tradition has it, but because Agamemnon was a prominent ruler at the time (1.3–9). Thucydides assumes that if he peels away the fabulous elements from the received stories, and replaces romantic motives with political or economic ones, he reaches the historical core that must have inspired the tradition.

Another variety of rationalism assumed that improbable elements found in myths and heroic legends were not poetic exaggerations and other deliberate elaborations but rather unintended distortions of historic truth that arose from misunderstanding. In the view of the Greek traveler Pausanias (1.23.8) and of the Roman encyclopedist Pliny the Elder (*Natural History* 7.202), for example, the Trojan Horse is a reminiscence of a siege engine like that later known as the battering ram. Whereas Thucydides assumes that, having removed supernatural elements and other improbabilities, he reaches the truthful core, these authors think they achieve it by disentangling misunderstandings.

But what if the historicity of a mythological narrative is less important than its message? This appears to be Hesiod's position, for after he relates the myth of Pandora in his *Works and Days*, he says, "But if you wish, I will sum up another story for you," whereupon he relates the Myth of the Ages.[16] Both these myths portray the human condition as a mix of benefits and miseries, and both represent miseries as a later arrival whose advent is irreversible. Although the myths bear similar implications, their stories cannot be reconciled, for things happened either in the way recounted in the Pandora myth or in the way recounted in the Myth of the Ages. When Hesiod offers his listeners a choice of myths that cover the same territory, he appears to care more about their underlying ideology than about their relative historicity.

Belief legends, religious legends, and memorates, focusing as they do upon a striking supernatural event, challenge listeners to take a stand of belief or disbelief. We find precisely this range of strongly felt attitudes in a scene of storytelling in Ovid's *Metamorphoses*. Several males sit talking, and when one of them relates how divine action on the part of the god Neptune resulted in the wondrous transformation of an unjustly drowned maiden, Perimele, into an island of the same name, most of the listeners are moved, but one of them, Pirithous, contemptuously rejects the account as invented (*ficta*). His reaction in turn prompts an old man, Lelex, to tell of a miraculous event of which he himself has personal knowledge. The gods Jupiter and Mercury, he says, once visited the hill-country of Phrygia in the guise of mortals. They were received hospitably in only a single household, that of the old couple Philemon and Baucis. After the divine travelers had revealed their identity and led the old couple to safety, they flooded the region, destroying its inhabitants. Jupiter granted the kindly couple the boon that neither of them would outlive the other, and when the end of their days came, they were transformed into two trees, which stand side by side. Lelex says that Bithynian peasants still point out these trees and worship them by hanging wreaths on their branches. He himself heard this story, he says, from responsible old men who had no reason to deceive him; moreover, he himself has visited the area, now a marsh, and seen the very trees. The listeners are moved by the old man's account (8.547–725).

Lelex's attitude is manifestly one of earnest belief, and his narration teems with credibility-enhancing devices: the characters are named, the locale is specified, and (considering the lifespan of trees) a temporal setting in the recent past is implied. In addition, Lelex attributes his story to reliable sources and also refers to personal experience, having himself seen the marsh created by the flood as well as the sacred trees, the existence of which, he thinks, attests to the truth of the tradition. Whereas it scarcely occurs to Hesiod that anyone might doubt his stories, Lelex sees it as his task to convince others of the historical truth of his.

Between Lelex's earnest credence and Pirithous's contemptuous rejection lies the interested uncertainty of the younger Pliny, who relates three stories of the apparent supernatural—a female apparition, a haunted house, and mysterious hair-trimming—and is unsure what to think. The question of belief or nonbelief seems to him unavoidable, and he solicits the opinion of an acquaintance in order to clarify his own thoughts. When it comes to ghosts, the basic question is: do they exist or not? This question is different from that which Hesiodic myths prompted in Socrates, which is not whether there are gods, but whether gods behave in the scandalous ways they are represented as doing.

Unlike narratives of supernatural beings, the humble anecdote and other realistic stories are the sort of credence narrative that listeners are typically content to accept casually as being true or, if not precisely true to history, then at least true to the character of the protagonist. When one hears that Alexander came upon the philosopher Diogenes lying in the sun and invited him to ask for anything he wanted, and Diogenes merely bade him move out of his light (261 "Alexander's Offer"), one feels that the story nicely captures the self-sufficiency and outspokenness of the eccentric philosopher. If Diogenes did not actually utter these words of indifference to power and wealth, if indeed Diogenes and Alexander never even met, these are nevertheless the sorts of words that the philosopher might well have said if he had had the opportunity. One cannot easily imagine Ovid's Pirithous bothering to take an indignant stand against the reliability of this anecdote or a Lelex arguing on its behalf, or a Pliny writing to an acquaintance asking if he believed it really happened, or a rationalist systematically peeling away its improbabilities to get at its core of historicity. A person who accepts or rejects an unrealistic myth in toto is likely to grant at least lukewarm acceptance to an anecdote. The principal lesson to be drawn is that shades of belief and nonbelief are closely related to narrative genre.

Still, anecdotes were taken seriously by ancient historians and biographers. Xenophon pauses in his historical narration to relate apothegms attributed to the brave statesman Theramenes (186 "The Arrest of Theramenes"), and Plutarch observes that the character of a person is often revealed better by a brief comment or humorous remark than by a grand deed (*Life of Alexander* 1).

As a rule, neither narrators nor their listeners regard folktales as true, although in forms such as the tall tale raconteurs often toy with the fuzziness of genre and the limits of credulity, a practice with a very long history, as Lucian's *True Stories* shows. Occasionally, however, we find straightforward folktales taken as true stories. Folk-narrative investigators report that some peasants in Germany, Russia, and elsewhere take, or used to take, folktales to be true, or hold that they were once true, saying that such things happened in the past.

An ancient instance of belief in the historicity of a folktale is provided by Herodotos. Recounting the novella "The Treasury of Rhampsinitos," the historian comes to the episode in which the Egyptian king, trying desperately to capture the clever thief, places his daughter in a brothel with instructions to service every man who comes to her; before sleeping with him, she is to ask each man what is the cleverest and wickedest thing he has ever done, and if the man proves to be the thief, she is to grab him. This scene is too much for Herodotos, who declares he does not believe it, implying of course that he takes the tale otherwise to be historic (2.121.e.1–2).

RELATIVE NUMBERS

Although it may seem that myths, legends, and folktales are uncountable and distributed more or less equally in number, they are in fact very unalike in their relative numbers. "Generally speaking, there are not so many myths in the world," folklorist Alan Dundes observes. The number of myths is much smaller than the number of folktales, and the number of folktales is in turn very much smaller than the number of legends. Dundes estimates that for every ten myths there are hundreds of folktales and thousands of legends (1984:6). These proportions probably also hold true for ancient Greece and Rome. Classical myths were relatively few in number and made up a small part of the ancient repertory of traditional narratives, and they were greatly outnumbered by folktales and legends. Doubtless the most common oral-narrative genre in Greco-Roman antiquity, quantitatively speaking, was the personal narrative.[17] A person may be an active bearer of traditional narratives or not, but he or she will tell narratives of self. Personal-experience narratives surely dominate most repertories.[18]

A pyramid chart illustrating the relative number of narratives in each of the broad categories of genre found in ancient Greece and Rome in, say, the first century BC might therefore look like the one below. At the top, fewest in number, are myths; next come folktales in their various forms (wonder tale, novella, joke, etc.); below them, the varieties of legend (heroic legend, historical legend, anecdote, etc.); and finally, numerically most abundant and so occupying the base, personal narratives. The absolute number of myths, legends, and so on as discrete stories is not the same as the relative frequency with which different genres and stories were told, a topic that would require a separate investigation.

A chart of their distribution today would be different not so much in its rough proportions as in the absence of certain kinds of story, for whole

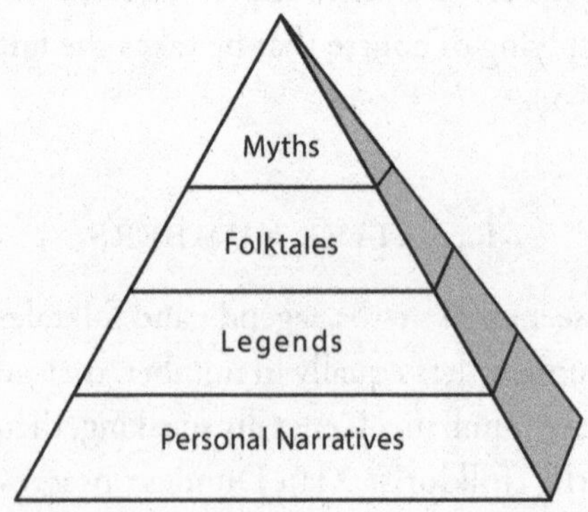

categories of oral narrative that were familiar to the ancients no longer exist in Western society, having suffered genre death, as one might call it.

Consider the fates of myths and wonder tales. Myths declined in status as credence narratives among intellectuals in the course of classical antiquity, and the eventual Christianization of the Greeks and Romans hastened the death of myth as a living and meaningful genre of oral story. Conversion to Christianity entailed one's acceptance of the Hebrew bible as embodying historical truth, and since Greek myth and Hebrew myth offer incompatible accounts of the origin of the cosmos, the creation of the first humans, the deities responsible, and so on, Greek myth was obliged to yield to Hebrew myth, the new truth.

The demise of the wonder tale, or traditional oral fairytale, in the West occurred many centuries later, almost in our own day. With the disintegration of traditional peasant society in Europe in the course of the nineteenth century and the first half of the twentieth century, the old oral culture mostly disappeared. Among the casualties were the most complex and demanding forms of the folktale, notably the wonder tale. Whereas in the past, persons sat gratefully around an oral storyteller, their descendants now place themselves in front of television sets viewing stories on an electronic screen.[19] The conversion of the fairytale from an oral genre to a predominantly book genre in the nineteenth century occurred in parallel with the decline of traditional peasant cultures in Europe. Like myth, the wonder tale ceased mostly to be a living oral genre, being saved from total oblivion by books and films.

Although the complex genres of oral narrative have disappeared from our lives, the simple forms—jokes, anecdotes, and contemporary legends—remain as popular as ever.[20] These stories require less skill to learn and to relate, and make modest demands on listeners.

NOTES

1. On Latin words for "witticism" see Cicero's dialogue *On the Orator* 2.216–291. See further Beard 2014:111–115.

2. On Greek and Latin words for "fable" see Dijk 1997:79–111.
3. *Works and Days* 106; cf. M. L. West 1978:177–178.
4. Perry 1952:63.
5. Lincoln 1999:3–43; Dijk 1997:110.
6. Dijk 1997:110.
7. Cf. Bødker 1965:207–209.
8. For a survey and discussion see Oring 2008.
9. Hansen 2002a:13.
10. See further Veyne 1988; Buxton 1994:155–165; Struck 2009; and Pirenne-Delforge 2009.
11. *Theogony* 613–616; *Works and Days* 105.
12. *Ad Herennium* 1.13: *Fabula est quae neque vera neque veri similes continent res, ut eae sunt quae tragoediis traditae sunt.*
13. Lamberton 1986:199–200. On ancient allegorism more generally see Hawes 2014:28–36.
14. On the ancient rationalists of myth and heroic legend see Stern 1996 and Hawes 2014.
15. Similarly, for example, Strabo 1.2.9.
16. *Works and Days* 106. Cf. M. L. West 1978:177.
17. Cf. Georgakopoulou 1997:4, 37.
18. Personal narratives that foreground the speaker are less frequent in narrative traditions such as that of rural Ireland in which personal modesty is expected of narrators (Glassie 1982:59; Cashman 2008:140–142).
19. Klintberg 1989:70; similarly, Lüthi 1975:7–8.
20. Cf. Röhrich 1991:10 and n. 6.

NOTES ON THE TALES

1. CUPID AND PSYCHE

Apuleius *Metamorphoses* 4.28–6.24. See also Fulgentius *Mythologies* 3.6.

Literature. ATU 425B *Son of the Witch*. Wright 1971. Anderson 2000:61–71. Hansen 2002a:100–114. Zimmerman et al. 2004.

2. THE TREASURY OF RHAMPSINITOS

Herodotos 2.121. See also schol. on Aristophanes *Clouds* 508 (= Charax *FGH* 103 F 5).

Literature. ATU 950 *Rhampsinitus*. Lloyd (1975–1988) 3:52–55. Hansen 2002a:357–371. Asheri et al. 2007:326–328.

3. THE PHARAOH AND THE COURTESAN

[a] Aelian *Historical Miscellany* 13.33. [b] Strabo 17.1.33. See also Herodotos 2.134–135; Diodoros of Sicily 1.64.140; Pliny the Elder *Natural History* 36.17.82; and Hyginus *Astronomica* 2.16.

Literature. Cf. ATU 510A *Cinderella*. Scobie 1977:17–18. Lloyd (1975–1988) 3:83–87. Anderson 2000:24–42. Stramaglia 2000:267–270. Hansen 2002a:85–89.

4. THE MUSES APPEAR TO HESIOD

Hesiod *Theogony* 22–35.

Literature. M. L. West 1966:158–167.

5. THE MUSES APPEAR TO ARCHILOCHOS

Mnesiepes, excerpt from a narrative inscription on two stones displayed in a precinct sacred to the poet Archilochos (= Gerber 1999b:16–25, testimonium 3).

Literature. Müller 1992. Clay 2004:9–24. Kivilo 2010:95–96.

6. THAMYRIS COMPETES AGAINST THE MUSES

[a] Homer *Iliad* 2:595–600. [b] Apollodoros *Library* 1.3.3. See also Euripides *Rhesos* 915–925, and schol. on Homer *Iliad* 2.595 Erbse.

Literature. Devereux 1987. Wilson 2009.

7. STESICHOROS'S *PALINODE*

[a] *Suda* s.v. Stesichoros. [b] Plato *Phaedrus* 243a–244a (= *PMG* 192). See also *PMG* 193; Isokrates *Helen* 64; Konon *Narrations* 18; and Pausanias 3.19.11.

Literature. Davison 1968:202–225. Burkert 1972:153. Lefkowitz 1981:32–34. Nagy 1990:419–423. M. K. Brown 2002:146–147. Kivilo 2010:73–75. Grossardt 2012.

8. ASKLEPIOS HEALS PANDAROS

IG IV^2, 1, nos. 121–122 (= Longo 1969:63–75, nos. 6–7; and LiDonnici 1995:88–91), an anonymous testimonial inscription from the sanctuary of Asklepios at Epidauros.

Literature. ATU 503 *The Gifts of the Little People*. Clouston (1887) 1:352–372. Hansen 2002a:147–151.

9. ASKLEPIOS REVEALS SECRETS OF THE GODS

[a] Thessalos *On the Virtues of Plants*, prologue 1–28. [b] Thessalos *On the Virtues of Plants*, epilogue 12–14 (Latin version P) (Friedrich 1968:273).

Literature. Friedrich 1968. Winkler 1985:257–273. Hansen 2003. Moyer 2011:208–273.

10. ATHENA SAVES THE LINDIANS

Aretalogical inscription from the sanctuary of Athena at Lindos, Rhodes (*FGH* 532 F 1).

Literature. Longo 1969:127–131, no. 70. Higbie 2003.

11. THE ALTAR OF THE VULTURE GOD

Konon *Narrations* 35.

Literature. ATU 301 *The Three Stolen Princesses*. M. K. Brown 2002:243–247. Hansen 2002a:352–357.

12. A FORTUNE IN WATER

Plutarch *Greek Questions* 54 (*Moralia* 4.303c): Aphrodite of Dexikreon.

Literature. Cf. ATU 1651A *Fortune in Salt*. Hansen 2002a:142–145.

13. THE RESCUE OF SIMONIDES

Cicero *On the Orator* 2.86.351–353. See also Kallimachos fr. 64 Trypanis; Phaedrus 4.26; Quintilian 11.2.11–16; Valerius Maximus 1.8.ext. 7; and, in general, *PMG* fr. 510. Cf. also Aelian *Nature of Animals* 13.1.

Literature. Marx 1889:34–35. Weinreich 1931:34–39. Slater 1972. Lefkowitz 1981:54–56. Farrell 1997. Ingemark and Ingemark 2004:140–142.

14. NARCISSUS

[a] Konon *Narrations* 24. [b] Pausanias 9.31.7. See also Pausanias 9.31.8–9, and Ovid *Metamorphoses* 3.339–510.

Literature. Cf. ATU 1336A *Not Recognizing Own Reflection*. Frazer (1898) 5:159–160. Wesselski 1935. M. K. Brown 2002:172–178. Hansen 2002a:257–261.

15. RHOIKOS AND THE NYMPH

Schol. on Apollonios of Rhodes 2.476, citing Charon of Lampsakos (*FGH* 262 F 12a). See also schol. on Theokritos 3.13, and Pindar fr. 165.

Literature. Larson 2001:73–75.

16. "THE GREAT GOD PAN IS DEAD!"

Plutarch *The Obsolescence of Oracles* 17 (*Moralia* 419a–e).

Literature. ATU 113A *Pan Is Dead*. ML 6070A *Fairies Send a Message*. Hansen 2002a:131–136. Lindow 2010.

17. BOGIES

[a] Zenobios 3.3 (= Sappho fr. 178 Campbell). [b] Schol. on Aristeides (3:42.16–19 Dindorf). See also schol. on Theokritos 15.40. [c] Diodoros of Sicily 20.41.3–5. [d] Schol. on Aristophanes *Wasps* 1030 (= Douris fr. 35 Müller). [e] Horace *Art of Poetry* 340. See also Porphyrio *Commentary on Horace* on *Art of Poetry* 340. [f] Tertullian *Against the Valentinians* 3.3 Fredouille.

Literature. Rohde 1925:590–593. Fontenrose 1959:100–104. Scobie 1977:7–10; 1979:250. Widdowson 1977. Green 1980. Johnston 1995; 1999:161–199. Anderson 2000:3. Hansen 2002a:18. Patera 2014.

18. THE WEREWOLF

Petronius *Satyrica* 61–63. See also Pliny the Elder *Natural History* 8.80–84.

Literature. ML 4005 *The Werewolf Husband*. Schuster 1930. Baldwin 1986. Salanitro 1998. Anderson 1999:58. Schmeling 2011:252–260. Kitchell 2014:196–197.

19. THE EMPOUSA

Philostratos *Life of Apollonios of Tyana* 4.25. See also Dion Chrysostomos *Oration* 5.

Literature. Ting 1966. Scobie 1977:7–10; 1979:245–250; 1983:24–30, 61–65. Johnston 1999:161–162. Stramaglia 1999:226–227; 2000:155–166. Patera 2014:249–278.

20. PHILINNION

[a] Phlegon of Tralles *On Marvels* 1. [b] Proklos *Commentary on Plato's Republic* 2:115 Kroll.

Literature. Cf. ATU 425B *Son of the Witch*. Hansen 1980; 1989; 1996:68–85; 2002a:392–397. Stramaglia 1999:215–257; 2000:167–184. Chesters 2011:216–234.

21. THE LAST PRINCESS AT TROY

Philostratos *Heroikos* 56.

Literature. Hansen 1996:98–101. Stramaglia 1999:376 n. 33. Cf. Grossardt (2006) 2:752–754.

22. THE GRATEFUL DEAD MAN

[a] Cicero *On Divination* 1.27.56. [b] Simonides (*Palatine Anthology* 7.77). See also Valerius Maximus 1.7.ext. 3, and Libanios 4.1101.

Literature. Motif E341 *The grateful dead*. Hansen 2002a:61.

23. MURDER AT THE INN

Cicero *On Divination* 1.27.57. See also Valerius Maximus 1.7.*ext*.10.

Literature. Felton 1999:20–21.

24. LETTER FROM THE MIDDLE OF THE EARTH

Pliny the Elder *Natural History* 2.248.

Literature. Speyer 1970:49.

25. THE HAUNTED HOUSE

Lucian *Lover of Lies* 29–32. See also Pliny the Younger *Letters* 7.27.

Literature. ATU 326A* *Soul Released from Torment*. Trenkner 1958:121–122. Felton 1999:65–73, 81–88. Stramaglia 1999:144–162. Ogden 2007:205–224. Baraz 2012:116–130.

26. THE HAUNTED BATHS

Plutarch *Kimon* 1.6.

Literature. Stramaglia 1999:185–213.

27. THE HAUNTED BATTLEFIELD

Pausanias 1.32.3–4.

Literature. Frazer (1898) 2:431–444. Collison-Morley 1912:24–27. Felton 1999:36. Stramaglia 1999:418–423.

28. THE HERO OF TEMESA

[a] Pausanias 6.6.7–11. [b] *Diegesis*, fragmentary summary of a now-lost poem by Kallimachos (fr. 98 Pfeiffer). See also Kallimachos *Causes* 4, fr. 98–99; Aelian *Historical Miscellany* 8.18; Strabo 6.1.5; and *Suda* s.v. Euthymos (3510).

Literature. ATU 300 *The Dragon-Slayer*. Fontenrose 1959:101–103; 1968:79–82. Visintin 1992. Felton 1999:26-27. B. Currie 2002. Hansen 2002a:127–128.

29. PERIANDER'S WIFE

Herodotos 5.92.η.

Literature. How and Wells (1928 [1912]) 2:54–55. Pellizer 1993. Felton 1999:78–81. Ogden 2007:195–204.

30. ABARIS THE HYPERBOREAN

[a] Herodotos 4.36. [b] Iamblichos *Life of Pythagoras* 28 (135–136).

On Empedokles see further Burkert (1972:154); on Epimenides, Burkert (1972:151) and Parker (1983:209–210).

Literature. Burkert 1972:149–150. Bremmer 1983:43–46. Asheri et al. 2007:607–608.

31. ARISTEAS OF PROKONNESOS

[a] Herodotos 4.14. [b] Herodotos 4.15. [c] Apollonios *On Marvels* 2. [d] Maximus of Tyre 10.2f. [e] Pliny the Elder *Natural History* 7.174.

Literature. Bolton 1962. Burkert 1972:147–149. Bremmer 1983:25–53. Asheri et al. 2007:583–586.

32. HERMOTIMOS OF KLAZOMENAI

Apollonios *On Marvels* 3. See also Diogenes Laertios 8.5; Pliny the Elder *Natural History* 7.174; Plutarch *On the Sign of Socrates* (*Moralia* 592c–e); and Tertullian *On the Soul* 44.

Literature. Rohde 1925:300, 331 n. 112. Burkert 1972:152. Scobie 1977:12–15. Bremmer 1983:25–53.

33. EPIMENIDES OF CRETE

[a] Apollonios *On Marvels* 1 (= Theopompos *Philippika FGH* 115 F 67b). [b] Diogenes Laertios 1.109 (= Theopompos *Philippika FGH* 115 F 67a).

Literature. ATU 766 *The Seven Sleepers*. Frazer (1898) 2:121–123. Burkert 1972:150–152. Hansen 2002a:397–402. Ogden 2007:264 nn. 39 and 44.

34. PHEREKYDES OF SYROS

Apollonios *On Marvels* 5.

Literature. Burkert 1972:144–145.

35. PYTHAGORAS

[a] Plutarch *Numa* 8.5. [b] Aelian *Historical Miscellany* 4.17. [c] Diogenes Laertios 8.11.

Literature. Bieler 1930. Burkert 1972. *EM* 2:382–383. Bremmer 1983:33.

36. PYTHAGORAS REMEMBERS AN EARLIER LIFE

Diodoros of Sicily 10.6.1–3. See also, for example, Diogenes Laertios 8.4–5.

Literature. Rohde 1925:598–601. Burkert 1972:138–141.

37. PYTHAGORAS DISCERNS A FRIEND'S SOUL IN A DOG

Diogenes Laertios 8.36 (= Xenophanes fr. 7 DK).

Literature. Kirk and Raven 1957:222–223, no. 268.

38. EMPEDOKLES RECALLS HIS EARLIER LIVES

Empedokles fr. 117 DK. These two lines of verse are quoted with minor variations by several authors, including Diogenes Laertios 8.77 and Athenaios 8.365e.

Literature. Burkert 1972:153–154. Chitwood 2004:50–51.

39. THE WOMAN WHO REMEMBERS TOO MUCH

Proklos *Commentary on Plato's Republic* 2:324–325 Kroll.

Literature. Festugière (1970) 3:283–84.

40. PASES THE MAGICIAN

Suda s.v. Pases.

Literature. ATU 745 *Hatch-Penny*. Cf. also ATU 1182A *The Copper Coin*. Hansen 2002a:188–190.

41. ATTACK BY STAR-STROKE

Porphyry *Life of Plotinos* 10.1–13.

Literature. Merlan 1953. Edwards 2000:52–71. Brisson 2009.

42. A WOMAN DIES FROM SPELLS

CIL VIII, 2756.

43. THE SOUL-DRAWING WAND

Proklos *Commentary on Plato's Republic* 2:122 Kroll (= Klearchos of Soli *On Sleep* F7 Wehrli).

Literature. Waele 1927. Bolton 1962:148. Bremmer 1983:50. Tsitsiridis 2013:64–69.

44. APOLLONIOS CURES A PLAGUE

Philostratos *Life of Apollonios of Tyana* 4.10.

Literature. Motif F493 *Spirit of plague*. Cf. Klintberg 2010:335–340.

45. THE MAGICIAN'S APPRENTICE

Lucian *Lover of Lies* 33–37.

Literature. ATU 325* *The Sorcerer's Apprentice*. ML 3020 *Inexperienced Use of the Black Book*. Anderson 2000:103–105. Hansen 2002a:35–38. Ogden 2007:231–270.

46. EVIL LANDLADIES

Augustine *City of God* 18.18.

Literature. Scobie 1983:258–271.

47. THE LANGUAGE OF BIRDS

Porphyry *On Abstinence* 3.3.

Literature. Frazer 1888.

48. THE ACQUISITION OF THE SIBYLLINE ORACLES

Dionysios of Halikarnassos *Roman Antiquities* 4.62. See also Pliny the Elder *Natural History* 13.27.88; Lactantius *Divine Institutes* 1.6.10–11; Servius *Commentary on Vergil's Aeneid* 6.72; Cassius Dio 2, fr. 11 (1:28–29 Boissevain).

Literature. Bouché-Leclercq (1880) 2:187–190. Hansen 1996:40–43, 126–137.

49. WHAT THE SIBYL WANTS

Petronius *Satyrica* 48.8. See also Pausanias 10.12.8; Pseudo-Justin Martyr *Exhortation to the Greeks* 35e; and Lucius Ampelius *Liber Memorialis* 8.16.

Literature. James 1892. Frazer (1898) 5:292–293. Bonner 1937. Pack 1956. Veyne 1964. M. S. Smith 1975:131–132. Schmeling 2011:206–207.

50. BACCHUS FORSAKES ANTONY

Plutarch *Antony* 75.

51. CATO EXPLAINS A PORTENT

Augustine *On Christian Doctrine* 2.77. See also Cicero *On Divination* 2.27.59.

52. CATO ON SOOTHSAYERS

Cicero *On Divination* 2.24.51. See also Cicero *On the Nature of the Gods* 1.26.71.

53. POLYKRATES'S RING

Herodotos 3.40–43. See also Valerius Maximus 6.9.ext. 5.

Literature. ATU 736A *The Ring of Polycrates*. ML 7050 *Ring Thrown into the Water and Recovered in a Fish*. Clouston (1887) 1:398–403. Saintyves 1912. Künzig 1934. Caillois 1938. Loomis 1941. *EM* 10:1164–1168. Asheri et al. 2007:440–442.

54. "ZEUS, WHY ME?"

Aelian *Historical Miscellany* 9.21. See also Plutarch *A Letter to Apollonios* 6 (*Moralia* 105b).

55. THE LAST DAYS OF MYKERINOS

Herodotos 2.133. See also Aelian *Historical Miscellany* 2.41.

Literature. How and Wells (1928 [1912]) 1:231–232. Lloyd (1975–1988) 3:81–83. Asheri et al. 2007:336.

56. KLEONYMOS'S NEAR-DEATH EXPERIENCE

Proklos *Commentary on Plato's Republic* 2:114–115 Kroll (= Klearchos of Soli *On Sleep* F8 Wehrli). See also Augustine *City of God* 22.28.

Literature. Bolton 1962:148–150. MacDonald and Willson 1986. Ogden 2007:171–172 and n. 3. Tsitsiridis 2013:69–77.

57. EURYNOOS'S NEAR-DEATH EXPERIENCE

Proklos *Commentary on Plato's Republic* 2:115 Kroll.

58. CURMA'S NEAR-DEATH EXPERIENCE

Augustine *On Caring for the Dead* 12.15 (*PL* 40:602). See also Plutarch *On the Soul* fr. 176 Sandbach, and Lucian *Lover of Lies* 25–26.

Literature. Ogden 2007:171–193.

59. THE ORIGIN OF THE SEPTUAGINT

Irenaeus *Against All Heresies* 3.21.2 (= Eusebios *History of the Church* 5.8.11–14). See also Pseudo-Aristeas *The Letter of Aristeas*; Philo of Alexandria *On the Life of Moses* 2.25–44; and Epiphanios *On Measures and Weights* (Wasserstein and Wasserstein 2006:116–124).

Literature. Speyer 1970:91. Honigman 2003. Wasserstein and Wasserstein 2006.

60. MIRACLES OF JESUS

Mark 5:21–43. See also Matthew 9:18–26; Luke 8:40–56.

Literature. Cotter 1999:220–222, 228–233.

61. PAUL AND BARNABAS MISTAKEN FOR PAGAN GODS

Acts of the Apostles 14.8–18.

Literature. Hansen 2002a:211–223.

62. THE DISCOVERY OF THE TRUE CROSS

Sokrates Scholastikos *History of the Church* 1.17 (= *PG* 67:117–121). See also, among many other versions, Rufinus *History of the Church* 10.7–8.

Literature. Borgehammar 1991. Drijvers 1992.

63. THE LAST DELPHIC ORACLE

Kedrenos *Compendium of Histories* 1 (p. 532 Bekker). See also Philostorgios *History of the Church* 7 (p. 77 Winkelmann) (*Artemii Passio* 35).

Literature. Fontenrose 1978:353 (Q263). Gregory 1983. Markopoulos 1985. Amidon 2007:88. Scott 2014:242–244.

64. "YOU HAVE WON, GALILEAN!"

[a] Philostorgios *History of the Church* 7.15. [b] Sozomenos *History of the Church* 6.2.10–11 (p. 238 Bidez). [c] Theodoretos *History of the Church* 3.25.6–7 (pp. 204–205 Parmentier and Scheidweiler).

Literature. Reinhardt 1891:18–26.

65. THE MURDER OF HYPATIA

Sokrates Scholastikos *History of the Church* 7.15. See also Damaskios *Life of Isidore* fr. 102 and 105; Philostorgios *History of the Church* 8.9; John of Nikiu *Chronicle* 84.87–103.

Literature. Dzielska 1995:1–26. Watts 2006.

66. CAPTURE OF A SATYR

Plutarch *Sulla* 27.

Literature. Hansen 1996:171–172.

67. CAPTURE OF A CENTAUR

Phlegon of Tralles *On Marvels* 34–35.

Literature. Hansen 1996:170–176. Mayor 2000:239–240 and 327 n. 12.

68. SIGHTINGS OF MERMEN AND MERMAIDS
Pliny the Elder *Natural History* 9.4.9–11.
Literature. Hansen 1996:172–173.

69. THE SELF-SUSTAINING BEAST
Athenaios 1.19d.

70. IN LOVE WITH A STATUE
[a] Clement of Alexandria *Exhortation* 4.57.3. [b] Arnobius *Against the Pagans* 6.22. [c] Pliny the Elder *Natural History* 36.21. Cf. also Lucian *Loves* 13–16. [d] Ovid *Metamorphoses* 10.243–297.
Literature. Reinhold 1971. Bömer (1980) 5:93–110. J. M. Miller 1988. Isager 1991:152–153. Németh 1997:125–131. Corso 2008. Kindt 2012:155–189.

71. ANIMAL OFFSPRING
Phlegon of Tralles *On Marvels* 22.
Literature. Hansen 1996:151–159.

72. THE UGLY MAN
[a] Galen *On Antidotes against Poisonous Bites* 14.253.18. [b] Soranos *Gynaecology* 1.39. See also Dionysios of Halikarnassos *On Imitation* fr. 6.1 Usener and Radermacher; Heliodoros *Aithiopika* 4.8; and Oppian *Cynegetica* 1.328–367.
Literature. Hansen 1996:152, 155–159.

73. MALE PARTURITION
Phlegon of Tralles *On Marvels* 26.
Literature. Hansen 1996:159–161.

74. SUDDEN CHANGE OF SEX
[a] Diodoros of Sicily 32.10.2–9. [b] Phlegon of Tralles *On Marvels* 6.
Literature. Hansen 1996:117–126.

75. PERIODIC ECSTASY
Apollonios *On Marvels* 40 (= Aristoxenos fr. 117 Wehrli).
Literature. Frazer (1921) 1:146–147.

76. THE LAUGHING TIRYNTHIANS
Athenaios 6.261d–e. Cf. Aelian *Historical Miscellany* 4.20.
Literature. Fontenrose 1978:32, 387 (L86). Fortenbaugh 1984:29, 191–194 (L30); 1995. Halliwell 2008:155–157.

77. THE MAN WHO LOSES HIS LAUGH

Athenaios 14.614a–b. See also Aelian *Historical Miscellany* 8.13 and DK 2:12, no. 21.

Literature. Cf. Motif H1194 *Task: making person laugh*. Frazer (1898) 5:200–204. Fontenrose 1978:69–70, 328 (Q185). Kindt 2012:36–54. Beard 2014:174–176.

78. A STRANGE TOMB

Aelian *Historical Miscellany* 13.3. See also Strabo 16.1.5.

79. THE LAME MAN AND THE BLIND MAN

[a] Leonidas of Alexandria (*Palatine Anthology* 9.12). [b] Plato the Younger (*Palatine Anthology* 9.13). See also *Palatine Anthology* 9.11 and 9.13b. For the legend of Orion and Kedalion, set in the heroic period, see Hesiod fr. 148a MW, and Fontenrose 1981:8–12.

Literature. Motif N886 *Blind man carries lame man*. Wallach 1943. Trenkner 1958:3.

80. INTAPHRENES'S WIFE

Herodotos 3.119. See also Sophocles *Antigone* 897–915, and Lucian *Toxaris* 61.

Literature. ATU 985 *Brother Chosen Rather Than Husband or Son*. How and Wells (1928 [1912]) 1:294–295. Beekes 1986. Hansen 2002a:62–66. Asheri et al. 2007:506–507.

81. A PARENT'S REQUEST

Herodotos 4.84. See also Herodotos 7.38–39.

Literature. How and Wells (1928 [1912]) 2:145. Mayor 1991. Asheri et al. 2007:642.

82. PLATO'S CHARACTERS

[a] Diogenes Laertios 3.35. [b] Athenaios 11.505e (*SSR* 5).

Literature. Riginos 1976:108, no. 58.

83. THE UNBREAKABLE GLASS BOWL

Petronius *Satyrica* 51. See also Pliny the Elder *Natural History* 36.66.195; Cassius Dio 57.21.5–7; and Isidore of Seville 16.16.6.

Literature. Lassen 1995; 2001. Anderson 1999:52–54. Ingemark and Ingemark 2004:114–116. Bennett and Smith 2007:235–237. Schmeling 2011:212–213.

84. THE DOLPHIN RIDER

Pliny the Younger *Letters* 9.33. See also Pliny the Elder *Natural History* 9.8.25–28; Athenaios 13.606d; Aulus Gellius *Attic Nights* 6.8; Pausanias 3.25.7 and 10.13.10; Pollux 9.80 (= Aristotle fr. 590 Rose); Apuleius *Metamorphoses* 4.31.6; and Aelian *Nature of Animals* 2.6 and 6.15.

Literature. Marx 1889:5–29. Frazer (1898) 3:398, 5:307–308. Stebbins 1929:74. Fontenrose 1951:142–144. Higham 1960. Kitchell 2014:53–57.

85. THE GRATEFUL DOLPHIN

Athenaios 13.606e–f (= Phylarchos *FGH* 81 F 26). See also Plutarch *The Cleverness of Animals* (*Moralia* 985a), and Aelian *Nature of Animals* 8.3.

Literature. Marx 1889:5–29. Stebbins 1929:62–63. Kitchell 2014:53–57.

86. ANDROKLES AND THE LION

[a] Aelian *Nature of Animals* 7.48. [b] Aulus Gellius *Attic Nights* 5.14.1. See also Aulus Gellius *Attic Nights* 5.14 (Perry 563a = Apion *FGH* 616 F 5); the Aesopic fable of the lion and the shepherd (Perry 563); Seneca the Younger *On Benefits* 2.19.1; Pliny the Elder *Natural History* 8.21.56–22.61; *Acts of Paul*; and *Acts of Xanthippe and Polyxene* 26–27, 37.

Literature. ATU 156 *Androcles and the Lion.* Marx 1889:55–70. Fries 1915. Brodeur 1922; 1924. Osborne 1966. *EM* 1:501–508. Scobie 1977:18–23. Schwarzbaum 1979:53 and n. 8. MacDonald 1983:21–23. Kitchell 2014:108–111. S. D. Smith 2014:229–238.

87. HOW OPHITEIA GETS ITS NAME

Pausanias 10.33.9–10.

Literature. ATU 178A *The Innocent Dog.* Liebrecht 1876:155–156. Baring-Gould 1882:132–143. Clouston (1887) 2:166–186. Marx 1889:95–124. Hartland 1892:127–129. Jacobs 1892:192–194, 259–264. Frazer (1898) 5:421–422. Rose 1929:294. Emeneau 1940. Ranelagh 1979:244–245, 264–265. Schmitt 1983. Brunvand 1984:31–34. *EM* 6:1362–1368. Kitchell 2014:47–52, 173–174.

88. XANTHIPPOS'S DOG

Plutarch *Themistokles* 10.5. See also Plutarch *Cato the Elder* 5.4.

Literature. Marx 1889:70–86. Kitchell 2014:47–52.

89. THE ACCIDENTAL KILLING OF A CAT

Diodoros of Sicily 1.83.6–9.

Literature. How and Wells (1928 [1912]) 1:199–200. Oldfather 1933:viii. Asheri et al. 2007:281–284. Kitchell 2014:24–25.

90. THE CHILDREN PLAY KING

Herodotos 1.114–116.

Literature. ATU 920 *The Son of the King and the Son of the Smith*. Hansen 2002a:408–414. Asheri et al. 2007:160–161.

91. THE CHILDREN PLAY PRIEST

Aelian *Historical Miscellany* 13.2.

Literature. ATU 1343* *Children Play at Hog-Killing*. Schönberger 1968. Hansen 2002a:79–85. Uther 2008:425–427.

92. THE CHILDREN PLAY WAR

Prokopios *The Gothic War* 1.20.

Literature. ATU 1343 *Hanging Game*. *EM* 6:481–485. Klintberg 2010:217, no. L14.

93. A CHILD STEALS FROM THE GODDESS

[a] Hypereides fr. 199 Jensen (= Pollux 9.74). [b] Aelian *Historical Miscellany* 5.16.

Literature. Motif H256 *Test of innocence: apple and gold offered*. *EM* 1:626–628. Hansen 2002a:79–85.

94. DAMON AND PHINTIAS

Iamblichos *On the Pythagorean Life* 33.234–236 (= Aristoxenos *Life of Pythagoras* fr. 31 Wehrli). See also Diodoros of Sicily 10.4.1–6; Porphyry *Life of Pythagoras* 59–61; Polyainos *Stratagems* 5.2.22; Cicero *Tusculan Disputations* 5.22.63 and *On Duties* 3.10.45; and Valerius Maximus 4.7.ext.1. A version of the legend in which the friends bear the names Selinuntius and Moerus was also in circulation (e.g., Hyginus *Fabulous Tales* 257).

Literature. Motif P315 *Friends offer to die for each other*. *EM* 2:1041–1044. Cf. Ben-Amos 2006:305–309.

95. FRIENDS UNKNOWN

Iamblichos *On the Pythagorean Life* 33.237–238.

96. ABAUCHAS'S CHOICE

Lucian *Toxaris* 61. See also Herodotos 3.119, and Sophocles *Antigone* 897–915.

Literature. ATU 985 *Brother Chosen Rather Than Husband or Son*. Hansen 2002a:62–66.

97. PLATO TEACHES A TYRANT ABOUT DEMOCRACY

Life of Aristophanes 46–49.

Literature. Riginos 1976:70–85, 176–178, no. 129. Lefkowitz 1981:111–112.

98. THE CITY OF FORBIDDEN EXPRESSION

Aelian *Historical Miscellany* 14.22.

99. ISMENIAS'S SUBTERFUGE

Aelian *Historical Miscellany* 1.21. See also Plutarch *Artaxerxes* 22.4.

100. QUEEN FOR A DAY

Aelian *Historical Miscellany* 7.1. See also Diodoros of Sicily 2.20.3–5, and Plutarch *Dialogue on Love* 9 (*Moralia* 753d–e).

Literature. *EM* 12:563–565.

101. THE ABSENTMINDED EMPEROR

Suetonius *Claudius* 39.

102. ZEUS'S LEDGER

Babrios 127 (Perry 313).

Literature. Crusius 1879:218–219. Schwarzbaum 1979:xiv.

103. THE GOLDEN AX

Aesopic fable (Hsr 183; Perry 173).

Literature. ATU 729 *The Merman's Golden Axe*. Hansen 2002a:17, 42–44.

104. THE JUDGE OF THE ANTS

Babrios 117 (Perry 306).

Literature. ATU 774K *St. Peter Stung by Bees*. Schwarzbaum 1979:xiii–xiv. Hansen 2002a:329–331.

105. TARPEIA'S REWARD

Livy 1.11.5–9. See also Dionysios of Halikarnassos *Roman Antiquities* 2.38–40; Plutarch *Romulus* 17; Plutarch *Parallel Stories* 15 (*Moralia* 309b–c); and Propertius 4.4.

Literature. Halliday 1963 [1927]:77–78. Krappe 1929. Dumézil 1947: 247–291. Burkert 1979:76–77. Wiseman 2004:145–146. Welch 2015.

106. THE CRANES OF IBYKOS

[a] *Suda* s.v. Ibykos. [b] Plutarch *On Talkativeness* (*Moralia* 509f–510a). See also Zenobios 1.37, and Antipatros of Sidon (*Palatine Anthology*

7.745). Iamblichos (*Life of Pythagoras* 27.126) relates a form of the story in which the victims are unnamed boys.

Literature. ATU 960A *The Cranes of Ibycus*. Hansen 2002a:89–92.

107. THE MURDER OF MITYS OF ARGOS

[a] Aristotle *Poetics* 9.11–12.1452a. See also Pseudo-Aristotle *On Marvelous Things Heard* 156. [b] Plutarch *On the Delays of Divine Vengeance* (*Moralia* 553d).

Literature. Rohde 1925:136 and 154, nn. 117–118. Else 1963:322–341. Fontenrose 1968:90. Hansen 1999. Velleman 2003:5–7. Bennett and Smith 2007:87–88. G. Currie 2010:29–32, 38.

108. AN EYE FOR AN EYE

Aelian *Historical Miscellany* 13.24. See also Valerius Maximus 6.5.ext. 3.

Literature. Szegedy-Maszak 1978:206.

109. THE TRIAL OF THE COURTESAN PHRYNE

[a] Athenaios 13.590d–e (= Hermippos fr. 68a I Wehrli). [b] Pseudo-Plutarch *Lives of the Ten Orators* 9: *Hypereides* (*Moralia* 849d–e). [c] Sextus Empiricus *Against the Mathematicians* 2.4. See also Quintilian 2.15.9, and Alkiphron 4.4.

Literature. Cooper 1995. Davidson 1999:133–135. McClure 2003:132–136.

110. THE PROBLEM OF DREAMT SEX

[a] Plutarch *Demetrios* 27. [b] Clement of Alexandria *Miscellanies* 4.18. See also Aelian *Historical Miscellany* 12.63, and cf. Iamblichos *Babyloniaka* fr. 35 Stephens and Winkler.

Literature. ATU 1804B *Payment with the Clink of Money*. Motif J1551.1 *Imagined intercourse, imagined payment*. Lucas 1903:261–262. Harkort 1956:85–118. *EM* 11:1314–1319.

111. THE DISPUTED CHILD

[a] *P. Oxy.* 2944 (fragmentary Greek papyrus found at Oxyrhynchus, Egypt). [b] Detail of a wall painting found in the so-called House of the Doctor at Pompeii, reproduced from Martha (1885:260). A color reproduction of the full painting can be seen in Clarke 2007, plate 8.

Literature. ATU 926 *Judgment of Solomon*. Turner 1973:8–14. Hansen 2002a:227–232.

112. ABUSIVE SON OF AN ABUSIVE FATHER

Aristotle *Nicomachean Ethics* 7.1149b.

Literature. ATU 980 *The Ungrateful Son* (4). Hansen 2002a:117–119.

113. TROPHONIOS AND AGAMEDES

Pausanias 9.37.4–7. See also Charax (*FGH* 103 F 5 = schol. on Aristophanes *Clouds* 508).

Literature. ATU 950 *Rhampsinitus*. Hansen 2002a:357–371. Bonnechère 2003.

114. THE DISHONEST BANKER

Konon *Narrations* 38. See also Stobaios 3.28.21. Cf. Herodotos 6.86.

Literature. ATU 961B *Money in the Stick*. M. K. Brown 2002:261–265. Hansen 2002a:279–284.

115. THE JOINT DEPOSITORS

Valerius Maximus 7.3.ext. 5. See also Iamblichos *Life of Pythagoras* 27.124.

Literature. ATU 1591 *The Three Joint Depositors*. *EM* 5:1274–1276. Hansen 2002a:427–429.

116. THE TWO THIEVES

Avianus 25 (Perry 581).

Literature. ATU 1525J *Thieves Cheated of Their Booty*. *EM* 9:515–516. Bennett and Smith 2007:10–11.

117. AESOP AND THE FIGS

Life of Aesop (Vita G) 2–3.

118. NEVER HEARD BEFORE

Life of Aesop (Vita G) 121–122.

Literature. ATU 921E *Never Heard Before* and/or ATU 1920F *He Who Says "That's a Lie!" Must Pay a Fine*. *EM* 8:1274–1279. Konstantakos 2010:263.

119. THE SLAVES TAKE OVER

Justin *Epitome of Pompeius Trogus's Historiae Philippicae* 18.3.6–16.

Literature. ATU 120 *The First to See the Sunrise*, mixed with ATU 981 *Wisdom of Hidden Old Man Saves Kingdom*. Hansen 2002a:471–472.

120. THE MILESIANS HOLD A PARTY

Herodotos 1.17–22.

Literature. Motif K2365.1 *Enemy induced to give up siege by pretending to have plenty of food*. Stender-Petersen 1953. Imellos 1971–1974. Asheri et al. 2007:88–91. Klintberg 2010:393, type W32 *The beseiged pretend to have cattle.*

121. SAVING LAMPSAKOS

Valerius Maximus 7.3.ext. 4. See also Pausanias 6.18.2–4, and *Suda* s.v. Anaxamenes (1989).

Literature. ATU 1871B *King Cannot Destroy the City.*

122. THE SUCKLING DAUGHTER

Valerius Maximus 5.4.7. See also Pliny the Elder *Natural History* 7.121, and Festus 228 Lindsay. The legend was told of different pairs of imprisoned fathers and pious daughters: Nonnos *Dionysiaka* 26.100–145; Valerius Maximus 5.4.ext. 1; Hyginus *Fabulous Tales* 254.3.

Literature. ATU 985* *The Suckled Prisoner*. Lambertz 1922:32–33. *EM* 6:414–415.

123. A DONKEY'S SHADOW

Pseudo-Plutarch *Lives of the Ten Orators* 8: *Demosthenes* (*Moralia* 848a = Perry 460). See also the corresponding Aesopic fable (Hsr 63; Perry 63); Diogenes Laertios 6.27; Diogeneianos 7.1; *Appendix Proverbiorum* 4.26; Apostolios 92; schol. on Plato *Phaedrus* 260c; Photios s.v. *onou skia*; and *Suda* s.v. *onou skia kai huper onou skias*.

Literature. ATU 1804D *The Shadow of the Donkey* and ATU 2200 *Catch Tales*. Dijk 1997:296–301. Hansen 2002a:75–79. Kitchell 2014:57–59.

124. THE HOAX

Galen *Commentary on Hippocrates's Epidemics* 2.6.29. The original Greek text is lost, and our knowledge of it is owed to an Arabic translation made in the ninth century AD. See also Pausanias 6.18.5.

Literature. Strohmaier 1976:118–119. Ogden 2007:40 n. 131. On the so-called Sokal Affair, see Sokal 1996.

125. ZEUS AND HERA WRANGLE OVER SEXUALITY

Apollodoros *Library* 3.6.7 (= Hesiod fr. 275 MW). See also schol. on Homer *Odyssey* 11.494; schol. on Lykophron 683; and Phlegon of Tralles *On Marvels* 4.

Literature. Frazer (1921) 1:360–367. Hansen 1996:113–116.

126. THE AFFAIR OF ARES AND APHRODITE

Homer *Odyssey* 8.266–369.

Literature. ATU 571B *Lover Exposed*. Petersmann 1981:52. Hansen 1995. *EM* 8:1056–1063. Klintberg 1999:102–104. Bennett and Smith 2007:192–194.

127. IPHIMEDEIA DESIRES POSEIDON

Apollodoros *Library* 1.7.4. See also Homer *Odyssey* 11.305–310.

128. HIPPOLYTOS AND PHAIDRA

Apollodoros *Epitome* 1.18–19.

Literature. Motif K2111 *Potiphar's wife*. Frazer (1921) 2:144–147. Yohannan 1968. Hansen 2002a:332–352.

129. THE HUSBAND'S UNTIMELY RETURN: 1

Apuleius *Metamorphoses* 9.5–7.

Literature. ATU 1419 *The Returning Husband Hoodwinked*. Lee 1972 [1909]:186–189. Dick 1941. Konstantakos 2006:587–589.

130. THE HUSBAND'S UNTIMELY RETURN: 2

Aristophanes *Women Celebrating the Thesmophoria* 498–501.

Literature. ATU 1419C *The One-Eyed Husband*. Hansen 2002a:225–227.

131. THE SIGNAL

Aesopic fable (Perry 420).

Literature. Rohde 1876.

132. THE WIDOW OF EPHESOS

Petronius *Satyrica* 111–112. See also Phaedrus *Appendix* 15 (Perry 543), and *Life of Aesop* (Vita G) 129 (Perry 388).

Literature. ATU 1510 *The Matron of Ephesus*. Scobie 1977:15–17. Anderson 1999:54–57. Courtney 2001:165–173. Hansen 2002a:266–279. Vannini 2010:231–269. Schmeling 2011:427–435.

133. SLEEPING WITH A GOD

Pseudo-Aischines *Letters* 10.

Literature. Lee 1972 [1909]:123–135. Weinreich 1911. Rohde 1925:155 n. 134. Trenkner 1958:133–134. Stramaglia 2000:85–96.

134. THE PERGAMENE BOY

Petronius *Satyrica* 85–87.

Literature. Mundo 1986. Lefèvre 1997. Anderson 1999:57–58. Schmeling 2011:358–365.

135. AESOP AND THE MASTER'S WIFE

Life of Aesop (Vita W) 75–76.

Literature. Stramaglia 2000:309–314. Konstantakos 2006; 2009. Orofino 2011. Cf. Tangherlini 2013:119–120.

136. THE KING'S TRUSTED FRIEND

Lucian *On the Syrian Goddess* 19–27.

Literature. Motif K2111 *Potiphar's wife*. Benveniste 1931. Krappe 1946. Lightfoot 2003:384–417.

137. DREAM-LOVERS

Athenaios 13.575 (= Chares of Mitylene *FGH* 125 F 5).

Literature. Wirkenhauser 1948.

138. THE ASTUTE PHYSICIAN

Lucian *On the Syrian Goddess* 17–18. See also, inter alia, Plutarch *Demetrios* 38; Appian *Roman History* 11.10; and Aristainetos 1.13.

Literature. Mesk 1913. Amundsen 1974. Pinault 1992:61–77. Stramaglia 2000:271–281. Lightfoot 2003:400.

139. HERO AND LEANDER

First Vatican Mythographer 1.28. The fullest sources for the legend of Hero and Leander are Ovid's *Heroides* 18–19 and Mousaios's little epic poem, *Hero and Leander*.

Literature. ATU 666* *Hero and Leander*. Färber 1961. Grant 1962:373–378. Cf. Durrell 1975:30.

140. XANTHOS, WHO LONGS FOR HIS WIFE

Parthenios 8.

Literature. Motif R151 *Husband rescues stolen wife*. Lightfoot 1999:412–418. Cf. Edmunds 2016.

141. ARISTON AND HIS FRIEND'S WIFE

Herodotos 6.61–62.

Literature. How and Wells (1928 [1912]) 2:88–89. Stramaglia 2000:283–290. Bayliss 2009.

142. OLYMPIANS IN THE BEDROOM

Athenaios 13.578f (= Machon *Anecdotes* vv. 218–225 Gow).

Literature. Gow 1965:45, 101–103.

143. HERAKLES FOOLED

Apollodoros *Library* 2.6.3.

144. NATURE FOOLED

[a] Athenaios 13.605f. See also *Palatine Anthology* 9.713–742. [b] Pliny the Elder *Natural History* 35.36.95. See also Aelian *Historical Miscellany* 2.3.

Literature. Carey 2003:102–111.

145. PAINTER FOOLED

Pliny the Elder *Natural History* 35.65. See also Pliny the Elder *Natural History* 35.66.

Literature. Pollitt 1974:63–66. Altick 1978:189. Isager 1991:136–140. Németh 1997:129. Carey 2003:102–111.

146. THE SCULPTOR POLYKLEITOS

Aelian *Historical Miscellany* 14.8.

147. MODELS FOR HELEN OF TROY

Dionysios of Halikarnassos *On Imitation* fr. 6.1 Usener and Radermacher. See also Cicero *On Invention* 2.1.1–3, and Pliny the Elder *Natural History* 35.64.

Literature. Carey 2003:106. King 2003:225.

148. HELEN'S CHALICE

Pliny the Elder *Natural History* 33.81.

Literature. Mayor 1994. Higbie 2003:89, 217–218.

149. ARCHILOCHOS: LETHAL IAMBICS

[a] Pseudo-Acron, schol. on Horace *Epode* 6.13 (Gerber 1999b:52, testimonium 26). [b] Gaitoulikos (*Palatine Anthology* 7.71). See further Gerber 1999b:47–57, testimonia 19–32.

Literature. Beavis 1988:193.

150. HIPPONAX: MORE LETHAL IAMBICS

Pseudo-Acron, schol. on Horace *Epode* 6.14 (Gerber 1999b:350, testimonium 11). See further Gerber 1999b:344–351, testimonia 3–11.

Literature. Kivilo 2010:127–128.

151. THE CICADA

Strabo 6.1.9. See also Strabo 6.1.6; Antigonos *Amazing Stories* 1; Paulos Silentarios (*Palatine Anthology* 6.54); anonymous (*Palatine Anthology* 9.584); and Clement of Alexandria *Exhortation* 1.

Literature. Beavis 1988:91–103. Kitchell 2014:30–32.

152. A SINGER'S COMPENSATION

Plutarch *On Listening to Lectures* 7 (*Moralia* 41d–e). See also Plutarch *On the Fortune of Alexander* (2) 1 (*Moralia* 333f–334a), and Aristotle *Nicomachean Ethics* 9.1.4 (1164a).

Literature. Motif J1551.3 *Singer repaid with promise of reward: words for words*. Harkort 1956:38–53. *EM* 11:1316–1317.

153. PINDAR'S SACRIFICE

Apothegms of Pindar 2.

154. PINDAR'S HOUSE

[a] *Ambrosian Life of Pindar* 2.10–14. See also Plutarch *Alexander* 11.6; Dion Chrysostomos *Oration* 2.33; Aelian *Historical Miscellany* 13.7; and *Thoman Life of Pindar* 5.11–16. [b] Pliny the Elder *Natural History* 7.29.109.

Literature. Slater 1971:146–150. Lefkowitz 1981:60. Berman 2015:176–177.

155. PHRYNICHOS FINED

Herodotos 6.21.

Literature. How and Wells (1928 [1912]) 2:72.

156. THE CHORUS OF AESCHYLUS'S *EUMENIDES*

Life of Aeschylus 9 (p. 371 Murray).

Literature. Lefkowitz 1981:70–72. Cf. Powers 2014:29–46.

157. SOPHOCLES ON HIMSELF AND EURIPIDES

Aristotle *Poetics* 25.1460b.

158. "I SEE A WEASEL"

Aristophanes *Frogs* 302–304.

Literature. Borthwick 1968. Kitchell 2014:193–196.

159. "MOTHER, I CALL TO YOU"

[a] Horace *Satires* 2.3.60–62. [b] Porphyrio *Commentary on Horace* on *Satires* 2.3.60. See also Cicero *Tusculan Disputations* 1.44.106.

Literature. Beare 1965:80–81, 362–363 n. 4.

160. SAVED BY EURIPIDES

[a] Plutarch *Nicias* 29. [b] Plutarch *Lysander* 15.3.

161. HOW MENANDER COMPOSES HIS PLAYS

Plutarch *On the Fame of the Athenians* 4 (*Moralia* 347e).

162. THE FIRST LINE OF PLATO'S *REPUBLIC*

Quintilian 8.6.63–64. See also Diogenes Laertios 3.37, and Dionysios of Halikarnassos *On the Composition of Words* 25.209.

Literature. Riginos 1976:185–186, no. 137.

163. OVID'S WORST LINES

Seneca the Elder *Controversiae* 2.2.12.

Literature. Wills 1996:416, 450–451.

164. THE ORIGIN OF THE STADIUM

Aulus Gellius *Attic Nights* 1.1.2. See also Diodoros of Sicily 4.14.1–2.

Literature. Frazer (1898) 4:81.

165. THE FIRST MARATHON

[a] Plutarch *On the Fame of the Athenians* 3 (*Moralia* 347c), including Herakleides of Pontos fr. 145 Schütrumpf. [b] Lucian *On a Slip of the Tongue* 3.

Literature. Allinson 1930. Matthews 1974. Badian 1979. Frost 1979.

166. THE ORIGIN OF NUDE ATHLETES

[a] *Etymologicum Magnum* s.v. *gymnasia*. [b] Schol. on Homer *Iliad* 23.683. [c] Pausanias 1.44.1. [d] Dionysios of Halikarnassos *Roman Antiquities* 7.72.2–3.

Literature. Frazer (1898) 2:537–538; 3:486. Fontenrose 1968:92–93. Sweet 1987:124–133. Golden 2004:111–112.

167. THE ORIGIN OF NUDE TRAINERS

Pausanias 5.6.7–8. See also Philostratos *On Athletic Exercise* 17.

Literature. Frazer (1898) 3:482.

168. POLYMESTOR THE SPRINTER

Philostratos *On Athletic Exercise* 13.

Literature. Motif F681 *Marvelous runner*. F681.6 *Marvelous runner catches wild game on the run*. F681.12 *Runner runs so swiftly that he does not snap the ears of wheat (bend grass)*. Golden 2004:138.

169. AGEUS THE LONG-DISTANCE RUNNER

Eusebios *Chronicon* 1.206 Schöne.

Literature. Golden 2004:4, 55–56. S. G. Miller 2004:25–27.

170. MILON THE WRESTLER

[a] Quintilian 1.9.5. See also Petronius *Satyrica* 25, and Favorinos fr. 106 Barigazzi. [b] Athenaios 10.412e–f. [c] Diodoros of Sicily 12.9.5–6.

[d] Pausanias 6.14.8. See also Pausanias 6.14.5–7; Strabo 6.1.12; and Valerius Maximus 9.12.ext. 9.

Literature. Otto 1890:341, no. 1744. Frazer (1898) 4:44. R. S. Robinson 1955:85–89. Fontenrose 1968:88–89. Crowther 1977:114–116. Hock and O'Neil 1986:330, no. 47. Golden 2004:103.

171. EUMASTAS THE STRONGMAN

IG XII, 3, no. 449.

Literature. R. S. Robinson 1955:90. Crowther 1977:111–115. Golden 2004:29, 64.

172. THEAGENES'S STATUE

[a] Pausanias 6.11.2–3. [b] Pausanias 6.11.6. See also Dion Chrysostomos *Oration* 31.95–97; *Suda* s.v. Nikon.

Literature. Frazer (1898) 4:38–39. R. S. Robinson 1955:105–106. Fontenrose 1968:75–76. Hansen 1999. Golden 2004:163.

173. POULYDAMAS THE PANCRATIAST

Pausanias 6.5.4–9. See also Valerius Maximus 9.12.ext. 10.

Literature. Frazer (1898) 4:16–19. Hansen 1996:137–139. Golden 2004:142.

174. KLEOMEDES RUNS AMOK

Pausanias 6.9.6–8. See also Plutarch *Romulus* 28.4–5.

Literature. Frazer (1898) 4:35. Rohde 1925:129–130. Fontenrose 1968; 1978:323 (Q166). Golden 2004:41.

175. ASTYLOS ANGERS HIS HOMETOWN

Pausanias 6.13.1. See also Dionysios of Halikarnassos *Roman Antiquities* 8.1.

Literature. Frazer (1898) 4:40–41. R. S. Robinson 1955:107. Young 1984:141–144. Golden 2004:18.

176. EXAINETOS PLEASES HIS HOMETOWN

Diodoros of Sicily 12.82.1, 13.34.1, and 13.82.7.

Literature. Golden 2004:66.

177. GLAUKOS THE BOXER

Pausanias 6.10.1–3. See also Philostratos *On Athletic Exercise* 20, and Lucian *In Defense of Images* 19.

Literature. Frazer (1898) 4:35–36. R. S. Robinson 1955:84–85. Fontenrose 1968:99–103. Golden 2004:71–72.

178. THE RELUCTANT DUELER
Diodoros of Sicily 17.100–101.
Literature. Baumgartner 1959:162. Golden 2004:54.

179. THE INFANT PINDAR ON MT. HELIKON
Ambrosian Life of Pindar 1.6–9. See also Aelian *Historical Miscellany* 12.45; Pausanias 9.23.2; and Philostratos *Imagines* 2.12.
Literature. Frazer (1898) 5:97. Slater 1971:149. Riginos 1976:18–20. Lefkowitz 1981:59. Kitchell 2014:16–17.

180. THE INFANT PLATO ON MT. HYMETTOS
Aelian *Historical Miscellany* 10.21. See also Aelian *Historical Miscellany* 12.45; Cicero *On Divination* 1.36.78 and 2.31.66; Valerius Maximus 1.6.ext. 2–3; and Pliny the Elder *Natural History* 11.18.55.
Literature. Riginos 1976:17–21, no. 3. Kitchell 2014:16–17.

181. YOUNG DEMOSTHENES IN COURT
Pseudo-Plutarch *Lives of the Ten Orators* 8: *Demosthenes* (*Moralia* 844c–d). See also Plutarch *Demosthenes* 6.1.
Literature. Worthington 2013:14–27.

182. A STATUE OF HOMER
Christodoros of Egyptian Thebes (*Palatine Anthology* 2.342–343).
Literature. Riginos 1976:19.

183. THEMISTOKLES AND THE MAN FROM SERIPHOS
Plato *Republic* 1.329e6–330a6. See also Herodotos 8.125; Plutarch *Themistokles* 18.5 and *Apothegms of Kings and Generals* (*Moralia* 185c); Origen *Against Celsus* 1.29; and Cicero *On Old Age* 3.8.
Literature. How and Wells (1928 [1912]) 2:276. Dillon 2004:186–187.

184. ARISTEIDES THE JUST
Plutarch *Aristeides* 7. See also Plutarch *Apothegms of Kings and Generals* (*Moralia* 186a–b); *Suda* s.v. Aristeides (3903); and Cornelius Nepos *Lives* 3.1.
Literature. Sansone 1989:185. Lang 1990:35–40, figures 2–4, and plate 1.

185. TIMON THE MISANTHROPE
Plutarch *Antony* 69.6–71.1. See further Strabo 17.1.9; Pausanias 1.30.4; Lucian *Timon, or the Misanthrope*; and *Palatine Anthology* 7.313–320.
Literature. Armstrong 1987. Henderson 1987:172. Pelling 1988:291–293.

186. THE ARREST OF THERAMENES

Xenophon *Hellenika* 2.3.54–56.

Literature. Russo 1997:60–62.

187. SOCRATES'S HARDIHOOD

Plato *Symposium* 219e–220b.

188. SOCRATES PONDERS A PROBLEM

Plato *Symposium* 220c–d.

189. DEMOSTHENES'S HANDICAPS

[a] Pseudo-Plutarch *Lives of the Ten Orators* 8: *Demosthenes* (*Moralia* 844d–e). [b] Plutarch *Demosthenes* 11.1–2. See further Cicero *On the Orator* 1.61.260–261 and *De Finibus* 5.2.5; and Quintilian 10.3.30.

Literature. Lefkowitz 1981:114 and n. 32. Worthington 2013:38–41.

190. "DELIVERY!"

Pseudo-Plutarch *Lives of the Ten Orators* 8: *Demosthenes* (*Moralia* 845b).

Literature. Worthington 2013:38.

191. ONLY HUMAN

Aelian *Historical Miscellany* 8.15. See also Plutarch *Table-Talk* 7.10 (*Moralia* 715c), and Stobaios 3.21.6.

Literature. Sternbach 1894:29–30. Cf. Beard 2007:85–92.

192. WHAT ALEXANDER SLEEPS UPON

Plutarch *Alexander* 8 (= Oneisikritos of Astypalaia *FGH* 134 F 38). See also Plutarch *On the Fortune of Alexander* 4 (*Moralia* 327f).

Literature. Riginos 1976:174–176.

193. CLEOPATRA'S WAGER

Pliny the Elder *Natural History* 9.58.119–121. See also Macrobius *Saturnalia* 3.17.14–18.

Literature. Friedländer (1913) 4:275–276. Ullman 1957. Flory 1988. Healy 1999:130–131. D. W. Roller 2010:132–133.

194. THE LAMPREY POOLS

Cassius Dio 54.23. See also Seneca the Younger *On Anger* 3.40.

Literature. Flory 1988:503–504. Hopkins 1993:8.

195. A PRINCIPLED MAN

Seneca the Elder *Controversiae* 10.4–8.

Literature. Cramer 1945:172–177.

196. NERO FIDDLES

Tacitus *Annals* 15.38–39. See also Suetonius *Nero* 38 and, on Nero's kithara-playing more generally, 20–25 and 41; and Cassius Dio 62.18.1.

Literature. Gyles 1947. Champlin 2003:48–49.

197. "WHERE WOULD HE BE NOW?"

Pliny the Younger *Letters* 4.22.

Literature. Hansen 2004:117.

198. A SLAVE'S EYE

Galen *On Recognizing and Treating Mental Illnesses* 5.17–18 Kühn.

Literature. Hopkins 1993:7.

199. THE PEOPLE OF AKRAGAS

Aelian *Historical Miscellany* 14.48a. See also Aelian *Historical Miscellany* 12.29; Diogenes Laertios 8.63; and Tertullian *Apology* 39.14.

Literature. *SSR* 285.

200. TOO MANY WORDS

Herodotos 3.46. See also Plutarch *Laconic Apothegms: Kleomenes* 7 (*Moralia* 223d) and *Spartans* 1 (*Moralia* 232d), and Sextus Empiricus *Against the Mathematicians* 2.23.

Literature. How and Wells (1928 [1912]) 1:268–269. Asheri et al. 2007:444. Bayliss 2009.

201. A SPARTAN MOTHER

Plutarch *Apothegms of Spartan Women* 16 (*Moralia* 241f). See also Plutarch *Apothegms of Spartan Women* 17 (*Moralia* 241f); Valerius Maximus 2.7.ext. 2; Seneca the Elder *Suasoriae* 2.8; and Sextus Empiricus *Outlines of Pyrrhonism* 3.216.

Literature. Hammond 1979–1980.

202. DISCUSSION AT THERMOPYLAE

Plutarch *Laconic Apothegms: Leonidas* 11 (*Moralia* 225d).

203. ALEXANDER THE GREAT BECOMES A GOD

Aelian *Historical Miscellany* 2.19. See further Aelian *Historical Miscellany* 5.12, and Athenaios 251b.

204. ON SPARTAN ADULTERY

Plutarch *Lykourgos* 15.10. See also Plutarch *Laconic Apothegms: Lykourgos* 20 (*Moralia* 228b–c).

Literature. ATU 1960A *The Great Ox*. Smither 1941. Hansen 2002a:176–178.

205. MENEKRATES, WHO CALLS HIMSELF ZEUS

[a] *Suda* s.v. Menekrates. [b] Athenaios 7.289a–c. For the legend of Salmoneus see Apollodoros *Library* 1.9.7; Vergil *Aeneid* 6.585–594; and Hyginus *Fabulous Tales* 61.

Literature. Weinreich 1933. Squillace 2012.

206. MENEKRATES-ZEUS WRITES TO KING PHILIP

Athenaios 7.289d–e. See also Aelian *Historical Miscellany* 12.51; Plutarch *Agesilaos* 21; Plutarch *Laconic Apothegms: Agesilaos* 59 (*Moralia* 213a); and Plutarch *Apothegms of Kings and Generals: Agesilaos* 5 (*Moralia* 191a).

207. PHILIP HOSTS MENEKRATES

Athenaios 7.289e–f. See also Aelian *Historical Miscellany* 12.51.

208. HANNON'S BIRDS

Aelian *Historical Miscellany* 14.30. Cf. Pliny the Elder *Natural History* 8.55.

209. THE WOMAN WHO HOLDS UP THE WORLD WITH HER FINGER

Alexander of Tralles *Therapeutica* (2:605 Puschmann).

Literature. Weinreich 1933:79–80.

210. THE HOUSE CALLED TRIREME

Athenaios 2.37b–e (= Timaios *FGH* 566 F 149).

Literature. Trenkner 1958:12 n. 2.

211. THE HAPPY SHIPOWNER

Athenaios 12.554e–f (= Herakleides of Pontos fr. 40 Schütrumpf). See also Aelian *Historical Miscellany* 4.25, and Horace *Letters* 2.2.128–140.

212. THE HAPPY PLAYGOER

Pseudo-Aristotle *On Marvelous Things Heard* 31.

213. ARS LONGA, VITA BREVIS

Lucian *Hermotimos* 1. See further Lucian *Hermotimos* 63; Hippokrates *Aphorisms* 1.1; and Seneca the Younger *On the Shortness of Life* 1.1.

Literature. Otto 1890:375, no. 1916. Mieder et al. 1992:28, no. 9.

214. WHICH CAME FIRST?

Plutarch *Table-Talk* 2.3 (*Moralia* 635e–638a). See also Censorinus *On the Birthday* 4.3–4, and Macrobius *Saturnalia* 7.16.1–14.

Literature. Chroust 1971–1980. Arnott 2007:9–11.

215. ALTER EGO

Diogenes Laertios 7.23. See also Aristotle *Nicomachean Ethics* 1166a.31–32.

Literature. Mieder et al. 1992:234, no. 41.

216. "GIVE ME A PLACE TO STAND, AND I'LL MOVE THE WORLD!"

[a] Plutarch *Marcellus* 14.7–8. [b] Pappos of Alexandria *Compilation* 8.11 (p. 1060 Hultsch). See also Simplicius *Commentary on Aristotle's Physics* (p. 1110 Diels).

Literature. Dijksterhuis 1987:14–18. Jaeger 2008:101–122.

217. LIFE IS LIKE THE OLYMPIC GAMES

Cicero *Tusculan Disputations* 5.3.8–9. See also Diogenes Laertios 8.8; Iamblichos *Life of Pythagoras* 12 and *Protrepticus* 53.19–25.

Literature. Kirk and Raven 1957:228–229, no. 278. Else 1963:335.

218. "THE DIE IS CAST"

[a] Suetonius *Julius Caesar* 31.2–32. [b] Plutarch *Pompey* 60.2. See also Suetonius *Julius Caesar* 31–33.

Literature. Otto 1890:12–13, no. 55. Dubuisson 1980:885–886. Cf. Strauss 2015:34–35.

219. "ET TU, BRUTE?"

Suetonius *Julius Caesar* 82.2. See also Plutarch *Julius Caesar* 66.5–7, and Cassius Dio 44.19.5.

Literature. Dubuisson 1980. Arnaud 1998. Strauss 2015:136–137, 254.

220. IN HOC SIGNO VINCES

Eusebios *Life of Constantine* 1.28–30. See also Eusebios *Life of Constantine* 1.27–32, and Lactantius *On the Deaths of the Persecutors* 44.5.

Literature. Cameron and Hall 1999:204–213.

221. TOXIC HONEY

Xenophon *Anabasis* 4.8.19–21.

Literature. Mayor 2003:145–148.

222. A NARROW ESCAPE

Lucian *Alexander the False Prophet* 55–57.

223. THE GREAT FISH

Pseudo-Kallisthenes *Life and Deeds of Alexander of Macedon* (A-text) 3.17 (1:106–107 Kroll). See also *Physiologus Graecus* 17 and *Physiologus Latinus* 24.

Literature. ATU 1960B *The Great Fish*. Motif J1761.1 *Whale thought to be island*. Runeberg 1902. Hansen 2002a:181–182.

224. THE DISCOVERY OF ARCHIMEDES'S TOMB

Cicero *Tusculan Disputations* 5.23.64–66.

Literature. Dijksterhuis 1987:32. Jaeger 2008:32–47.

225. COUNTING ONE'S BLESSINGS

[a] Diogenes Laertios 1.33. [b] Favorinos *On Fortune* 17 Barigazzi. [c] Plutarch *Caius Marius* 46.1.

Literature. Riginos 1976:58–59, no. 21. Meeks 1974:167–168.

226. SOCRATES

Plato *Phaedo* 118.

Literature. Gnilka 1979:8–10. Crooks 1998.

227. THEOPHRASTOS'S LAMENT

Cicero *Tusculan Disputations* 3.69. See also Diogenes Laertios 5.40–41.

Literature. Fortenbaugh 1984:45, 237–240 (L68).

228. VESPASIAN'S LAST WORDS

[a] Suetonius *Vespasian* 23. See also Cassius Dio 66.1. [b] Suetonius *Vespasian* 24. See also Cassius Dio 66.17.

229. PYTHAGORAS

Diogenes Laertios 8.39.

Literature. Fairweather 1973:235.

230. AESCHYLUS

[a] *Life of Aeschylus* 10–11. [b] Aelian *Nature of Animals* 7.16. See also Valerius Maximus 9.12.ext. 2, and Pliny the Elder *Natural History* 10.3.7.

Literature. ATU 934 *Tales of the Predestined Death*. Cf. ATU 225A *The Tortoise Lets Itself Be Carried by Birds*. Crusius 1882. Lefkowitz 1981:72–73. Hadjicosti 2005.

231. EURIPIDES

Suda s.v. Euripides (3695). See also Athenaios 13.598d (= Hermesianax of Colophon); Adaios (*Palatine Anthology* 7.51); Ion (*Palatine Anthology*

7.44); Diodoros of Sicily 13.103.5; Stephanos of Byzantium (p. 176.1 Meineke); Diogeneianos 7.52; *Life of Euripides* 36–61 Méridier; Pausanias 1.2.2; Valerius Maximus 9.12.ext. 4; Ovid *Ibis* 595–596; Hyginus *Fabulous Tales* 247; and Aulus Gellius *Attic Nights* 15.20.9.

Literature. Nestle 1898. Lefkowitz 1981:96–97.

232. PHILEMON

[a] Lucian *Long-Lived Persons* 25. [b] *Suda* s.v. Philemon (2) (= Aelian fr. 11 Herscher). See also *Suda* s.v. Philemon (1); Plutarch *Old Men in Public Affairs* (*Moralia* 785b); Valerius Maximus 9.12.ext. 6; and Apuleius *Florida* 16.

Literature. Lefkowitz 1981:115–116.

233. DIOGENES THE CYNIC

Aelian *Historical Miscellany* 8.14. See also Diogenes Laertios 6.76–79; Plutarch *On the Eating of Meat* 1.6 (*Moralia* 995c–d = *SSR* 93); Plutarch *On Whether Fire or Water Is More Useful* 2 (*Moralia* 956b = *SSR* 93); Epiktetos 3.25.58 (= *SSR* 99); Jerome *Against Jovinian* 5.17 (= *SSR* 99); and *Suda* s.v. Diogenes (= *SSR* 96).

234. ZENON

Diogenes Laertios 7.28. See also Diogenes Laertios 7.31 (= *Palatine Anthology* 7.118), and *Suda* s.v. *aueis*.

235. CLEOPATRA

Plutarch *Antony* 85–86. See also Strabo 17.795; Velleius Paterculus *Roman History* 2.87; Cassius Dio 51.14; Suetonius *Augustus* 17.4; and Aelian *Nature of Animals* 9.61.

Literature. Pelling 1988:318–323. Kostuch 2009. Kitchell 2014:33.

236. PETRONIUS ARBITER

Tacitus *Annals* 16.18–19. See also Pliny the Elder *Natural History* 37.7.20. For a somewhat similar death scene see the anonymous work *The Spanish War* (33), by one of Caesar's continuators.

Literature. Courtney 2001:5–11. Schmeling 2011:xiii–xvii.

237. ARCHIMEDES

Valerius Maximus 8.7.ext. 7. See also Livy 25.31; Pliny the Elder *Natural History* 7.37.125; Plutarch *Marcellus* 19.4–6; and Cicero *De Finibus* 5.19.50.

Literature. Dijksterhuis 1987:30–32. Jaeger 2008:77–100.

238. THE SEVEN SAGES AND THE PRIZE OF WISDOM

Plutarch *Solon* 4. For the sources see Wiersma (1933–1934), and Fontenrose (1978:293).

Literature. Wiersma 1933–1934. Fontenrose 1978:293 (Q76). On the tradition of the Seven Sages generally, see Snell 1971; Martin 1998; Engels 2010; and Kurke 2011.

239. THALES ON LIFE AND DEATH

Diogenes Laertios 1.35.

240. A QUESTION OF RESPONSIBILITY

Plutarch *Pericles* 36.3.

Literature. O'Sullivan 1995.

241. A PROBLEM OF IDENTITY

Plutarch *Theseus* 23.1.

Literature. Lerner 2016.

242. SECUNDUS THE SILENT PHILOSOPHER

Life of Secundus, ad init.

Literature. ATU 823A* *A Mother Dies of Fright When She Learns That She Was about to Commit Incest with Her Son*. Perry 1964. Hansen 2002a:284–287.

243. PLATO

Aelian *Historical Miscellany* 2.30. See also, among many other sources (Riginos 1976:43), Diogenes Laertios 3.5.

Literature. Gigon 1946. Riginos 1976:43–48, no. 14.

244. AXIOTHEA

Themistios *Sophistes* 295c.

Literature. Gigon 1946:12–13.

245. EPICURUS

[a] Diogenes Laertios 10.2. [b] Sextus Empiricus *Against the Mathematicians* 10.18.

Literature. Cf. Gigon 1946.

246. ARISTIPPOS ON THE PHILOSOPHER'S ADVANTAGE

Diogenes Laertios 2.68 (*SSR* 105).

Literature. Hock and O'Neil 1986:45–46.

247. ARISTIPPOS ON THE BENEFITS OF PHILOSOPHY
Diogenes Laertios 2.68 (*SSR* 104).

248. ANTISTHENES ON THE BENEFITS OF PHILOSOPHY
Diogenes Laertios 6.6.

249. DIOGENES ON THE BENEFITS OF PHILOSOPHY
Diogenes Laertios 6.63. See also *Gnomologium Vaticanum* 182 (*SSR* 361).

250. KRATES ON THE BENEFITS OF PHILOSOPHY
Diogenes Laertios 6.86. Cf. Teles 44.2–9.

251. THE MOST USEFUL MAN IN EPHESOS
Strabo 14.1.25 (DK 22 B 121). See also Diogenes Laertios 9.2.
Literature. T. M. Robinson 1987:161.

252. PROTAGORAS'S BOOKS BURNED
Diogenes Laertios 9.51–52. See also Aristotle fr. 67 Rose; Cicero *On the Nature of the Gods* 1.23.63; Eusebios *Preparation for the Gospel* 14.19.10; schol. on Plato *Republic* 600c; *Suda* s.v. Protagoras.
Literature. Cramer 1945. Herren 2013.

253. SINNING AGAINST PHILOSOPHY
Aelian *Historical Miscellany* 3.36. See also the texts collected in Düring 1957:341–344 (T 44a–e, 45a–d).
Literature. Riginos 1976:63.

254. THALES IN THE WELL
Plato *Theaetetus* 174a. See also Diogenes Laertios 1.34 and 6.28; Aesopic fable (Hsr 40; Perry 40); Aristophanes *Clouds* 171–173; Pseudo-Kallisthenes *Life and Deeds of Alexander of Macedon* 1.14; Antipatros of Sidon (*Palatine Anthology* 7.172); Horace *Art of Poetry* 457–460; and Valerius Maximus 7.2.ext. 13.
Literature. ATU 1871A *Star Gazer Falls into Well.* Brecht 1930:43–44. Kirk and Raven 1957:78–79, no. 74. Megas 1970:9 and 211, no. 7 (Greek Folklore Archives, type *34C). Blumenberg 1976. *EM* 1:929–930; cf. *EM* 1:275.

255. THALES AND THE OLIVE PRESSES
Aristotle *Politics* 1.4.6–18 (1259a9). See also Diogenes Laertios 1.26, and Cicero *On Divination* 1.49.111.
Literature. Kirk and Raven 1957:78–79, no. 75.

256. SIMONIDES'S VIEW

Aristotle *Rhetorica* 2.16.2–4 (1391a).

Literature. Bell 1978.

257. ARISTIPPOS'S VIEW

Diogenes Laertios 2.69 (*SSR* 106). See also the pseudo-Aesopic *Sententiae* 19 (Perry 1952:252).

258. DIOGENES ON BEING LAUGHED AT

Diogenes Laertios 6.58 (*SSR* 431).

Literature. Halliwell 2008:380.

259. DIOGENES AND THE LANTERN

[a] Diogenes Laertios 6.41 (*SSR* 272). [b] Arsenios *Violetum* p. 197.22–24 Waltz (*SSR* 272). See also Tertullian *Against Marcio* 1.1, and Phaedrus 3.19.

Literature. ATU 1871F *Diogenes and the Lantern*. Motif J1303 *Aesop with the lantern*. Zeitz 1936:230–234. Sayre 1938:99–100. Hock and O'Neil 1986:321. Jedrkiewicz 1989:116–127.

260. THE MEETING OF DIOGENES AND ALEXANDER

Diogenes Laertios 6.60 (*SSR* 34).

261. ALEXANDER'S OFFER

[a] Diogenes Laertios 6.38 (*SSR* 33). See also Cicero *Tusculan Disputations* 5.32.92; Valerius Maximus 4.3.ext. 4; and Arrian *Anabasis* 7.2.1–2. [b] Plutarch *On Exile* 15 (*Moralia* 605d–e) (*SSR* 32). See also Plutarch *Alexander* 14.2–5 (*Moralia* 671d–e), and Diogenes Laertios 6.32.

Literature. ATU 1871C *The Cynic Wants Sunlight*. *EM* 3:676–681. Sayre 1938:82–87. Cf. Riginos 1976:74–85. Gray 1986. Hansen 1997. Dillon 2004:188.

262. DIOGENES ON PERSONAL ATTIRE

Aelian *Historical Miscellany* 9.34 (*SSR* 288). See also Aristotle *Nicomachean Ethics* 4.7.15.

263. DIOGENES ON TEMPLE THEFT

Diogenes Laertios 6.45 (*SSR* 462).

264. DIOGENES ON A PUBLIC READING

Diogenes Laertios 6.38 (*SSR* 391). See also *Gnomologium Vaticanum* 348.

265. DIOGENES VISITS A BROTHEL

Favorinos *Thoughts and Responses of Philosophers* (*Codex Bodleianus Baroccianus* 50, fol. 108b, no. 6) (*SSR* 211B).

266. DIOGENES ON THE CITY OF MYNDOS

Diogenes Laertios 6.57 (*SSR* 286).

267. "WATCH OUT!"

Diogenes Laertios 6.41 (*SSR* 457). See also Cicero *On the Orator* 2.279.

Literature. Süss 1969:5.

268. KRATES AND HIPPARCHIA

[a] Apuleius *Florida* 14. See also Diogenes Laertios 6.85–93. [b] Diogenes Laertios 6.96–97. See also Apuleius *Florida* 14.

Literature. Clay 1996:372–373.

269. MONIMOS ON WEALTH

Stobaios 4.31.89 (*SSR* 4). The remark is also attributed to Diogenes (Arsenios *Violetum* p. 209.11 Waltz [*SSR* 220]).

270. DIOGENES CRITICIZES PLATO

Plutarch *On Moral Virtue* 12 (*Moralia* 452d) (*SSR* 61). See also Stobaios 3.13.68.

Literature. Riginos 1976:111–112, no. 63.

271. PLATO CRITICIZES DIOGENES

Gnomonologium Vaticanum 445 (*SSR* 60). See also Theon *Progymnasmata* 98.14–17.

Literature. Riginos 1976:117, no. 73.

272. PLATO CHARACTERIZES DIOGENES

Aelian *Historical Miscellany* 14.33 (*SSR* 59). See also Diogenes Laertios 6.54.

Literature. Riginos 1976:115, no. 70.

273. DIOGENES ON PLATO'S THEORY OF IDEAS

Diogenes Laertios 6.53 (*SSR* 62). The anecdote was also told of Antisthenes and Plato (Riginos 1976:148).

Literature. Riginos 1976:147–148, no. 103.

274. DIOGENES ON A DEFINITION OF PLATO'S

Diogenes Laertios 6.40 (*SSR* 63).

Literature. Riginos 1976:149, no. 104.

275. DIOGENES ON THE IMPOSSIBILITY OF MOTION

Diogenes Laertios 6.39 (*SSR* 479).

276. A SONG BEFORE DYING

Aelian *Historical Miscellany* fr. 190 Wilson (= Stobaios 3.29.58). See also Ammianus Marcellinus *History* 28.4.15 (= D. A. Campbell [1991] 3:56–57, no. 43).

277. THE ENTRANCE TO PLATO'S CLASSROOM

Schol. on Aristeides (3:464.12–15 Dindorf). See also Philoponos *Commentary on Aristotle* On the Soul 1.3 (*CAG* 15: 117.26–27 Hayduck), and Olympiodoros *Prolegomena* (*CAG* 12.1: 8.39–9.1 Busse).

Literature. Saffrey 1968. Riginos 1976:138–140, no. 98.

278. THE DELIAN PROBLEM

Plutarch *On the E at Delphi* 6 (*Moralia* 386e). See also Plutarch *On the Sign of Socrates* 7 (*Moralia* 579a–d).

Literature. De Lacy and Einarson (1959) 7:397–399. Riginos 1976:141–145, no. 99. Fontenrose 1978, Q200.

279. THE WORST PUNISHMENT

Aelian *Historical Miscellany* 7.15.

280. THE INVENTION OF HUNTING

Xenophon *On Hunting* 1.1–2. See also, for lists of "first inventors," Pliny the Elder *Natural History* 7.56.191–7.60.214, and Hyginus *Fabulous Tales* 274, 277.

Literature. Kleingünther 1933.

281. THE INVENTION OF BOARD GAMES

[a–b] Suetonius *On Games among the Greeks* 1. [c] Herodotos 1.94. See also Athenaios 1.19, and Isidore of Seville *Etymologies* 18.60.

Literature. Roscher (1884–1937) 3:1268–1271. How and Wells (1928 [1912]) 1:103. Asheri et al. 2007:146.

282. THE ORIGINAL LANGUAGE

Herodotos 2.2.

Literature. How and Wells (1928 [1912]) 1:155–156. Lloyd (1975–1988) 2:4–12. Campbell and Grieve 1982. D. J. Taylor 1984. Asheri et al. 2007:242–243. Cf. Arvidsson 2006:22–28.

283. THALES INSCRIBES A TRIANGLE IN A CIRCLE

Diogenes Laertios 1.24 (= Pamphile fr. 1).

Literature. Kirk and Raven 1957:84.

284. THALES MEASURES THE HEIGHT OF THE PYRAMIDS

Diogenes Laertios 1.27 (= Hieronymos fr. 21 Hiller). See also Plutarch *Symposium of the Seven Sages* 2 (*Moralia* 147a), and Pliny the Elder *Natural History* 36.17.82.

Literature. Kirk and Raven 1957:83–84. Jedrkiewicz 2000.

285. THALES PREDICTS AN ECLIPSE

[a] Diogenes Laertios 1.23 (= Eudemos viii, fr. 144 Wehrli). [b] Herodotos 1.74.2.

Literature. How and Wells (1928 [1912]) 1:93–94. Kirk and Raven 1957: 79–83, nos. 76–78. Mosshammer 1981. Asheri et al. 2007:134–135.

286. THE PYTHAGOREAN THEOREM

Proklos *Commentary on the First Book of Euclid's Elements* p. 426 Friedlein. See also Diogenes Laertios 8.12.

Literature. Kirk and Raven 1957:229–231, no. 281. Burkert 1972:428–429; cf. Burkert 1983:39. Maor 2007.

287. "EUREKA!"

Vitruvius 9.9–12.

Literature. Dijksterhuis 1987:18–21. Jaeger 2008:17–31.

288. THE ORIGIN OF HUMAN MISERIES

Hesiod *Works and Days* 53–105. See also Hesiod *Theogony* 570–593.

Literature. M. L. West 1978:155–172. Hansen 2013.

289. THE ROCK OF TANTALOS

Athenaios 7.281b–c (= *Return of the Atreidai* fr. 3 West). See also Homer *Odyssey* 11.582–592; Pindar *Olympian* 1.52–69; and Pausanias 10.31.12.

Literature. ATU 981A* *Life by a Silk Thread.* Comparetti 1873. Roscher (1884–1937) 5:75–86. Frazer (1898) 5:392. Radermacher 1908. Aly 1969 [1921]:17. Olrik 1922:264–269. Bächtold-Stäubli 1928. *EM* 8:813–815.

290. THE SWORD OF DAMOCLES

Cicero *Tusculan Disputations* 5.20.61–62. See also Horace *Odes* 3.1.17–20, and Eusebios *Preparation for the Gospel* 8.14.29–30.

Literature. ATU 981A* *Life by a Silk Thread.* Motif F833.2 *Sword of Damocles.* Comparetti 1873. Wageningen 1905. Olrik 1922:264–269. Bächtold-Stäubli 1928. *EM* 8:813–815. Klintberg 2010:202–203, type K191E.

291. KING MIDAS

Hyginus *Fabulous Tales* 191. See also Aristotle *Politics* 1.3.16 (1257b16); Konon *Narrations* 1; Alexander Polyhistor *FGH* 273 F76, quoted by Pseudo-Plutarch *On Streams* 10.1; Ovid *Metamorphoses* 11.85–193; and Servius *Commentary on Vergil's Aeneid* 10.142.

Literature. ATU 775 *Midas' Short-Sighted Wish.* Otto 1890:49, no. 220, and 222, no. 1110. Bömer (1980) 5:259–287. L. E. Roller 1983. M. K. Brown 2002:49–57.

292. WEALTH AND HAPPINESS

Xenophon *Education of Cyrus* 8.3.35 ff. See also Horace *Letters* 1.7.46–98.

Literature. Cf. ATU 754 *Lucky Poverty.* Trenkner 1958:122–126.

293. WATER AND A LOAF OF BREAD

Aelian *Historical Miscellany* 4.13. See also Stobaios 3.17.29.

294. GOLD VS. FIGS

Athenaios 3.78f, quoting Ananios fr. 3 (Gerber 1999b:506–507).

295. UNTOUCHED BY GRIEF

[a] Julian the Apostate *Letter 37 (413a–c, to Himerios)* (no. 201 Bidez). [b] Pseudo-Kallisthenes *Life and Deeds of Alexander of Macedon* 3.33.2–4 van Thiel. See also Lucian *Demonax* 25.

Literature. ATU 844 *The Luck-Bringing Shirt.* Rohde 1914:599–600. *EM* 6:808–812. Cf. Hansen 2002a:92–95.

296. THE HAPPY MUTE

Pseudo-Aristotle *On Marvelous Things Heard* 178.

297. PYRRHOS AND KINEAS

Plutarch *Pyrrhos* 14.

Literature. Fries 1939.

298. THE THIRD CUP OF WINE

[a] *Life of Aesop* (Vita G) 68. [b] Euboulos fr. 93 Hunter 1983. See also Apuleius *Florida* 20.

Literature. Perry 1962:294–299. Schwarzbaum 1972:286–288. Hunter 1983:183–189. Cf. Gerber 1988. Faraone 1999:125–126.

299. THE DIFFERENT STAGES OF LIFE

Babrios 74. See also the fable of the years of a human being (Perry 105).

Literature. ATU 173 *Human and Animal Life Spans Are Readjusted.* Schwarzbaum 1972. *EM* 8:842–846.

300. THE DIFFERENT KINDS OF PEOPLE

Aesopic fable (Perry 240). See also Kallimachos fr. 192 Trypanis (Perry 431).

301. THE DIFFERENT KINDS OF WOMEN

Phokylides fr. 2 Gerber 1999a:392–393 (= Stobaios 4.22.192). See also Semonides fr. 7 Gerber 1999b:304–314.

Literature. Motif A1371.2 *Bad women combination of nine different animals.* Bolte 1901. Kakridis 1967:57–66. Lloyd-Jones 1975.

302. THE FOX AND THE CRANE

Plutarch *Table-Talk* 1.5 (*Moralia* 614d–615a) (= Perry 426). See also Phaedrus 1.26.

Literature. ATU 60 *Fox and Crane Invite Each Other*. Bormann and Benndorf 1902. Peterson 1981. *EM* 5:503–511. Arnott 2007:52–54. Kitchell 2014:70–72.

303. THE DOG WITH A PIECE OF MEAT

Aesopic fable (Hsr 136; Perry 133). See also Irenaeus *Against All Heresies* 2.11; Babrios 79; Pseudo-Dositheus 11 (p. 126 Hsr); and Aphthonios 35 (p. 149 Hsr).

Literature. ATU 34A *The Dog Drops His Meat for the Reflection. EM* 6:1343–1347. Kitchell 2014:47–52.

304. THE RAVEN WITH A PIECE OF MEAT

Aesopic fable (Hsr 126; Perry 124). See also Apuleius *Florida* 25; Babrios 77; Pseudo-Dositheus 9 (p. 125 Hsr); and Aphthonios 29 (p. 146 Hsr).

Literature. ATU 57 *The Raven with Cheese in His Mouth. EM* 11:135–139. Arnott 2007:109–116.

305. THE KING OF THE APES

Phaedrus 4.13, supplemented by a prose paraphrase (Perry 569).

Literature. ATU 48* *Flatterer Rewarded, Honest One Punished.*

306. THE APE WITH IMPORTANT ANCESTORS

Aesopic fable (Hsr 14; Perry 14). See also Babrios 81.

Literature. Motif J954.2 *Fox claims that certain statues are of his ancestors.* McDermott 1938:110–118. Kitchell 2014:5, 70–72.

307. THE SOUR GRAPES

Aesopic fable (Hsr 15a; Perry 15). See also Babrios 19, and Phaedrus 4.3.

Literature. ATU 59 *The Fox and the Sour Grapes.* Stahl 1980. *EM* 5:527–534. Hansen 1982. Kitchell 2014:70–72.

308. THE ANT AND THE CICADA

Aesopic fable (Hsr 114 [Ib]). See also Babrios 140 (Perry 373); Pseudo-Dositheus 17; Theophylaktos Simokattes *Letters* 61 and fable 2 (p. 154 Hsr); Aphthonios 1 (p. 133 Hsr); and Avianus 34. Cf. the fable of the ant and the dung-beetle (Hsr 114; Perry 112).

Literature. ATU 280A *The Ant and the Cricket. EM* 6:161–164. Beavis 1988:91–103, 198–209.

309. THE LION'S SHARE

Babrios 67 (Perry 339). See also Phaedrus 1.5, and the fable of the lion, donkey, and fox (Hsr 154; Perry 149).

Literature. ATU 51 *The Lion's Share. EM* 8:1224–1228. B. M. Jensen 2004. Kitchell 2014:108–111.

310. THE RACE OF THE TORTOISE AND THE HARE

Aesopic fable (Hsr 254; Perry 226). See also Libanios 2 (pp. 130–131 Hsr).

Literature. ATU 275A *The Race between Hare and Tortoise.* Ross 1955:71–85. Kitchell 2014:82–85, 186–188.

311. THE LION AND THE MOUSE

Aesopic fable (Hsr 155; Perry 150). See also Babrios 107; Pseudo-Dositheus 2 (p. 121 Hsr); and Julian the Apostate *Letter* 67 Wright.

Literature. ATU 75 *The Help of the Weak.* Brugsch 1878. Marx 1889:127–131, 140–146. *EM* 6:1023–1029. Kitchell 2014:108–111, 123–126.

312. THE PLUMP DOG

Babrios 100 (Perry 346). See also Phaedrus 3.7.

Literature. ATU 201 *The Lean Dog Prefers Liberty to Abundant Food and a Chain.* Kitchell 2014:47–52.

313. THE TRANSFORMED WEASEL

Aesopic fable (Hsr 50; Perry 50). See also Babrios 32.

Literature. ATU 218 *A Cat Transformed to a Maiden Runs after a Mouse.* Zielinski 1889. Rohde 1901. Kitchell 2014:193–196.

314. THE GOOSE THAT LAYS GOLDEN EGGS

Aesopic fable (Hsr 89; Perry 87). See also Babrios 123, and Avianus 33.

Literature. ATU 219E** *The Hen That Laid the Golden Eggs.* Arnott 2007:30–31.

315. THE TORTOISE THAT WISHES TO FLY

Aesopic fable (Hsr 259; Perry 230). See also Babrios 115; Avianus 2; and Phaedrus 2.6 (Perry 490).

Literature. ATU 225A *The Tortoise Lets Itself Be Carried by Birds.* Cf. Crusius 1882. *EM* 4:1290–1295. Arnott 2007:2–4. Kitchell 2014:186–188.

316. THE KING OF THE FROGS

Aesopic fable (Hsr 44; Perry 44). See also Phaedrus 1.2.

Literature. ATU 277 *The King of the Frogs.* Jacobsen 1952. *EM* 5:408–410. Kitchell 2014:72–73.

317. THE ASTRONOMER

Aesopic fable (Hsr 40; Perry 40). See also Plato *Theaetetus* 174a; Diogenes Laertios 1.34 and 6.28; Aristophanes *Clouds* 171–173; Pseudo-Kallisthenes *Life and Deeds of Alexander of Macedon* 1.14; Antipatros of Sidon (*Palatine Anthology* 7.172); Horace *Art of Poetry* 457–460; Valerius Maximus 7.2.ext. 13.

Literature. ATU 1871A *Star Gazer Falls into Well.* Brecht 1930:43–44. Blumenberg 1976. *EM* 1:929–930.

318. THE SHEPHERD WHO CRIES "WOLF!"

Aesopic fable (Hsr 226; Perry 210).

Literature. ATU 1333 *The Shepherd Who Cried "Wolf!" Too Often. EM* 6:1083–1084. Hansen 2002a:402–404. Kitchell 2014:199–201.

319. "HERE IS RHODES!"

Aesopic fable (Hsr 33; Perry 33).

320. THE BELLY AND THE FEET

Aesopic fable (Hsr 132; Perry 130). See also Babrios 134 (Perry 362); Dion Chrysostomos *Oration* 33.16; Maximus of Tyre 15.5; Paul 1

Corinthians 12; Livy 2.32.9–12; Lucius Annaeus Florus *Epitome of Titus Livius* 1.23; Dionysios of Halikarnassos *Roman Antiquities* 6.83–86; Plutarch *Coriolanus* 6–7.1 and *Agis and Kleomenes* 2.3–4; Sextus Aurelius Victor *On Illustrious Men* 18.1–5; Quintilian 5.11.19.

Literature. ATU 293 *The Debate of the Belly and the Members*. Maspero 1879. Prato 1885. Nestle 1927. Gombel 1934. Perry 1965: xxvi–xxvii. Hale 1968. Barié 1970. Abrahams 1970:214–215. Dundes and Pagter 1978:100–101. Schwarzbaum 1979:xliv n. 53. Peil 1985. *EM* 8:1418–1422.

321. THE OAK AND THE REED

Aesopic fable (Hsr 71; Perry 70). See also Sophocles *Antigone* 712–714; Loukillios (*Palatine Anthology* 10.122); Babrios 336; Aphthonios (p. 149 Hsr); Avianus 16; and Macrobius *Saturnalia* 7.8.6.

Literature. ATU 298C* *The Reeds Bend before the Wind (Flood)*. *EM* 1:1386–1389.

322. THE MOUNTAIN IN LABOR

Diogeneianos 8.75. See also Athenaios 14.616d; Horace *Art of Poetry* 136–142; and Phaedrus 4.24 (Perry 520).

Literature. ATU 299 *The Mountain Gives Birth to a Mouse*. *EM* 2:141. Otto 1890:234–235, no. 1173. Perry 1965:xxx–xxxiv.

323. THE ATTENTIVE DONKEY

Zenobios 5.42.

Literature. ATU 1211 *The Cow Chewing Its Cud*. Perry 1965:xxx–xxxiv. Hansen 2002a:35–38. Kitchell 2014:57–59.

324. MARGITES

[a] Hesychios *Lexicon* M 267 (= *Margites* fr. 4b West). [b] Eustathios *Commentary on Homer's Odyssey* 1669.48 (= *Margites* fr. 4c West). See also Suetonius *On Slanders* 7.185 Taillardat.

Literature. Radermacher 1908. Gostoli 2007. Cf. Hansen 2002a: 251–255.

325. MELETIDES

Suetonius *On Slanders* 7.188 Taillardat.

326. KOROIBOS

Zenobios 4.58. See also Diogeneianos 5.56.

Literature. Gow 1931. Marcovich 1976. Hansen 2002a:97–99.

327. MORYCHOS

Zenobios 5.13.

328. AKKO

[a] Zenobios 1.53. [b] Suetonius *On Slanders* 7.194–195 Taillardat.

Literature. ATU 1336A *Not Recognizing Own Reflection*. Pauly et al. (1893–1980) 1:1171–1173. Winkler 1982. Hansen 2002a:258.

329. THE FOOLISH KYMAIANS

[a] Strabo 13.3.6. [b] *Philogelos* 154. [c] *Philogelos* 178.

330. THE FOOLISH ABDERITES

[a] Lucian *How to Write History* 1. [b] *Philogelos* 124.

Literature. ATU 1543A *The Greedy Dreamer*. Andreassi 2004:119–120.

331. CARRYING THE LOAD

Aristophanes *Frogs* 19–30.

Literature. ATU 1242A *Relief for the Donkey*. *EM* 4:18–21. Hansen 2002a:66–69.

332. ACQUIRING SENSE

Life of Aesop (Vita G) 131 (Perry 386).

Literature. ATU 1542** *The Maiden's Honor*. Lee 1972 [1909]:108–109. Stramaglia 2000:312–314. Hansen 2002a:251–255. Kurke 2011:213–217. Kitchell 2014:17–18.

333. SEEING THE DOCTOR

Philogelos 6.

334. THE TRAINED DONKEY

Philogelos 9.

Literature. ATU 1682 *The Horse Learns Not to Eat*. Hansen 2002a:187–188. Andreassi 2004:85–86. Kitchell 2014:57–59.

335. THE BOOKS

Philogelos 17.

Literature. Hansen 2001:94–95.

336. THE SLAVE

Philogelos 18.

Literature. Andreassi 2004:91.

337. A CALL OF NATURE

Philogelos 132. See also *Philogelos* 42.

338. THE TWINS

Philogelos 29.

Literature. ATU 1284C *"You, or Your Brother?"* Christensen 1939:163, 224–225, no. 87. Hansen 2001:90–91. Andreassi 2004:94–96.

339. THE FUNERAL

Philogelos 40.

340. THE BALL IN THE WELL

Philogelos 33.

Literature. ATU 1336A *Not Recognizing Own Reflection.* Hansen 2002a:257–261. Andreassi 2004:96–98.

341. THE EDUCATED SON

Philogelos 54.

342. THE TRAVELERS

Philogelos 56.

Literature. ATU 1284 *Person Does Not Know Himself.* Cf. ATU 1383 *The Woman Does Not Know Herself.* Hansen 2002a:327–329. Andreassi 2004:106–112.

343. THE GRATEFUL FATHER

Philogelos 98.

Literature. Andreassi 2004:117–118.

344. A PAIR OF TWINS

Philogelos 101.

Literature. Baldwin 1983:79, no. 101.

345. THE FUGITIVES

Philogelos 96.

Literature. ATU 1341A *The Fool and the Robbers.* Megas 1970:178 and 244, no. 61 (Greek Folklore Archives, type *1298). Hansen 2002a:136–138. Andreassi 2004:112–117.

346. THE PILLOW

[a] Suetonius *On Slanders* 7.189–190 Taillardat. [b] *Philogelos* 21.

Literature. Hansen 2001:87. Andreassi 2004:92–94.

347. TOO HEALTHY

Aesopic fable (Hsr 180; Perry 170).

348. WHAT DOES IT TASTE LIKE?

Phaedrus 3.4 (Perry 496).

349. ALL IN THE FAMILY

Philogelos 45.

Literature. Andreassi 2004:101–103.

350. THE STRONGEST THING

Athenaios 10.451b (= Diphilos *Theseus* fr. 49).

Literature. ATU 2031 *Stronger and Strongest*. Hansen 2002a:415–424.

351. CAESAR'S SOLDIERS SING

Suetonius *Julius Caesar* 49. See also Suetonius *Julius Caesar* 2.

Literature. ATU 2031 *Stronger and Strongest*. Hansen 2002a:415–424.

352. NOT AT HOME

[a] *Philogelos* 193. [b] Cicero *On the Orator* 2.68.276.

Literature. ATU 1594 *The Donkey Is Not at Home*. S. West 1992. Hansen 2001:95–97. Andreassi 2004:120–123.

353. THE PORTENT

Plutarch *Symposium of the Seven Sages* 3 (*Moralia* 149c–e). See also Phaedrus 3.3 (Perry 495).

Literature. Hansen 1996:155–159. Konstantakos 2010:277. Kitchell 2014:17–18.

354. THE DEAF JUDGE

Nikarchos (*Palatine Anthology* 11.251).

Literature. Cf. ATU 1698A *Search for the Lost Animal*. Hansen 2002a:190–192.

355. THE SCYTHIAN

Aelian *Historical Miscellany* 7.6. See also *Gnomologium Vaticanum* 534.

Literature. Motif J1309.1 *Man asks naked Indian if he is not cold*. Dorson 1946. Hancock 1963. Glassie 1964. Marzolph (1992) 1:225–229.

356. THE COLD READING

Philogelos 201.

Literature. Hansen 2001. See further Lateiner 1993 and Hyman 1996.

357. THE COVETOUS MAN AND THE ENVIOUS MAN

Avianus 22 (Perry 580).

Literature. ATU 1331 *The Covetous and the Envious*. *EM* 9:1331–1335.

358. UNCOMFORTABLE SLEEP

[a] Aelian *Historical Miscellany* 9.24. [b] Seneca the Younger *On Anger* 2.25.

Literature. ATU 1290B* *Sleeping on a Feather*. Cf. ATU 704 *The Princess on the Pea*. Hansen 1997.

359. THE SUITOR

Aelian *Historical Miscellany* 12.24. See also Athenaios 6.273c and 12.541b–c, and Herodotos 6.126–130.

Literature. Gorman and Gorman 2014.

360. NOISE POLICY

Athenaios 12.518c–d.

361. THE AFFLICTION OF WORK

Athenaios 12.518d (= Timaios *FGH* 566 F 48). See also Diodoros of Sicily 8.18.2, and Seneca the Younger *On Anger* 2.25.2.

Literature. Hansen 1997.

362. EXCURSIONS TO THE COUNTRY

Athenaios 12.519c–d.

363. CHAMBER POTS

Athenaios 12.519e.

364. PIPED WINE

Athenaios 12.519d.

365. POLICY ON PARTIES

Athenaios 12.521c.

366. DANCING HORSES

Athenaios 12.520c. See also Athenaios 12.520c–f; Longos *Daphnis and Chloe* 1.28–31; Aelian *Nature of Animals* 8.19; and Pliny the Elder *Natural History* 8.208.

Literature. Liebrecht 1879:110–111. Trenkner 1958:176. Bennett and Smith 2007:148–150.

367. TOPSY-TURVY LAND

[a] Aristeides *Orations* 48 (2:475–476 Dindorf). [b] Tertullian *Against the Valentinians* 20.3 Fredouille.

Literature. ATU 1935 *Topsy Turvy Land*. Kenner 1970. Hansen 2002a:439–445.

368. FROZEN SPEECH

Plutarch *Progress in Virtue* 7 (*Moralia* 79a).

Literature. ATU 1889F *Frozen Words (Music) Thaw*. Hansen 2002a:146–147.

369. THIN MEN

[a] Athenaios 12.552b. See also Aelian *Historical Miscellany* 9.14; Aelian *Historical Miscellany* 10.6; and Athenaios 12.551–552. [b] Loukillios (*Palatine Anthology* 11.103).

Literature. Motif X924 *Lie: remarkably thin persons*. Cameron 1991.

GLOSSARY

ANALOGISM. The representation of nonhuman characters, particularly animals, as behaving in tales like human beings in one way or another. Thus in the fable of the fox and crane (302), the two animals exchange dinner parties. In the fable of the belly and the feet (320), the different parts of the body converse with one another.

ANECDOTE. Credence narrative consisting of a brief incident that culminates in a memorable utterance or action by a named person. When, for example, the monarch Alexander meets the philosopher Diogenes lying in the sun, and offers to grant him any wish, Diogenes asks only that he stand out of his light (261).

ANIMAL TALE. Simple folktale featuring animals as characters, or animals and humans. Animal tales are told primarily to amuse, whereas fables are told to instruct.

APOTHEGM (Greek *apophthegma*). Pointed utterance attributed to a particular person. Apothegms typically have the form "A, asked such and such by B, said C."

ARETALOGY (Greek *aretalogia*). Form of religious legend that tells of a miracle performed by a deity. An example is the narrative of Athena's bringing about a sudden rain shower that saves the parched inhabitants of Lindos when they are besieged by the Persians (10).

BELIEF LEGEND. Legend built around a particular folk belief (whence the name), or superstition. An example is the story of the helpful ghost; see 22 "The Grateful Dead Man."

CATCH TALE. Formulaic narrative that induces the listener to ask a particular question for which the narrator has a ready answer that makes the listener appear foolish, as in 123, "A Donkey's Shadow."

CHAIN TALE. Cumulative tale constructed upon a succession of phenomena on a particular theme, such as strong, stronger, and strongest (350 and 351).

COMIC TALE. Humorous folktale, an umbrella category that includes both punch-line and non-punch-line narratives. See also "Joke."

CONTEMPORARY LEGEND. Short legend telling of an unusual event set in the very recent past. An example is the Roman legend of the craftsman who invents unbreakable glass (83). "Contemporary legend" has come to be the preferred scholarly term, whereas the popular term remains "urban legend."

CREDENCE NARRATIVE. Story that narrators have formed in such a way as to present, or imply, a claim to historicity, such as employing named characters and locating the events in a particular setting in time and space.

EMIC GENRE. Native and local, as opposed to scholarly and cross-cultural, genre. In the United States, for example, "ghost story" and "dirty joke" are emic genres of story. The complementary term is "etic genre."

EPIMYTHIUM (Greek *epimythion*) or "after-tale." Moral, or generalized point, of a fable that, if present, appears after the narration of the fable. For example, an epimythium for the fable of the tortoise and the hare (310) states: "The story shows that hard work often trumps a careless nature." Cf. "Promythium."

ETIC GENRE. Analytic category of narrative devised by investigators for the purpose of multicultural comparison. An example is "belief legend." See also "Emic genre."

FABLE. Simple fictional tale that features animals and/or humans, gods, plants, and the like as characters, and serves to convey the narrator's message metaphorically. An example is the tale of the ant and the cicada (308).

FABLE-PROVERB. Same as "short fable."

FAIRYTALE (from French *conte de fées*). Same as "wonder tale" and "magic tale," the terms preferred by folklorists, since few fairytales actually feature fairies. However, some investigators restrict the term "fairytale" to the literary fairytale (German *Kunstmärchen*). See also "Wonder tale."

FOLK NARRATIVE. Umbrella term for the different genres of traditional, predominantly oral, narrative, namely myth, legend, folktale, and their subgenres.

GENRE, NARRATIVE. Conventionalized narrative form, such as "joke."

HERO (Greek *heros*). In Greek heroic legend, (1) a member of the heroic age, which is characterized by the presence of demigods, the offspring of a mortal and an immortal. Achilleus, son of the mortal Peleus and the nymph Thetis, is an example. In Greek historic legend, (2) a mortal who dies and continues to exist as a powerful dead person, or revenant, often receiving worship at the site of his or her supposed grave. An example is the Hero of Temesa (28).

HEROIC LEGEND. Legend set in the age of heroes, which in Greek tradition is the period that follows the mythic era and precedes our own, the historic era. The traditions about the Trojan War are heroic legends.

HISTORIC LEGEND. Legend set in the historic era, featuring allegedly real persons and events belonging to the relatively recent past, such as the traditions that developed around the Athenian heroes Harmodios and Aristogeiton.

JOKE. Succinct, fictional comic tale featuring generic characters and consisting of a setup and a punch line. For example, a man complains that the slave he bought died (= setup). "By the gods," the seller replies, "he never did anything like that when he was with me" (= punch line) (336).

LEGEND. Traditional credence narrative set in the familiar world following the mythic, or formative, era of the cosmos.

MAGIC TALE (from German *Zaubermärchen*). Same as "wonder tale." See also "Fairytale."

MEMORATE. First-person credence narrative of a supernatural experience. An example is Hesiod's report of his encounter with the Muses (4).

MILESIAN TALE. Ribald novella. See also "Novella."

MYTH. Traditional credence narrative whose principal characters are gods and other supernatural beings, whose events are set in the remote past during the formative era of the cosmos, and whose central topics include the origins of the physical world, the gods, and human beings, as well as the establishment of cosmic order. An example is the story of the creation of the first woman, Pandora (288).

MYTHOLOGY. Collective term for two genres of traditional story, myth and heroic legend, which focus respectively upon supernatural beings and heroic beings, the era of the gods and the era of the demigods, and provide between them a more or less continuous account of events from the beginning of the cosmos to the end of the heroic age. "Classical mythology" designates Greek mythology after its adoption and incorporation by the Romans.

NOVELLA (Italian *novella*, pl. *novelle*). Traditional fiction focusing upon realistic domestic and urban themes such as love, cleverness, and thievery, and featuring ordinary people as protagonists. See also "Milesian tale."

ORACLE. In historic legend, either (1) a shrine at which an inquirer poses a question to a god and receives a response via a priestess or priest, or (2) the oracular response itself. When an oracular shrine is mentioned in ancient legend, it is regularly the renowned oracle of Apollon at Delphi, whose priestess was known as the Pythia. In the story of the Hero of Temesa (28), for example, the inhabitants of Temesa consult the Delphic oracle and act upon the response they get.

PARADOXOGRAPHER (modern compound based upon Greek *paradoxon* "something extraordinary"). Person who writes about marvels.

PAROEMIOGRAPHER (Greek *paroimiographos*). Person who writes about proverbs.

PERSONAL-EXPERIENCE FABLE or PERSONAL FABLE. Form that combines two narrative models, the personal narrative as a first-person account of the speaker's own experience and the fable as a simple metaphoric narrative with an application to the immediate situation.

PERSONAL-EXPERIENCE NARRATIVE or PERSONAL NARRATIVE. First-person narrative presented as an account of something actually experienced by the narrator.

PROMYTHIUM (Greek *promythion*) or "fore-tale." Generalized point, or application, of a fable that, if present, introduces the narration of the tale. Promythia are common in early fable compilations but rare later. Cf. "Epimythium."

RELIGIOUS LEGEND. Credence narrative set in the historical period that recounts the epiphany of a deity who performs a wonder of some kind or otherwise affects human affairs in a significant way. An example is the Phrygian flood story of Philemon and Baucis.

RELIGIOUS TALE. Traditional fictional narrative focusing upon an aspect of the relationship of humans and gods. An instance is the tale of Hermes and the ants (104).

SACRED STORY (from Greek *hieros logos*). Greek emic genre that appears to be an esoteric credence narrative associated with a sacred rite. Since ancient authors were reluctant to disclose the content of individual sacred stories, little is known of the genre.

SHORT FABLE. An ultrashort narrative, usually no more than a single sentence, that can be classified as a fable, a proverb, or both, such as 322 "The Mountain in Labor."

TALL TALE or LYING TALE. Traditional fictional narrative with humorous, outrageous exaggeration, often recounted by a narrator in a tone of mock seriousness as a personal-experience narrative. An example is 368 "Frozen Speech."

TYRANT (Greek *tyrannos*). Absolute ruler of a city-state who gained power by usurpation and maintained it by force. Individual tyrants ranged from just monarchs to despots. Several Sicilian tyrants, such as Dionysios the Younger, play a major role in the ancient anecdotal tradition.

URBAN LEGEND. Early and still popular term for "contemporary legend."

VICARIOUS NARRATIVE. A retelling of someone else's narrative.

WONDER TALE (German *Wundermärchen*). Complex (that is, poly-episodic) traditional tale of fantasy that features a mix of the natural and the supernatural. In a typical wonder tale an adolescent male or female leaves home, encounters the supernatural, is tested, and ends happily by rising socially (e.g., a royal marriage) and/or financially. An example is the tale of Cupid and Psyche (1). Identical with "magic tale." See also "Fairytale."

BIBLIOGRAPHY

Abrahams, Roger D. 1970. *Deep Down in the Jungle: Negro Narrative Folklore from the Streets of Philadelphia.* 1st rev. ed. Chicago: Aldine.

Allinson, Francis G. 1930. "The Original 'Marathon Runner.'" *Classical Weekly* 24 (October 1):152.

Almqvist, Bo. 2008. "Midwife to the Fairies (ML 5070) in Icelandic Tradition." In *Legends and Landscape*, edited by Terry Gunnell, 273–322. Reykjavik: University of Iceland Press.

Altick, Richard D. 1978. *The Shows of London.* Cambridge: Belknap Press.

Aly, Wolf. 1969 [1921]. *Volksmärchen, Sage und Novelle bei Herodot und seinen Zeitgenossen: Eine Untersuchung über die volkstümlichen Elemente der altgriechischen Prosaerzählung.* 2nd ed. Göttingen: Vandenhoeck & Ruprecht.

Amidon, Philip R., trans. and comm. 2007. *Philostorgius: Church History.* Atlanta: Society of Biblical Literature.

Amundsen, Darrell W. 1974. "Romanticizing the Ancient Medical Profession: The Characterization of the Physician in the Graeco-Roman Novel." *Bulletin of the History of Medicine* 48:320–337.

Anderson, Graham. 1999. "The Novella in Petronius." In *Latin Fiction: The Latin Novel in Context*, edited by Heinz Hofmann, 52–63. London: Routledge.

———. 2000. *Fairytale in the Ancient World.* London: Routledge.

Andreassi, Mario. 2004. *Le Facezie del Philogelos: Barzellette Antiche e Umorismo Moderno.* Lecce: Pensa MultiMedia Editore.

Armstrong, A. MacC. 1987. "Timon of Athens—A Legendary Figure?" *Greece & Rome* 34:7–11.

Arnaud, Pascal. 1998. "'Toi Aussi, Mon Fils, Tu Mangeras ta Part de Nôtre Pouvoir'—Brutus le Tyran?" *Latomus* 57:61–71.

Arnott, W. Geoffrey. 2007. *Birds in the Ancient World from A to Z.* London: Routledge.

Arvidsson, Stefan. 2006. *Aryan Idols: Indo-European Mythology as Ideology and Science*, translated by Sonia Wichmann. Chicago: University of Chicago Press.

Asheri, David, Alan Lloyd, and Aldo Corcella. 2007. *A Commentary on Herodotus Books I–IV*, edited by Oswyn Murray and Alfonso Moreno, with a contribution by Maria Brosius. Translated by Barbara Graziosi et al. Oxford: Oxford University Press.

Bächtold-Stäubli, Hanns. 1928. "Der Mühlstein am Faden." *Schweizerisches Archiv für Volkskunde* 28:119–129.

Badian, Ernst. 1979. "The Name of the Runner: A Summary of the Evidence." *American Journal of Ancient History* 4:163–166.

Baldwin, Barry, trans. and comm. 1983. *The Philogelos or Laughter-Lover*. Amsterdam: J. C. Gieben.

———. 1986. "Why the Werewolf Urinates." *Petronian Society Newsletter* 16:9.

———. 1992. "Jokes Old and New." *Classical Outlook* 69:77–81.

Baraz, Yelena. 2012. "Pliny's Epistolary Dreams and the Ghost of Domitian." *TAPA* 142:105–132.

Barié, Paul. 1970. "Menenius Agrippa erzählt eine politische Fabel: Ein Beispiel für Ideologiekritik im altsprachliche Unterricht." *Das altsprachliche Unterricht* 4:50–77.

Baring-Gould, S. 1882. *Curious Myths of the Middle Ages*. Boston: Roberts Brothers.

Barrett, W. S., ed. and comm. 1964. *Euripides: Hippolytos*. Oxford: Clarendon Press.

Barrick, Mac E. 1976. "The Migratory Anecdote and the Folk Concept of Fame." *Mid-South Folklore* 4:39–47.

Barton, Tamsyn. 1994. *Ancient Astrology*. London: Routledge.

Bascom, William. 1965. "The Forms of Folklore: Folk Narratives." *JAF* 78:3–20.

Bauman, Richard. 1986. *Story, Performance, and Event: Contextual Studies of Oral Narrative*. Cambridge: Cambridge University Press.

———. 1992. "Genre." In *Folklore, Cultural Performances, and Popular Entertainments: A Communications-Centered Handbook*, edited by Richard Bauman, 53–59. New York: Oxford University Press.

Baumgartner, Walter. 1959. *Zum alten Testament und seiner Umwelt: Ausgewählete Aufsätze.* Leiden: E. J. Brill.

Bausinger, Hermann. 1961. "Schildbürgergeschichten: Betrachtungen zum Schwank." *Der Deutschunterricht* 13. 1:18–44.

Bayliss, Andrew J. 2009. "Using Few Words Wisely?: 'Laconic Swearing' and Spartan Duplicity." In *Sparta: Comparative Approaches*, edited by Stephen Hodkinson, 231–260. Swansea: Classical Press of Wales.

Beard, Mary. 2007. *The Roman Triumph*. Cambridge: Harvard University Press.

———. 2014. *Laughter in Ancient Rome: On Joking, Tickling, and Cracking Up*. Berkeley: University of California Press.

Beare, W. 1965. *The Roman Stage: A Short History of Latin Drama in the Time of the Republic*. New York: Barnes and Noble.

Beavis, Ian C. 1988. *Insects and Other Invertebrates in Classical Antiquity*. Exeter: University of Exeter Press.

Beekes, Robert S. P. 1986. "'You Can Get New Children . . .': Turkish and Other Parallels to Ancient Greek Ideas in Herodotus, Thucydides, Sophocles and Euripides." *Mnemosyne* 34:225–239.

Bell, J. M. 1978. "Κίμβιξ καὶ σοφός: Simonides in the Anecdotal Tradition." *Quaderni Urbinati di Cultura Classica* 28:29–86.

Ben-Amos, Dan. 1969. "Analytical Categories and Ethnic Genres." *Genre* 2:275–301.

———, ed. 1976. *Folklore Genres*. Austin: University of Texas Press.

———, ed. and comm. 2006. *Folktales of the Jews*. Vol. 1. Philadelphia: Jewish Publication Society.

Bennett, Gillian, and Paul Smith. 1993. *Contemporary Legend: A Folklore Bibliography*. New York: Garland.

———, eds. 2007. *Urban Legends: A Collection of International Tall Tales and Terrors*. Westport, CT: Greenwood Press.

Benveniste, É. 1931. "La Légende de Kombabos." In *Méanges Syriens offerts à René Dussaud, Secrétaire Perpétuel de l'Académie des Inscriptions et Belles-Lettres, par ses Amis et ses Élèves*, 1:249–258. Paris: Librarie Orientaliste Paul Geuthner.

Berman, Daniel W. 2015. *Myth, Literature, and the Creation of the Topography of Thebes*. Cambridge: Cambridge University Press.

Bieler, Ludwig. 1930. "Zu Porphyrios Vita Pythagorae 27." *Wiener Studien* 48:201–205.

Blumenberg, Hans. 1976. "Der Sturz des Protophilosophen—Zur Komik der reinen Theorie, anhand einer Rezeptionsgeschichte der Thales-Anekdote." In *Das Komische*, edited by Wolfgang Preisendanz and Rainer Warning, 11–64. Munich: Wilhelm Fink.

Bødker, Laurits. 1965. *Folk Literature (Germanic)*. Vol. 2 of *International Dictionary of Regional European Ethnology and Folklore*. Copenhagen: Rosenkilde og Bagger.

Bolte, Johannes. 1901. "Ein dänisches Märchen von Petrus und dem Ursprunge der bösen Weiber." *Zeitschrift des Vereins für Volkskunde* 11:252–262.

Bolton, J. D. P. 1962. *Aristeas of Proconnesus*. Oxford: Clarendon Press.

Bömer, Franz, comm. 1980. *P. Ovidius Naso: Metamorphosen, Kommentar.* Vol. 5, *Buch 10–11*. Heidelberg: Carl Winter Universitätsverlag.

Bonnechère, Pierre. 2003. *Trophonios de Lébadée: Cultes et Mythes d'une Cité Béotienne au Miroir de la Mentalité Antique*. Leiden: E. J. Brill.

Bonner, Campbell. 1937. "The Sibyl and Bottle Imps." In *Quantulacumque: Studies Presented to Kirsopp Lake by Pupils, Colleagues, and Friends,* edited by Robert P. Casey, Silva Lake, and Agnes K. Lake, 1–8. London: Christophers.

Borgehammar, Stephan. 1991. *How the Holy Cross Was Found: From Event to Medieval Legend*. Stockholm: Almqvist & Wiksell International.

Bormann, Eugen, and O. Benndorf. 1902. "Aesopische Fabel auf einem römischen Grabstein." *Jahreshefte des österreichischen archäologischen Instituts* 5:1–8.

Borthwick, E. K. 1968. "Seeing Weasels: The Superstitious Background of the Empusa Scene in the *Frogs*." *CQ* NS 18:200–206.

Bouché-Leclercq, August. 1879–1882. *Histoire de la Divination dans l'Antiquité*. 4 vols. Paris: E. Leroux.

Bowie, Ewen. 2013. "'Milesian Tales.'" In *The Romance between Greece and the East*, edited by Tim Whitmarsh and Stuart Thomson, 243–257. New York: Cambridge University Press.

Brecht, Franz Josef. 1930. *Motiv- und Typengeschichte des griechischen Spottepigramms. Philologus*, Supplementband 22.2.

Bremmer, Jan. 1983. *The Early Greek Concept of the Soul*. Princeton: Princeton University Press.

———. 1997. "Jokes, Jokers, and Jokebooks in Ancient Greek Culture." In Bremmer and Roodenburg, 11–28. Cambridge: Polity Press.

Bremmer, Jan, and Herman Roodenburg, eds. 1997. *A Cultural History of Humour from Antiquity to the Present Day*. Cambridge: Polity Press.

Brillante, Carlo. 2009. *Il Cantore e la Musa: Poesia e Modelli Culturali nella Grecia Arcaica*. Studi e Testi di Storia Antica 18. Pisa: Editioni ETS.

Brisson, Luc. 2009. "The Philosopher and the Magician (Porphyry, *Vita Plotini* 10.1–13), Magic and Sympathy." In Dill and Walde, 189–202.

Brodeur, Arthur Gilchrist. 1922. "Androcles and the Lion." *Modern Philology* 11:197–213.

———. 1924. "The Grateful Lion: A Study in the Development of Mediæval Narrative." *Publications of the Modern Language Association of America* 39:485–524.

Brown, Carolyn S. 1987. *The Tall Tale in American Folklore and Literature*. Knoxville: University of Tennessee Press.

Brown, Malcolm Kenneth. 2002. *The* Narratives *of Konon: Text, Translation, and Commentary of the* Diegeseis. Munich: K. G. Saur.

Brugsch, H. 1878. "Aesopische Fabeln in einem ägyptischen Papyrus." *Zeitschrift für ägyptische Sprache und Altertumskunde* 16:47–50.

Brunvand, Jan Harold. 1984. *The Choking Doberman and Other "New" Urban Legends.* New York: W. W. Norton.

———. 1993. *The Baby Train & Other Lusty Urban Legends*. New York: W. W. Norton.

———. 2001. *Encyclopedia of Urban Legends*. Santa Barbara: ABC CLIO.

Burkert, Walter. 1972. *Lore and Science in Ancient Pythagoreanism*. Translated by Edwin L. Minar Jr. Cambridge: Harvard University Press.

———. 1979. *Structure and History in Greek Mythology and Ritual*. Berkeley: University of California Press.

———. 1983. *Homo Necans: The Anthropology of Ancient Greek Sacrificial Ritual and Myth*. Translated by Peter Bing. Berkeley: University of California Press.

Buxton, Richard. 1987. "Wolves and Werewolves in Greek Thought." In *Interpretations of Greek Mythology*, edited by Jan Bremmer, 60–79. London: Croom Helm.

———. 1994. *Imaginary Greece: The Contexts of Mythology*. Cambridge: Cambridge University Press.

Bynum, Caroline Walker. 1984. "Women's Stories, Women's Symbols: A Critique of Victor Turner's Theory of Liminality." In *Anthropology and the Study of Religion*, edited by Robert L. Moore and Frank E. Reynolds, 105–125. Chicago: Center for the Scientific Study of Religion.

Caillois, Roger. 1938. "L'Anneau de Polycrate." In *Travaux du 1er Congrès International de Folklore, Tenu à Paris, du 23 au 28 Août 1937 à l'Ecole du Louvre*, 165–168. Tours: Arrault.

Cameron, Alan. 1991. "How Thin Was Philetas?" *CQ* 41:534–538.

———. 2004. *Greek Mythography in the Roman World*. New York: Oxford University Press.

Cameron, Averil, and Stuart G. Hall, trans. and comm. 1999. *Eusebius: Life of Constantine*. Oxford: Clarendon Press.

Campbell, D. A. 1990–1992. *Greek Lyric.* 4 vols. Cambridge: Harvard University Press.

Campbell, Robin N., and Robert Grieve. 1982. "Royal Investigations of the Origin of Language." *Historiographia Linguistica* 9:43–74.

Carey, Sorcha. 2003. *Pliny's Catalogue of Culture: Art and Empire in the* Natural History. Oxford: Oxford University Press.

Carnahan, James R. 1892. *Pythian Knighthood, Its History and Literature; Being an Account of the Origin and Growth of the Order of Knights of Pythias.* 2nd ed. Cincinnati: Pettibone.

Carnes, Pack. 1985. *Fable Scholarship: An Annotated Bibliography*. New York: Garland.

Cashman, Ray. 2008. *Storytelling on the Northern Irish Border: Characters and Community*. Bloomington: Indiana University Press.

Cataudella, Quintino. 1957. *La Novella Greca: Prolegomeni e Testi in Traduzioni Originali*. Naples: Edizioni Scientifiche Italiane.

Champlin, Edward. 2003. *Nero*. Cambridge: Harvard University Press.

Chesters, Timothy. 2011. *Ghost Stories in Late Renaissance France: Walking by Night*. Oxford: Oxford University Press.

Chitwood, Ava. 2004. *Death by Philosophy: The Biographical Tradition in the Life and Death of the Archaic Philosophers Empedocles, Heraclitus, and Democritus*. Ann Arbor: University of Michigan Press.

Christensen, Arthur. 1939. *Moboernes Vise Gerninger*. Copenhagen: Det Schønbergske Forlag.

Christiansen, Reidar. 1958. *The Migratory Legends: A Proposed List of Types with a Systematic Catalogue of the Norwegian Variants. FFC* 175. Helsinki: Academia Scientiarum Fennica.

Chroust, Anton-Hermann. 1971–1980. "Which Came First, the Chicken or the Egg? Censorinus *de Die Natali* IV.3–4, a Fragment of Aristotle's *On Philosophy*." *Classica et Mediaevalia* 32:221–225.

Clarke, John R. 2007. *Looking at Laughter: Humor, Power, and Transgression in Roman Visual Culture, 100 B.C.–A.D. 250*. Berkeley: University of California Press.

Clay, Diskin. 1996. "Picturing Diogenes." In *The Cynics: The Cynic Movement in Antiquity and Its Legacy*, edited by R. Bracht-Branham and Marie-Odile Goulet-Cazé, 366–387. Berkeley: University of California Press.

———. 2004. *Archilochos Heros: The Cult of Poets in the Greek Polis.* Cambridge, MA: Center for Hellenic Studies.

Clouston, W. A. 1887. *Popular Tales and Fictions: Their Migrations and Transformations.* 2 vols. Edinburgh: William Blackwood and Sons.

———. 1888. *The Book of Noodles: Stories of Simpletons; or, Fools and Their Follies*. London: Elliot Stock.

Clover, Carol J. 1986. "Warrior Maidens and Other Sons." *Journal of English and Germanic Philology* 85:35–49.

———. 1993. "Regardless of Sex: Men, Women, and Power in Early Northern Europe." *Speculum* 68:363–387.

Cobet, Justus. 2002. "The Organization of Time in the *Histories*." In *Brill's Companion to Herodotus*, edited by Egbert J. Bakker, I. J. F. de Jong, and H. van Wees, 387–412. Leiden: E. J. Brill.

Collison-Morley, Lacy. 1912. *Greek and Roman Ghost Stories*. Oxford: B. H. Blackwell; London: Simpkin, Marshall.

Commentaria in Aristotelem Graeca. 1882–1909. 23 vols. Berlin: G. Reimer.

Comparetti, D. 1873. "Die Strafe des Tantalus nach Pindar." *Philologus* 32:227–251.

Cooper, Craig. 1995. "Hyperides and the Trial of Phryne." *Phoenix* 49:303–318.

Corpus Inscriptionum Latinarum. 1867 ff. Berlin-Brandenburgische Akademie der Wissenschaften. Berlin.

Corso, Antonio. 2008. "Ancient Greek Sculptors as Magicians." In *Greek Magic: Ancient, Medieval and Modern*, edited by J. C. B. Petropoulos, 21–27. London: Routledge.

Cotter, Wendy. 1999. *Miracles in Greco-Roman Antiquity: A Sourcebook*. London: Routledge.

Courtney, Edward. 2001. *A Companion to Petronius*. Oxford: Oxford University Press.

Cramer, Frederick H. 1945. "Book Burning and Censorship in Ancient Rome: A Chapter from the History of Freedom of Speech." *Journal of the History of Ideas* 6: 157–196.

Crooks, J. 1998. "Socrates' Last Words: Another Look at an Ancient Riddle." *CQ* 48:117–125.

Crowther, Nigel B. 1977. "Weightlifting in Antiquity: Achievement and Training." *Greece & Rome* 24:111–120.

Crusius, Otto. 1879. "De Babrii Aetate." *Leipziger Studien zur Classischen Philologie* 2:125–248.

———. 1882. "Die Tradition vom Tode des Aischylos." *RhM* 37:308–312.

Currie, Bruno. 2002. "Euthymos of Locri: A Case Study in Heroization in the Classical Period." *JHS* 122:24–44.

Currie, Gregory. 2010. *Narratives and Narrators: A Philosophy of Stories*. Oxford: Oxford University Press.

Davidson, James. 1999. *Courtesans and Fishcakes: The Consuming Passions of Classical Athens*. New York: HarperPerennial.

Davison, J. A. 1968. *From Archilochos to Pindar: Papers on Greek Literature of the Archaic Period*. London: MacMillan; New York: St. Martin's Press.

Dégh, Linda. 1969. *Folktales and Society: Story-Telling in a Hungarian Peasant Community*. Translated by Emily M. Schossberger. Bloomington: Indiana University Press.

Dégh, Linda. 1971. "The 'Belief Legend' in Modern Society." In *American Folk Legend: A Symposium*, edited by Wayland D. Hand, 55–68. Berkeley: University of California Press.

———. 1972. "Folk Narrative." In *Folklore and Folklife: An Introduction*, edited by Richard M. Dorson, 53–83. Chicago: University of Chicago Press.

———. 1995. "Manipulation of Personal Experience." In *Narratives in Society: A Performer-Centered Study of Narration*, 70–78. *FFC* 255. Helsinki: Academia Scientiarum Fennica.

———. 1996. "What Is a Belief Legend?" *Folklore* 107:33–46.

———. 2001. *Legend and Belief: Dialectics of a Folklore Genre*. Bloomington: Indiana University Press.

Dégh, Linda, and Andrew Vázsonyi. 1971. "Legend and Belief." *Genre* 4:281–304.

De Lacy, Philip H., and Benedict Einarson, trans. and comm. 1959. *Plutarch: Moralia.* Vol. 7. Cambridge: Harvard University Press.

Detienne, Marcel. 1986. *The Creation of Mythology*. Translated by Margaret Cook. Chicago: University of Chicago Press.

Devereux, George. 1987. "Thamyris and the Muses (an Unrecognized Oedipal Myth)." *American Journal of Philology* 108:199–201.

Dick, Hugh G. 1941. "The Lover in a Cask: A Tale of a Tub." *Italica* 18:12–13.

Dickens, Charles. 2008. *Great Expectations*. Edited by Margaret Cardwell. Introduction and Notes by Robert Douglas-Fairhurst. Oxford: Oxford University Press.

Dickie, Matthew W. 2001. *Magic and Magicians in the Greco-Roman World*. London: Routledge.

Diels, Hermann. 1951–1952. *Die Fragmente der Vorsokratiker: Griechisch und Deutsch.* Edited by Walther Kranz. 6th ed. 3 vols. Berlin: Weidmann.

Dijk, Gert-Jan van. 1997. ΑΙΝΟΙ, ΛΟΓΟΙ, ΜΥΘΟΙ*: Fables in Archaic, Classical, and Hellenistic Literature, with a Study of the Theory and Terminology of the Genre*. Leiden: E. J. Brill.

Dijksterhuis, E. J. 1987. *Archimedes*. Translated by C. Dikshoorn. Princeton: Princeton University Press.

Dill, Ueli, and Christine Walde, eds. 2009. *Antike Mythen: Medien, Transformationen und Konstruktionen*. Berlin: Walter de Gruyter.

Dillon, John M. 2004. *Morality and Custom in Ancient Greece*. Bloomington: Indiana University Press.

Dorson, Richard M. 1946. "Comic Indian Anecdotes." *Southern Folklore Quarterly* 10:113–128.

Drijvers, Jan W. 1992. *Helena Augusta: The Mother of Constantine the Great and the Legend of Her Finding of the True Cross*. Brill's Studies in Intellectual History 27. Leiden: E. J. Brill.

Dubuisson Michel. 1980. "Toi Aussi, Mon Fils!" *Latomus* 39:885–890.

Dumézil, Georges. 1947. *Tarpeia: Essais de Philologie Comparative Indo-Européenne*. 4th ed. Paris: Gallimard.

Dundes, Alan, ed. 1984. *Sacred Narrative: Readings in the Theory of Myth*. Berkeley: University of California Press.

Dundes, Alan, and Carl R. Pagter. 1978. *Work Hard and You Shall Be Rewarded: Urban Folklore from the Paperwork Empire*. Bloomington: Indiana University Press.

Düring, Ingemar. 1957. *Aristotle in the Ancient Biographical Tradition*. Gothenburg: Elanders Boktryckeri.

Durrell, Lawrence. 1975. *Prospero's Cell: A Guide to the Landscape and Manners of the Island of Coryra*. New ed. London: Faber and Faber.

Dzielska, Maria. 1995. *Hypatia of Alexandria*. Translated by F. Lyra. Cambridge: Harvard University Press.

Ebner, Martin, Holger Gzella, Heinz-Günther Nesselrath, and Ernst Ribbat, eds. 2001. *Lukian: Die Lügenfreunde oder: Der Ungläubige*. Stuttgart: Wissenschaftliche Buchgesellschaft.

Edmunds, Lowell, ed. 2014. *Approaches to Greek Myth*. 2nd ed. Baltimore: Johns Hopkins University Press.

———. 2016. *Stealing Helen: The Myth of the Abducted Wife in Comparative Perspective*. Princeton: Princeton University Press.

Edwards, M. J. 2000. "Birth, Death, and Divinity in Porphyry's *Life of Plotinus*." In *Greek Biography and Panegyric in Late Antiquity*, edited by Tomas Hägg and Philip Rousseau, 52–71. Berkeley: University of California Press.

Ellis, Bill. 1983. "De Legendis Urbis: Modern Legends in Ancient Rome." *JAF* 96:200–208.

———. 1991. "Wars and Rumors of War." *FOAFtale News* 22 (June):8.

———. 2001. *Aliens, Ghosts, and Cults: Legends We Live*. Jackson: University Press of Mississippi.

Ellison, Ralph. 1995. *The Collected Essays of Ralph Ellison*, edited by John F. Callahan. New York: Modern Library.

Else, Gerald F. 1963. *Aristotle's Poetics: The Argument*. Cambridge: Harvard University Press.

El-Shamy, Hasan M., ed. and trans. 1980. *Folktales of Egypt*. Chicago: University of Chicago Press.

Emeneau, M. B. 1940. "A Classical Indian Folk-tale as a Reported Modern Event: The Brahman and the Mongoose." *Proceedings of the American Philosophical Society* 83:503–513.

Engels, Johannes. 2010. *Die sieben Weisen: Leben, Lehren und Legenden.* Munich: Verlag C. H. Beck.

Esar, Evan. 1952. *The Humor of Humor: The Art and Techniques of Popular Comedy Illustrated by Comic Sayings, Funny Stories, and Jocular Traditions through the Centuries.* New York: Bramhall House.

Fairweather, Janet. 1973. "The Death of Heraclitus." *GRBS* 14:233–239.

Faraone, Christopher A. 1999. *Ancient Greek Love Magic.* Cambridge: Harvard University Press.

Färber, Hans. 1961. *Hero und Leander: Musaios und die weiteren antiken Zeugnisse Gesammelt und Übersetzt.* Munich: Ernst Heimeran Verlag.

Farrell, Joseph. 1997. "The Phenomenology of Memory in Roman Culture." *CJ* 92:373–383.

Felton, D. 1999. *Haunted Greece and Rome: Ghost Stories from Classical Antiquity.* Austin: University of Texas Press.

Festugière, A. J., trans. and comm. 1970. *Proclus: Commentaire sur la République.* 3 vols. in 2. Paris: J. Vrin.

Finkelberg, Margalit. 2014. "Boreas and Oreithyia: A Case-Study in Multichannel Transmission of Myth." In *Between Orality and Literacy: Communication and Adaptation in Antiquity*, edited by Ruth Scodel, 87–100. Leiden: E. J. Brill.

Flory, Marleen B. 1988. "Pearls for Venus." *Historia* 37:498–504.

Fontenrose, Joseph. 1945. "Philemon, Lot, and Lycaon." *University of California Publications in Classical Philology* 13:93–119.

———. 1951. "White Goddess and Syrian Goddess." *University of California Publications in Semitic Philology* 11:125–148.

———. 1959. *Python: A Study of Delphic Myth and Its Origins.* Berkeley: University of California Press.

———. 1968. "The Hero as Athlete." *California Studies in Classical Antiquity* 1:73–104.

———. 1978. *The Delphic Oracle: Its Responses and Operations, with a Catalogue of Responses.* Berkeley: University of California Press.

———. 1981. *Orion: The Myth of the Hunter and the Huntress.* University of California Publications in Classical Studies 23. Berkeley: University of California Press.

Fortenbaugh, Wm. 1984. *Quellen zur Ethik Theophrasts.* Amsterdam: B. R. Grüner.

———. 1995. "Theophrastus, Source no. 709 FHS & G." In *Greek Literary Theory after Aristotle: A Collection of Papers in Honour of D. M. Schenkeveld*, edited by J. G. J. Abbenes, S. R. Slings, and I. Sluiter, 1–16. Amsterdam: VU University Press.

Fowler, Robert L. 2000. *Early Greek Mythography*. Vol. 1. Oxford: Oxford University Press.

Frazer, J. G. 1888. "The Language of Animals." *Archaeological Review* 1:81–91, 161–181.

———, trans. and comm. 1898. *Pausanias's Description of Greece*. 6 vols. London: MacMillan.

———, trans. and comm. 1921. *Apollodorus: The Library*. 2 vols. London: William Heinemann; Cambridge: Harvard University Press.

Freud, Sigmund. 1960. *Jokes and Their Relation to the Unconscious*. Translated by James Strachey. Vol. 8 of *The Standard Edition of the Complete Psychological Works of Sigmund Freud* (1905). London: Hogarth Press and the Institute of Psycho-Analysis.

Friedländer, Ludwig. 1910. "Das Märchen vom Amor und Psyche und andere Spuren des Volksmärchens im Altertum." In *Darstellungen aus der Sittengeschichte Roms in der Zeit von August bis zum Ausgang der Antonine*. 8th ed. 1:527–569. Leipzig: S. Hirzel.

———. 1913. *Roman Life and Manners under the Early Empire*. Translated by A. B. Gough. 4 vols. London: George Routledge; New York: E. P. Dutton.

Friedrich, Hans-Veit, ed. 1968. *Thessalos von Tralles: Griechisch und Lateinisch*. Beiträge zur Klassischen Philologie 28. Meisenheim am Glan: Verlag Anton Hain.

Fries, Carolus (Carl). 1915. "De Androcli Leone." *Wochenschrift für klassische Philologie* 48:1150–1151.

———. 1939. "Buddha und Kineas." *Zeitschrift der deutschen morganländischen Gesellschaft* 93:73–74.

Frost, Frank J. 1979. "The Dubious Origins of the 'Marathon.'" *American Journal of Ancient History* 4:159–163.

Fulk, R. D. 2002. "Myth in Historical Perspective: The Case of Pagan Deities in the Anglo-Saxon Royal Genealogies." In Schrempp and Hansen, 225–239.

Gantz, Timothy. 1993. *Early Greek Myth: A Guide to Literary and Artistic Sources*. Baltimore: Johns Hopkins University Press.

Gemoll, Wilhelm. 1924. *Das Apophthegma: Literarhistorische Studien*. Vienna: Hölder-Pichler-Tempsky A. G.; Leipzig: G. Freytag G.M.B.H.

Georgakopoulou, Alexandra. 1997. *Narrative Performances: A Study of Modern Greek Storytelling*. Amsterdam: John Benjamins.

Gerber, Douglas E. 1988. "The Measure of Bacchus." *Mnemosyne* 41:39–45.

———, ed. and trans. 1999a. *Greek Elegiac Poetry from the Seventh to the Fifth Centuries BC*. Cambridge: Harvard University Press.

———, ed. and trans. 1999b. *Greek Iambic Poetry from the Seventh to the Fifth Centuries BC*. Cambridge: Harvard University Press.

Giannantoni, Gabriele, ed. and comm. 1990. *Socratis et Socraticorum Reliquiae*. 4 vols. Naples: Bibliopolis.

Gigon, Olof. 1946. "Antike Erzählungen über die Berufung zur Philosophie." *Museum Helveticum* 3:1–21.

Glassie, Henry. 1964. "A Choctaw 'Me All Face' Story." *JAF* 77:258.

———. 1982. *Passing the Time in Ballymenone: Culture and History in an Ulster Community*. Philadelphia: University of Pennsylvania Press.

Gnilka, Christian. 1979. "Ultima Verba." *Jahrbuch für Antike und Christentum* 22:5–21.

Golden, Mark. 2004. *Sport in the Ancient World from A to Z*. London: Routledge.

Goldhill, Simon. 2009. "The Anecdote: Exploring the Boundaries between Oral and Literate Performance in the Second Sophistic." In *Ancient Literacies: The Culture of Reading in Greece and Rome*, edited by W. A. Johnson and H. N. Parker, 96–113. Oxford: Oxford University Press.

Goldstein, Diane E., Sylvia Ann Grider, and Jeannie Banks Thomas. 2007. *Haunting Experiences: Ghosts in Contemporary Folklore*. Logan: Utah State University Press.

Gombel, Heinrich. 1934. *Die Fabel "vom Magen und den Gliedern" in der Weltliteratur (mit besonderer Berücksichtigung der romanischen Fabelliteratur)*. Beihefte zur Zeitschrift für romanische Philologie 80. Halle: M. Niemeyer.

Gorman, Robert J., and Vanessa B. Gorman. 2007. "The *Tryphe* of the Sybarites: A Historiographical Problem in Athenaeus." *JHS* 127:38–60.

———. 2014. *Corrupting Luxury in Ancient Greek Literature*. Ann Arbor: University of Michigan Press.

Gostoli, Antonietta. 2007. *Omero: Margite: Introduzione, Testimonianze, Testo Critico, Traduzione e Commento*. Pisa: Fabrizio Serra Editore.

Gow, A. S. F. 1931. "*Metra Thalasses.*" *CR* 45:10–12.

———. 1965. *Machon: The Fragments*. Cambridge: Cambridge University Press.

Graf, Fritz. 1993. *Greek Mythology: An Introduction*. Translated by Thomas Marier. Baltimore: Johns Hopkins University Press.

———. 1997. "Cicero, Plautus, and Roman Laughter." In Bremmer and Roodenburg, 29–39.

Grant, Michael. 1962. *Myths of the Greeks and Romans*. New York: Mentor.

Gray, V. J. 1986. "Xenophon's *Hiero* and the Meeting of the Wise Man and Tyrant in Greek Literature." *CQ* 36:115–123.

Green, A. E. 1980. "Some Thoughts on Threatening Children." In *Folklore Studies in Honour of Herbert Halpert: A Festschrift*, edited by Kenneth S. Goldstein and Neil V. Rosenberg, 187–210. St. Johns: Memorial University of Newfoundland.

Gregory, T. E. 1983. "Julian and the Last Oracle at Delphi." *GRBS* 24:355–366.

Grider, Silvia Ann. 2007. "Haunted Houses." In Goldstein et al., 143–170.

Grimm, Brothers. 1981. *The German Legends of the Brothers Grimm*. Edited and translated by Donald Ward. 2 vols. Philadelphia: Institute for the Study of Human Issues.

———. 1985. *Die Kinder- und Hausmärchen der Brüder Grimm. Urfassung 1812/1814*. Lindau: AntiquaVerlag.

———. 2014. *The Original Folk and Fairy Tales of the Brothers Grimm: The Complete First Edition*. Translated and edited by Jack Zipes. Princeton: Princeton University Press.

Grossardt, Peter. 2006. *Einführung, Übersetzung und Kommentar zum* Heroikos *von Flavius Philostrat*. Schweizerische Beiträge zum Altertumswissenschaft 33. 2 vols. Basel: Schwabe Verlag.

———. 2012. *Stesichoros zwischen kultischer Praxis, mythischer Tradition und eigenem Kunstanspruch: Zur Behandlung des Helenamythos im Werk des Dichters aus Himera*. Leipziger Studien zur Klassischen Philologie 9. Tübingen: Narr Verlag.

Guthke, Karl S. 1992. *Last Words: Variations on a Theme in Cultural History*. Princeton: Princeton University Press.

Gyles, Mary Francis. 1947. "Nero Fiddled While Rome Burned." *CJ* 2:211–217.

Hadjicosti, Ioanna L. 2005. "Death by a Turtle: The Route of a Motif from *Telegonia* to the *Vita* of Aeschylus." *Eranos* 103:78–82.

Hale, David G. 1968. "Intestine Sedition: The Fable of the Belly." *Comparative Literature Studies* 5:377–388.

Halliday, William Reginald. 1963 [1927]. *Greek and Roman Folklore*. New York: Cooper Square Publishers.

Halliwell, Stephen. 2008. *Greek Laughter: A Study of Cultural Psychology from Homer to Early Christianity*. Cambridge: Cambridge University Press.

Hammond, Mason. 1979–1980. "A Famous Exemplum of Spartan Toughness." *CJ* 75:97–109.

Hancock, Cecily. 1963. "The 'Me All Face' Story: European Literary Background of an American Comic Indian Anecdote." *JAF* 76:340–342.

Haney, Jack V. 1999. *An Introduction to the Russian Folktale*. Armonk, NY: M. E. Sharp.

Hansen, William. 1977. "An Oral Source for the *Menaechmi*." *Classical World* 70:385–390.

———. 1980. "An Ancient Greek Ghost Story." In *Folklore on Two Continents: Essays in Honor of Linda Dégh*, edited by Nikolai Burlakoff and Carl Lindahl, 71–77. Bloomington: Trickster Press.

———. 1982. "The Applied Message in Storytelling." In *Folklorica: Festschrift for Felix J. Oinas*, edited by Egle Victoria Žygas and Peter Voorheis, 99–109. Indiana University Uralic and Altaic Series 141. Bloomington: Research Institute for Inner Asian Studies, 1982.

———. 1983. "Greek Mythology and the Study of the Ancient Greek Oral Story." *Journal of Folklore Research* 20:101–112.

———. 1989. "Contextualizing the Story of Philinnion." *Midwestern Folklore* 15:101–108.

———. 1995. "The Stuck Couple in Ancient Greece." *FOAFtale News* 36 (January):2–3.

———. 1996. *Phlegon of Tralles' Book of Marvels*. Exeter: University of Exeter Press.

———. 1997. "Idealization as a Process in Ancient Greek Story-Formation." *Symbolae Osloenses* 72:118–123.

———, ed. 1998. *Anthology of Ancient Greek Popular Literature*. Bloomington: Indiana University Press.

———. 1999. "Poetic Justice: The Murder of Mitys of Argos." *FOAFtale News* 45 (May):4.

———. 2001. "The Seer and the Computer: On *Philogelos* and Modern Jokes." *Classical Bulletin* 77:87–102.

———. 2002a. *Ariadne's Thread: A Guide to International Tales Found in Classical Literature*. Ithaca: Cornell University Press.

———. 2002b. "Meanings and Boundaries: Reflections on Thompson's 'Myths and Folktales.'" In Schrempp and Hansen, 19–28.

———. 2003. "Strategies of Authentication in Ancient Popular Literature." In *The Ancient Novel and Beyond*, edited by Stelios Panayotakis, Maaike Zimmerman, and Wytse Keulen, 301–314. Leiden: E. J. Brill.

———. 2004. "Reading Embedded Narration." In *Myth and Symbol II: Symbolic Phenomena in Ancient Greek Culture*, edited by Synnøve des Bouvrie, 111–121. Papers from the Norwegian Institute at Athens 7. Bergen: Norwegian Institute at Athens.

———. 2005. *Classical Mythology: A Guide to the Mythical World of the Greeks and Romans*. Oxford: Oxford University Press.

———. 2008. "Classical Antiquity." In *The Greenwood Encyclopedia of Folktales and Fairy Tales*, edited by Donald Haase, 1:211–215. Westport, CT: Greenwood Press, 2008.

———. 2010. "King Kroisos Questions Apollon." *Fabula* 51:178–186.

———. 2013. "Packaging Greek Mythology." In *Writing Down the Myths*, edited by Joseph Falaky Nagy, 19–43. Turnhout: Brepols.

———. 2014. "Mythic Gaps." In *Festskrift Synnøve des Bouvrie/Liber Festivus Sunnivae des Bouvrie*. Special issue of *Nordlit: Tidsskrift i Litteratur og Kultur* 33:65–75.

Hard, Robin, trans. and comm. 2012. *Diogenes the Cynic: Sayings and Anecdotes with Other Popular Moralities*. Oxford: Oxford University Press.

Harkort, Fritz. 1956. "Die Schein- und Schattenbußen im Erzählgut." Unpublished dissertation, Kiel.

Harrison, S. J. 1998. "The Milesian Tales and the Roman Novel." *Groningen Colloquia on the Novel* 9:61–73.

Hartland, E. Sidney. 1892. "Report on Folk-Tale Research." *Folklore* 3:111–129.

Hausrath, August, ed. 1959–1970. *Corpus Fabularum Aesopicarum*. 2nd ed. Edited by Herbert Hunger. Leipzig: B. G. Teubner.

Hausrath, August, and August Marx, eds. and trans. 1922 [1913]. *Griechische Märchen, Fabeln, Schwänke, und Novellen aus dem klassischen Altertum*. 2nd ed. Jena: Eugen Diederichs Verlag.

Havelock, Christine Mitchell. 1995. *The Aphrodite of Knidos and Her Successors: A Historical Review of the Female Nude in Greek Art*. Ann Arbor: University of Michigan Press.

Hawes, Greta. 2014. *Rationalizing Myth in Antiquity*. Oxford: Oxford University Press.

Healy, John F. 1999. *Pliny the Elder on Science and Technology*. Oxford: Oxford University Press.

Henderson, Jeffrey, ed. and comm. 1987. *Aristophanes: Lysistrata*. Oxford: Clarendon Press.

Henningsen, Gustav. 1965. "The Art of Perpendicular Lying: Concerning a Commercial Collection of Norwegian Sailors' Tall Tales." *Journal of the Folklore Institute* 2:180–219.

Henrichs, Albert. 2003. "*Hieroi Logoi* and *Hierai Bibloi*: The (Un)Written Margins of the Sacred in Ancient Greece." *HSCP* 101:207–266.

Henssen, Gottfried. 1953. "Deutsche Schreckmärchen und ihre europäischen Anverwandten." *Zeitschrift für Volkskunde* 51:84–97.

Herrin, Judith. 2013. "Book Burning as Purification in Early Byzantium." In *Margins and Metropolis: Authority across the Byzantine Empire*, 335–356. Princeton: Princeton University Press.

Higbie, Carolyn. 2003. *The Lindian Chronicle and the Greek Creation of Their Past*. Oxford: Oxford University Press.

Higham, T. F. 1960. "Nature Note: Dolphin-Riders. Ancient Stories Vindicated." *Greece & Rome* 7:82–86.

Hock, Ronald F., and Edward N. O'Neil. 1986. *The Chreia in Ancient Rhetoric*. Vol. 1, *The* Progymnasmata. Atlanta: Scholars Press.

———, trans. and eds. 2002. *The Chreia and Ancient Rhetoric*. Vol. 2, *Classroom Exercises*. Atlanta: Society of Biblical Literature.

Holbek, Bengt. 1985. "Parallelen zur Rattenfängersage in der dänischen Volksüberlieferung." In *Geschichten und Geschichte: Erzählforschertagung in Hameln, Oktober 1984*, edited by Norbert Humburg, 129–134. Hildesheim: Lax.

———. 1987. *Interpretation of Fairy Tales: Danish Folklore in a European Perspective*. *FFC* 239. Helsinki: Academia Scientiarum Fennica.

———. 1991. "On the Borderline between Legend and Tale: The Story of the Old Hoburg Man in Danish Folklore." *Arv* 47:179–191.

Holtzmann, Oscar, trans. and ed. 1912. *Der Tosephtatraktat Berakot: Text, Übersetzung, und Erklärung.* Giessen: A. Töpelmann.

Holzberg, Niklas. 2002. *The Ancient Fable: An Introduction*. Translated by Christine Jackson-Holzberg. Bloomington: Indiana University Press.

Honigman, Sylvie. 2003. *The Septuagint and Homeric Scholarship in Alexandria: A Study in the Narrative of the* Letter of Aristeas. London: Routledge.

Honko, Lauri. 1964. "Memorates and the Study of Folk Belief." *Journal of the Folklore Institute* 1:5–19.

———. 2014 [1989]. "Folkloristic Theories of Genre." In *Theoretical Milestones: Selected Writings of Lauri Honko*, edited by Pekka Hakamies and Anneli Honko, 55–77. *FFC* 304. Helsinki: Academia Scientiarum Fennica.

Hopkins, Keith. 1993. "Novel Evidence for Slavery." *Past and Present* 138:3–27.

How, W. W., and J. Wells. 1928 [1912]. *A Commentary on Herodotus*. 2 vols. Oxford: Clarendon Press.

Hunter, R.C. 1983. *Eubulus: The Fragments.* Cambridge: Cambridge University Press.

Hyman, Ray. 1996. "'Cold Reading': How to Convince Strangers That You Know All about Them." In *The Outer Edge: Classic Investigations of the Paranormal*, edited by Joe Nickell, Barry Karr, and Tom Genoni, 70–84. Amherst, NY: Committee for the Scientific Investigation of Claims of the Paranormal.

Imellos, Stephanos D. 1971–1974. "Neugriechische und antike Erzählungen über den Betrug von Feinden durch eine List." *Byzantinisch-Neugriechische Jahrbücher* 21:1–9.

Ingemark, Camilla Asplund. 2008. "The Octopus in the Sewers: An Ancient Legend Analogue." *Journal of Folklore Research* 45:145–170.

Ingemark, Camilla Asplund, and Dominic Ingemark. 2004. *Sagor och Svartkonst under Antiken.* Lund: Historiska Media.

Inscriptiones Graecae. 1873 ff. Berlin-Brandenburgische Akademie der Wissenschaften. Berlin.

Isager, Jacob. 1991. *Pliny on Art and Society: The Elder Pliny's Chapters on the History of Art.* London: Routledge.

Jacobs, Joseph. 1892. *Celtic Fairy Tales.* London: David Nutt.

Jacobsen, Eric. 1952. "The Fable Is Inverted, or Donne's Aesop." *Classica et Mediaevalia* 13:1–37.

Jacoby, Felix, ed. 1923–1958. *Die Fragmente der griechischen Historiker.* Berlin: Weidmann; Leiden: E. J. Brill.

Jaeger, Mary. 2008. *Archimedes and the Roman Imagination.* Ann Arbor: University of Michigan Press.

James, M. R. 1892. "The Sibyl in Petronius." *CR* 6:74.

Jason, Heda, and Aharon Kempinski. 1981. "How Old Are Folktales?" *Fabula* 22:1–27.

Jauhiainen, Marjatta. 1998. *The Type and Motif Index of Finnish Belief Legends and Memorates. FFC* 267. Helsinki: Academia Scientiarum Fennica.

Jedrkiewicz, Stefano. 1989. *Sapere e Paradosso nell'Antichità: Esopo e la Favola.* Rome: Edizioni dell'Ateneo.

———. 2000. "Savant et *Trickster*: Thalès Devant les Pyramides." *Lexis* 18:77–91.

Jensen, Brian Møller. 2004. "*Societas Leonina* or the Lion's Share: An Analysis of *Aesopica* 149, Phaedrus 1.5, and Babrius 1.67." *Eranos* 102:97–104.

Jensen, Kr. Sandfeld. 1896–1898. "Himmelbreve." *Dania* 3:193–228.

Johnston, Sarah Iles. 1995. "Defining the Dreadful: Remarks on the Greek Child-Killing Demon." In *Ancient Magic and Ritual Power*, edited by Marvin Mayer and Paul Mirecki, 361–387. Leiden: E. J. Brill.

———. 1999. *Restless Dead: Encounters between the Living and the Dead in Ancient Greece.* Berkeley: University of California Press.

Joshel, Sandra R. 2010. *Slavery in the Roman World.* Cambridge: Cambridge University Press.

Kakridis, Johannes Theoph. 1967. *Die alte Hellenen im neugreichischen Volksglauben*. Munich: Ernst Heimeran Verlag.

Karadagli, Triantaphyllia. 1981. *Fabel und Ainos: Studien zur Griechischen Fabel.* Beiträge zur Klassischen Philologie 135. Königstein: Verlag Anton Hain.

Kassel, Rudolf. 1956. "Reste eines hellenistischen Spassmacherbuches auf einem Heidelberger Papyrus?" *RhM* 99:242–245.

Kennedy, George, trans. and comm. 1991. *Aristotle* On Rhetoric*: A Theory of Civic Discourse*. New York: Oxford University Press.

Kenner, Hedwig. 1970. *Das Phänomen der verkehrten Welt in der griechisch-römischen Antike*. Klagenfurt: Ernst Ploetz.

Ker, James. 2009. *The Deaths of Seneca*. Oxford: Oxford University Press.

Kindt, Julia. 2012. *Rethinking Greek Religion*. Cambridge: Cambridge University Press.

King, Ross. 2003. *Michelangelo and the Pope's Ceiling*. New York: Walker.

Kirk, G. S., and J. E. Raven. 1957. *The Presocratic Philosophers: A Critical History with a Selection of Texts*. Cambridge: Cambridge University Press.

Kitchell, Kenneth F., Jr. 2014. *Animals in the Ancient World from A to Z*. London: Routledge.

Kivilo, Maarit. 2010. *Early Greek Poets' Lives: The Shaping of the Tradition. Mnemosyne*, Supplement 322. Leiden: E. J. Brill.

Kleingünther, A. 1933. *Protos Heuretes: Untersuchungen zur Geschichte einer Fragestellung. Philologus*, Supplement 26. Leipzig.

Klintberg, Bengt af. 1989. "Legends Today." In *Nordic Folklore: Recent Studies*, edited by Reimund Kvideland and Henning K. Sehmsdorf, 70–89. Bloomington: Indiana University Press.

———. 1990. "Do the Legends of Today and Yesterday Belong to the Same Genre?" In *Storytelling in Contemporary Societies*, edited by Lutz Röhrich and Sabine Wienker-Piepho, 113–123. Tübingen: Gunter Narr Verlag.

———. 1999. *Råttan I Pizzan: Folksägner i Vår Tid*. Stockholm: Norstedts Förlag.

———. 2010. *The Types of the Swedish Folk Legend. FFC* 300. Helsinki: Academia Scientiarum Fennica.

Konstantakos, Ioannis. 2006. "Aesop Adulterer and Trickster: A Study of the *Vita Aesopi* ch. 75–76." *Athenaeum* 94:563–600.

———. 2009. "Cuckoo's Fruit: Erotic Imagery in *Vita Aesopi* ch. 75–76." In Αντιφίλησις*: Studies on Classical, Byzantine, and Modern Greek Literature and Culture in Honour of John-Theophanes A. Papademetriou*, edited by Eleni Karamalengou and Eugenia Makrygianni, 453–460. Stuttgart: Franz Steiner Verlag.

———. 2010. "Aesop and Riddles." *Lexis* 28:257–290.

Kostuch, Lucyna. 2009. "Cleopatra's Snake or Octavian's? The Role of the Cobra in the Triumph over the Egyptian Queen." *Klio* 91:115–124.

Krappe, Alexander H. 1927. "Tiberius and Thrasyllus." *American Journal of Philology* 48:359–366.

———. 1929. "Die Sage von der Tarpeja." *RhM* 78:248–267.

———. 1946. "Seleukos and Kombabos." *Byzantina-Metabyzantina* 1:189–199.

Kristensen, Evald Tang. 1892–1901. *Danske Sagn som De Har Lydt i Folkemunde*. 6 vols. Århus and Silkeborg: Århus Folkeblads Trykkeri; Jacob Zeuners Bogtrykkeri; Silkeborg Ny Bogtrykkeri.

Künzig, Johannes. 1934. "Der im Fischbauch Wiedergefundene Ring in Sage, Legende, Märchen und Lied." In *Volkskundliche Gaben John Meier zum Siebzigsten Geburtstage Dargebracht*, 85–103. Berlin: Walter de Gruyter.

Kurke, Leslie. 2011. *Aesopic Conversations: Popular Tradition, Cultural Dialogue, and the Invention of Greek Prose*. Princeton: Princeton University Press.

Labov, William, and Joshua Waletsky. 1967. "Narrative Analysis: Oral Versions of Personal Experience." In *Essays on the Verbal and Visual Arts: Proceedings of the 1966 Annual Spring Meeting of the American Ethnological Society*, edited by June Helm, 12–44. Seattle: American Ethnological Society, distributed by the University of Washington Press.

Lamberton, Robert. 1986. *Homer the Theologian: Neoplatonist Allegorical Reading and the Growth of the Epic Tradition*. Berkeley: University of California Press.

Lambertz, M. 1922. *Vom goldenen Horn: Griechische Märchen aus dem Mittelalter*. Leipzig: Verlag der Wiener Graphischen Werkstätte.

Lang, Mabel L. 1990. *Ostraka*. Vol. 25 of *The Athenian Agora*. Princeton: American School of Classical Studies at Athens.

Larson, Jennifer. 2001. *Greek Nymphs: Myth, Cult, Lore*. Oxford: Oxford University Press.

Lassen, Henrik R. 1995. "'The Improved Product': A Philological Investigation of a Contemporary Legend." *Contemporary Legend* 5:1–37.

———. 2001. "A Regenerative Approach to Oral Traditions of the Past? Modern Contemporary Legends and Their Medieval and Ancient Counterparts." In *Inclinate Aurem: Oral Perspectives on Early European Verbal Culture*, edited by Jan Helldén, Minna Skafte Jensen, and Thomas Pettitt, 255–280. Odense: Odense University Press.

Lateiner, Donald. 1993. "The Perception of Deception and Gullibility in Specialists of the Supernatural (Primarily) in Athenian Literature." In *Nomodeiktes: Greek Studies in Honor of Martin Oswald*, edited by Ralph M.

Rosen and Joseph Farrell, 179–195. Ann Arbor: University of Michigan Press.

Lattimore, Richmond. 1962. *Themes in Greek and Latin Epitaphs*. Urbana: University of Illinois Press.

Lee, A. C. 1972 [1909]. *The Decameron: Its Sources and Analogues*. New York: Haskell House.

Lefèvre, Eckard. 1997. "Der Ephebe von Pergamon (Petron c. 85-87)." In *Der antike Roman und seine mittelalterliche Rezeption*, edited by Michelangelo Picone and Bernhard Zimmermann, 129–135. Basel: Birkhäuser Verlag.

Lefkowitz, Mary. 1981. *The Lives of the Greek Poets*. London: Duckworth.

Legman, G. 1975. *Rationale of the Dirty Joke: An Analysis of Sexual Humor*. 2nd series. New York: Breaking Point.

Lerner, Ben. 2016. "The Custodians: How the Whitney Is Transforming the Art of Museum Conservation." *The New Yorker* (January 11):50–59.

Levine, Daniel B. 2002–2003. "Poetic Justice: Homer's Death in the Ancient Biographical Tradition." *CJ* 98:141–160.

LiDonnici, Lynn R. 1995. *The Epidaurian Miracle Inscriptions: Text, Translation, and Commentary*. Atlanta: Scholars Press.

Liebrecht, Felix. 1876. "Zum Pantschatantra." *Jahrbuch für romanische und englische Literatur* 3:146–162.

———. 1879. "Zu den Avadânas." In *Zur Volkskunde: Alte und Neue Aufsätze*, 109–121. Heilbronn: Verlag von Gebr. Henninger.

Lightfoot, J. L., ed. and comm. 1999. *Parthenius of Nicaea: The Poetical Fragments and the* Ἐρωτικὰ Παθήματα. Oxford: Clarendon Press.

———, ed. and comm. 2003. *Lucian: On the Syrian Goddess*. Oxford: Oxford University Press.

Lincoln, Bruce. 1999. *Theorizing Myth: Narrative, Ideology, and Scholarship*. Chicago: University of Chicago Press.

Lindahl, Carl, ed. 2004. *American Folktales from the Collections of the Library of Congress*. 2 vols. Armonk, NY: M. E. Sharpe.

Lindow, John. 2010. "Cats and Dogs, Trolls and Devils: At Home in Some Migratory Legend Types." *Western Folklore* 69:163–179.

Lloyd, Alan B. 1975–1988. *Herodotus: Book II*. 3 vols. Leiden: E. J. Brill.

Lloyd-Jones, Hugh. 1975. *Females of the Species: Semonides on Women*. London: Duckworth.

Loiperdinger, Martin. 2004. "Lumière's Arrival of the Train: Cinema's Founding Myth." *Moving Image* 4:89–118.

Longo, Vincenzo. 1969. *Aretalogie nel Mondo Greco*. Vol. 1. Genoa: Istituto di Filologia Classica e Medioevale.

Loomis, C. Grant. 1941. "The Ring of Polycrates in the Legends of the Saints." *JAF* 54:44–47.

Lucas, Hans. 1903. "Ein Märchen bei Petron." In *Beiträge zur Alten Geschichte und Griechisch-Römischen Alterthumskunde. Festschrift zu Otto Hirschfelds Sechzigstem Geburtstage*, 257–269. Berlin: Weidmannsche Buchhandlung.

Luppe, Wolfgang. 2006. "Sex mit einem Esel." *Zeitschrift für Papyrologie und Epigraphik* 158:93–94.

Lüthi, Max. 1975. *Volksmärchen und Volkssage: Zwei Grundformen Erzählender Dichtung.* 3rd ed. Bern: Francke Verlag.

———. 1986. *The European Folktale: Form and Nature*, translated by John D. Niles. Bloomington: Indiana University Press.

MacDonald, Dennis Ronald. 1983. *The Legend and the Apostle: The Battle for Paul in Story and Canon.* Philadelphia: Westminster Press.

MacDonald, Jeffery L., and Margaret Willson. 1986. "The Near-Death Experience." *International Folklore Review* 4:68–73.

Maor, Eli. 2007. *The Pythagorean Theorem: A 4,000-Year History*. Princeton: Princeton University Press.

Marcovich, M. 1976. "Aelian, *Varia Historia* 13.15." *Živa Antika* 26:49–51.

Markopoulos, A. 1985. "Kedrenos, Pseudo-Symeon, and the Last Oracle at Delphi." *GRBS* 26:207–210.

Martha, Jules. 1885. *Manuel d'Archéologique Étrusque et Romaine.* Paris: A. Quantin.

Martin, Richard P. 1998. "The Seven Sages as Performers of Wisdom." In *Cultural Poetics in Archaic Greece: Cult, Performance, Politics*, edited by Carol Dougherty and Leslie Kurke, 108–128. New York: Oxford University Press.

Marx, August. 1889. *Griechische Märchen von dankbaren Tieren und Verwandtes.* Stuttgart: W. Kohlhammer.

Marzolph, Ulrich. 1992. *Arabia Ridens: Die humoristische Kurzprosa der frühen adab-Literatur im internationalen Traditionsgeflecht.* 2 vols. Frankfurt am Main: Vittorio Klostermann.

Maspero, Gaston. 1879. "Fragment d'une Version Égyptienne de la Fable des Membres et d'Estomac." In *Études Égyptiennes: Romans et Poesies du Papyrus Harris No. 500 Conservé au British Museum*, 260–264. Paris: Imprimerie Nationale.

Matthews, Victor J. 1974. "The *Hemerodromoi*: Ultra Long-Distance Running in Antiquity." *Classical World* 68:161–169.

Mayor, Adrienne. 1991. "Home in a Body Bag: Classical Parallels for a Persian Gulf Rumor." *FOAFtale News* 24 (December):5.

———. 1992. "Ambiguous Guardians: The 'Omen of the Wolves' (A.D. 402) and the 'Choking Doberman' (1980s)." *Journal of Folklore Research* 29:253–268.

Mayor, Adrienne. 1994. "Libation Titillation: Wine Goblets and Women's Breasts." *Studies in Popular Culture* 16:61–71.

———. 1995. "The Nessus Shirt in the New World: Smallpox Blankets in History and Legend." *JAF* 108:54–77.

———. 2000. *The First Fossil Hunters: Paleontology in Greek and Roman Times.* Princeton: Princeton University Press.

———. 2003. *Greek Fire, Poison Arrows, and Scorpion Bombs: Biological and Chemical Warfare in the Ancient World.* Woodstock, NY: Duckworth Overlook.

———. 2010. *The Poison King: The Life and Legend of Mithradates, Rome's Deadliest Enemy*. Princeton: Princeton University Press.

McClure, Laura I. 2003. *Courtesans at Table: Gender and Greek Literary Culture in Athenaeus.* New York: Routledge.

McDermott, William C. 1938. *The Ape in Antiquity*. Baltimore: Johns Hopkins University Press.

Meeks, Wayne. 1974. "The Image of the *Androgyne*: Some Uses of a Symbol in Earliest Christianity." *History of Religions* 13:165–208.

Megas, Georgios A., ed. 1970. *Folktales of Greece*, translated by Helen Colaclides. Chicago: University of Chicago Press.

Merkelbach, R., and M. L. West, eds. 1967. *Fragmenta Hesiodea.* Oxford: Clarendon Press.

Merlan, Philip. 1953. "Plotinus and Magic." *Isis* 44:341–348.

Mesk, J. 1913. "Antiochus und Stratonike." *RhM* 68:366–394.

Meuli, Karl. 1954. "Herkunft und Wesen der Fabel." *Schweizerisches Archiv für Volkskunde* 50:65–88.

Mieder, Wolfgang, Stewart A. Kingsbury, and Kelsie B. Harder, eds. 1992. *A Dictionary of American Proverbs*. New York: Oxford University Press.

Migne, J.-P., ed. 1844–1845. *Patrologia Latina.* Paris.

———, ed. 1857–1858. *Patrologia Graeca.* Paris.

Miller, Jane M. 1988. "Some Versions of Pygmalion." In *Ovid Renewed*, edited by Charles Martindale, 205–214. Cambridge: Cambridge University Press.

Miller, Stephen G. 2004. *Arete: Greek Sports from Ancient Sources.* 3rd ed. Berkeley: University of California Press.

Minchin, Elizabeth. 2001. *Homer and the Resources of Memory: Some Applications of Cognitive Theory to the* Iliad *and the* Odyssey. Oxford: Oxford University Press.

Mongold, Roger. 1999. "Poetic Justice: Cactus Murder." *FOAFtale News* 44 (May):11.

Mosshammer, Alden A. 1981. "Thales' Eclipse." *TAPA* 111:145–155.

Moyer, Ian S. 2011. *Egypt and the Limits of Hellenism*. Cambridge: Cambridge University Press.

Mullen, Patrick B. 1978. *I Heard the Old Fishermen Say: Folklore of the Texas Gulf Coast*. Austin: University of Texas Press.

Müller, Carl Werner. 1992. "Die Legende von der Erwählung des Dichters Archilochos." *Fabula* 33:102–107.

Mundo, R. Di. 1986. "La Novella dell'Efebo di Pergamo: Struttura del Racconto." *Materiali e Contributi* 4:83–94.

Nagy, Gregory. 1990. *Pindar's Homer: The Lyric Possession of an Epic Past*. Baltimore: Johns Hopkins University Press.

Németh, György. 1997. "Love of Statues." *Hungarian Polis Studies* 2:115–139.

Nestle, Wilhelm. 1898. "Die Legende vom Tode des Euripides." *Philologus* 57:134–149.

———. 1927. "Die Fabel des Menenius Agrippa." *Klio* 21:350–360.

Nicastro, Nicholas. 2008. *Circumference: Eratosthenes and the Ancient Quest to Measure the Globe*. New York: St. Martin's Press.

Nicolson, Frank W. 1891. "Greek and Roman Barbers." *HSCP* 2:41–56.

Ogden, Daniel. 2002. *Magic, Witchcraft, and Ghosts in the Greek and Roman Worlds: A Sourcebook*. Oxford: Oxford University Press.

———. 2007. *In Search of the Sorcerer's Apprentice: The Traditional Tales of Lucian's* Lover of Lies. Swansea: Classical Press of Wales.

Oldfather, C. H., trans. and comm. 1933. *Diodorus of Sicily*. Vol. 1. Cambridge: Harvard University Press.

Olrik, Axel. 1922. *Ragnarök: Die Sage vom Weltuntergang*, translated by Wilhelm Ranisch. Berlin: Walter de Gruyter.

Oring, Elliott. 1992. *Jokes and Their Relations*. Lexington: University Press of Kentucky.

———. 2003. *Engaging Humor*. Urbana: University of Illinois Press.

———. 2008. "Legendry and the Rhetoric of Truth." *JAF* 121:127–166.

Orofino, Giacomella. 2011. "The Long Voyage of a Trickster Story from Ancient Greece to Tibet." *Aion* 33:101–115.

Orso, Ethelyn G. 1979. *Modern Greek Humor: A Collection of Jokes and Ribald Tales*. Bloomington: Indiana University Press.

Osborne, Robert E. 1966. "Paul and the Wild Beasts." *Journal of Biblical Literature* 85:225–230.

O'Sullivan, Neil. 1995. "Pericles and Protagoras." *Greece & Rome* 42:15–23.

Otto, August. 1890. *Die Sprichwörter und Sprichwörtlichen Redensarten der Römer*. Leipzig: B. G. Teubner.

The Oxyrhynchus Papyri. 1898 ff. Egypt Exploration Fund: Graeco-Roman Branch. London.

Pack, Roger. 1956. "The Sibyl in a Lamp." *TAPA* 87:190–191.

Page, D. L., ed. 1962. *Poetae Melici Graeci*. Oxford: Clarendon Press.

Pàmias, Jordi. 2014. "The Reception of Greek Myth." In Edmunds, 44–83.

Panati, Charles. 1987. *Extraordinary Origins of Everyday Things*. New York: Harper & Row.

Parker, Robert. 1983. *Miasma: Pollution and Purification in Early Greek Religion*. Oxford: Clarendon Press.

Patera, Maria. 2014. *Figures Grecques de l'Épouvante de l'Antiquité au Présent: Peurs Enfantines et Adultes*. *Mnemosyne*, Supplement 376. Leiden: E. J. Brill.

Pauly, A., G. Wissowa, and W. Kroll, eds. 1893–1980. *Realencyclopädie der klassischen Altertumswissenschaft*. 24 vols. Stuttgart.

Peil, Dietmar. 1985. *Der Streit der Glieder mit dem Magen: Studien zur Überlieferungs- und Deutungsgeschichte der Fabel des Menenius Agrippa von der Antike bis ins 20. Jahrhundert*. Mikrokosmos 16. Frankfurt am Main: P. Lang.

Pelling, C. B. R., ed. 1988. *Plutarch: Life of Antony*. Cambridge: Cambridge University Press.

Pellizer, Ezio. 1993. "Periandro di Corinto e il Forno Freddo." In *Tradizione e Innovazione nella Cultura Greca da Omero all'Età Ellenistica: Scritti in Onore de Bruno Gentili, a cura di Roberto Pretagostini*, 2:801–811. Rome: Gruppo Editoriale Internazionale.

Perry, Ben E. 1940. "The Origin of the Epimythium." *TAPA* 71:391–419.

———. 1952. *Aesopica: A Series of Texts Relating to Aesop or Ascribed to Him or Closely Connected with the Literary Tradition That Bears His Name*. Urbana: University of Illinois Press.

———. 1959. "Fable." *Studium Generale* 12:17–37.

———. 1962. "Demetrius of Phalerum and the Aesop Fables." *TAPA* 93:287–346.

———. 1964. *Secundus the Silent Philosopher: The Greek Life of Secundus*. Ithaca, NY: American Philological Association.

———. 1965. *Babrius and Phaedrus*. Cambridge: Harvard University Press; London: William Heinemann.

Petersmann, Hubert. 1981. "Homer und das Märchen." *Wiener Studien* 94:43–68.

Peterson, Per. 1981. *Rävens och Tranans Gästabud: En Studie över en Djurfabel i Verbal och Ikonografisk Tradition*. Uppsala: Almqvist & Wiksell.

Pike, Kenneth L. 1971. *Language in Relation to a Unified Theory of the Structure of Human Behavior*. 2nd ed. The Hague: Mouton.

Pinault, Jody R. 1992. *Hippocratic Lives and Legends*. Leiden: E. J. Brill.

Pirenne-Delforge, Vinciane. 2009. "Under Which Conditions Did the Greeks 'Believe' in Their Myths? The Religious Criteria of Adherence." In Dill and Walde, 38–54.

Pollitt, J. J. 1974. *The Ancient View of Greek Art: Criticism, History, and Terminology*. New Haven: Yale University Press.

Powers, Melinda. 2014. *Athenian Tragedy in Performance: A Guide to Contemporary Studies and Historical Debates*. Iowa City: University of Iowa Press.

Prato, Stanislao. 1885. "L'Apologo di Menenio Agrippa 'Le Membra Ribellate allo Stomaco' nelle Varie Redazioni Straniere." *Archivio per le Tradizioni Populari* 4:25–40.

Pronko, Leonard C. 1975. *Georges Feydeau*. New York: Frederick Ungar.

Propp, Vladimir Yakovlevich. 2012. *The Russian Folktale*. Edited and translated by Sibelan Forrester. Detroit: Wayne State University Press.

Radermacher, Ludwig. 1908. "Motiv und Personlichkeit, 1: Margites." *RhM* 63:445–464.

Radt, Stefan, ed. 1977. *Tragicorum Graecorum Fragmenta*. Vol. 4. Göttingen: Vandenhoeck & Ruprecht.

Rammel, Hal. 1990. *Nowhere in America: The Big Rock Candy Mountain and Other Comic Utopias*. Urbana: University of Chicago Press.

Ranelagh, E. L. 1979. *The Past We Share: The Near Eastern Ancestry of Western Folk Literature*. London: Quartet Books.

Ranke, Kurt et al., eds. 1977–2015. *Enzyklopädie des Märchens: Handwörterbuch zur historischen und vergleichenden Erzählforschung*. 15 vols. Berlin: Walter de Gruyter.

Reinhardt, Gustav. 1891. *Der Tod des Kaisers Julian, nach den Quellen dargestellt*. Cöthen: S. Bühling.

Reinhold, Meyer. 1971. "The Naming of Pygmalion's Animated Statue." *CJ* 66:316–319.

Riginos, Alice S. 1976. *Platonica: The Anecdotes Concerning the Life and Writings of Plato*. Leiden: E. J. Brill.

Robinson, Rachel S. 1955. *Sources for the History of Greek Athletics in English Translation*. Cincinnati: Published by the Author.

Robinson, T. M. 1987. *Heraclitus: Fragments, a Text and Translation with a Commentary*. Toronto: University of Toronto Press.

Rohde, Erwin. 1876. "Eine griechische Novelle." *RhM* 31:628–630.

———. 1901. "Ein griechisches Märchen." In *Kleine Schriften: Beiträge zur Geschichte des Romans und der Novelle zur Sagen-, Märchen- und Altherthumskunde*, 2:212–215. Tübingen: J. C. B. Mohr.

Rohde, Erwin. 1914. "Über griechische Novellendichtung und ihren Zusammenhang mit dem Orient." In *Der griechische Roman und seine Vorläufer*, 578–601. 3rd ed. Leipzig: Breitkopf und Härtel.

———. 1925. *Psyche: The Cult of Souls and Belief in Immortality among the Greeks*, translated by W. B. Hillis. London: Kegan Paul, Trench, Trubner; New York: Harcourt, Brace.

Röhrich, Lutz. 1977. *Der Witz: Figuren, Formen, Funktionen*. Stuttgart: J. B. Metzler.

———. 1991. *Folktales and Reality*. Translated by Peter Tokofsky. Bloomington: Indiana University Press.

Roller, Duane W. 2010. *Cleopatra: A Biography*. Oxford: Oxford University Press.

Roller, Lynn E. 1983. "The Legend of Midas." *Classical Antiquity* 2:299–313.

Roscher, W. H., ed. 1884–1937. *Ausführliches Lexikon der Griechischen und Römischen Mythologie*. 7 vols. Leipzig: B. G. Teubner.

Rose, H. J. 1929. *A Handbook of Greek Mythology, Including Its Extension to Rome*. New York: E. P. Dutton.

Ross, W. D., ed. and comm. 1955. *Aristotle's Physics*. Oxford: Clarendon Press.

Rouse, W. H. D. 1902. *Greek Votive Offerings: An Essay in the History of Greek Religion*. Cambridge: The University Press.

Runeberg, J. 1902. "Le Conte de l'Ile-Poisson." *Mémoires de la Société Néo-Philologique à Helsingfors* 3:343–395.

Russo, Joseph. 1997. "Prose Genres for the Performance of Traditional Wisdom in Ancient Greece: Proverb, Maxim, Apothegm." In *Poet, Public, and Performance in Ancient Greece*, edited by Lowell Edmunds and Robert W. Wallace, 49–64. Baltimore: Johns Hopkins University Press.

Saffrey, Henri-Dominique. 1968. "ΑΓΕΩΜΕΤΡΗΤΟΣ ΜΗΔΕΙΣ ΕΙΣΙΤΩ: Une Inscription Légendaire." *Revue des Études Grecques* 81:67–87.

Saintyves, P. 1912. "L'Anneau de Polycrate: Essai sur l'Origine Liturgique du Thème de l'Anneau Jeté à la Mer et Retrouvé dans le Ventre d'un Poisson." *Revue de l'Histoire des Religions* 66:49–80.

Salanitro, Maria. 1998. "Il Racconto del Lupo Mannaro in Petronio: Tra Folclore e Letteratura." *Atene e Roma* 43:156–167.

Sansone, David, ed. and comm. 1989. *Plutarch: The Lives of Aristeides and Cato*. Warminster: Aris & Phillips.

Sayre, Farrand. 1938. *Diogenes of Sinope: A Study of Greek Cynicism*. Baltimore: J. H. Furst.

Schmeling, Gareth. 2002. "*Humano capiti*: Body-Parts and Beautiful Women in Petronius and Lucian." In *Hommages à Carl Deroux*, edited by Pol Defosse, 2:404–408. Brussels: Collection Latomus 267.

———. 2011. *A Commentary on the* Satyrica *of Petronius*. Oxford: Oxford University Press.

Schmitt, Jean-Claude. 1983. *The Holy Greyhound: Guinefort, Healer of Children Since the Thirteenth Century*. Translated by Martin Thom. Cambridge: Cambridge University Press; Paris: Éditions de la Maison des Sciences de l'Homme.

Schönberger, Otto. 1968. "Das Verbrechen des Makareus." *Antike und Abendland* 14:36–40.

Schrempp, Gregory. 1995. "Our Funny Universe: On Aristotle's Metaphysics, Oring's Theory of Humor, and Other Appropriate Incongruities." *Humor* 8:219–228.

Schrempp, Gregory, and William Hansen, eds. 2002. *Myth: A New Symposium*. Bloomington: Indiana University Press.

Schuster, Mauriz. 1930. "Der Werwolf und die Hexen." *Wiener Studien* 48:149–178.

Schwarzbaum, Haim. 1972. "The Zoologically Tinged Stages of Man's Existence (AT 173 & 828)." *Folklore Research Center Studies* 3:267–290.

———. 1979. *The Mishle Shu'alim (Fox Fables) of Rabbi Berechiah Ha-Nakdan: A Study in Comparative Folklore and Fable Lore*. Kiron: Institute for Jewish and Arab Folklore Research.

Scobie, Alexander. 1969. *Aspects of the Ancient Romance and Its Heritage*. Beiträge zur klassischen Philologie 30. Meisenheim am Glan: Verlag Anton Hain.

———. 1977. "Some Folktales in Graeco-Roman and Far Eastern Sources." *Philologus* 121:1–23.

———. 1979. "Storytellers, Storytelling, and the Novel in Graeco-Roman Antiquity." *RhM* 122:229–259.

———. 1983. *Apuleius and Folklore: Toward a History of ML 3045, AaTh 567, 449A*. London: Folklore Society.

Scott, Michael. 2014. *Delphi: A History of the Center of the Ancient World*. Princeton: Princeton University Press.

Siegmund, Wolfdietrich, ed. 1984. *Antiker Mythos in unseren Märchen*. Kassel: Erich Röth Verlag.

Slater, William J. 1971. "Pindar's House." *GRBS* 12:141–152.

Slater, William J. 1972. "Simonides' House." *Phoenix* 26:232–240.

Smith, Martin S., ed. 1975. *Petronius: Cena Trimalchionis*. Oxford: Clarendon Press.

Smith, Steven D. 2014. *Man and Animal in Severan Rome: The Literary Imagination of Claudius Aelianus*. Cambridge: Cambridge University Press.

Smither, Paul C. 1941. "The Tall Story of the Bull." *Journal of Egyptian Archaeology* 27:158–159.

Snell, Bruno. 1971. *Leben und Meinungen der Sieben Weisen*. 4th ed. Munich: Heimeran Verlag.

Sokal, Alan D. 1996. "A Physicist Experiments with Cultural Studies." *Lingua Franca* (May/June):62–64.

Speyer, Wolfgang. 1970. *Bücherfunde in der Glaubenswerbung der Antike, mit einem Ausblick auf Mittelalter und Neuzeit*. Hypomnemata 24. Göttingen: Vandenhoeck & Ruprecht.

Squillace, Giuseppe. 2012. *Menecrate di Siracusa: Un Medico del IV Secolo a.C. tra Sicilia, Grecia e Macedonia*. Spudasmata 141. Hildesheim: Olms.

Stahl, Sandra K. D. 1975. "The Local Character Anecdote." *Genre* 8:283–302.

———. 1977a. "The Oral Personal Narrative in Its Generic Context." *Fabula* 18:18–39.

———. 1977b. "The Personal Narrative as Folklore." *Journal of the Folklore Institute* 14:9–30.

———. 1980. "Sour Grapes: Fable, Proverb, Unripe Fruit." In *Folklore on Two Continents: Essays in Honor of Linda Dégh*, edited by Nikolai Burlakoff and Carl Lindahl, 160–168. Bloomington: Trickster Press.

———. 1983. "Personal Experience Stories." In *Handbook of American Folklore*, edited by Richard M. Dorson, 268–276. Bloomington: Indiana University Press.

———. 1989. *Literary Folkloristics and Personal Narrative*. Bloomington: Indiana University Press.

Stapleton, Alfred. 1900. *All about the Merry Tales of Gotham*. Nottingham: R. N. Pearson.

Stebbins, Eunice B. 1929. *The Dolphin in the Literature and Art of Greece and Rome*. Menasha, WI: George Banta.

Stender-Petersen, Adolf. 1953. "A Varangian Stratagem." In *Varangica*, 189–198. Aarhus: Bianco Lunos Bogtrykkeri.

Stern, Jacob, trans. and comm. 1996. *Palaephatus: Peri Apiston, On Unbelievable Tales*. Wauconda, IL: Bolchazy-Carducci.

Sternbach, Leo. 1894. "Excerpta Vaticana." *Wiener Studien* 16:8–37.

Stramaglia, Antonio. 1999. *Res Inauditae, Incredulae: Storie di Fantasmi nel Mondo Greco-Latino.* Bari: Levante Editori.

———. 2000. Ερως*: Antiche Trame Greche d'Amore.* Bari: Levante Editori.

Strauss, Barry. 2015. *The Death of Caesar: The Story of History's Most Famous Assassination.* New York: Simon & Schuster.

Strohmaier, Gotthard. 1976. "Übersehenes zur Biographie Lukians." *Philologus* 120:117–122.

Struck, Peter T. 2009. "The Invention of Mythic Truth in Antiquity." In Dill and Walde, 26–37.

Süss, Wilhelm. 1969. *Lachen, Komik und Witz in der Antike.* Zurich: Artemis Verlag.

Swahn, Jan-Öjvind. 1955. *The Tale of Cupid and Psyche (Aarne-Thompson 425 & 428).* Lund: C. W. K. Gleerup.

Swales, John M. 1990. *Genre Analysis: English in Academic and Research Settings.* Cambridge: Cambridge University Press.

Sweet, Waldo E. 1987. *Sport and Recreation in Ancient Greece: A Sourcebook with Translations.* New York: Oxford University Press.

Sydow, C. W. von. 1948. "Kategorien der Prosa-Volksdichtung." In *Selected Papers on Folklore, Published on the Occasion of His 70th Birthday*, 60–88. Copenhagen: Rosenkilde og Bagger.

Szedegy-Maszak, A. 1978. "Legends of the Greek Lawgivers." *GRBS* 19:199–209.

Tangherlini, Timothy R., ed. and trans. 2013. *Danish Folktales, Legends, and Other Stories.* Seattle: University of Washington Press; Copenhagen: Museum Tusculanum Press.

Taylor, Archer. 1970. "The Anecdote: A Neglected Genre." In *Medieval Literature and Folklore Studies*, edited by J. Mandel and B. A. Rosenberg, 223–228. New Brunswick, NJ: Rutgers University Press.

Taylor, Daniel J. 1984. "Another Royal Investigation of the Origin of Language?" *Historiographia Linguistica* 11:500–502.

Taylor, Michael W. 1991. *The Tyrant Slayers: The Heroic Image in Fifth Century B.C. Athenian Art and Politics.* 2nd ed. Salem, NH: Ayer.

Thiele, Just Mathias. 1968 [1843–1860]. *Danmarks Folkesagn*, edited by Per Skar. 3 vols. Copenhagen: Rosenkilde og Bagger.

Thierfelder, Andreas, ed. 1968. *Philogelos: Der Lachfreund von Hierokles und Philagrius.* Munich: Ernst Heimeran Verlag.

Thomas, Gerald. 1977. *The Tall Tale and Philippe d'Alcripe: An Analysis of the Tall Tale Genre with Particular Reference to Philippe d'Alcripe's* La Nouvelle Fabrique des Excellents Traits de Vérité *Together with an Annotated*

Translation of the Work. St. John's: Department of Folklore, Memorial University of Newfoundland, in association with the American Folklore Society.

Thomas, Jeannie Banks. 2007. "Gender and Ghosts." In Goldstein et al., 81–110.

Thomas, Rosalind. 1989. *Oral Tradition and Written Record in Classical Athens*. Cambridge: Cambridge University Press.

Thompson, Stith. 1955–1958. *A Motif-Index of Folk-Literature: A Classification of Narrative Elements in Folktales, Ballads, Myths, Fables, Mediaeval Romances, Exempla, Fabliaux, Jest-Books and Local Legends*. Rev. ed. 6 vols. Bloomington: Indiana University Press.

———. 1966 [1929]. *Tales of the North American Indians*. Bloomington: Indiana University Press.

Ting, Nai-tung. 1966. "The Holy Man and the Snake-Woman: A Study of a Lamia Story in Asian and European Literature." *Fabula* 8:145–191.

Toner, Jerry. 2009. *Popular Culture in Ancient Rome*. Cambridge: Polity Press.

Trenkner, Sophie. 1958. *The Greek Novella in the Classical Period*. Cambridge: Cambridge University Press.

Tsitsiridis, Stavros. 2013. *Beiträge zu den Fragmenten des Klearchos von Soloi*. Berlin: Walter de Gruyter.

Turner, Eric G. 1973. *The Papyrologist at Work*. Durham, NC: Duke University Press.

Ullman, B. L. 1957. "Cleopatra's Pearls." *CJ* 52:193–201.

Uther, Hans-Jörg. 2004. *The Types of International Folktales: A Classification and Bibliography*. *FFC* 284–286. Helsinki: Academia Scientiarum Fennica.

———. 2008. *Handbuch zu den* Kinder- und Hausmärchen *der Brüder Grimm*. Berlin: Walter de Gruyter.

Vannini, Giulio, ed. and comm. 2010. *Petronii Arbitri 'Satyricon' 100-115: Edizione Critica e Commento*. Berlin: Walter de Gruyter.

Velleman, J. David. 2003. "Narrative Explanation." *Philosophical Review* 112:1–25.

Verdenius, W. J. 1962. "Ainos." *Mnemosyne* 15:389.

Veyne, Paul. 1964. "La Sibylle dans la Bouteille." In *Hommages à Jean Bayet*, edited by Marcel Renard and Robert Schilling, 718–721. Brussels: Collection Latomus 70.

———. 1988. *Did the Greeks Believe in Their Myths? An Essay on the Constitutive Imagination*. Translated by Paula Wissing. Chicago: University of Chicago Press.

Visintin, Monica. 1992. *La Vergine e l'Eroe: Temesa e la Leggenda di Euthymos di Locri*. Bari: Edipuglia.

Waele, Dr. F. J. M de. 1927. *The Magic Staff or Rod in Graeco-Italian Antiquity*. Ghent: Erasmus.

Wageningen, J. van. 1905. "De Damoclis Gladio." *Mnemosyne* new series 33:317–329.

Wallach, Luitpold. 1943. "The Parable of the Blind and the Lame: A Study in Comparative Literature." *Journal of Biblical Literature* 62:333–339.

Wasserstein, Abraham, and David J. Wassersetin. 2006. *The Legend of the Septuagint: From Classical Antiquity to Today*. Cambridge: Cambridge University Press.

Watts, Edward. 2006. "The Murder of Hypatia: Acceptable or Unacceptable Violence?" In *Violence in Late Antiquity: Perceptions and Practices*, edited by H. A. Drake, 333–342. Aldershot, England; Burlington, VT: Ashgate.

Wehrli, Fritz. 1967–1969. *Die Schule des Aristoteles*. 2nd ed. 10 vols. Basel: B. Schwabe.

Weinreich, Otto. 1911. *Der Trug des Nektanebos: Wandlungen eines Novellenstoffs*. Leipzig: B. G. Teubner.

———. 1931. *Fabel, Aretalogie, Novelle: Beiträge zu Phädrus, Petron, Martial und Apuleius*. Sitzungsberichte der Heidelberger Akademie der Wissenschaften, Phil.-hist. Kl. 7. Heidelberg: Carl Winters Universitätshandlung.

———. 1933. *Menekrates Zeus and Salmoneus: Religionsgeschichtliche Studien zur Psychopathologie des Gottmenschentums in Antike und Neuzeit*. Tübinger Beiträge zur Altertumswissenschaft 18. Stuttgart: W. Kohlhammer.

Welch, Tara S. 2015. *Tarpeia: Workings of a Roman Myth*. Columbus: Ohio State University Press.

Wesselski, Albert. 1935. "Narkissos oder das Spiegelbild." *Archiv Orientální* 7:37–63, 328–350.

West, Martin L., ed. and comm. 1966. *Hesiod: Theogony*. Oxford: Clarendon Press.

———, ed. and comm. 1978. *Hesiod: Works and Days*. Oxford: Clarendon Press.

———, ed. and trans. 2003. *Homeric Hymns, Homeric Apocrypha, Lives of Homer*. Cambridge, MA: Harvard University Press.

West, Stephanie. 1992. "Not at Home: Nasica's Witticism and Other Stories." *CQ* 42:287–288.

Widdowson, J. D. A. 1977. *If You Don't Be Good: Verbal Social Control in Newfoundland*. St. Johns: Memorial University of Newfoundland.

Wiersma, W. 1933–1934. "The Seven Sages and the Prize of Wisdom." *Mnemosyne* 3rd series 1:150–154.

Wilde, Larry. 1983. *The Last Official Irish Joke Book*. New York: Bantam.

Wills, Jeffrey. 1996. *Repetition in Latin Poetry: Figures of Allusion*. Oxford: Clarendon Press.

Wilson, Peter. 2009. "Thamyris the Thracian: The Archetypal Wandering Poet?" In *Wandering Poets in Ancient Greek Culture: Travel, Locality, and Pan-Hellenism*, edited by Richard Hunter and Ian Rutherford, 46–79. Cambridge: Cambridge University Press.

Winkler, John J. 1982. "Akko." *Classical Philology* 77:137–138.

———. 1985. *Auctor & Actor: A Narratological Reading of Apuleius's* The Golden Ass. Berkeley: University of California Press.

Wirkenhauser, Alfred. 1948. "Doppelträume." *Biblica* 29:100–111.

Wiseman, T. P. 2004. *The Myths of Rome*. Exeter: University of Exeter Press.

Worthington, Ian. 2013. *Demosthenes of Athens and the Fall of Classical Greece*. Oxford: Oxford University Press.

Wright, James R. G. 1971. "Folk-Tale and Literary Technique in *Cupid and Psyche*." *CQ* 21:273–284.

Yohannan, John D., ed. 1968. *Joseph and Potiphar's Wife in World Literature: An Anthology of the Story of the Chaste Youth and the Lustful Stepmother*. New York: New Directions.

Young, David C. 1984. *The Olympic Myth of Greek Amateur Athletics*. Chicago: Ares.

Zeitz, Heinrich. 1936. "Der Aesoproman und seine Geschichte." *Aegyptus* 16: 225–256.

Zielinski, Th. 1889. "Das Wiesel als Braut." *RhM* 44:156–157.

Zimmerman, Maaike, et al., eds. and comm. 2004. *Apuleius Madaurensis: Metamorphoseon, Books IV 28–35, V and VI 1–24: The Tale of Cupid and Psyche. Text, Introduction, and Commentary*. Groningen: Egbert Forsten.

Zipes, Jack, ed. 2000. *The Oxford Companion to Fairy Tales: The Western Fairy Tale Tradition from Medieval to Modern*. Oxford: Oxford University Press.

ANCIENT SOURCES

The language in which the author writes, or in which a work is composed, is indicated by (G) or (L).

Acts of the Apostles (G). New Testament book. 1st cent. AD.
Acts of Paul (G). 2nd cent. AD.
Acts of Xanthippe and Polyxene (G). 3rd cent. AD.
Adaios (G). Epigrammatic poet. 4th cent. AD.
Aelian (G). Sophist. 2nd–3rd cent. AD.
Aesopic fables (G). Anonymous compilations of Aesopic fables in Greek prose. 2nd cent. AD ff.
Alexander of Tralles (G). Medical writer. 6th cent. AD.
Alexander Polyhistor (G). Historian. 1st cent. BC.
Alkiphron (G). Sophist. 2nd–3rd cent. AD.
Ammianus Marcellinus (L). Historian. 4th cent. AD.
Ampelius, Lucius (L). Historian. 2nd–3rd cent. AD?
Ananios (G). Poet. 6th cent. BC.
Antigonos (G). Paradoxographer. 3rd cent. BC.
Antipatros of Sidon (G). Epigrammatic poet. 2nd cent. BC.
Aphthonios (G). Sophist. 4th cent. AD?
Apion (G). Historian. 1st cent. AD.
Apollodoros (G). Mythographer. 1st cent. AD.
Apollonios (G). Paradoxographer. 2nd cent. BC?
Apostolios (G). Paroemiographer. 15th cent. AD.
Apothegms of Pindar (G). Compilation of apothegms. Date uncertain.
Appendix Proverbiorum (G). Compilation of proverbs. Date uncertain.
Appian (G). Historian. 2nd cent. AD.
Apuleius (L). Novelist. 2nd cent. AD.
Aristainetos (G). Epistolographer. 4th–5th cent. AD.
Aristeides (G). Rhetorician. 2nd cent. AD.
Aristophanes (G). Comic poet. 5th–4th cent. BC.
Aristotle (G). Philosopher. 4th cent. BC.
Arnobius (L). Theologian. 3rd–4th cent. AD.

Arrian (G). Historian. 2nd cent. AD.
Arsenios (G). Compiler of proverbs and anecdotes. 15th–16th cent. AD.
Athenaios (G). Sophist. 2nd–3rd cent. AD.
Augustine (L). Theologian. 5th cent. AD.
Avianus (L). Fabulist. 4th cent. AD?
Babrios (G). Fabulist. 2nd cent. AD.
Cassius Dio (G). Historian. 2nd–3rd cent. AD.
Censorinus (L). Scholar. 3rd cent. AD.
Charax (G). Historian. 2nd cent. AD?
Chares of Mytilene (G). Historian. 4th cent. BC.
Charon of Lampsakos (G). Historian. 5th cent. BC.
Christodoros of Egyptian Thebes (G). Epigrammatic poet. 6th cent. AD.
Cicero (L). Orator and philosopher. 2nd–1st cent. BC.
CIL VIII, 2756 (L). Epitaph composed by Aelius Proculinus. 2nd cent. AD?
Clement of Alexandria (G). Theologian. 2nd–3rd cent. AD.
Codex Bodleianus Baroccianus 50 (G). Miscellany. 10th cent. AD.
Cornelius Nepos (L). Biographer. 1st cent. BC.
Damaskios (G). Philosopher. 6th–5th cent. BC.
Diegesis (G). Narrative of a lost poem by Kallimachos. Date uncertain.
Diodoros of Sicily (G). Historian. 1st cent. BC.
Diogeneianos (G). Paroemiographer. 2nd cent. AD?
Diogenes Laertios (G). Biographer. 3rd cent. AD?
Dion Chrysostomos (G). Sophist. 1st–2nd cent. AD.
Dionysios of Halikarnassos (G). Rhetorician and historian. 1st cent. BC.
Diphilos (G). Comic poet. 4th–3rd cent. BC.
Empedokles (G). Philosopher. 5th cent. BC.
Epiktetos (G). Philosopher. 1st–2nd cent. AD.
Epiphanios (G). Ecclesiastical writer. 4th–5th cent. AD.
Etymologicum Magnum (G). Lexicon. 12th cent. AD.
Euboulos (G). Comic poet. 4th cent. BC.
Eudemos (G). Philosopher. 4th cent. BC.
Euripides (G). Tragedian. 5th cent. BC.
Eusebios (G). Ecclesiastical writer. 3rd–4th cent. AD.
Eustathios (G). Commentator. 12th cent. AD.
Favorinos (G). Philosopher and rhetorician. 2nd cent. AD.
Festus, Sextus Pompeius (L). Scholar. 2nd cent. AD.
First Vatican Mythographer (L). Mythological compendium. 10th cent. AD?
Florus, Lucius Annaeus (L). Historian. 2nd cent. AD.
Fulgentius (L). Mythographer. 5th–6th cent. AD.

Gaitoulikos (G). Epigrammatic poet. 1st cent. AD.
Galen (G). Medical writer. 2nd cent. AD.
Gellius, Aulus (L). Grammarian. 2nd cent. AD.
Gnomologium Vaticanum. (G). Compilation of apothegms. 14th cent. AD.
Heliodoros (G). Novelist. 3rd–4th cent. AD?
Herakleides of Pontos (G). Philosopher and historian. 4th cent. BC.
Hermesianax of Colophon (G). Elegiac poet. 4th–3rd cent. BC.
Hermippos (G). Comic poet. 5th cent. BC.
Herodotos (G). Historian. 5th cent. BC.
Hesiod (G). Epic poet. 8th–7th cent. BC.
Hesychios (G). Lexicographer. 5th cent. AD.
Hierokles and Philagrios (G). Compilers of the jokebook *Philogelos*. 4th cent. AD? Cited as *Philogelos*.
Hieronymos (G). Philosopher. 4th–3rd cent. BC.
Hippokrates (G). Medical writer. 5th cent. BC.
Homer (G). Epic poet. 8th cent. BC.
Horace (L). Poet. 1st cent. BC.
Hyginus (L). Mythographer. 2nd cent. AD?
Hypereides (G). Orator. 4th cent. BC.
Iamblichos (G). Novelist. 2nd cent. AD.
Iamblichos (G). Philosopher. 4th cent. AD.
IG IV^2, 1, nos. 121–122 (G). Testimonial inscription displayed in the sanctuary of Asklepios at Epidauros. 4th cent. BC.
IG XII, 3, no. 449 (G). Inscription on a boulder found on the island of Thera. 6th cent. BC.
Ion (G). Poet. 5th cent. BC.
Irenaeus (G). Theologian. 2nd cent. AD.
Isidore of Seville (L). Encyclopedist. 7th cent. AD.
Isokrates (G). Orator. 5th–4th cent. BC.
Jerome (= Eusebios Hieronymos) (L). Ecclesiastical writer. 4th–5th cent. AD.
John of Nikiu (G). Ecclesiastical writer. 7th cent. AD.
Julian the Apostate (G). Philosopher. 4th cent. AD.
Justin (L). Scholar. 3rd cent. AD.
Juvenal (L). Satirist. 1st–2nd cent. AD.
Kallimachos (G). Poet. 3rd cent. BC.
Kedrenos, George (G). Historian. 12th cent. AD.
Konon (G). Mythographer. 1st cent. BC–1st cent. AD.
Lactantius (L). Ecclesiastical writer. 5th or 6th cent. AD.
Leonidas of Alexandria (G). Poet. 3rd cent. BC.

Libanios (G). Rhetorician and sophist. 4th cent. AD.
Life of Aeschylus (G). Biography. Date uncertain.
Life of Aesop (G). Comic novel. 1st or 2nd cent. AD.
Life of Aristophanes (G). Biography. Date uncertain.
Life of Euripides (G). Biography. Date uncertain.
Life of Secundus the Silent Philosopher (G). Popular philosophy. 2nd cent. AD.
Lives of Pindar (Ambrosian, Thoman) (G). Dates uncertain.
Livy (L). Historian. 1st cent. BC–1st cent. AD.
Longos (G). Novelist. 2nd–3rd cent. AD?
Loukillios (G). Poet. 1st cent. AD.
Lucian (G). Sophist. 2nd cent. AD.
Luke (G). Gospel writer. 1st cent. AD.
Machon (G). Writer of anecdotes. 3rd cent. BC.
Macrobius (L). Grammarian and compiler. 4th cent. AD.
Margites (G). Heroic-comic poem. 7th cent. BC?
Mark (G). Gospel writer. 1st cent. AD.
Matthew (G). Gospel writer. 1st cent. AD.
Maximus of Tyre (G). Sophist. 2nd cent. AD.
Menander (G). Comic poet. 4th–3rd cent. BC.
Mnesiepes (G). Builder of a hero shrine for the poet Archilochos. 3rd cent. BC.
Mousaios (G). Epic poet. 5th–6th cent. AD.
Nikarchos (G). Epigrammatic poet. 1st cent. AD.
Nonnos (G). Epic poet. 5th cent. AD?
Olympiodoros (G). Commentator on Aristotle. 6th cent. AD.
Oneisikritos of Astypalaia (G). Historian. 4th cent. BC.
Oppian (G). Epic poet. 2nd–3rd cent. AD.
Origen (G). Theologian. 2nd–3rd cent. AD.
Ovid (L). Poet. 1st cent. BC–1st cent. AD.
Palatine Anthology (G). Compilation of short poems. Different authors and dates.
Pamphile (G). Historian. 1st cent. AD.
Pappos of Alexandria (G). Mathematician. 3rd–4th cent. AD?
P. Oxy. 2944 (G). Papyrus fragment. 1st cent. BC or 2nd cent. AD.
Parthenios (G). Mythographer. 1st cent. BC.
Paul (G). New Testament author. 1st cent. AD.
Paulos Silentarios (G). Christian poet. 6th cent. AD.
Pausanias (G). Travel writer. 2nd cent. AD.
Petronius (L). Novelist. 1st cent. AD.
Phaedrus (L). Fabulist. 1st cent. BC–1st cent. AD.

Philiskos (G). Rhetorician. 4th cent. BC.
Philo of Alexandria (= Philo Judaeus) (G). Philosopher and theologian. 1st cent. AD.
Philogelos. See Hierokles and Philagrios.
Philoponos, Ioannes (G). Philosopher and commentator. 6th cent. AD.
Philostorgios (G). Ecclesiastical writer. 4th–5th cent. AD.
Philostratos (G). Sophist. 2nd–3rd cent. AD.
Philostratos (G). Sophist. 3rd cent. AD.
Phlegon of Tralles (G). Paradoxographer. 2nd cent. AD.
Phokylides (G). Poet. 6th cent. BC.
Photios (G). Theologian. 9th cent. AD.
Phylarchos (G). Historian. 3rd cent. BC.
Physiologus Graecus (G). Allegorical treatise on the properties of animals, etc. 2nd–3rd cent. AD.
Physiologus Latinus (L). Latin translation of the foregoing. 7th or 8th cent. AD.
Pindar (G). Poet. 5th cent. BC.
Plato (G). Philosopher. 5th–4th cent. BC.
Plato the Younger (G). Poet. Date uncertain.
Pliny the Elder (L). Encyclopedist. 1st cent. AD.
Pliny the Younger (L). Epistolographer. 1st cent. AD.
Plutarch (G). Biographer and philosopher. 1st–2nd cent. AD.
Pollux (G). Grammarian. 2nd cent. AD.
Polyainos (G). Writer on military strategies. 2nd cent. AD.
Pompeiian wall painting in the House of the Doctor. Before AD 79.
Porphyrio, Pomponius (L). Commentator. 3rd cent. AD.
Porphyry (G). Philosopher. 3rd cent. AD.
Proklos (G). Philosopher and commentator. 5th cent. AD.
Prokopios (G). Historian. 6th cent. AD.
Propertius (L). Poet. 1st cent. BC.
Pseudo-Acron (L). Scholiast. Date uncertain.
Pseudo-Aesop (G). Gnomic literature. Date uncertain.
Pseudo-Aischines (G). Epistolographer. 2nd cent. AD?
Pseudo-Aristeas (G). Epic poet. Date uncertain.
Pseudo-Aristotle (G). Paradoxographer. Date uncertain.
Pseudo-Dositheus (G). Fabulist. 2nd AD.
Pseudo-Justin Martyr (G). Christian apologist. 3rd–5th cent. AD.
Pseudo-Kallisthenes (G). Biographer. After 4th cent. BC.
Pseudo-Plutarch (G). Essayist. Date uncertain.
Quintilian (L). Rhetorician. 1st cent. AD.

Return of the Atreidai (G). Epic poem. After 7th cent. BC.
Rufinus (L). Ecclesiastical writer. 4th–5th cent. AD.
Scholiasts (G and L). Commentators. Different, mostly uncertain dates.
Semonides (G). Iambic poet. 7th cent. BC.
Seneca the Elder (L). Orator. 1st cent. BC–1st cent. AD.
Seneca the Younger (L). Philosopher and tragic poet. 1st cent. AD.
Servius (L). Commentator. 4th–5th cent. AD.
Sextus Empiricus (G). Philosopher. 2nd cent. AD.
Simonides (G). Lyric poet. 6th–5th cent. BC.
Simplicius (G). Philosopher and commentator. 6th cent. AD.
Sokrates Scholastikos (G). Ecclesiastical writer. 5th cent. AD.
Sophocles (G). Tragic poet. 5th cent. BC.
Soranos (G). Medical writer. 2nd cent. AD.
Sozomenos (G). Ecclesiastical writer. 5th cent. AD.
Spanish War (L). Continuation of Caesar's *Civil War*. 1st cent. BC.
Stephanos of Byzantium (G). Grammarian. 5th–6th cent. AD?
Stesichoros (G). Lyric poet. 7th–6th cent. BC.
Stobaios (G). Anthologist. 5th cent. AD.
Strabo (G). Geographer. 1st cent. BC–1st cent. AD.
Suda (G). Lexicon. 10th cent. AD.
Suetonius (L and G). Biographer and essayist. 2nd cent. AD.
Tacitus (L). Historian. 1st–2nd cent. AD.
Teles (G). Philosopher. 3rd cent. BC.
Tertullian (L). Ecclesiastical writer. 2nd–3rd cent. AD.
Themistios (G). Orator. 4th cent. AD.
Theodoretos (G). Ecclesiastical writer. 5th cent. AD.
Theon, Aelius (G). Rhetorician. 1st–2nd AD.
Theophylaktos Simokattes (G). Ecclesiastical writer. 7th cent. AD.
Theopompos (G). Historian. 4th cent. BC.
Thessalos (G). Medical and astrological writer. 1st cent. AD.
Timaios (G). Historian. 4th–3rd cent. BC.
Valerius Maximus (L). Historian. 1st cent. AD.
Velleius Paterculus (L). Historian. 1st cent. AD.
Victor, Sextus Aurelius (L). Biographer. 4th cent. AD.
Vitruvius (L). Writer on architecture. 1st cent. BC.
Xenophanes (G). Philosopher. 6th cent. BC.
Xenophon (G). Historian and essayist. 5th–4th cent. BC.
Zenobios (G). Paroemiographer. 2nd cent. AD.

LIST OF INTERNATIONAL STORIES

INTERNATIONAL FOLKTALE TYPES	PRESENT BOOK
ATU 34A *The Dog Drops His Meat for the Reflection*	The Dog with a Piece of Meat
ATU 48* *Flatterer Rewarded, Honest One Punished*	The King of the Apes
ATU 51 *The Lion's Share*	The Lion's Share
ATU 57 *The Raven with Cheese in His Mouth*	The Raven with a Piece of Meat
ATU 59 *The Fox and the Sour Grapes*	The Sour Grapes
ATU 60 *Fox and Crane Invite Each Other*	The Fox and the Crane
ATU 75 *The Help of the Weak*	The Lion and the Mouse
ATU 113A *Pan Is Dead*	"The Great God Pan Is Dead!"
ATU 120 *The First to See the Sunrise*	The Slaves Take Over
ATU 156 *Androcles and the Lion*	Androkles and the Lion
ATU 173 *Human and Animal Life Spans Are Readjusted*	The Different Stages of Life
ATU 178A *The Innocent Dog*	How Ophiteia Gets Its Name
ATU 201 *The Lean Dog Prefers Liberty to Abundant Food and a Chain*	The Plump Dog
ATU 218 *A Cat Transformed to a Maiden Runs after a Mouse*	The Transformed Weasel
ATU 219E** *The Hen That Laid the Golden Eggs*	The Goose That Lays Golden Eggs
ATU 225A *The Tortoise Lets Itself Be Carried by Birds*	Aeschylus; The Tortoise That Wishes to Fly
ATU 275A *The Race between Hare and Tortoise*	The Race of the Tortoise and the Hare
ATU 277 *The King of the Frogs*	The King of the Frogs

ATU 280A *The Ant and the Cricket*	The Ant and the Cicada
ATU 293 *The Debate of the Belly and the Members*	The Belly and the Feet
ATU 298C* *The Reeds Bend before the Wind (Flood)*	The Oak and the Reed
ATU 299 *The Mountain Gives Birth to a Mouse*	The Mountain in Labor
ATU 300 *The Dragon-Slayer*	The Hero of Temesa
ATU 301 *The Three Stolen Princesses*	The Altar of the Vulture God
ATU 325* *The Sorcerer's Apprentice*	The Magician's Apprentice
ATU 326A* *Soul Released from Torment*	The Haunted House
ATU 425B *Son of the Witch*	Cupid and Psyche; Philinnion
ATU 503 *The Gifts of the Little People*	Asklepios Heals Pandaros
ATU 510A *Cinderella*	The Pharaoh and the Courtesan
ATU 571B *Lover Exposed*	The Affair of Ares and Aphrodite
ATU 666* *Hero and Leander*	Hero and Leander
ATU 704 *The Princess on the Pea*	Uncomfortable Sleep
ATU 729 *The Merman's Golden Axe*	The Golden Ax
ATU 736A *The Ring of Polycrates*	Polykrates's Ring
ATU 745 *Hatch-Penny*	Pases the Magician
ATU 754 *Lucky Poverty*	Wealth and Happiness
ATU 766 *The Seven Sleepers*	Epimenides of Crete
ATU 774K *St. Peter Stung by Bees*	The Judge of the Ants
ATU 775 *Midas' Short-Sighted Wish*	King Midas
ATU 823A* *A Mother Dies of Fright When She Learns That She Was about to Commit Incest with Her Son*	Secundus the Silent Philosopher
ATU 844 *The Luck-Bringing Shirt*	Untouched by Grief
ATU 920 *The Son of the King and the Son of the Smith*	The Children Play King
ATU 921E *Never Heard Before*	Never Heard Before
ATU 926 *Judgment of Solomon*	The Disputed Child
ATU 934 *Tales of the Predestined Death*	Aeschylus
ATU 950 *Rhampsinitus*	The Treasury of Rhampsinitos; Trophonios and Agamedes
ATU 960A *The Cranes of Ibycus*	The Cranes of Ibykos
ATU 961B *Money in the Stick*	The Dishonest Banker
ATU 980 *The Ungrateful Son*	Abusive Son of an Abusive Father

ATU 981 *Wisdom of Hidden Old Man Saves Kingdom*	The Slaves Take Over
ATU 981A* *Life by a Silk Thread*	The Rock of Tantalos; The Sword of Damocles
ATU 985 *Brother Chosen Rather Than Husband or Son*	Intaphrenes's Wife; Abauchas's Choice
ATU 985* *The Suckled Prisoner*	The Suckling Daughter
ATU 1211 *The Cow Chewing Its Cud*	The Attentive Donkey
ATU 1242A *Relief for the Donkey*	Carrying the Load
ATU 1284 *Person Does Not Know Himself*	The Travelers
ATU 1284C *"You, or Your Brother?"*	The Twins
ATU 1290B* *Sleeping on a Feather*	Uncomfortable Sleep
ATU 1331 *The Covetous and the Envious*	The Covetous Man and the Envious Man
ATU 1333 *The Shepherd Who Cried "Wolf!" Too Often*	The Shepherd Who Cries "Wolf!"
ATU 1336A *Not Recognizing Own Reflection*	Narcissus; Akko; The Ball in the Well
ATU 1341A *The Fool and the Robbers*	The Fugitives
ATU 1343 *Hanging Game*	The Children Play War
ATU 1343* *Children Play at Hog-Killing*	The Children Play Priest
ATU 1383 *The Woman Does Not Know Herself*	The Travelers
ATU 1419 *The Returning Husband Hoodwinked*	The Husband's Untimely Return: 1
ATU 1419C *The One-Eyed Husband*	The Husband's Untimely Return: 2
ATU 1510 *The Matron of Ephesus*	The Widow of Ephesos
ATU 1525J *Thieves Cheated of Their Booty*	The Two Thieves
ATU 1542** *The Maiden's Honor*	Acquiring Sense
ATU 1543A *The Greedy Dreamer*	The Foolish Abderites
ATU 1591 *The Three Joint Depositors*	The Joint Depositors
ATU 1594 *The Donkey Is Not at Home*	Not at Home
ATU 1651A *Fortune in Salt*	A Fortune in Water
ATU 1682 *The Horse Learns Not to Eat*	The Trained Donkey
ATU 1698A *Search for the Lost Animal*	The Deaf Judge

ATU 1804B *Payment with the Clink of Money*	The Problem of Dreamt Sex
ATU 1804D *The Shadow of the Donkey*	A Donkey's Shadow
ATU 1871A *Star Gazer Falls into Well*	Thales in the Well; The Astronomer
ATU 1871B *King Cannot Destroy the City*	Saving Lampsakos
ATU 1871C *The Cynic Wants Sunlight*	Alexander's Offer
ATU 1871F *Diogenes and the Lantern*	Diogenes and the Lantern
ATU 1889F *Frozen Words (Music) Thaw*	Frozen Speech
ATU 1920F *He Who Says "That's a Lie!" Must Pay a Fine*	Never Heard Before
ATU 1935 *Topsy Turvy Land*	Topsy-Turvy Land
ATU 1960A *The Great Ox*	On Spartan Adultery
ATU 1960B *The Great Fish*	The Great Fish
ATU 2031 *Stronger and Strongest*	The Strongest Thing; Caesar's Soldiers Sing
ATU 2200 *Catch Tales*	A Donkey's Shadow

INTERNATIONAL LEGEND TYPES

ML 3020 *Inexperienced Use of the Black Book*	The Magician's Apprentice
ML 4005 *The Werewolf Husband*	The Werewolf
ML 6070A *Fairies Send a Message*	"The Great God Pan Is Dead!"
ML 7050 *Ring Thrown into the Water and Recovered in a Fish*	Polykrates's Ring

SELECT MOTIFS

A1371.2 *Bad women combination of nine different animals*	The Different Kinds of Women
E341 *The grateful dead*	The Grateful Dead Man
F493 *Spirit of plague*	Apollonios Cures a Plague
F681 *Marvelous runner*	Polymestor the Sprinter
F833.2 *Sword of Damocles*	The Sword of Damocles
H256 *Test of innocence: apple and gold offered*	A Child Steals from the Goddess
H1194 *Task: making person laugh*	The Man Who Loses His Laugh

J954.2 *Fox claims that certain statues are of his ancestors*	The Ape with Important Ancestors
J1303 *Aesop with the lantern*	Diogenes and the Lantern
J1309.1 *Man asks naked Indian if he is not cold*	The Scythian
J1551.3 *Singer repaid with promise of reward: words for words*	A Singer's Compensation
J1761.1 *Whale thought to be island*	The Great Fish
K2111 *Potiphar's wife*	Hippolytos and Phaidra; The King's Trusted Friend
K2365.1 *Enemy induced to give up siege by pretending to have plenty of food*	The Milesians Hold a Party
N886 *Blind man carries lame man*	The Lame Man and the Blind Man
P315 *Friends offer to die for each other*	Damon and Phintias
R151 *Husband rescues stolen wife*	Xanthos, Who Longs for His Wife
X924 *Lie: remarkably thin persons*	Thin Men

INDEX